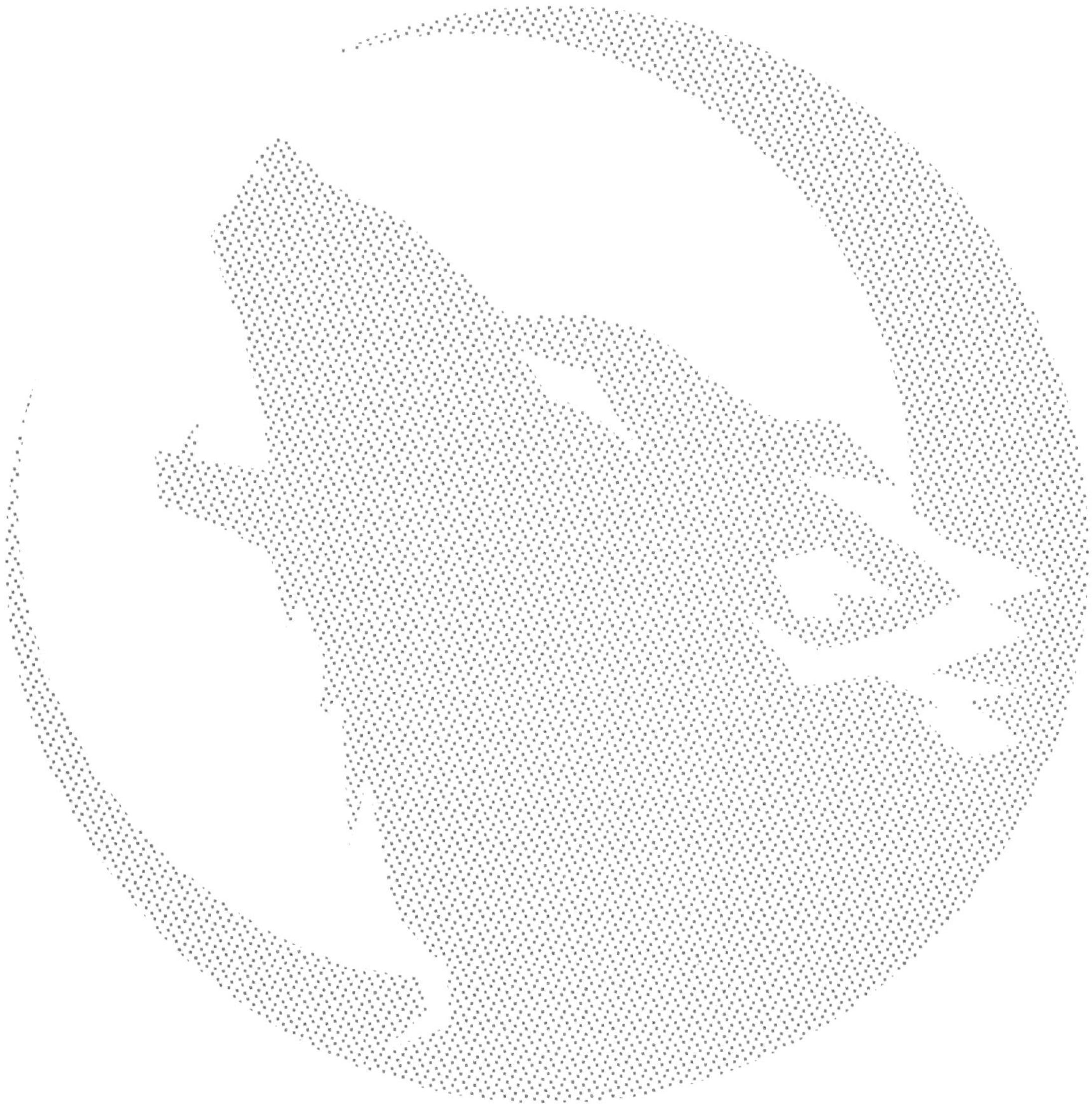

ROGUE'S CHALLENGE

Book Nine in the ElfQuest Graphic Novel Series

stories by Wendy & Richard Pini
art by Wendy Pini & friends

WHAT IS HERE...

Cover by Wendy Pini
"Daughter's Day" by Sarah Byam & Wendy Pini,
    Paul Abrams and Charles Barnett
"How Shall I Keep From Singing - Parts 1 & 2"
    by Sarah Byam, Wendy & Richard Pini,
    Paul Abrams and Charles Barnett
"The Enemy's Face" by Sarah Byam & Wendy Pini,
    Paul Abrams and Charles Barnett
"Rogue's Challenge" by Wendy & Richard Pini,
    Wendy Pini and John Byrne
Bridging pages by Wendy & Richard Pini

Elfquest - Rogue's Challenge

(Previously published in
single magazine issues as
Elfquest: Hidden Years 6-9 ^{1}/2.)

Published by Warp Graphics, Inc.,
under its Father Tree Press imprint.
Entire contents copyright © 1994
Warp Graphics, Inc. All rights reserved.

43 Haight Avenue
Poughkeepsie NY 12603

Printed in Canada.
First printing.
ISBN 0-936861-26-6

For a catalog of Elfquest
books, graphic novels, and music,
call 1-800-288-2131.

Daughter's Day

...FAILED TO
PREVENT THE
HIGH ONES'
ACCIDENT...

...FAILED TO
PREEMPT ALL
THOSE VOICES...
THOSE HE FIRST
HEARD SCREAM-
ING PAINFULLY
THROUGH
SUNTOP'S MIND...
CALLING
THROUGH
TIME...

...FAILED
TO INSPIRE
HIS PEOPLE
TO SEEK A
HIGHER AND
BETTER WAY
OF LIFE.

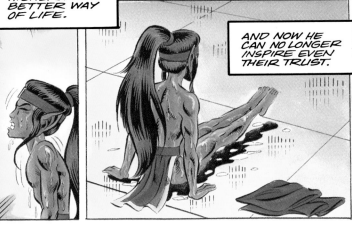

AND NOW HE
CAN NO LONGER
INSPIRE EVEN
THEIR TRUST.

SARAH BYAM ✷ WORDS
PAUL ABRAMS ✷ PENCILS
CHARLES BARNETT ✷ INKS
PATY ✷ COLORS
WENDY PINI ✷ EDITOR

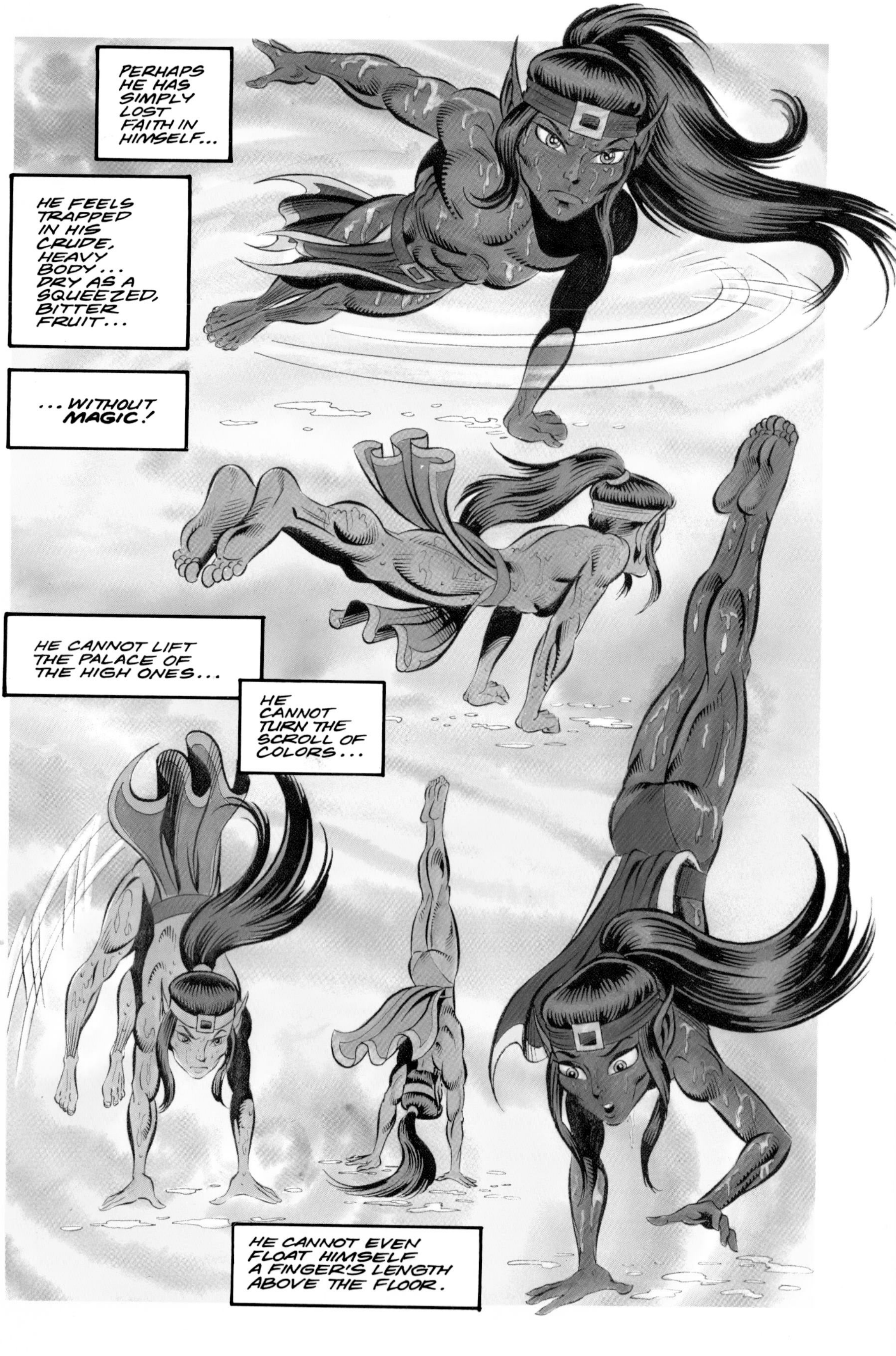
PERHAPS HE HAS SIMPLY LOST FAITH IN HIMSELF...
HE FEELS TRAPPED IN HIS CRUDE, HEAVY BODY... DRY AS A SQUEEZED, BITTER FRUIT...
...WITHOUT MAGIC!
HE CANNOT LIFT THE PALACE OF THE HIGH ONES...
HE CANNOT TURN THE SCROLL OF COLORS...
HE CANNOT EVEN FLOAT HIMSELF A FINGER'S LENGTH ABOVE THE FLOOR.

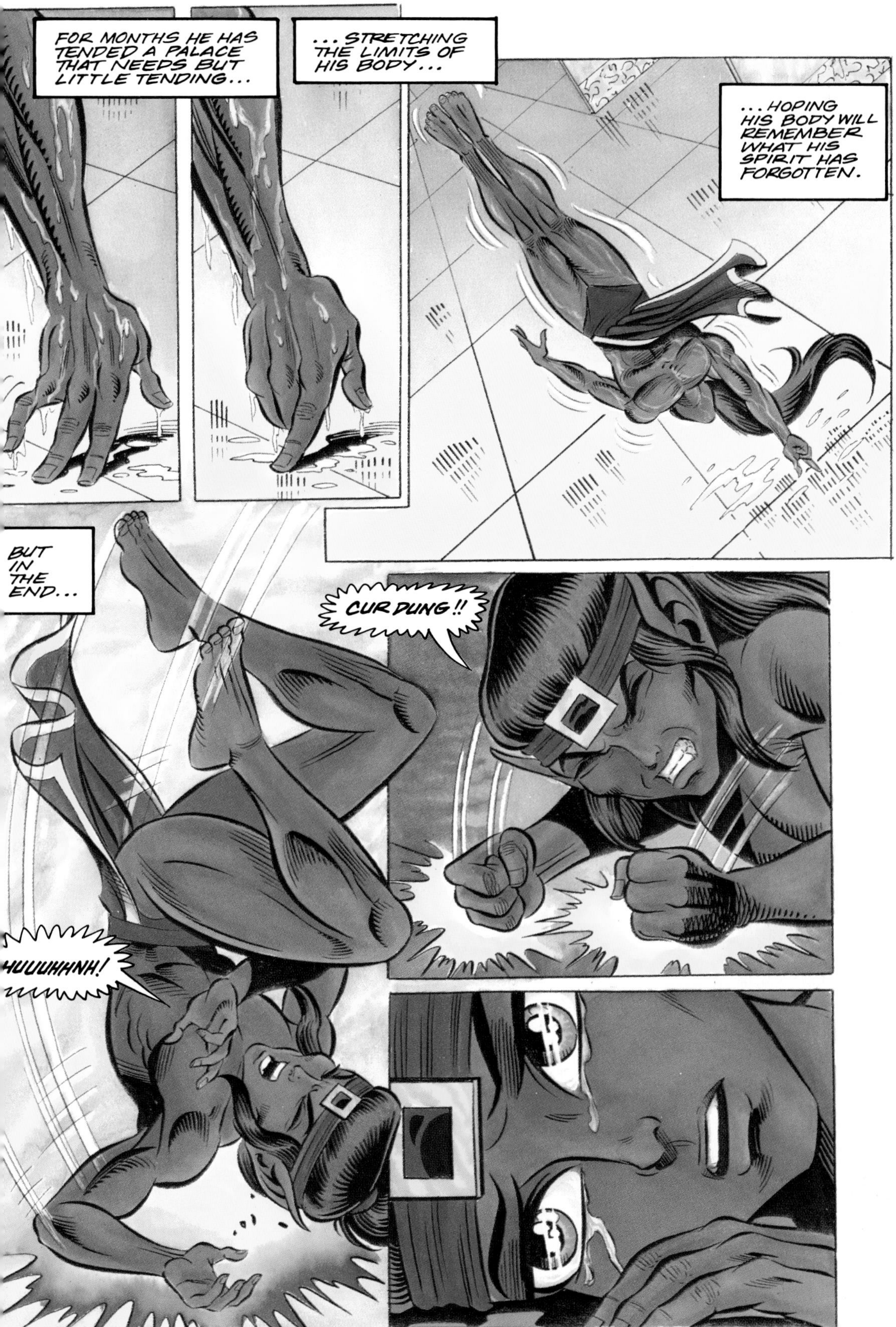
FOR MONTHS HE HAS TENDED A PALACE THAT NEEDS BUT LITTLE TENDING...
...STRETCHING THE LIMITS OF HIS BODY...
...HOPING HIS BODY WILL REMEMBER WHAT HIS SPIRIT HAS FORGOTTEN.
BUT IN THE END...
CUR DUNG!!
HUUUHHNH!

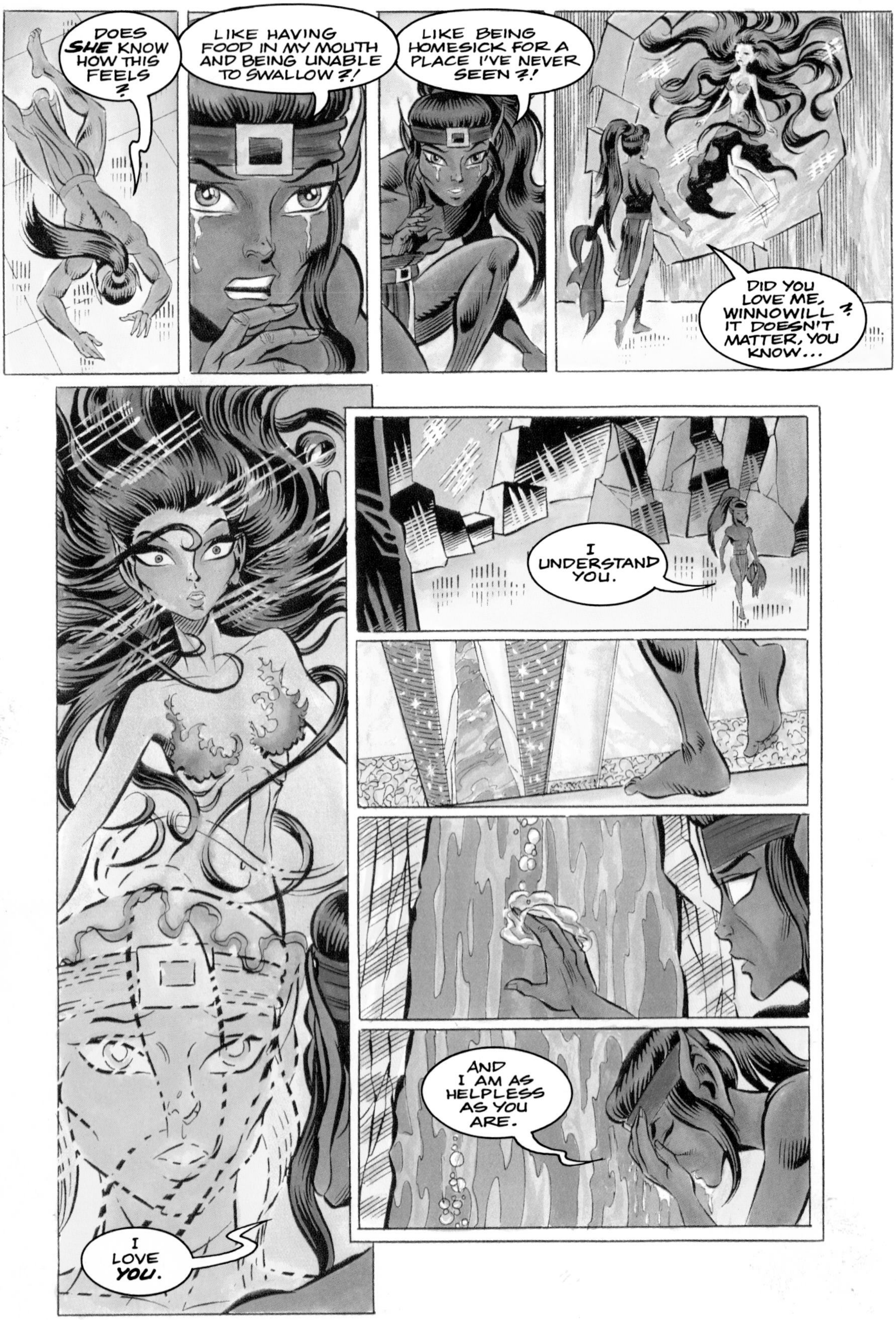
DOES SHE KNOW HOW THIS FEELS ?
LIKE HAVING FOOD IN MY MOUTH AND BEING UNABLE TO SWALLOW ?!
LIKE BEING HOMESICK FOR A PLACE I'VE NEVER SEEN ?!
DID YOU LOVE ME, WINNOWILL ? IT DOESN'T MATTER, YOU KNOW...
I UNDERSTAND YOU.
AND I AM AS HELPLESS AS YOU ARE.
I LOVE YOU.

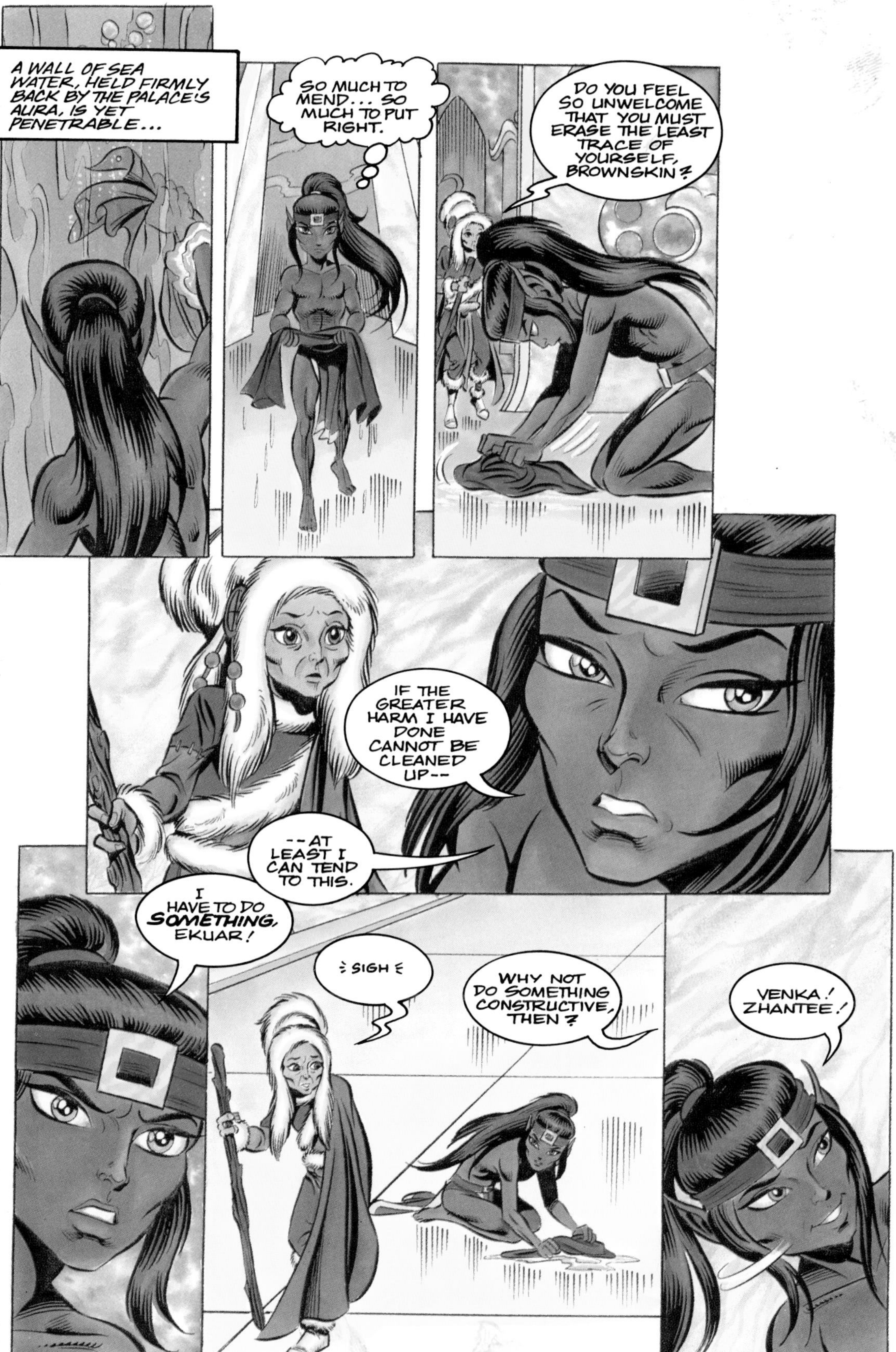
A WALL OF SEA WATER, HELD FIRMLY BACK BY THE PALACE'S AURA, IS YET PENETRABLE...
SO MUCH TO MEND... SO MUCH TO PUT RIGHT.
DO YOU FEEL SO UNWELCOME THAT YOU MUST ERASE THE LEAST TRACE OF YOURSELF, BROWNSKIN?
IF THE GREATER HARM I HAVE DONE CANNOT BE CLEANED UP--
--AT LEAST I CAN TEND TO THIS.
I HAVE TO DO SOMETHING, EKUAR!
SIGH
WHY NOT DO SOMETHING CONSTRUCTIVE, THEN?
VENKA! ZHANTEE!

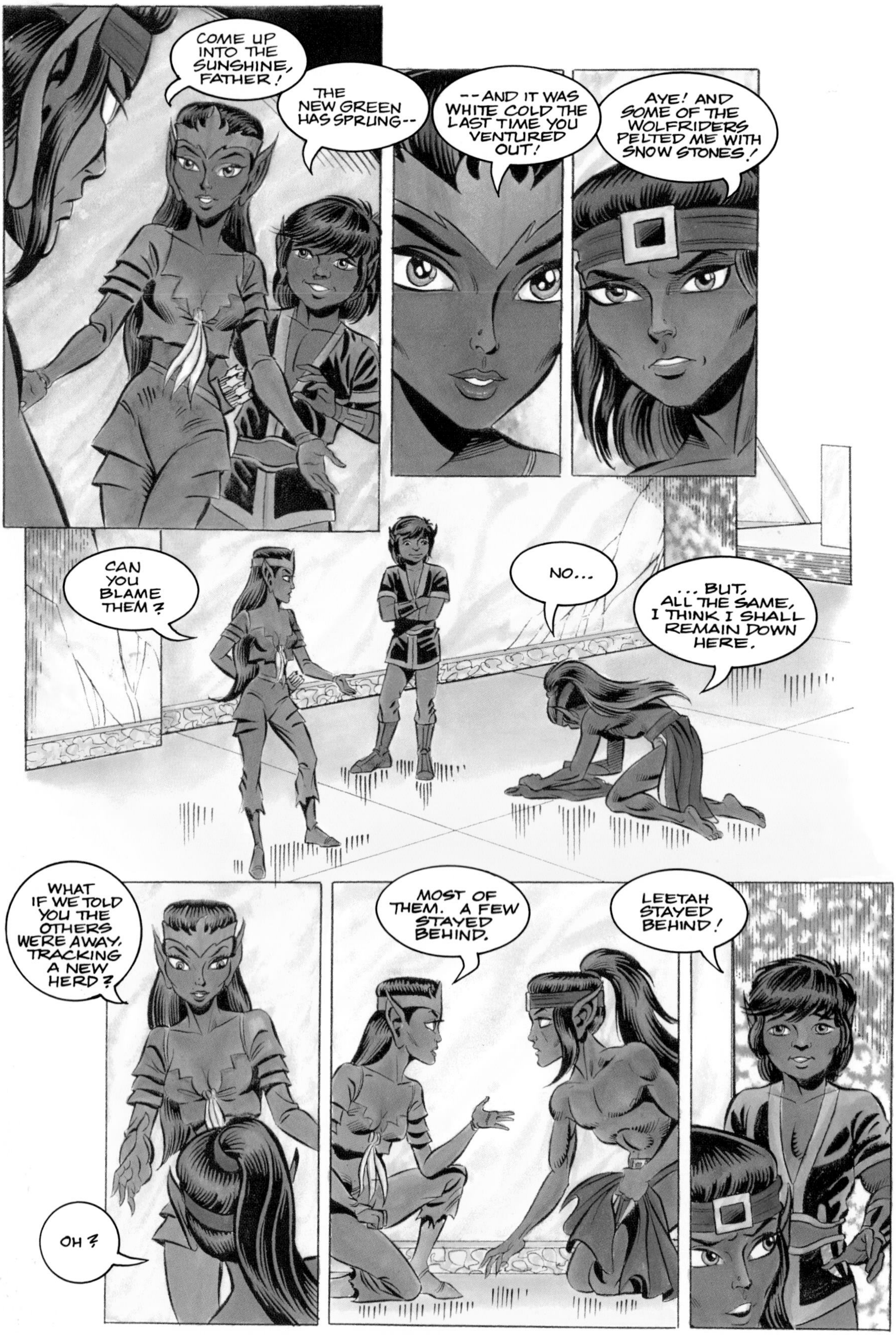
COME UP INTO THE SUNSHINE, FATHER!
THE NEW GREEN HAS SPRUNG--
--AND IT WAS WHITE COLD THE LAST TIME YOU VENTURED OUT!
AYE! AND SOME OF THE WOLFRIDERS PELTED ME WITH SNOW STONES!
CAN YOU BLAME THEM?
NO...
...BUT, ALL THE SAME, I THINK I SHALL REMAIN DOWN HERE.
WHAT IF WE TOLD YOU THE OTHERS WERE AWAY, TRACKING A NEW HERD?
OH?
MOST OF THEM. A FEW STAYED BEHIND.
LEETAH STAYED BEHIND!

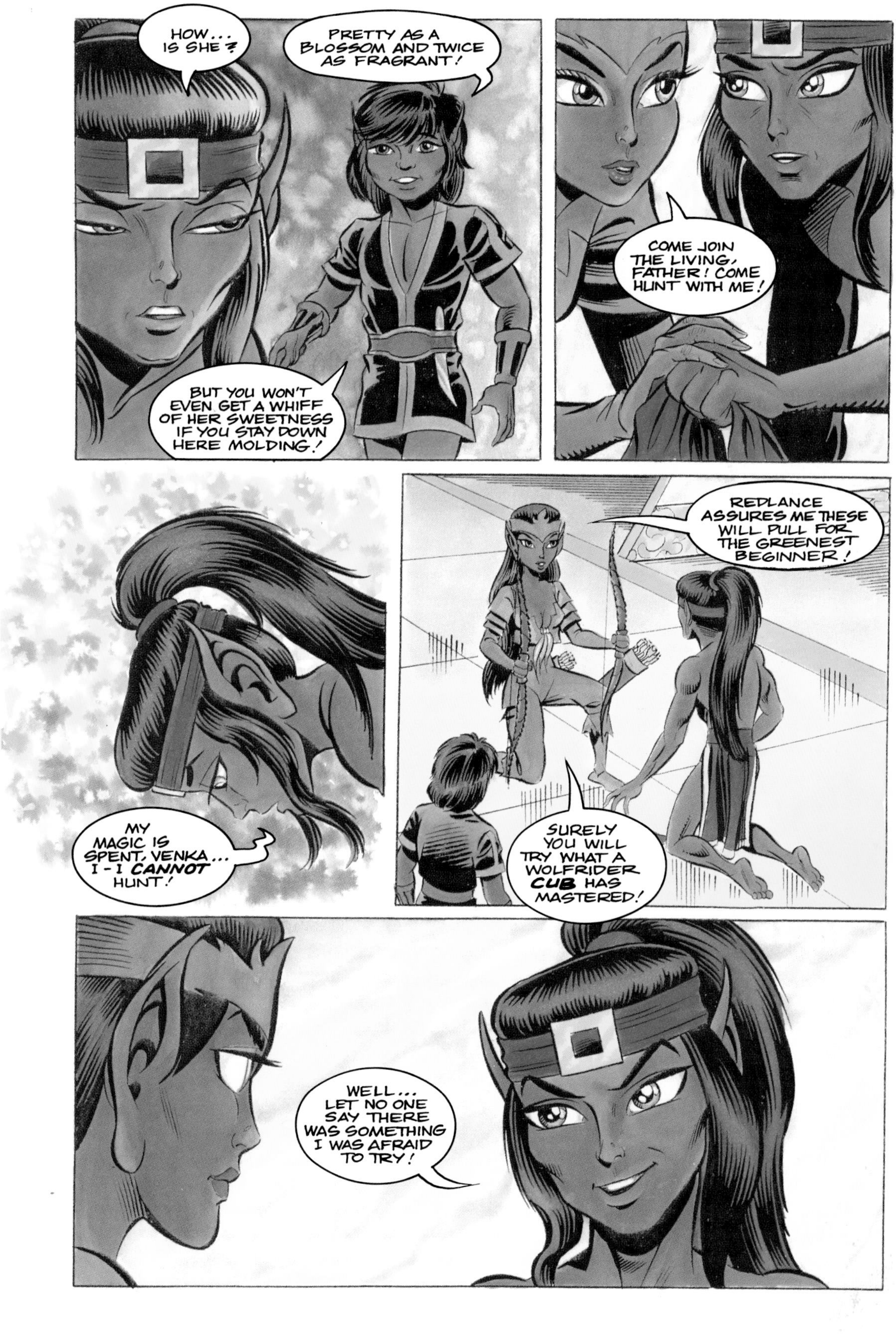
HOW... IS SHE?
PRETTY AS A BLOSSOM AND TWICE AS FRAGRANT!
BUT YOU WON'T EVEN GET A WHIFF OF HER SWEETNESS IF YOU STAY DOWN HERE MOLDING!
COME JOIN THE LIVING, FATHER! COME HUNT WITH ME!
MY MAGIC IS SPENT, VENKA... I-I CANNOT HUNT!
REDLANCE ASSURES ME THESE WILL PULL FOR THE GREENEST BEGINNER!
SURELY YOU WILL TRY WHAT A WOLFRIDER CUB HAS MASTERED!
WELL... LET NO ONE SAY THERE WAS SOMETHING I WAS AFRAID TO TRY!

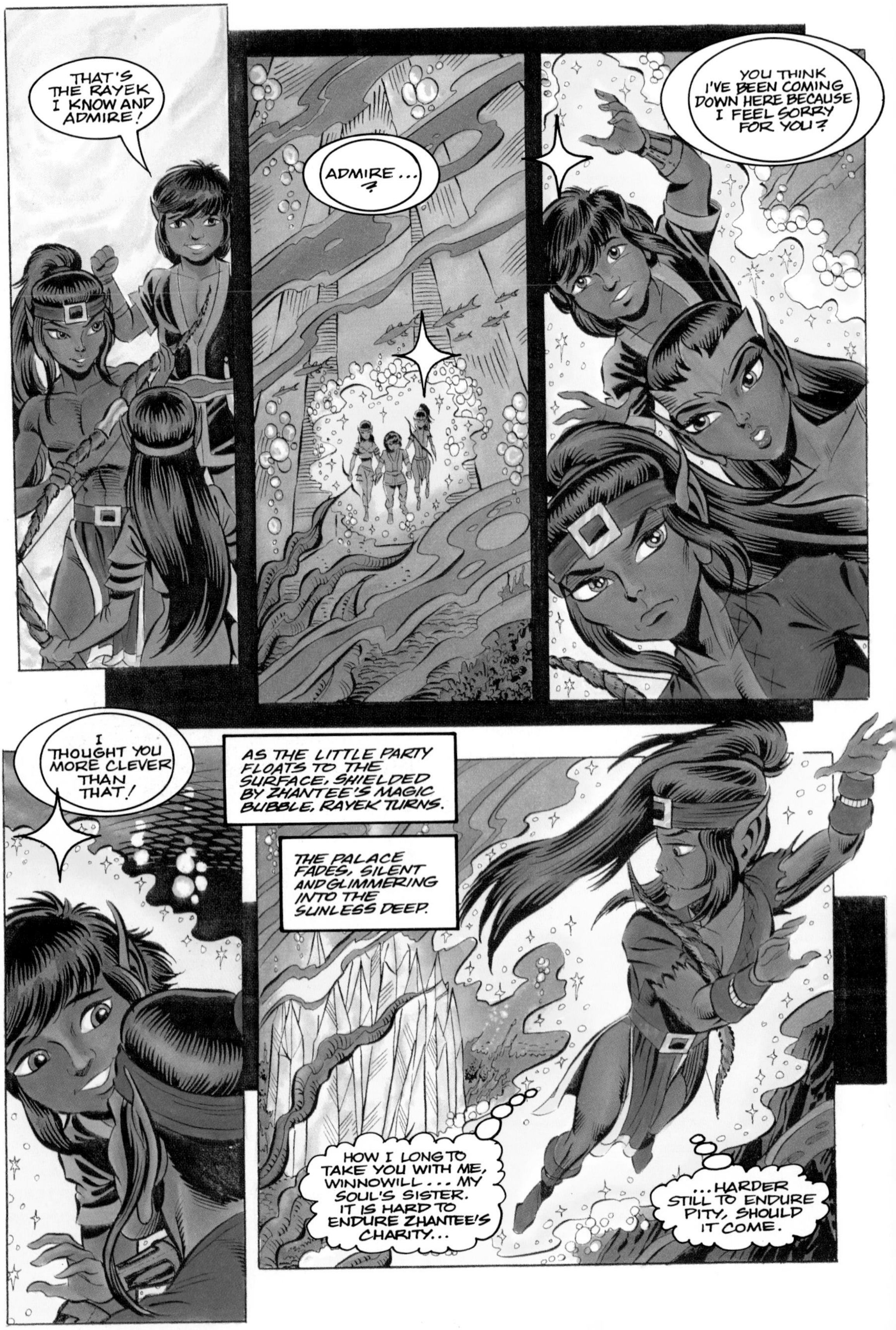
THAT'S THE RAYEK I KNOW AND ADMIRE!
ADMIRE...?
YOU THINK I'VE BEEN COMING DOWN HERE BECAUSE I FEEL SORRY FOR YOU?
I THOUGHT YOU MORE CLEVER THAN THAT!
AS THE LITTLE PARTY FLOATS TO THE SURFACE, SHIELDED BY ZHANTEE'S MAGIC BUBBLE, RAYEK TURNS.
THE PALACE FADES, SILENT AND GLIMMERING INTO THE SUNLESS DEEP.
HOW I LONG TO TAKE YOU WITH ME, WINNOWILL... MY SOUL'S SISTER. IT IS HARD TO ENDURE ZHANTEE'S CHARITY...
...HARDER STILL TO ENDURE PITY, SHOULD IT COME.

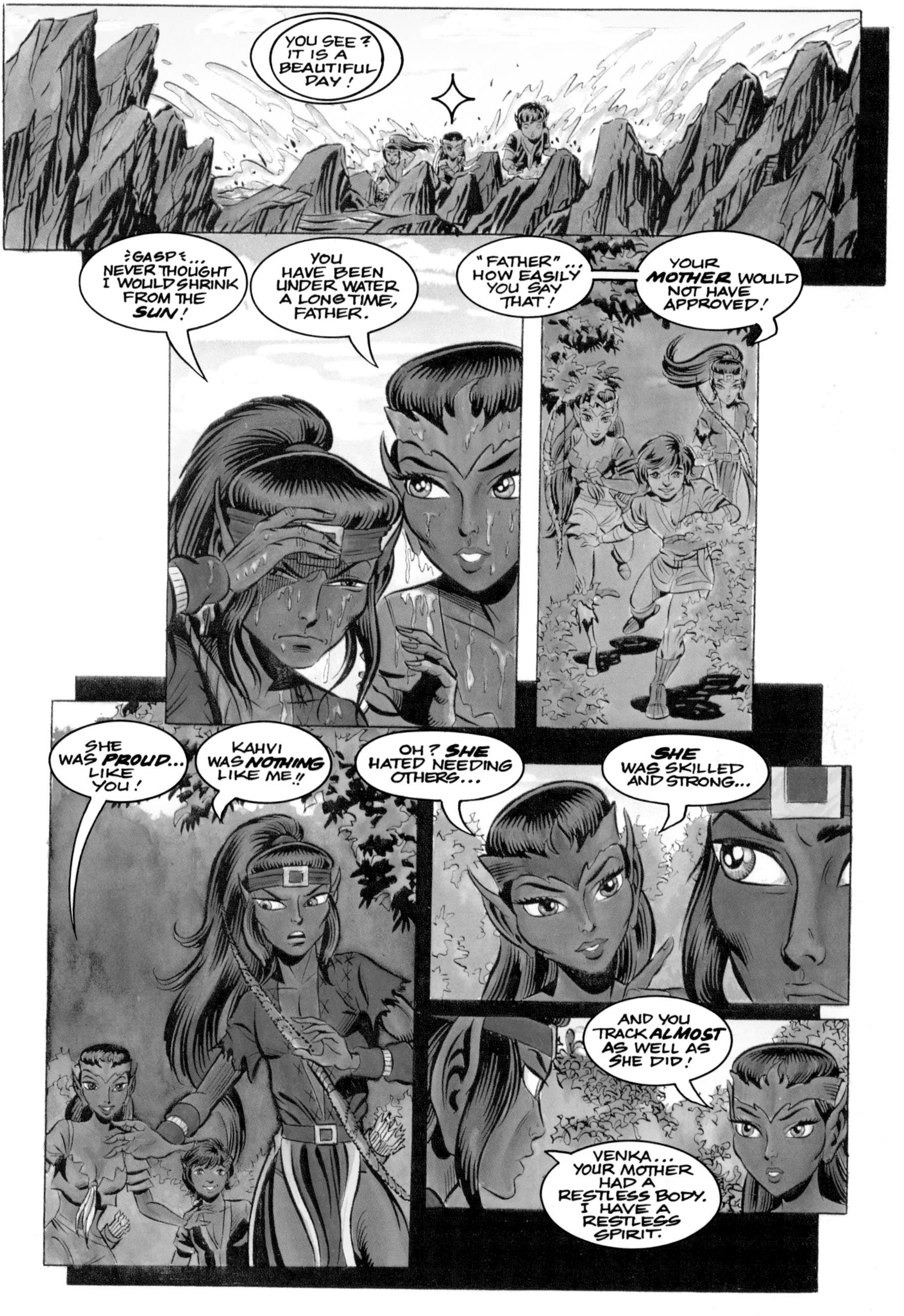
YOU SEE? IT IS A BEAUTIFUL DAY!
:GASP:... NEVER THOUGHT I WOULD SHRINK FROM THE SUN!
YOU HAVE BEEN UNDER WATER A LONG TIME, FATHER.
"FATHER"... HOW EASILY YOU SAY THAT!
YOUR MOTHER WOULD NOT HAVE APPROVED!
SHE WAS PROUD... LIKE YOU!
KAHVI WAS NOTHING LIKE ME!!
OH? SHE HATED NEEDING OTHERS...
SHE WAS SKILLED AND STRONG...
AND YOU TRACK ALMOST AS WELL AS SHE DID!
VENKA... YOUR MOTHER HAD A RESTLESS BODY. I HAVE A RESTLESS SPIRIT.

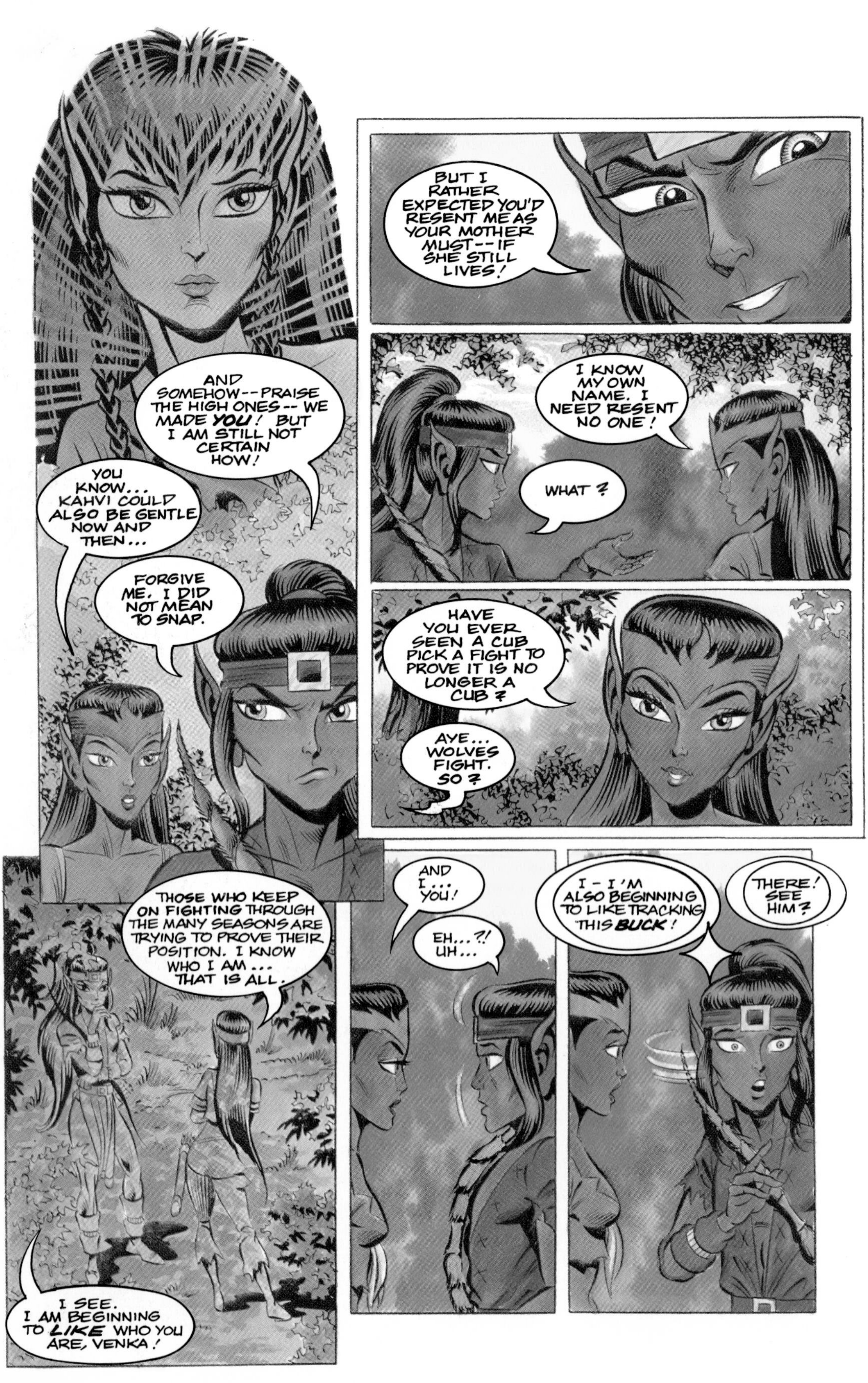
AND SOMEHOW--PRAISE THE HIGH ONES-- WE MADE YOU! BUT I AM STILL NOT CERTAIN HOW!
YOU KNOW... KAHVI COULD ALSO BE GENTLE NOW AND THEN...
FORGIVE ME. I DID NOT MEAN TO SNAP.
BUT I RATHER EXPECTED YOU'D RESENT ME AS YOUR MOTHER MUST--IF SHE STILL LIVES!
I KNOW MY OWN NAME. I NEED RESENT NO ONE!
WHAT ?
HAVE YOU EVER SEEN A CUB PICK A FIGHT TO PROVE IT IS NO LONGER A CUB ?
AYE... WOLVES FIGHT. SO ?
THOSE WHO KEEP ON FIGHTING THROUGH THE MANY SEASONS ARE TRYING TO PROVE THEIR POSITION. I KNOW WHO I AM... THAT IS ALL.
I SEE. I AM BEGINNING TO LIKE WHO YOU ARE, VENKA!
AND I... YOU!
EH...?! UH...
I-I'M ALSO BEGINNING TO LIKE TRACKING THIS BUCK!
THERE! SEE HIM ?

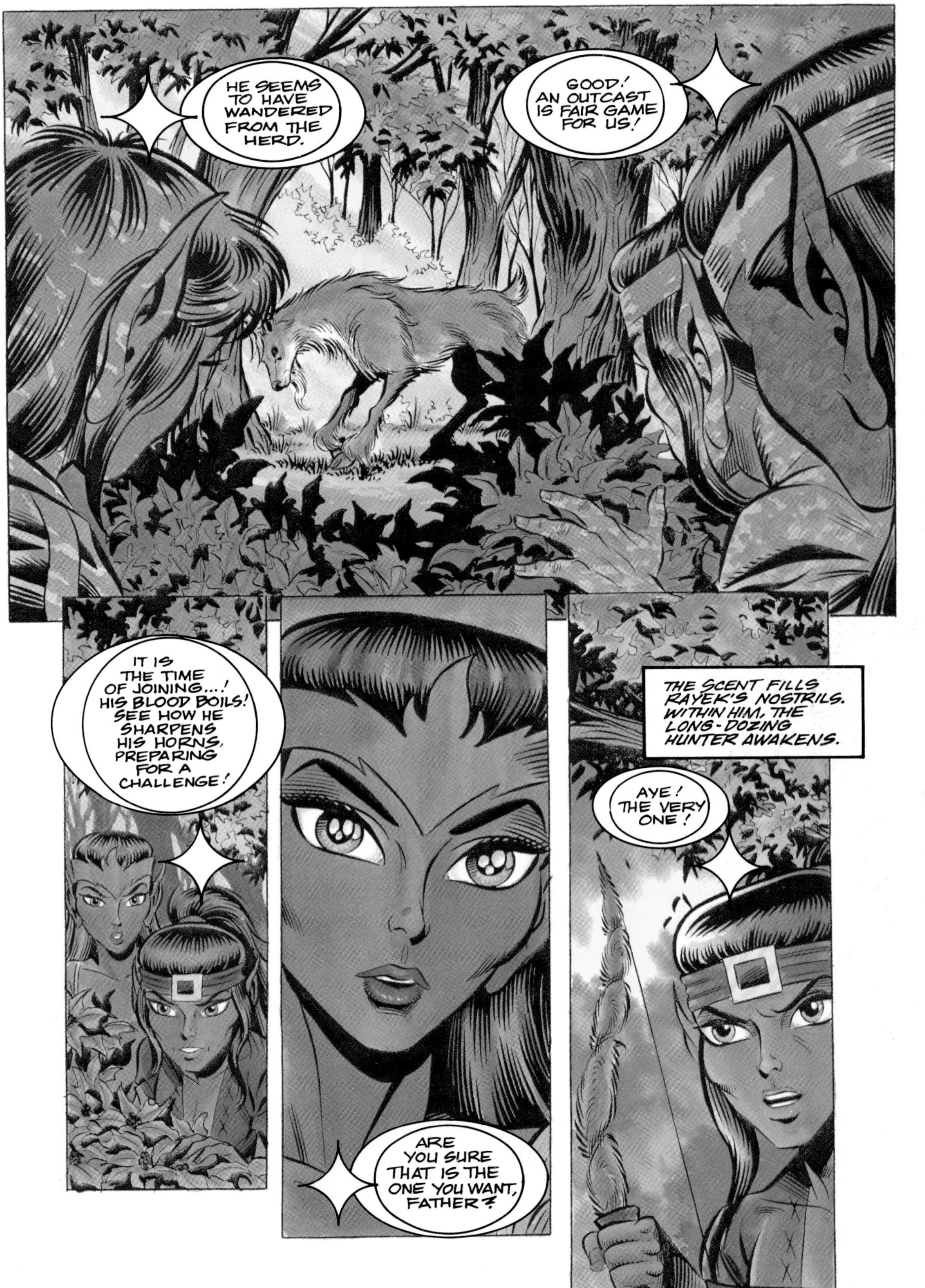
HE SEEMS TO HAVE WANDERED FROM THE HERD.
GOOD! AN OUTCAST IS FAIR GAME FOR US!
IT IS THE TIME OF JOINING...! HIS BLOOD BOILS! SEE HOW HE SHARPENS HIS HORNS, PREPARING FOR A CHALLENGE!
ARE YOU SURE THAT IS THE ONE YOU WANT, FATHER?
THE SCENT FILLS RAYEK'S NOSTRILS. WITHIN HIM, THE LONG-DOZING HUNTER AWAKENS.
AYE! THE VERY ONE!

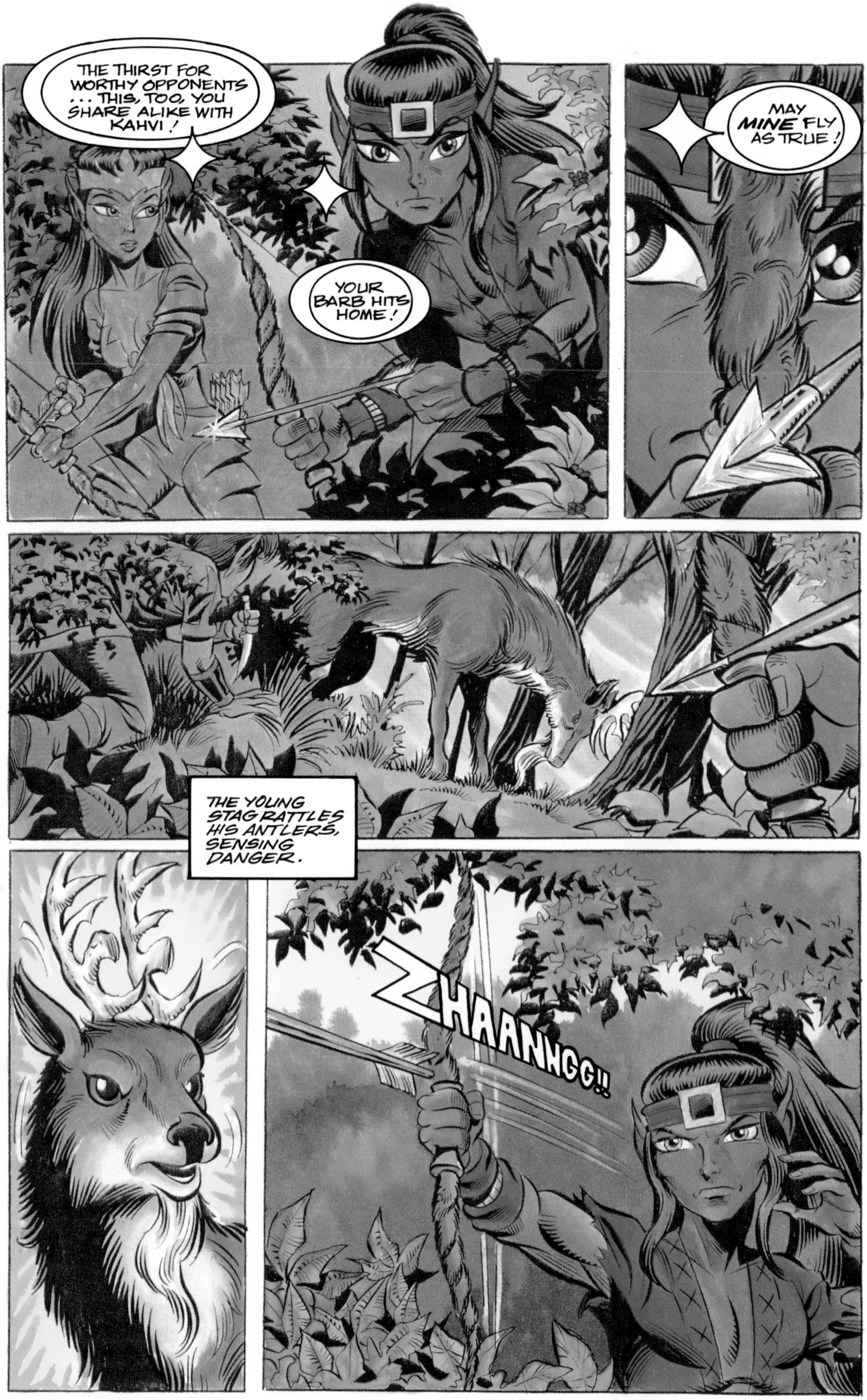
THE THIRST FOR WORTHY OPPONENTS . . . THIS, TOO, YOU SHARE ALIKE WITH KAHVI!
YOUR BARB HITS HOME!
MAY MINE FLY AS TRUE!
THE YOUNG STAG RATTLES HIS ANTLERS, SENSING DANGER.
ZHAANNGG!!

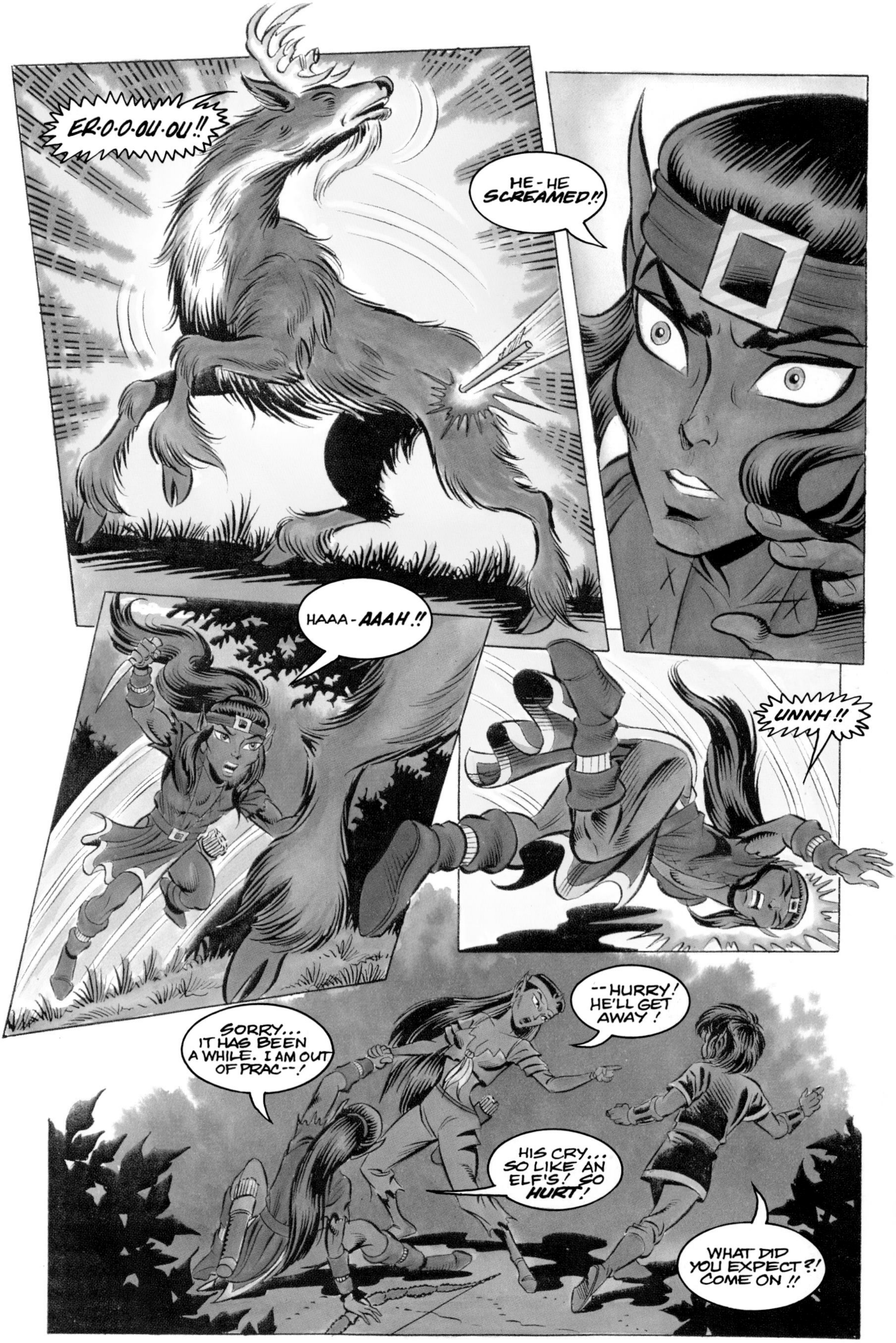
ER-O-O-OU-OU!!
HE-HE SCREAMED!!
HAAA-AAAH!!
UNNH!!
SORRY... IT HAS BEEN A WHILE. I AM OUT OF PRAC--!
--HURRY! HE'LL GET AWAY!
HIS CRY... SO LIKE AN ELF'S! SO HURT!
WHAT DID YOU EXPECT?! COME ON!!

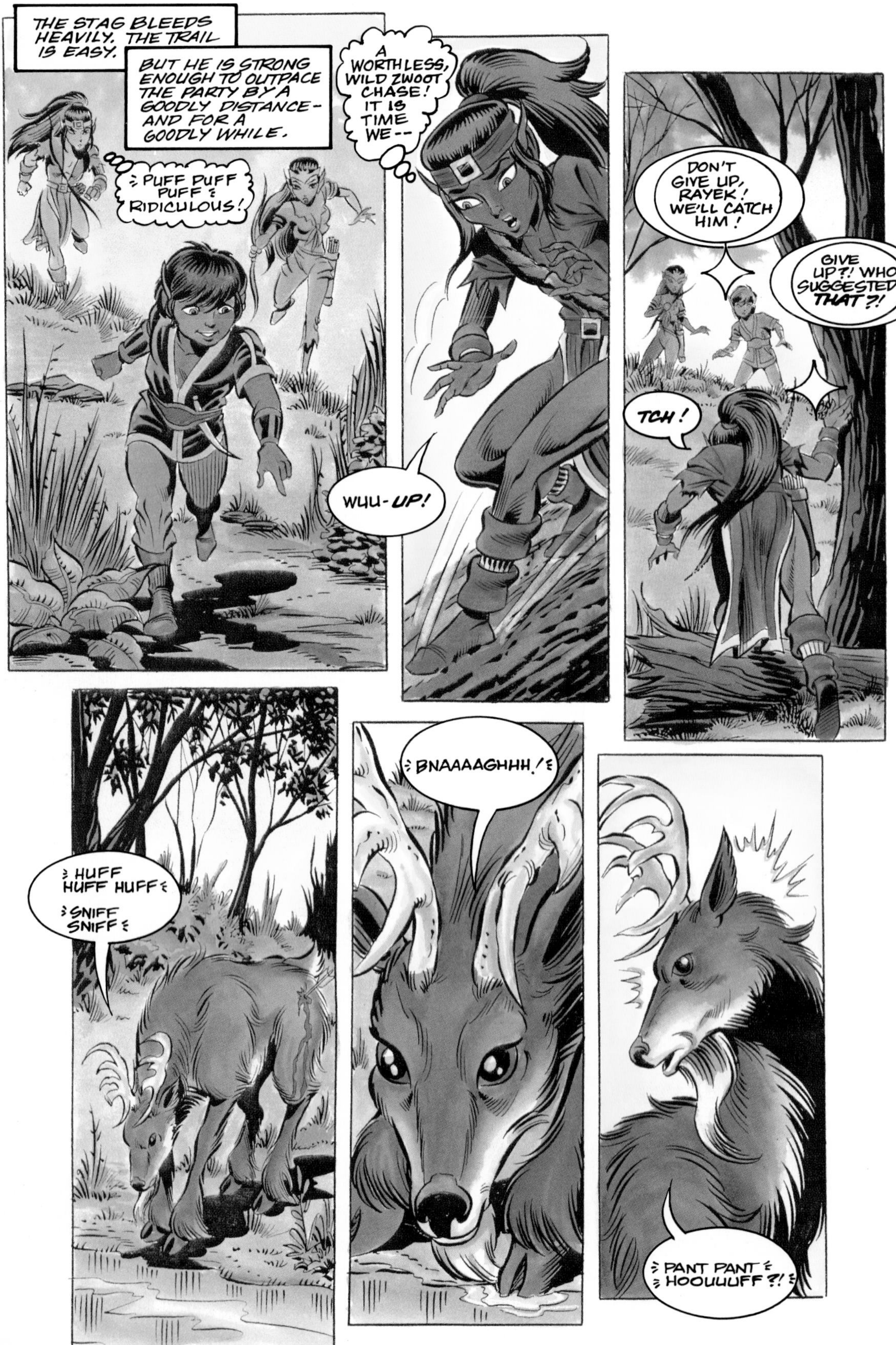
THE STAG BLEEDS HEAVILY. THE TRAIL IS EASY.
BUT HE IS STRONG ENOUGH TO OUTPACE THE PARTY BY A GOODLY DISTANCE - AND FOR A GOODLY WHILE.
PUFF PUFF PUFF RIDICULOUS!
A WORTHLESS, WILD ZWOOT CHASE! IT IS TIME WE--
WUU-UP!
DON'T GIVE UP, RAYEK! WE'LL CATCH HIM!
GIVE UP?! WHO SUGGESTED THAT?!
TCH!
HUFF HUFF HUFF
SNIFF SNIFF
BNAAAAGHHH!
PANT PANT HOOUUUFF?!

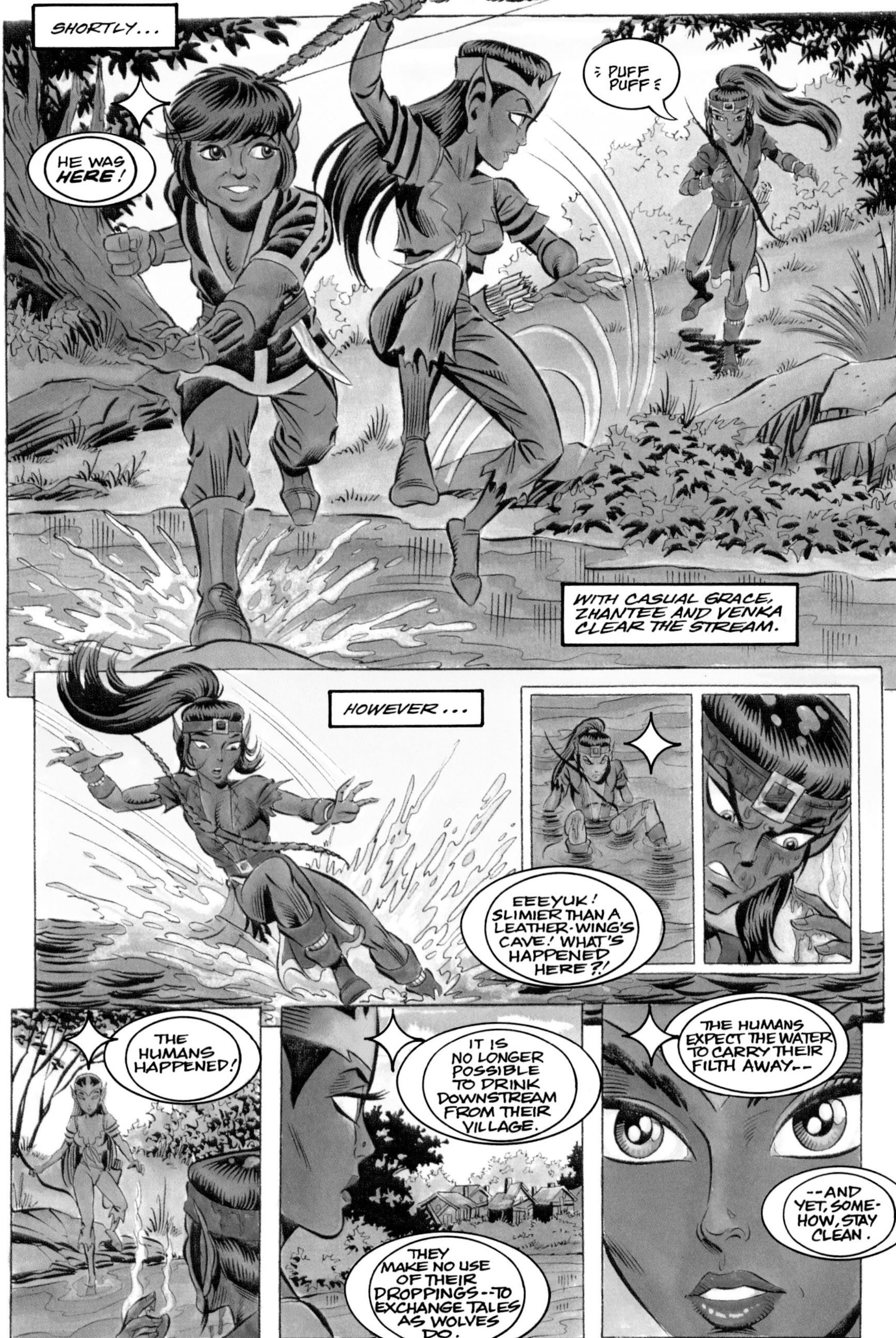
SHORTLY...
HE WAS HERE!
PUFF PUFF
WITH CASUAL GRACE, ZHANTEE AND VENKA CLEAR THE STREAM.
HOWEVER...
EEEYUK! SLIMIER THAN A LEATHER-WING'S CAVE! WHAT'S HAPPENED HERE?!
THE HUMANS HAPPENED!
IT IS NO LONGER POSSIBLE TO DRINK DOWNSTREAM FROM THEIR VILLAGE.
THEY MAKE NO USE OF THEIR DROPPINGS--TO EXCHANGE TALES AS WOLVES DO.
THE HUMANS EXPECT THE WATER TO CARRY THEIR FILTH AWAY--
--AND YET, SOME-HOW, STAY CLEAN.

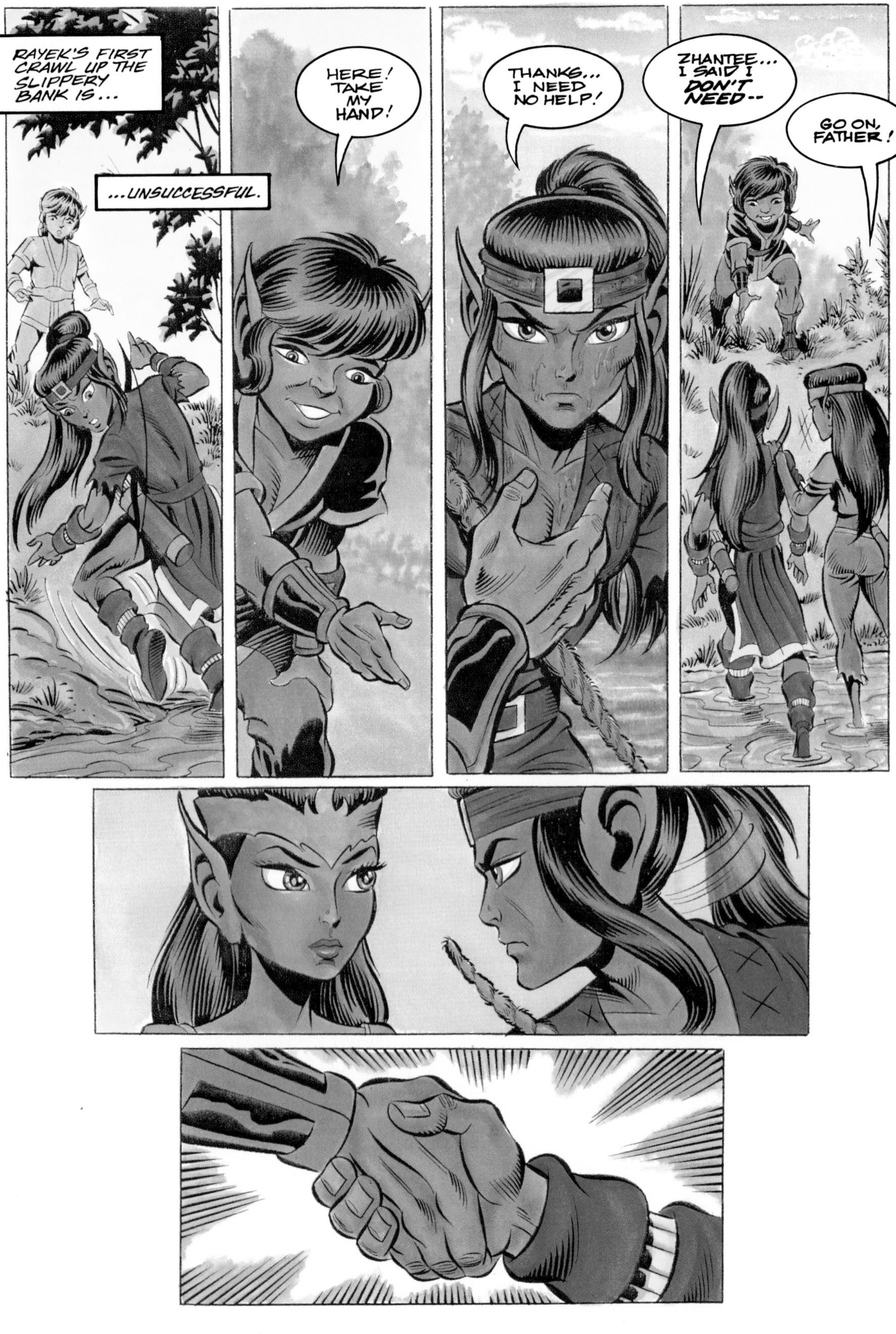
RAYEK'S FIRST CRAWL UP THE SLIPPERY BANK IS...
...UNSUCCESSFUL.
HERE! TAKE MY HAND!
THANKS... I NEED NO HELP!
ZHANTEE... I SAID I DON'T NEED--
GO ON, FATHER!

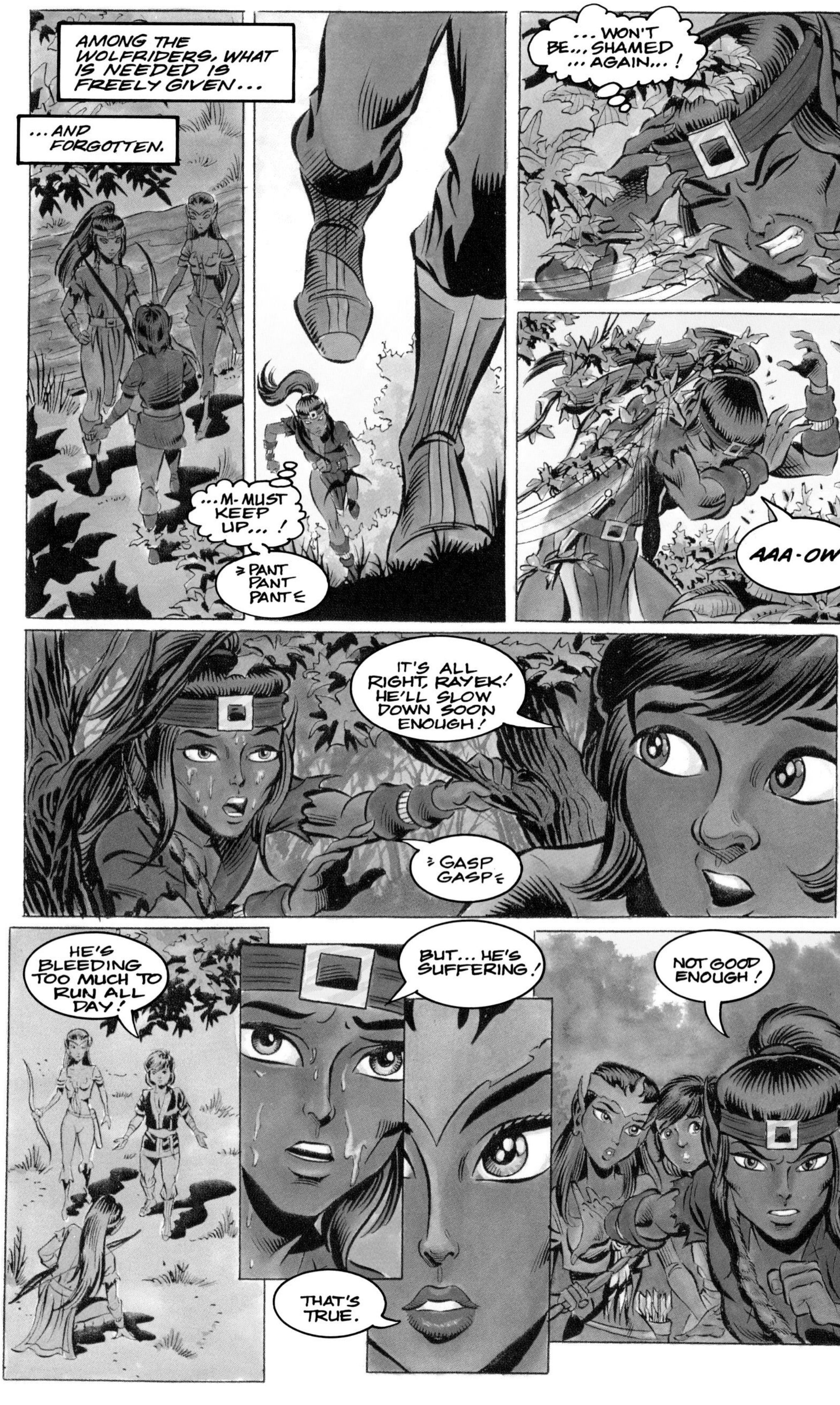
AMONG THE WOLFRIDERS, WHAT IS NEEDED IS FREELY GIVEN...
...AND FORGOTTEN.
...M-MUST KEEP UP...!
PANT PANT PANT
...WON'T BE...SHAMED ...AGAIN...!
AAA-OW!
IT'S ALL RIGHT, RAYEK! HE'LL SLOW DOWN SOON ENOUGH!
GASP GASP
HE'S BLEEDING TOO MUCH TO RUN ALL DAY!
BUT... HE'S SUFFERING!
THAT'S TRUE.
NOT GOOD ENOUGH!

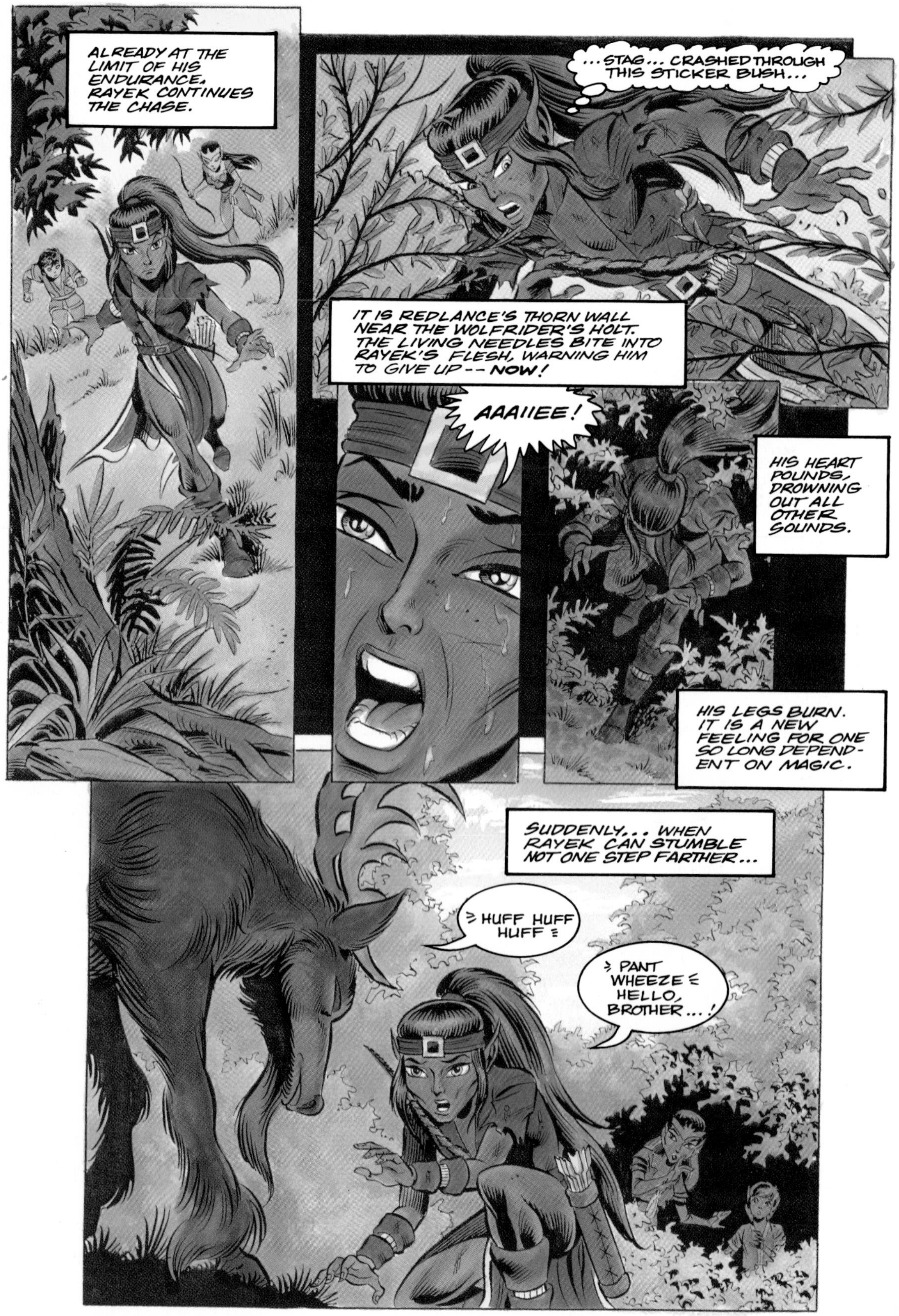
ALREADY AT THE LIMIT OF HIS ENDURANCE, RAYEK CONTINUES THE CHASE.
...STAG... CRASHED THROUGH THIS STICKER BUSH...
IT IS REDLANCE'S THORN WALL NEAR THE WOLFRIDER'S HOLT. THE LIVING NEEDLES BITE INTO RAYEK'S FLESH, WARNING HIM TO GIVE UP -- NOW!
AAAIIEE!
HIS HEART POUNDS, DROWNING OUT ALL OTHER SOUNDS.
HIS LEGS BURN. IT IS A NEW FEELING FOR ONE SO LONG DEPENDENT ON MAGIC.
SUDDENLY... WHEN RAYEK CAN STUMBLE NOT ONE STEP FARTHER...
HUFF HUFF HUFF
PANT WHEEZE HELLO, BROTHER...!

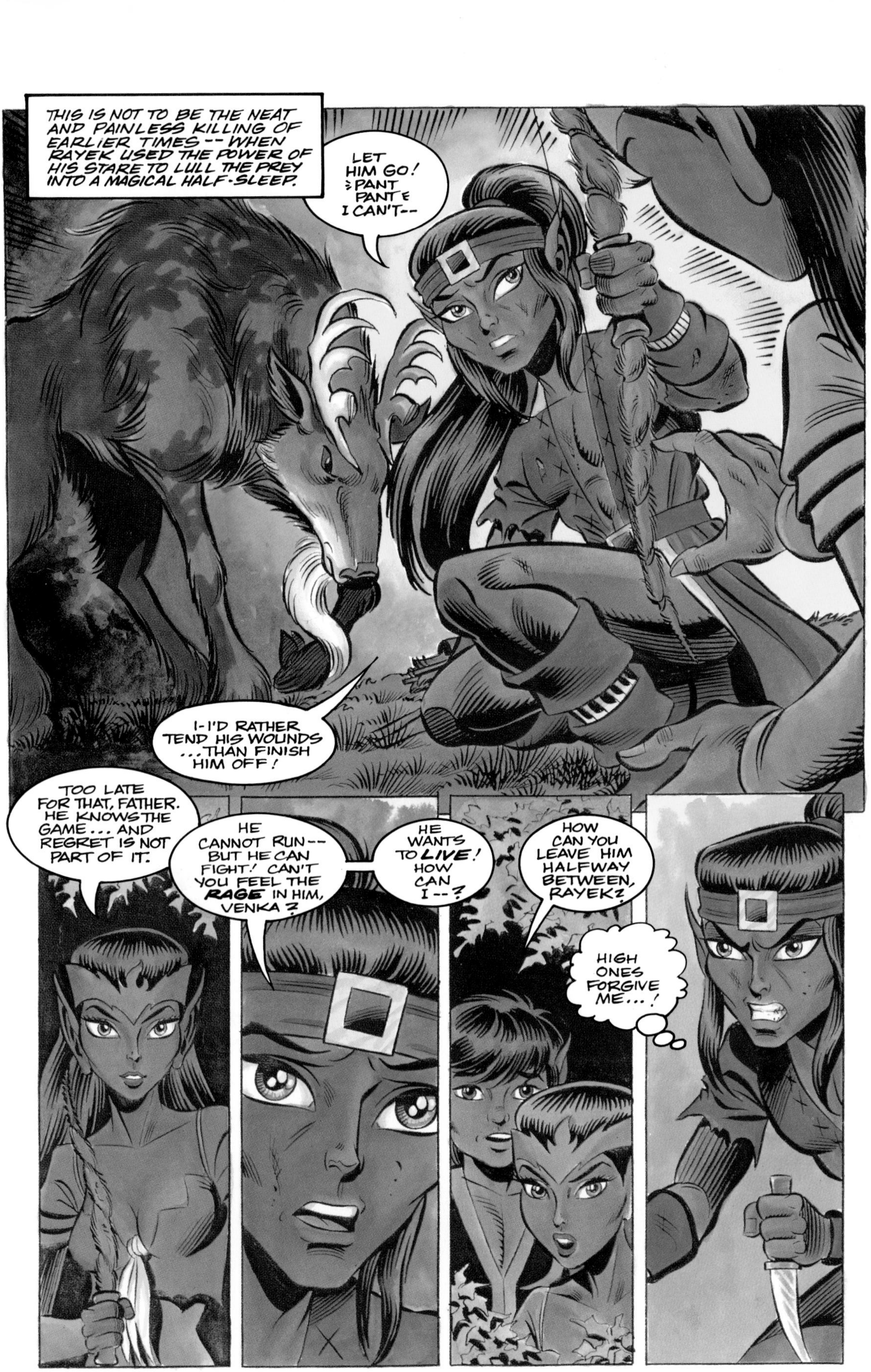
THIS IS NOT TO BE THE NEAT AND PAINLESS KILLING OF EARLIER TIMES -- WHEN RAYEK USED THE POWER OF HIS STARE TO LULL THE PREY INTO A MAGICAL HALF-SLEEP.
LET HIM GO! ≥PANT PANT≤ I CAN'T--
I-I'D RATHER TEND HIS WOUNDS ...THAN FINISH HIM OFF!
TOO LATE FOR THAT, FATHER. HE KNOWS THE GAME... AND REGRET IS NOT PART OF IT.
HE CANNOT RUN-- BUT HE CAN FIGHT! CAN'T YOU FEEL THE RAGE IN HIM, VENKA?
HE WANTS TO LIVE! HOW CAN I--?
HOW CAN YOU LEAVE HIM HALFWAY BETWEEN, RAYEK?
HIGH ONES FORGIVE ME...!

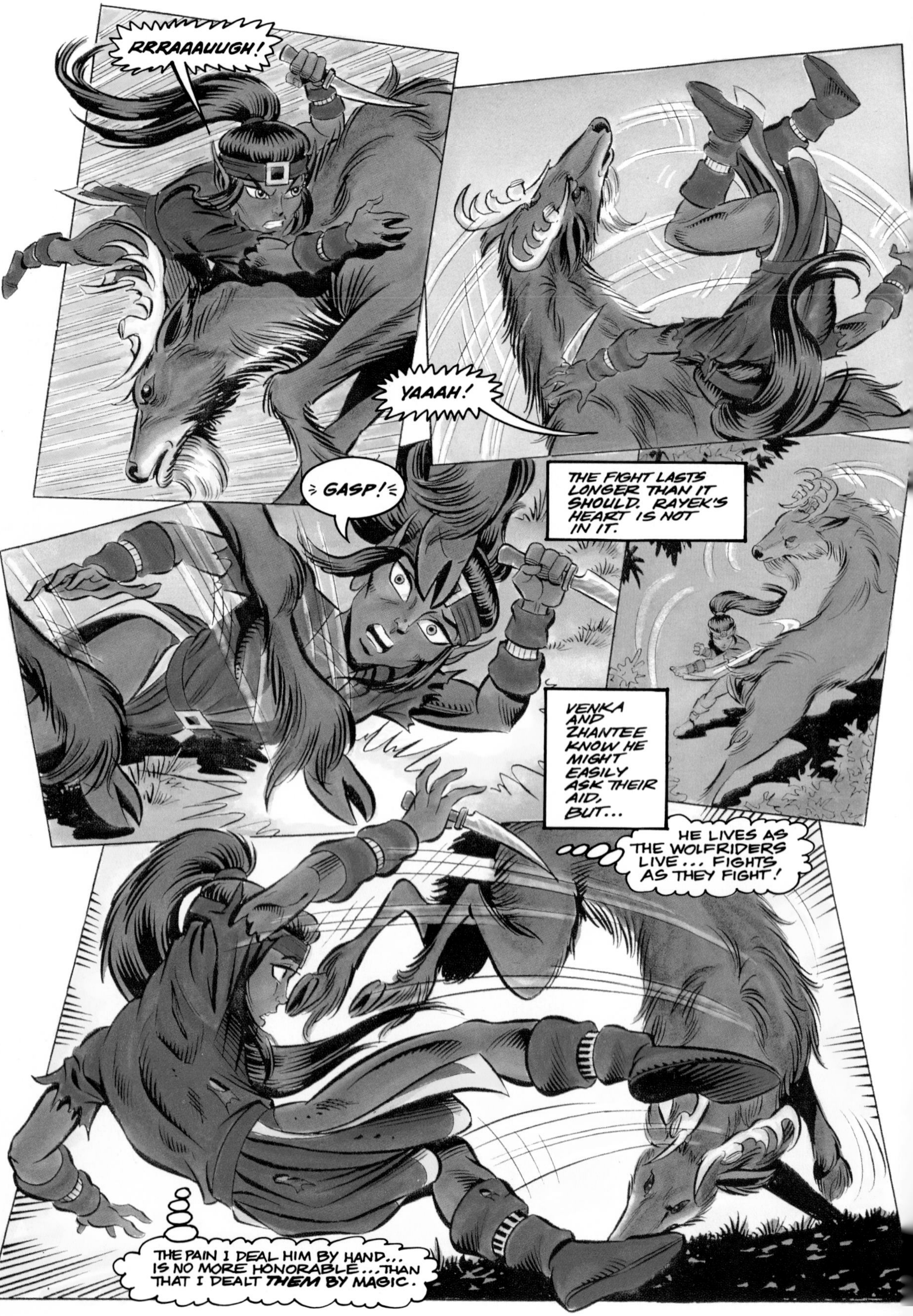
RRRAAAUUGH!
YAAAH!
GASP!
THE FIGHT LASTS LONGER THAN IT SHOULD. RAYEK'S HEART IS NOT IN IT.
VENKA AND ZHANTEE KNOW HE MIGHT EASILY ASK THEIR AID, BUT...
HE LIVES AS THE WOLFRIDERS LIVE... FIGHTS AS THEY FIGHT!
THE PAIN I DEAL HIM BY HAND... IS NO MORE HONORABLE... THAN THAT I DEALT THEM BY MAGIC.

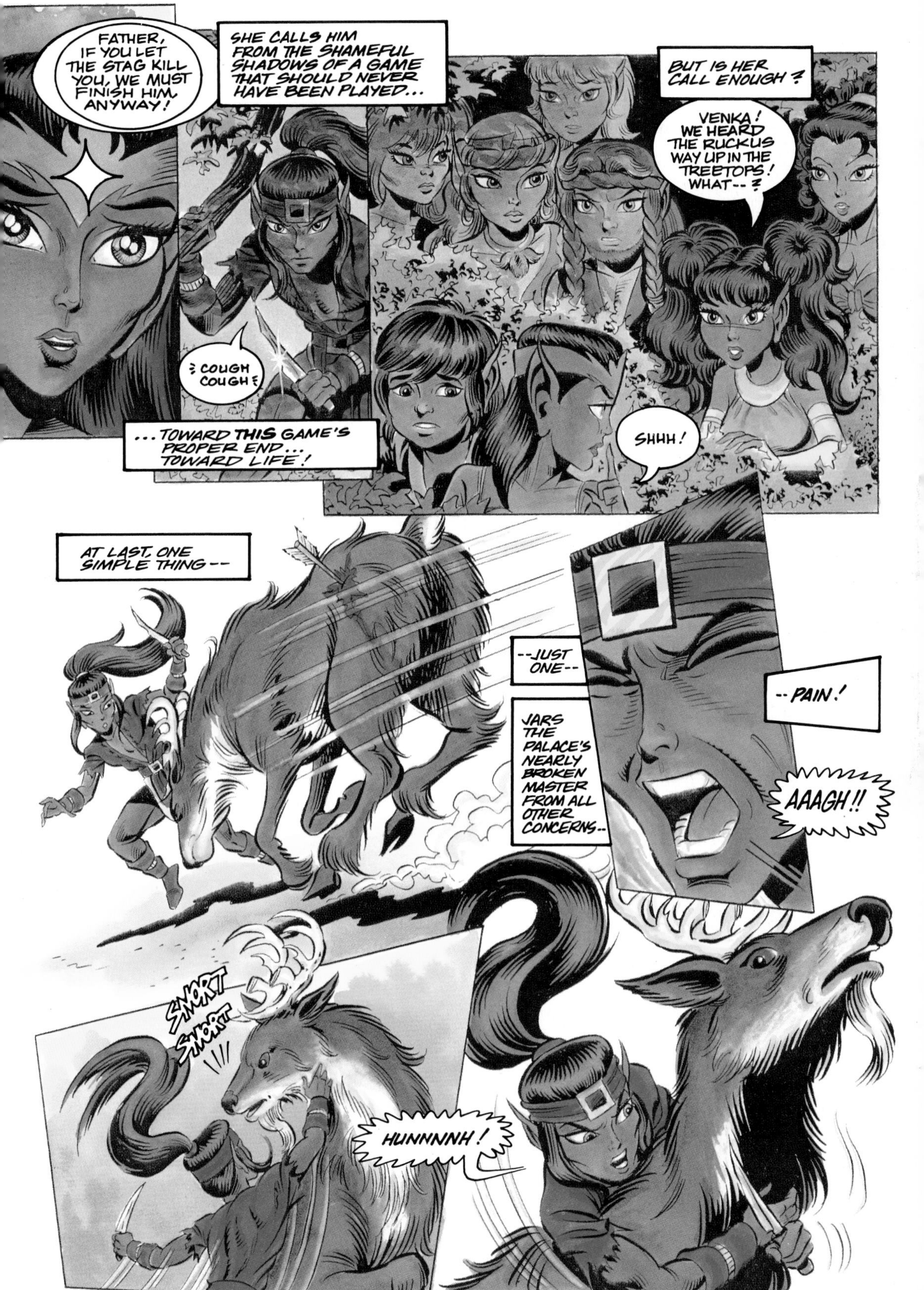
FATHER, IF YOU LET THE STAG KILL YOU, WE MUST FINISH HIM, ANYWAY!
SHE CALLS HIM FROM THE SHAMEFUL SHADOWS OF A GAME THAT SHOULD NEVER HAVE BEEN PLAYED...
COUGH COUGH
...TOWARD THIS GAME'S PROPER END... TOWARD LIFE!
BUT IS HER CALL ENOUGH?
VENKA! WE HEARD THE RUCKUS WAY UP IN THE TREETOPS! WHAT--?
SHHH!
AT LAST, ONE SIMPLE THING--
--JUST ONE--
JARS THE PALACE'S NEARLY BROKEN MASTER FROM ALL OTHER CONCERNS--
--PAIN!
AAAGH!!
SNORT SNORT
HUNNNNH!

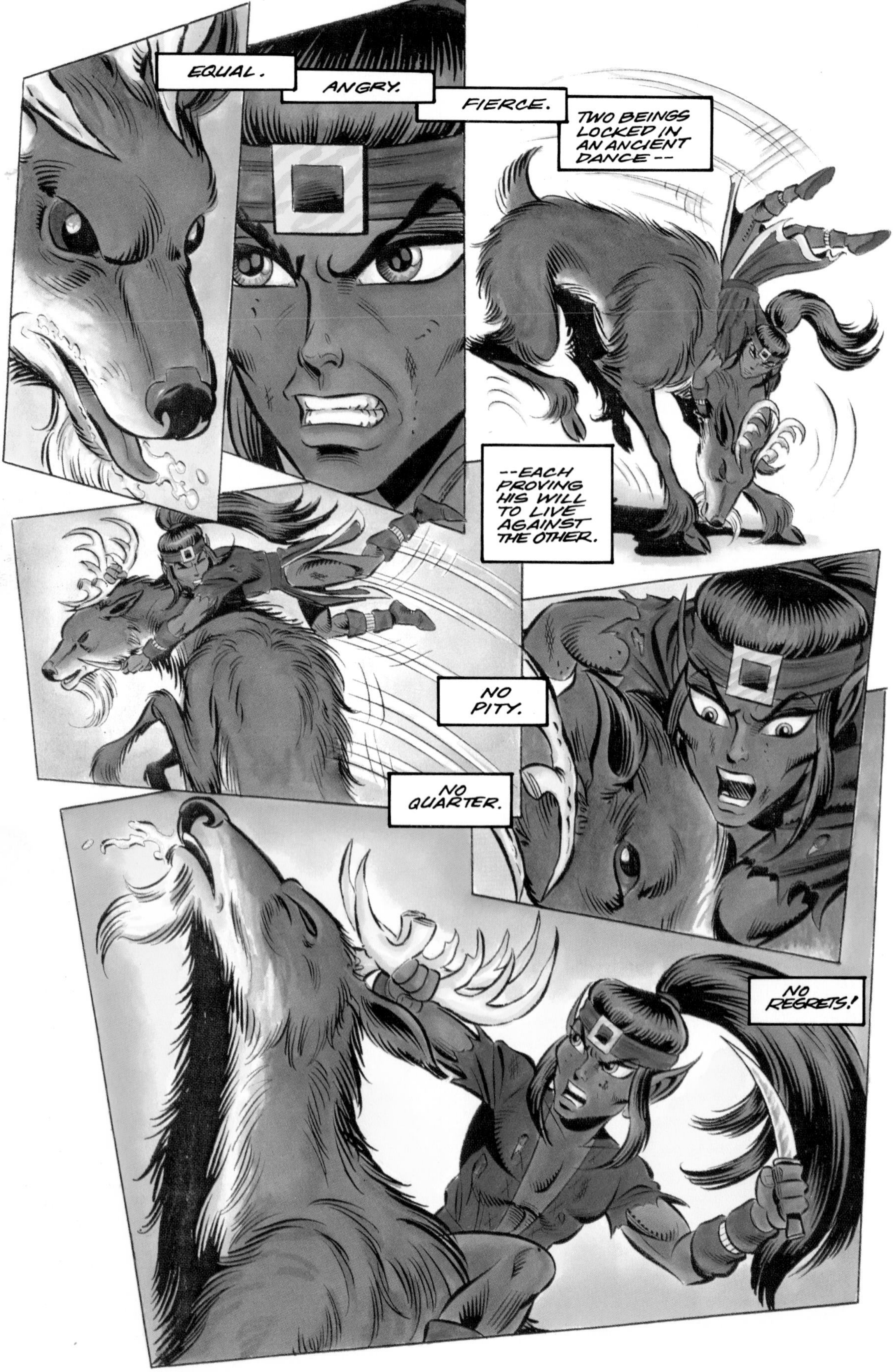
EQUAL.
ANGRY.
FIERCE.
TWO BEINGS LOCKED IN AN ANCIENT DANCE--
--EACH PROVING HIS WILL TO LIVE AGAINST THE OTHER.
NO PITY.
NO QUARTER.
NO REGRETS!

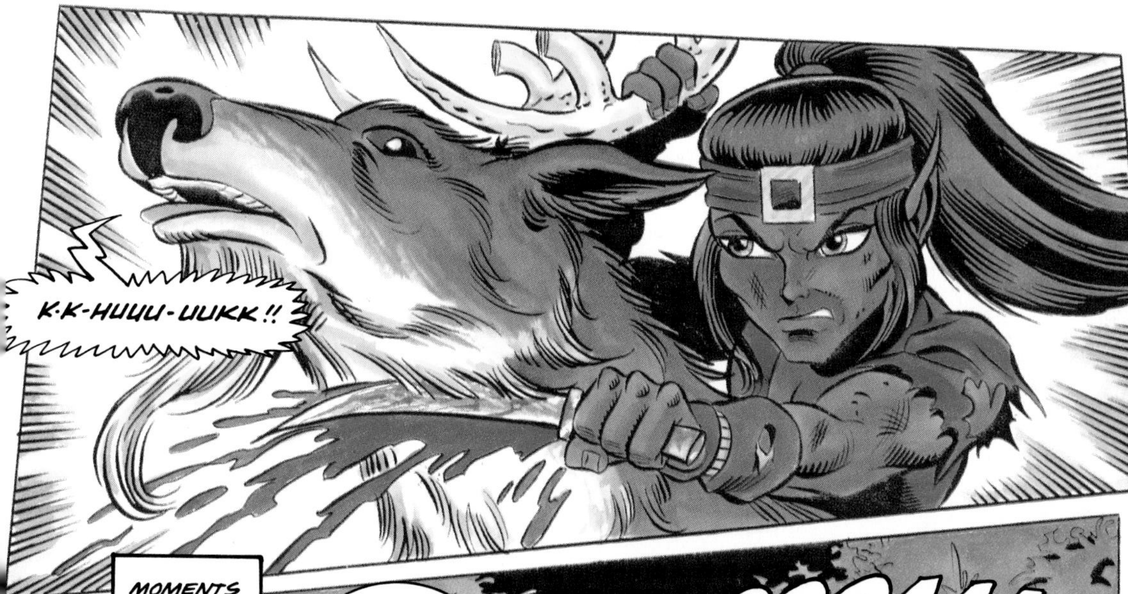
K-K-HUUU-UUKK!!

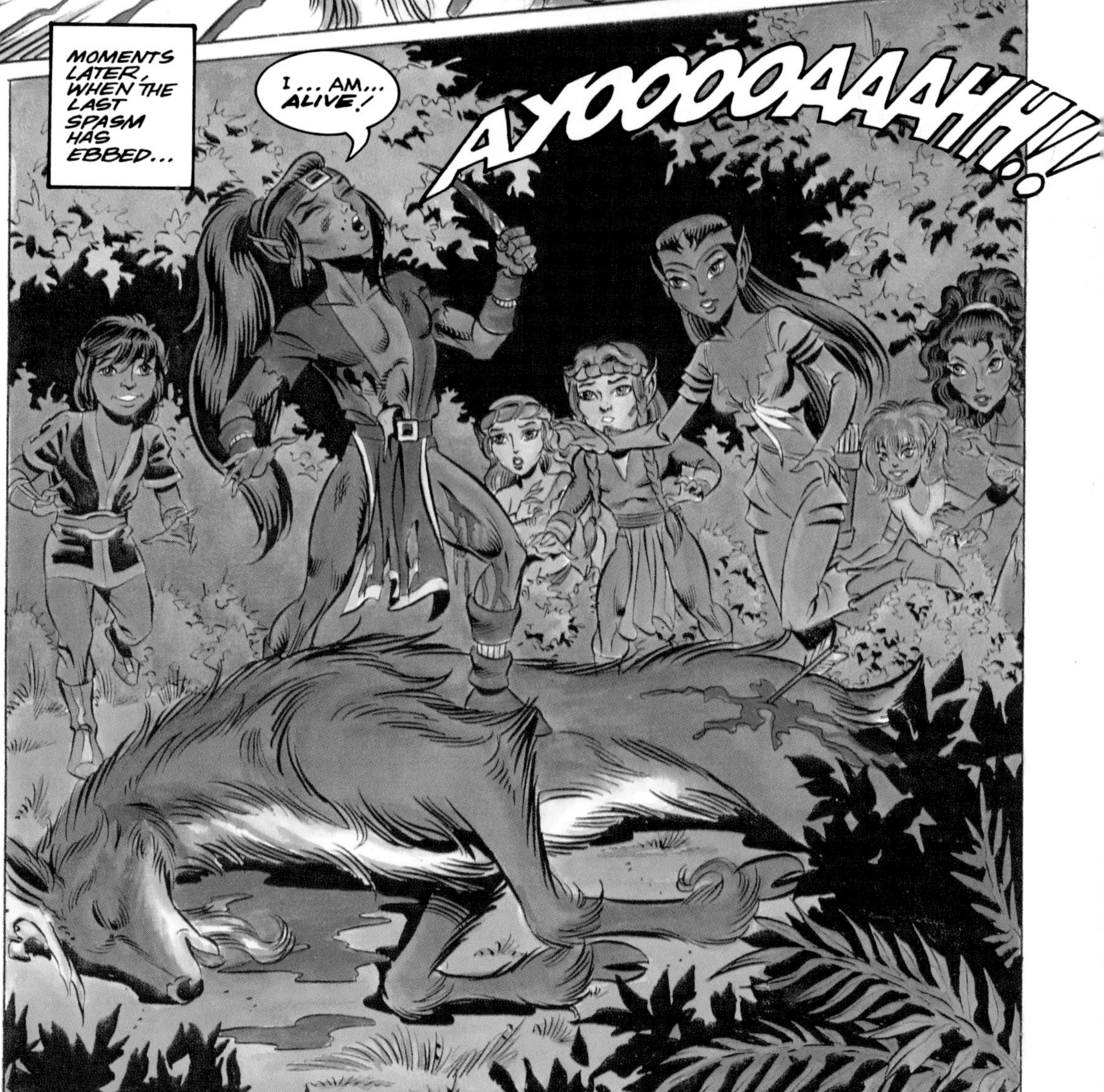
MOMENTS LATER, WHEN THE LAST SPASM HAS EBBED...
I... AM... ALIVE!
AYOOOOAAAHH!!

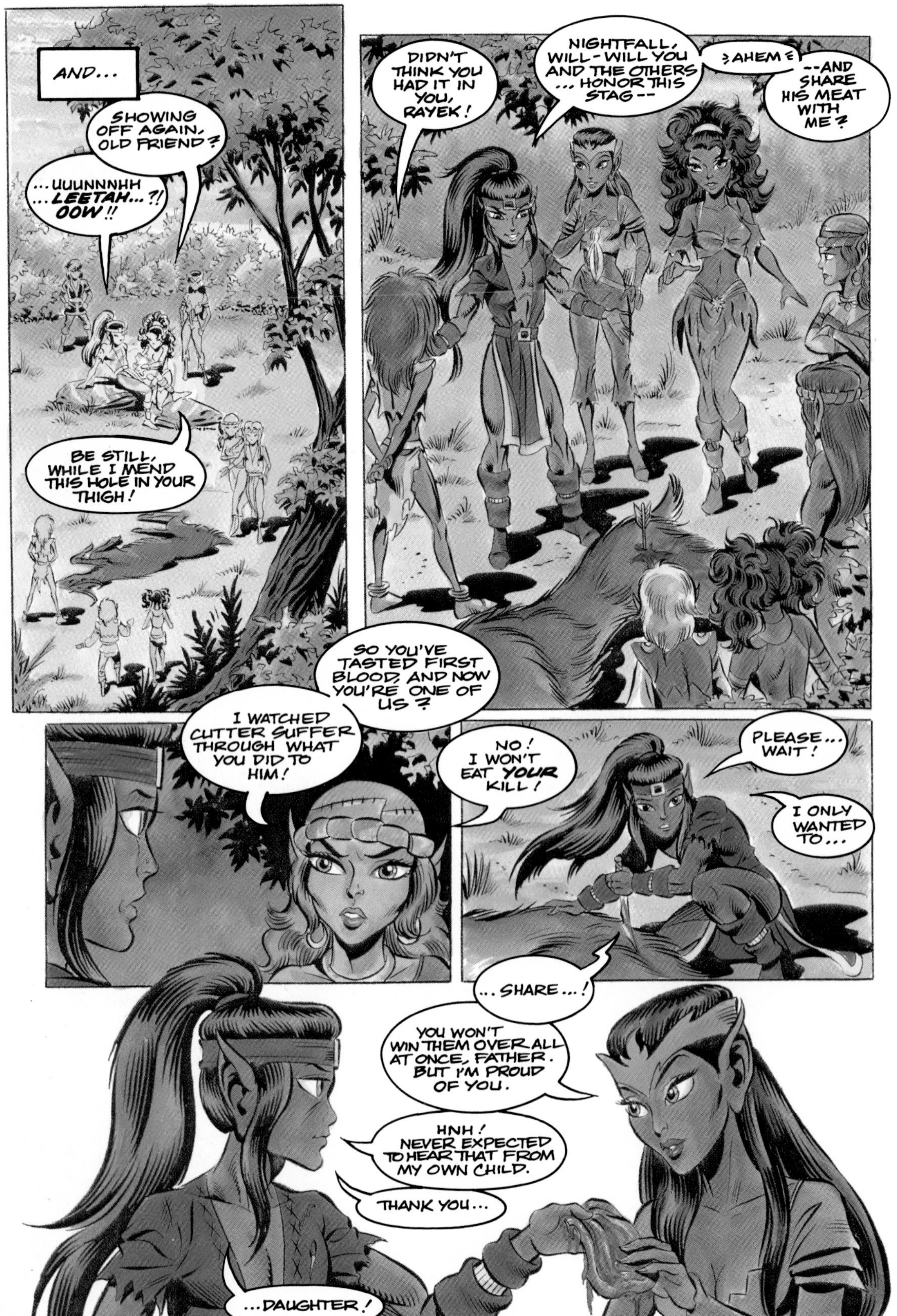
AND...
SHOWING OFF AGAIN, OLD FRIEND?
...UUUNNNHH ...LEETAH...?! OOW!!
BE STILL, WHILE I MEND THIS HOLE IN YOUR THIGH!
DIDN'T THINK YOU HAD IT IN YOU, RAYEK!
NIGHTFALL, WILL-WILL YOU AND THE OTHERS ... HONOR THIS STAG--
AHEM
--AND SHARE HIS MEAT WITH ME?
SO YOU'VE TASTED FIRST BLOOD, AND NOW YOU'RE ONE OF US?
I WATCHED CUTTER SUFFER THROUGH WHAT YOU DID TO HIM!
NO! I WON'T EAT YOUR KILL!
PLEASE... WAIT!
I ONLY WANTED TO...
...SHARE...!
YOU WON'T WIN THEM OVER ALL AT ONCE, FATHER. BUT I'M PROUD OF YOU.
HNH! NEVER EXPECTED TO HEAR THAT FROM MY OWN CHILD.
THANK YOU...
...DAUGHTER!

SIX TURNS OF THE SEASONS HAVE PASSED SINCE THE WOLFRIDERS CAUGHT UP WITH RAYEK - AND FOILED HIS PLAN TO RESCUE THE HIGH ONES - IN THE DARK AGES OF THE WORLD OF TWO MOONS.

THE LOVING SUPPORT OF VENKA, ZHANTEE AND EKUAR HAS BOTH SURPRISED AND HUMBLED THE ROGUE MAGIC USER... ENABLING HIM, FINALLY, TO REGAIN HIS POWERS.

HIS FIRST SERVICE AS RENEWED MASTER OF THE PALACE IS THE TRANSPORTATION OF CUTTER AND LEETAH'S CHILDREN... THIS TIME, HAPPILY, ON A MISSION OF HEALING AND GROWTH.*

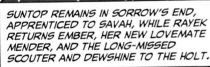

SUNTOP REMAINS IN SORROW'S END, APPRENTICED TO SAVAH, WHILE RAYEK RETURNS EMBER, HER NEW LOVEMATE MENDER, AND THE LONG-MISSED SCOUTER AND DEWSHINE TO THE HOLT.

NO SENDING OF THANKS COMES FROM THE WOLFRIDERS' CHIEF, NOR DOES RAYEK EXPECT IT. THE DEED SPEAKS FOR ITSELF.

IN ANY CASE, OTHER PURSUITS NOW ABSORB HIS FULL ATTENTION. AT LONG LAST THE ABILITY TO ACCURATELY TRANSLATE OF THE SCROLL OF COLORS LIES WITHIN HIS GRASP!

AH, CHILDREN! COME IN! COME IN!

*SEE ELFQUEST - THE HIDDEN YEARS - ED.

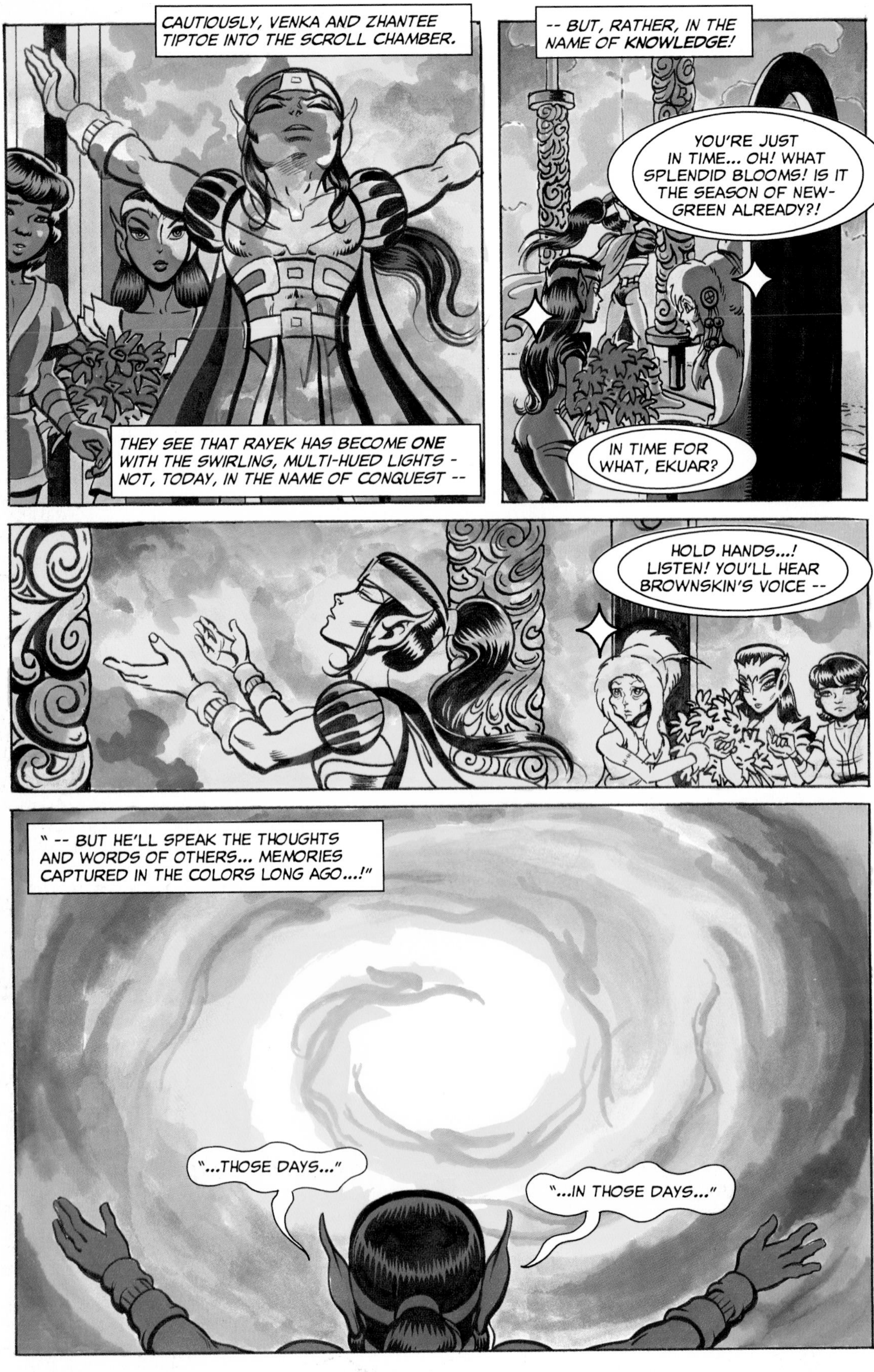
CAUTIOUSLY, VENKA AND ZHANTEE TIPTOE INTO THE SCROLL CHAMBER.
THEY SEE THAT RAYEK HAS BECOME ONE WITH THE SWIRLING, MULTI-HUED LIGHTS - NOT, TODAY, IN THE NAME OF CONQUEST --
-- BUT, RATHER, IN THE NAME OF KNOWLEDGE!
YOU'RE JUST IN TIME... OH! WHAT SPLENDID BLOOMS! IS IT THE SEASON OF NEW-GREEN ALREADY?!
IN TIME FOR WHAT, EKUAR?
HOLD HANDS...! LISTEN! YOU'LL HEAR BROWNSKIN'S VOICE --
" -- BUT HE'LL SPEAK THE THOUGHTS AND WORDS OF OTHERS... MEMORIES CAPTURED IN THE COLORS LONG AGO...!"
"...THOSE DAYS..."
"...IN THOSE DAYS..."

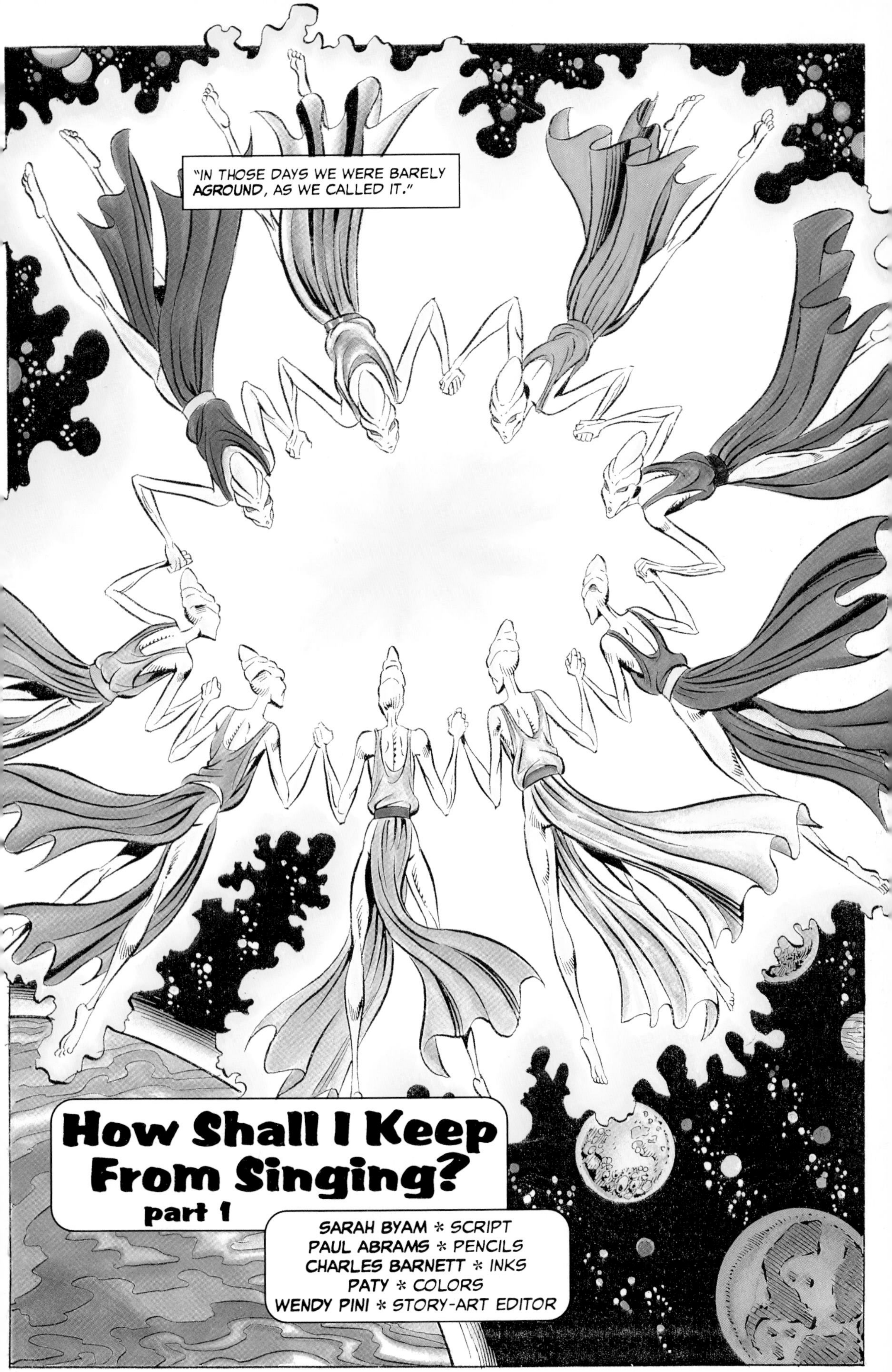
"IN THOSE DAYS WE WERE BARELY AGROUND, AS WE CALLED IT."
How Shall I Keep From Singing?
part 1
SARAH BYAM * SCRIPT
PAUL ABRAMS * PENCILS
CHARLES BARNETT * INKS
PATY * COLORS
WENDY PINI * STORY-ART EDITOR

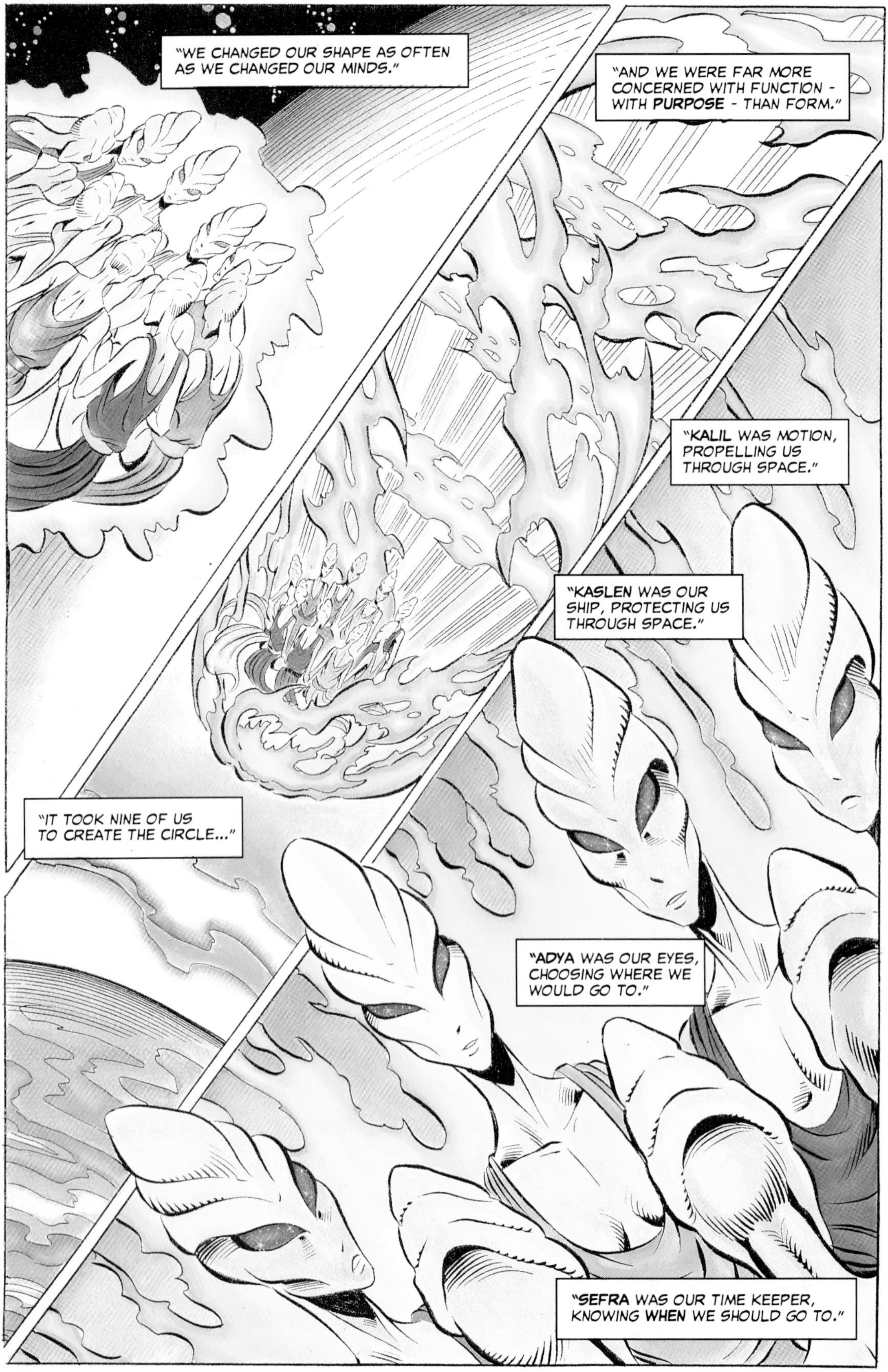
"WE CHANGED OUR SHAPE AS OFTEN AS WE CHANGED OUR MINDS."
"AND WE WERE FAR MORE CONCERNED WITH FUNCTION - WITH PURPOSE - THAN FORM."
"KALIL WAS MOTION, PROPELLING US THROUGH SPACE."
"KASLEN WAS OUR SHIP, PROTECTING US THROUGH SPACE."
"IT TOOK NINE OF US TO CREATE THE CIRCLE..."
"ADYA WAS OUR EYES, CHOOSING WHERE WE WOULD GO TO."
"SEFRA WAS OUR TIME KEEPER, KNOWING WHEN WE SHOULD GO TO."

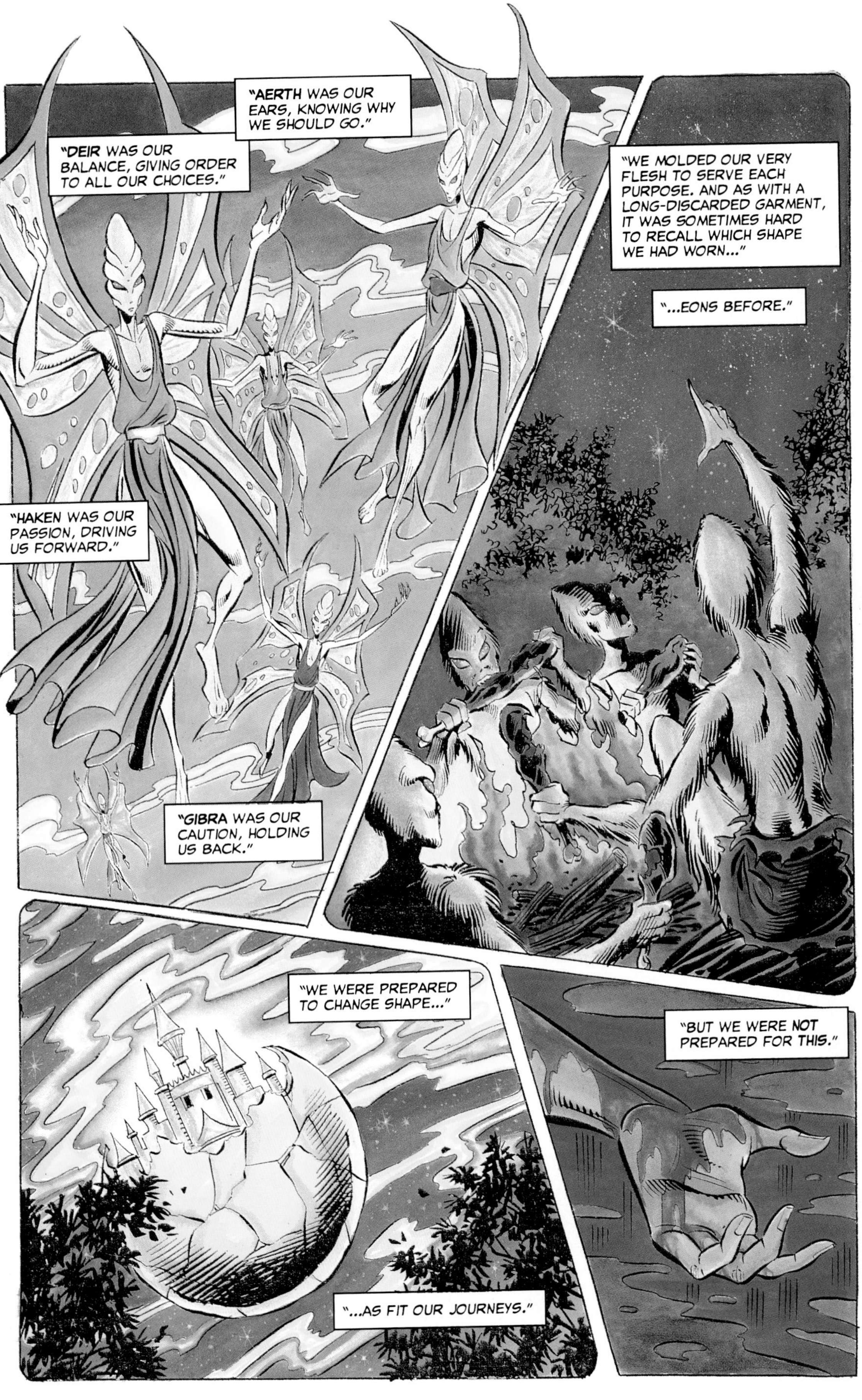
"DEIR WAS OUR BALANCE, GIVING ORDER TO ALL OUR CHOICES."
"AERTH WAS OUR EARS, KNOWING WHY WE SHOULD GO."
"HAKEN WAS OUR PASSION, DRIVING US FORWARD."
"GIBRA WAS OUR CAUTION, HOLDING US BACK."
"WE MOLDED OUR VERY FLESH TO SERVE EACH PURPOSE. AND AS WITH A LONG-DISCARDED GARMENT, IT WAS SOMETIMES HARD TO RECALL WHICH SHAPE WE HAD WORN..."
"...EONS BEFORE."
"WE WERE PREPARED TO CHANGE SHAPE..."
"...AS FIT OUR JOURNEYS."
"BUT WE WERE NOT PREPARED FOR THIS."

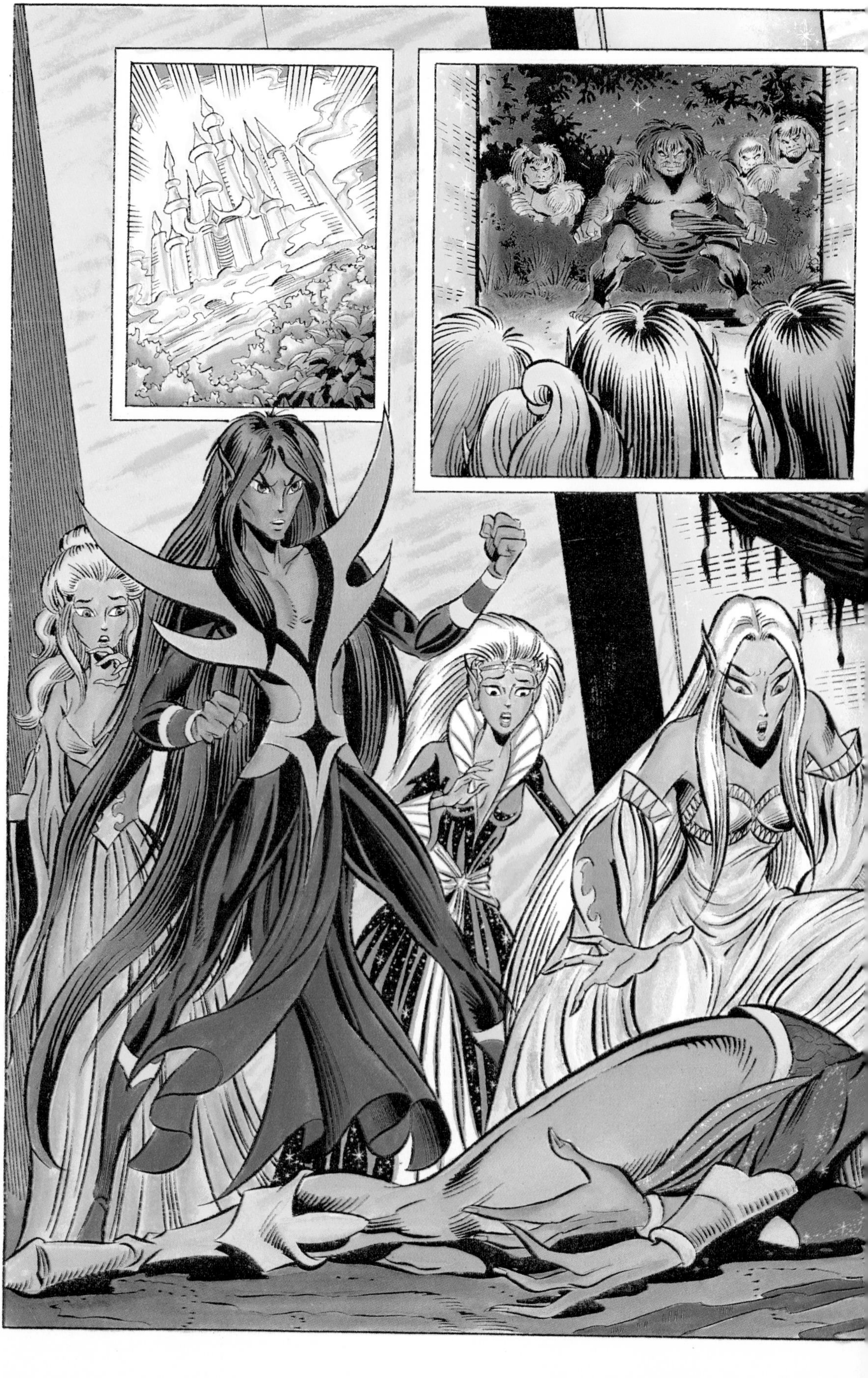

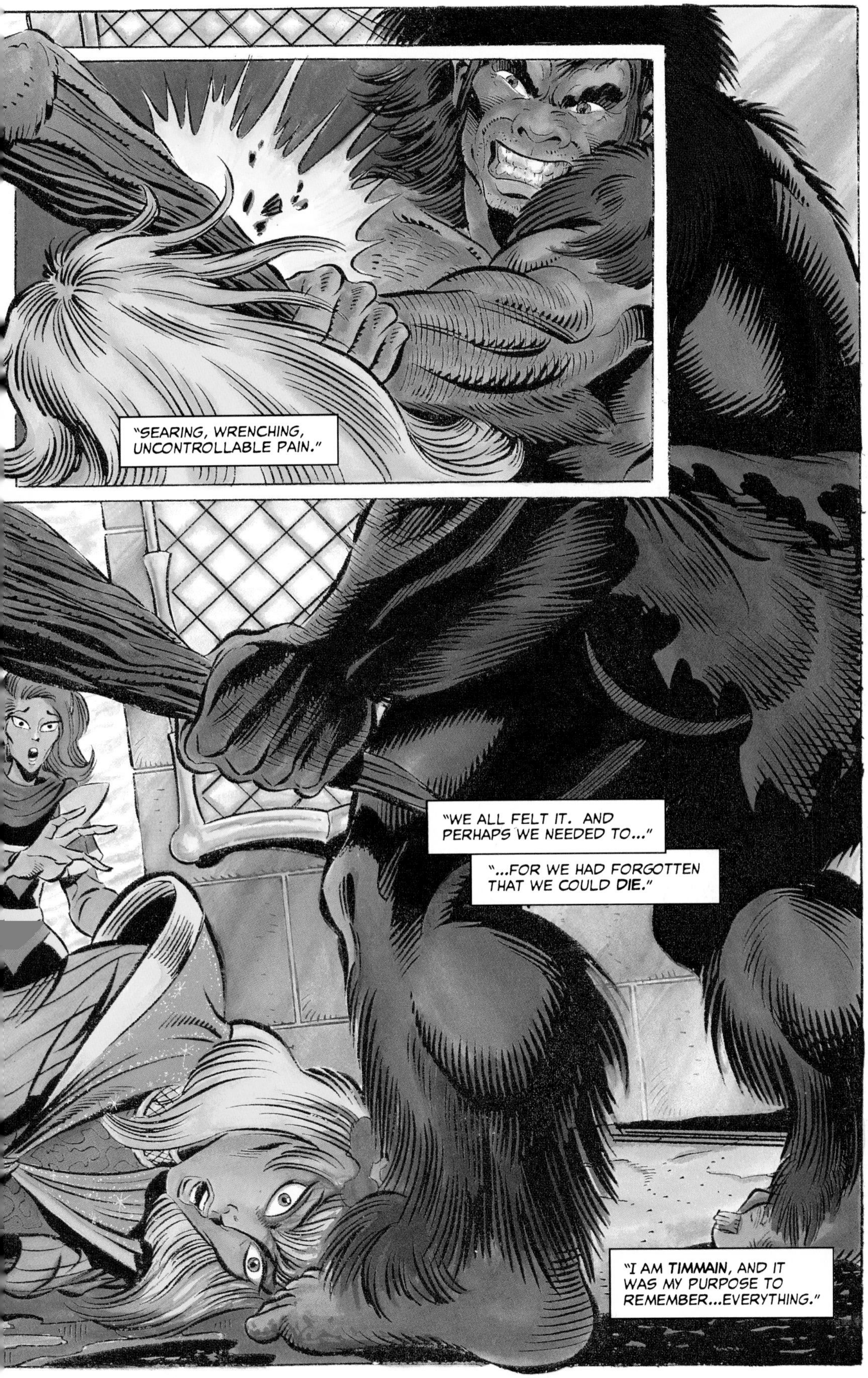
"SEARING, WRENCHING, UNCONTROLLABLE PAIN."
"WE ALL FELT IT. AND PERHAPS WE NEEDED TO..."
"...FOR WE HAD FORGOTTEN THAT WE COULD DIE."
"I AM TIMMAIN, AND IT WAS MY PURPOSE TO REMEMBER...EVERYTHING."

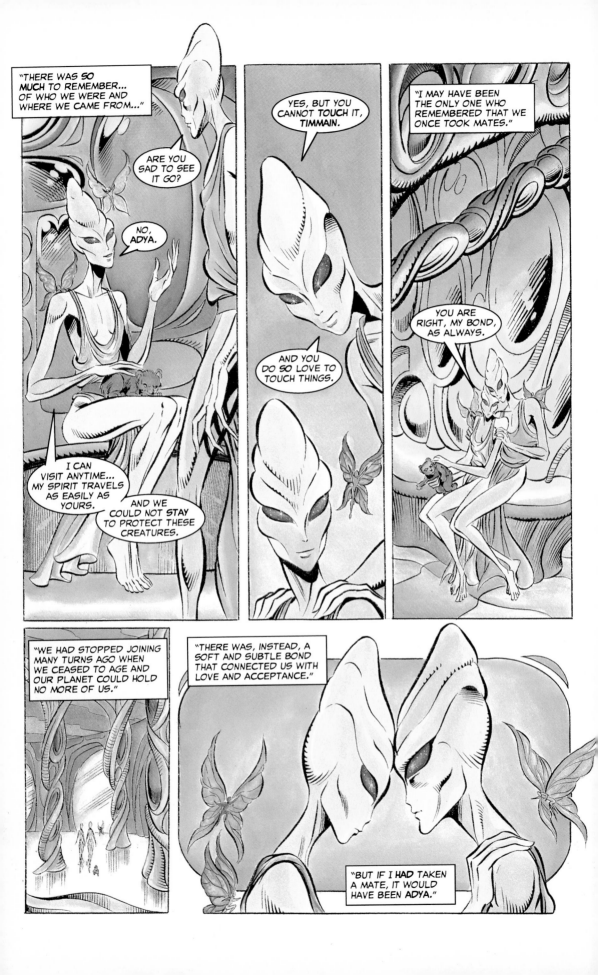

"THERE WAS SO MUCH TO REMEMBER... OF WHO WE WERE AND WHERE WE CAME FROM..."

ARE YOU SAD TO SEE IT GO?

NO, ADYA.

I CAN VISIT ANYTIME... MY SPIRIT TRAVELS AS EASILY AS YOURS.

AND WE COULD NOT STAY TO PROTECT THESE CREATURES.

YES, BUT YOU CANNOT TOUCH IT, TIMMAIN.

AND YOU DO SO LOVE TO TOUCH THINGS.

"I MAY HAVE BEEN THE ONLY ONE WHO REMEMBERED THAT WE ONCE TOOK MATES."

YOU ARE RIGHT, MY BOND, AS ALWAYS.

"WE HAD STOPPED JOINING MANY TURNS AGO WHEN WE CEASED TO AGE AND OUR PLANET COULD HOLD NO MORE OF US."

"THERE WAS, INSTEAD, A SOFT AND SUBTLE BOND THAT CONNECTED US WITH LOVE AND ACCEPTANCE."

"BUT IF I HAD TAKEN A MATE, IT WOULD HAVE BEEN ADYA."

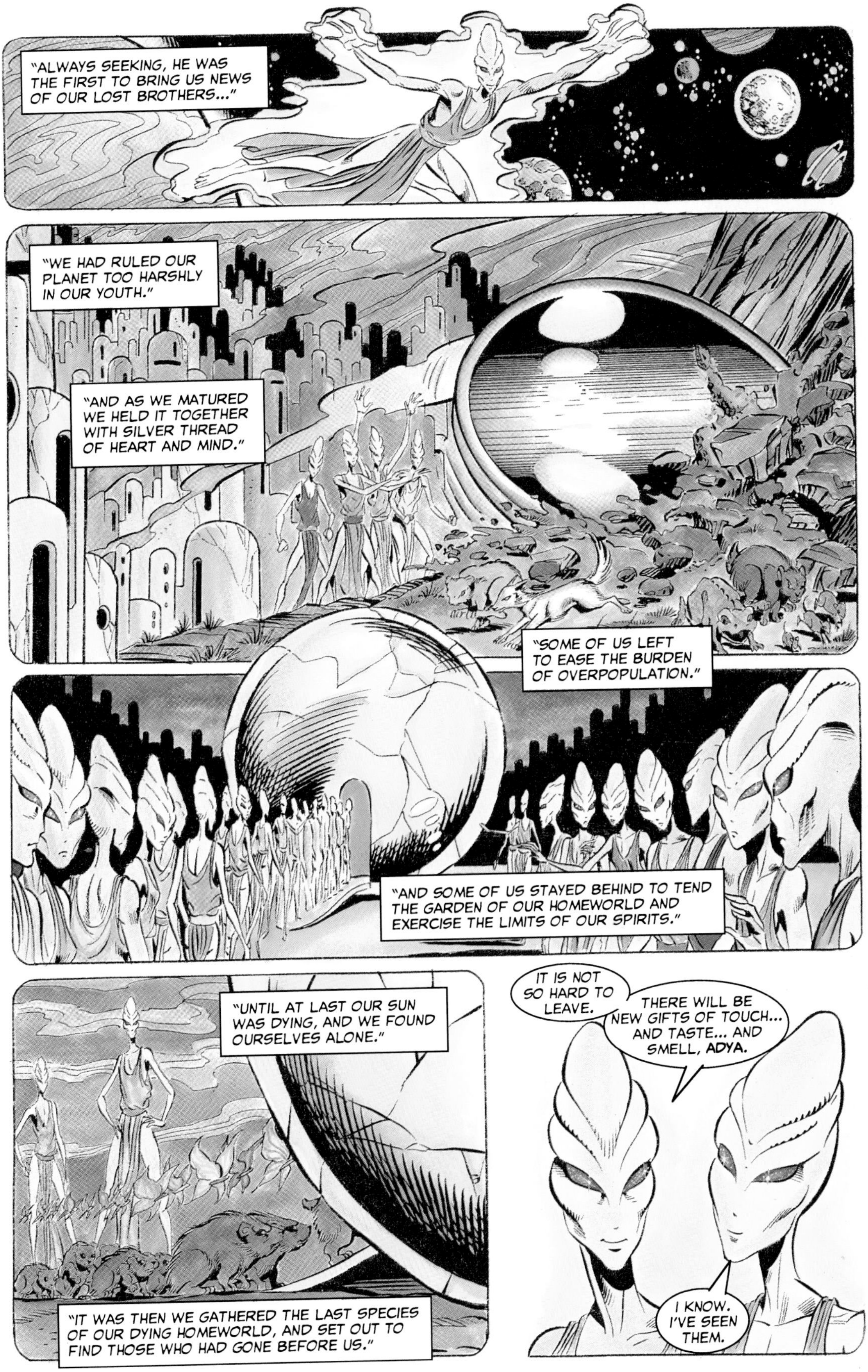
"ALWAYS SEEKING, HE WAS THE FIRST TO BRING US NEWS OF OUR LOST BROTHERS..."
"WE HAD RULED OUR PLANET TOO HARSHLY IN OUR YOUTH."
"AND AS WE MATURED WE HELD IT TOGETHER WITH SILVER THREAD OF HEART AND MIND."
"SOME OF US LEFT TO EASE THE BURDEN OF OVERPOPULATION."
"AND SOME OF US STAYED BEHIND TO TEND THE GARDEN OF OUR HOMEWORLD AND EXERCISE THE LIMITS OF OUR SPIRITS."
"UNTIL AT LAST OUR SUN WAS DYING, AND WE FOUND OURSELVES ALONE."
"IT WAS THEN WE GATHERED THE LAST SPECIES OF OUR DYING HOMEWORLD, AND SET OUT TO FIND THOSE WHO HAD GONE BEFORE US."
IT IS NOT SO HARD TO LEAVE.
THERE WILL BE NEW GIFTS OF TOUCH... AND TASTE... AND SMELL, ADYA.
I KNOW. I'VE SEEN THEM.

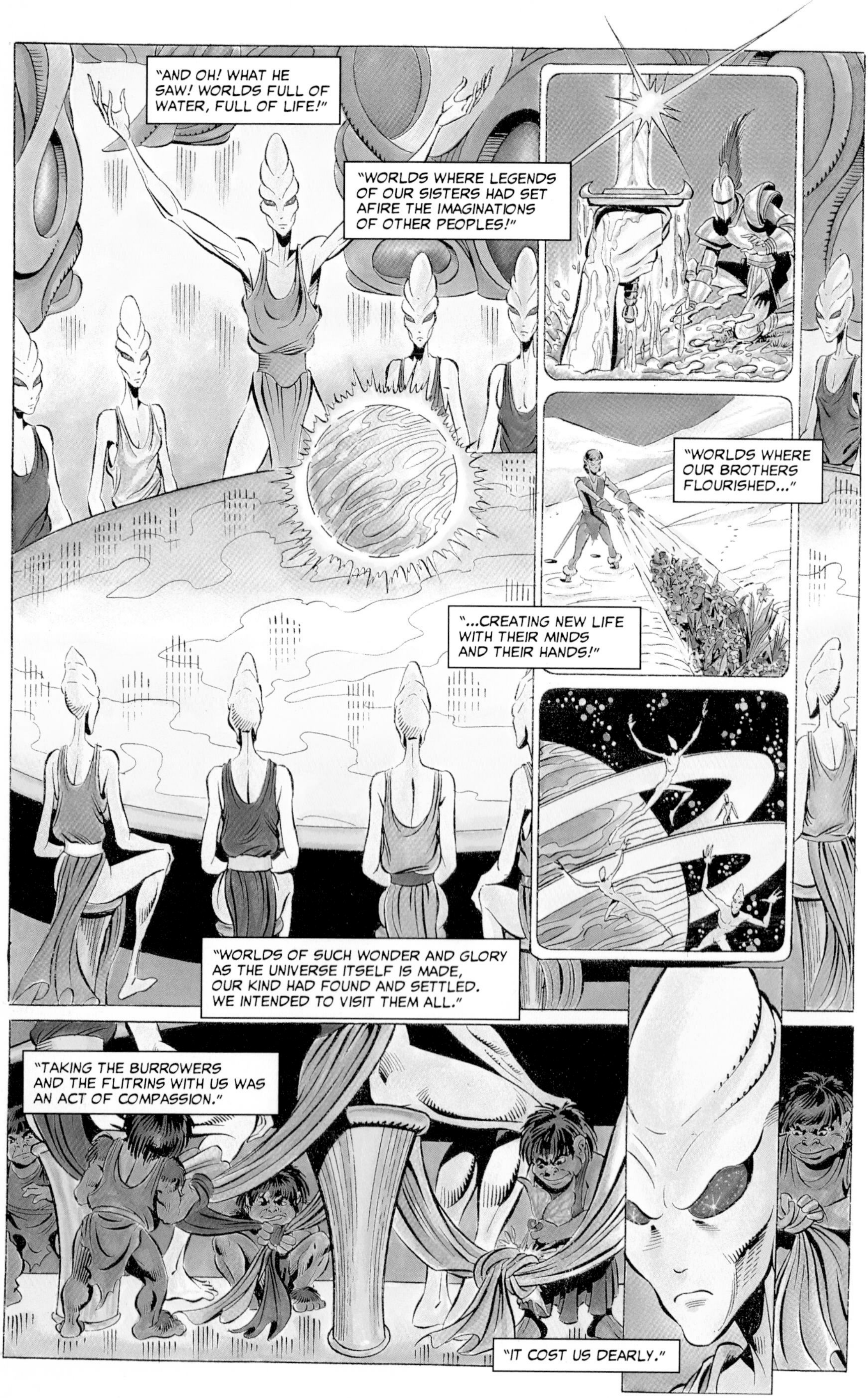
"AND OH! WHAT HE SAW! WORLDS FULL OF WATER, FULL OF LIFE!"
"WORLDS WHERE LEGENDS OF OUR SISTERS HAD SET AFIRE THE IMAGINATIONS OF OTHER PEOPLES!"
"WORLDS WHERE OUR BROTHERS FLOURISHED..."
"...CREATING NEW LIFE WITH THEIR MINDS AND THEIR HANDS!"
"WORLDS OF SUCH WONDER AND GLORY AS THE UNIVERSE ITSELF IS MADE, OUR KIND HAD FOUND AND SETTLED. WE INTENDED TO VISIT THEM ALL."
"TAKING THE BURROWERS AND THE FLITRINS WITH US WAS AN ACT OF COMPASSION."
"IT COST US DEARLY."

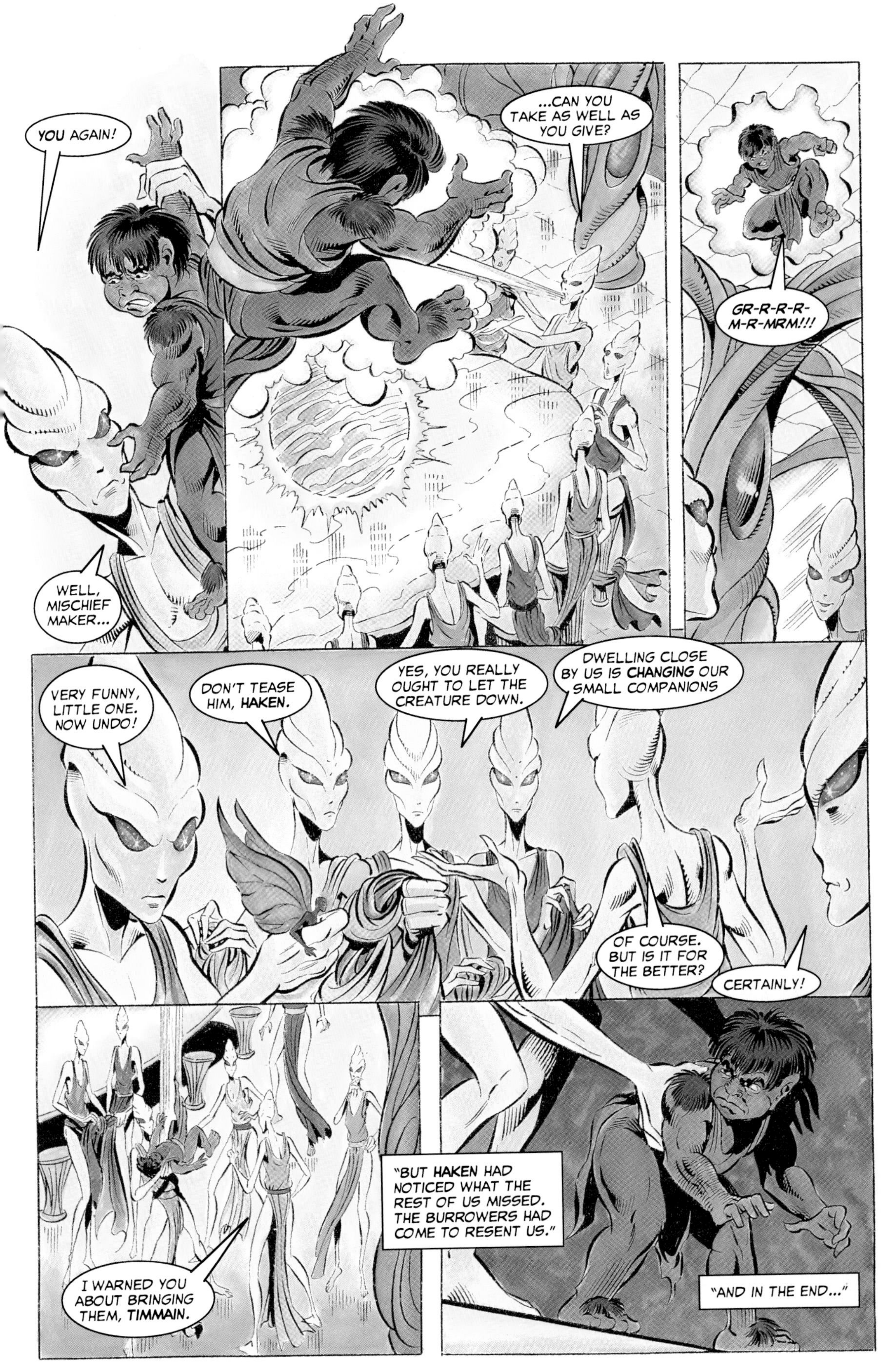
YOU AGAIN!
WELL, MISCHIEF MAKER...
...CAN YOU TAKE AS WELL AS YOU GIVE?
GR-R-R-R-M-R-MRM!!!
VERY FUNNY, LITTLE ONE. NOW UNDO!
DON'T TEASE HIM, HAKEN.
YES, YOU REALLY OUGHT TO LET THE CREATURE DOWN.
DWELLING CLOSE BY US IS CHANGING OUR SMALL COMPANIONS
OF COURSE. BUT IS IT FOR THE BETTER?
CERTAINLY!
I WARNED YOU ABOUT BRINGING THEM, TIMMAIN.
"BUT HAKEN HAD NOTICED WHAT THE REST OF US MISSED. THE BURROWERS HAD COME TO RESENT US."
"AND IN THE END..."

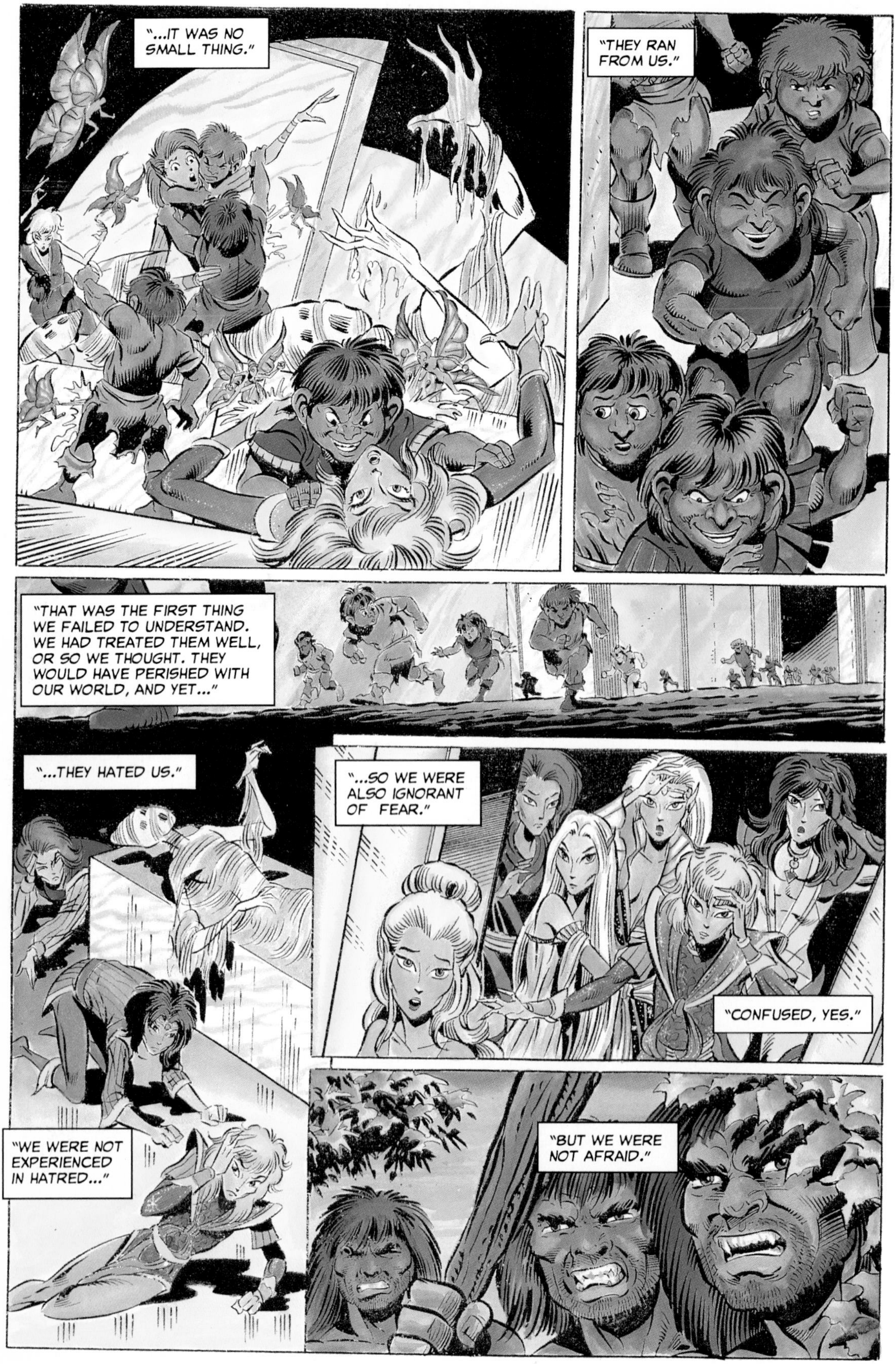
"...IT WAS NO SMALL THING."
"THEY RAN FROM US."
"THAT WAS THE FIRST THING WE FAILED TO UNDERSTAND. WE HAD TREATED THEM WELL, OR SO WE THOUGHT. THEY WOULD HAVE PERISHED WITH OUR WORLD, AND YET..."
"...THEY HATED US."
"WE WERE NOT EXPERIENCED IN HATRED..."
"...SO WE WERE ALSO IGNORANT OF FEAR."
"CONFUSED, YES."
"BUT WE WERE NOT AFRAID."

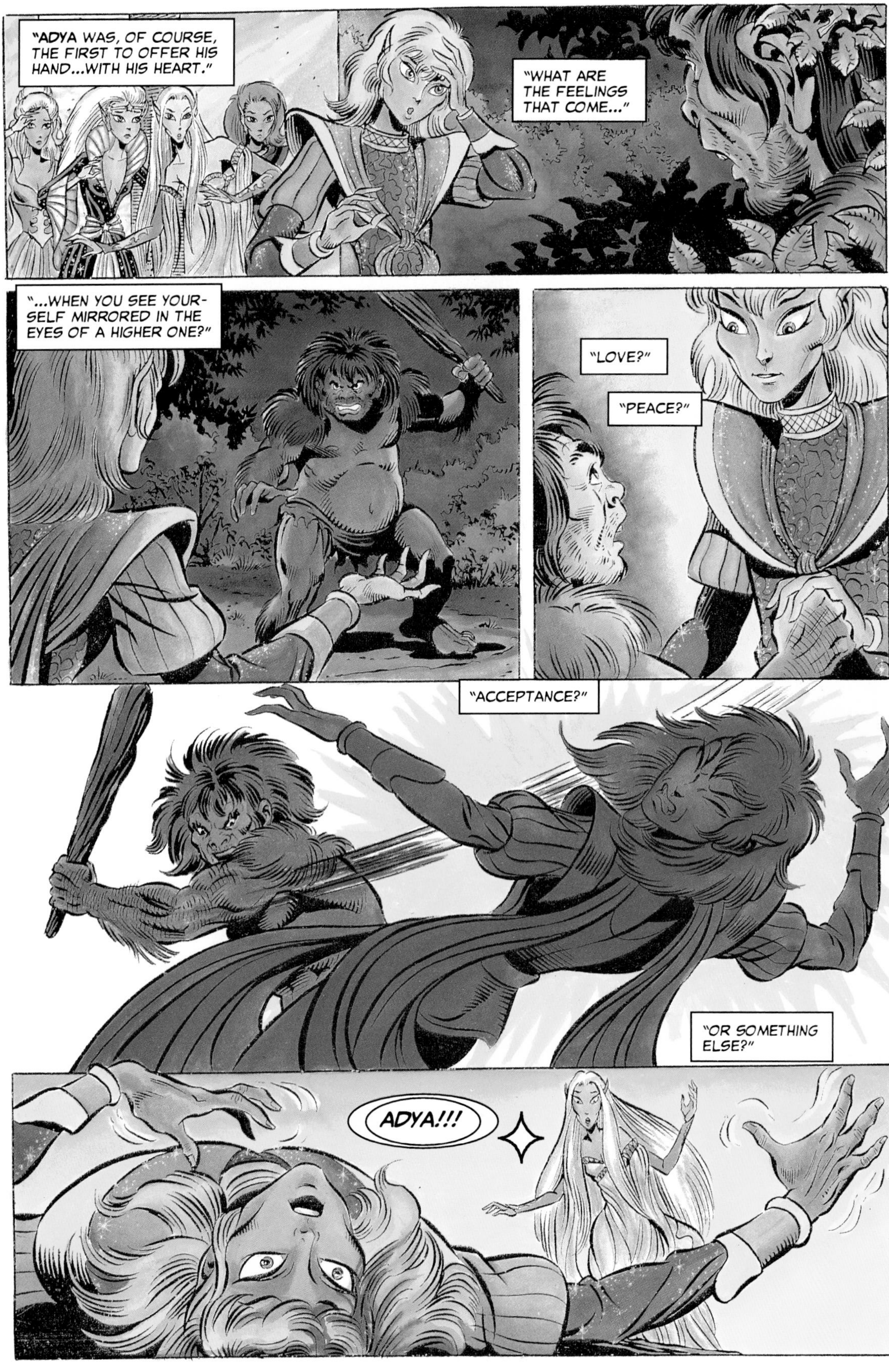
"ADYA WAS, OF COURSE, THE FIRST TO OFFER HIS HAND...WITH HIS HEART."
"WHAT ARE THE FEELINGS THAT COME..."
"...WHEN YOU SEE YOURSELF MIRRORED IN THE EYES OF A HIGHER ONE?"
"LOVE?"
"PEACE?"
"ACCEPTANCE?"
"OR SOMETHING ELSE?"
ADYA!!!

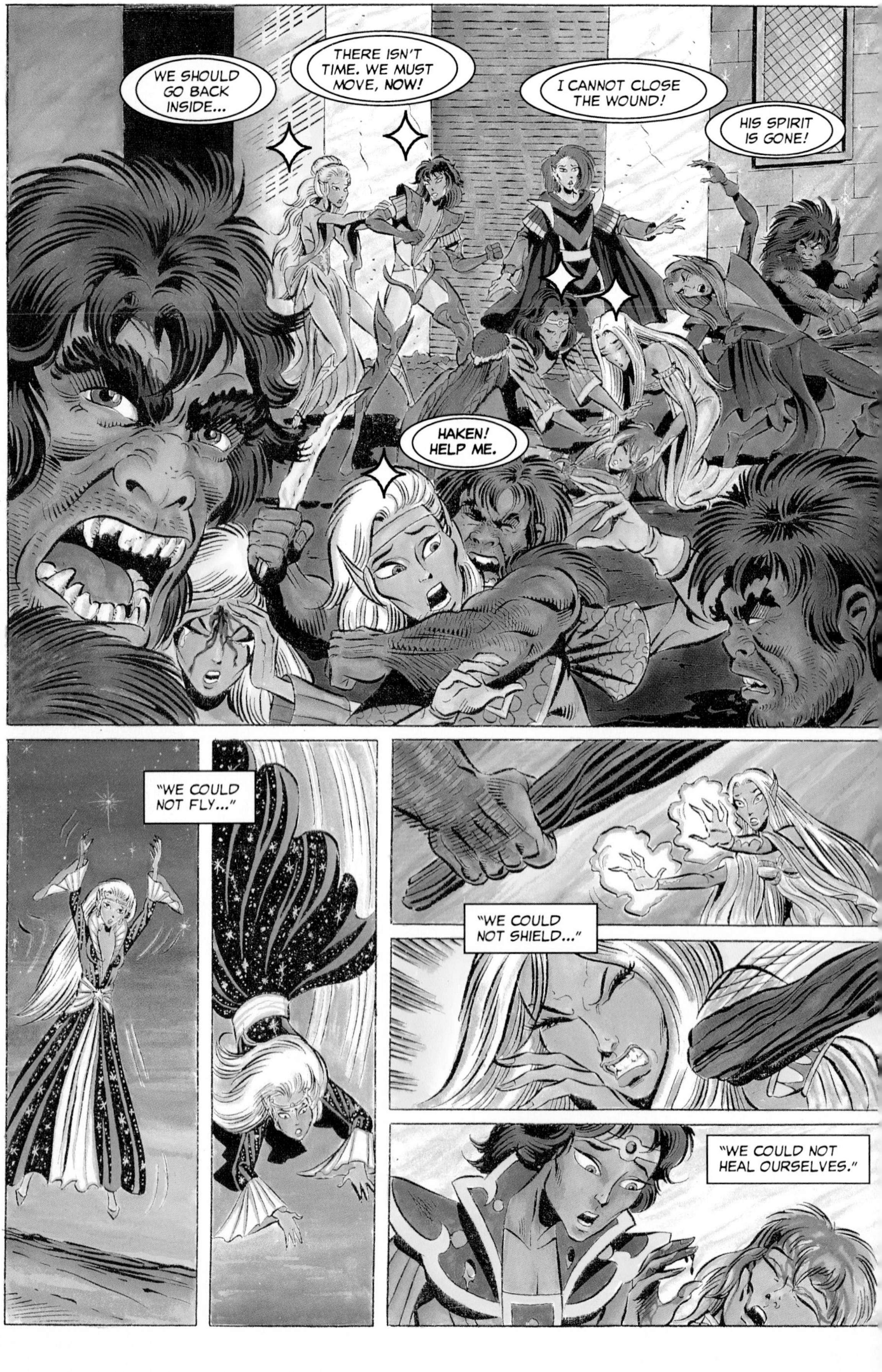

WE SHOULD GO BACK INSIDE...
THERE ISN'T TIME. WE MUST MOVE, NOW!
I CANNOT CLOSE THE WOUND!
HIS SPIRIT IS GONE!
HAKEN! HELP ME.
"WE COULD NOT FLY..."
"WE COULD NOT SHIELD..."
"WE COULD NOT HEAL OURSELVES."

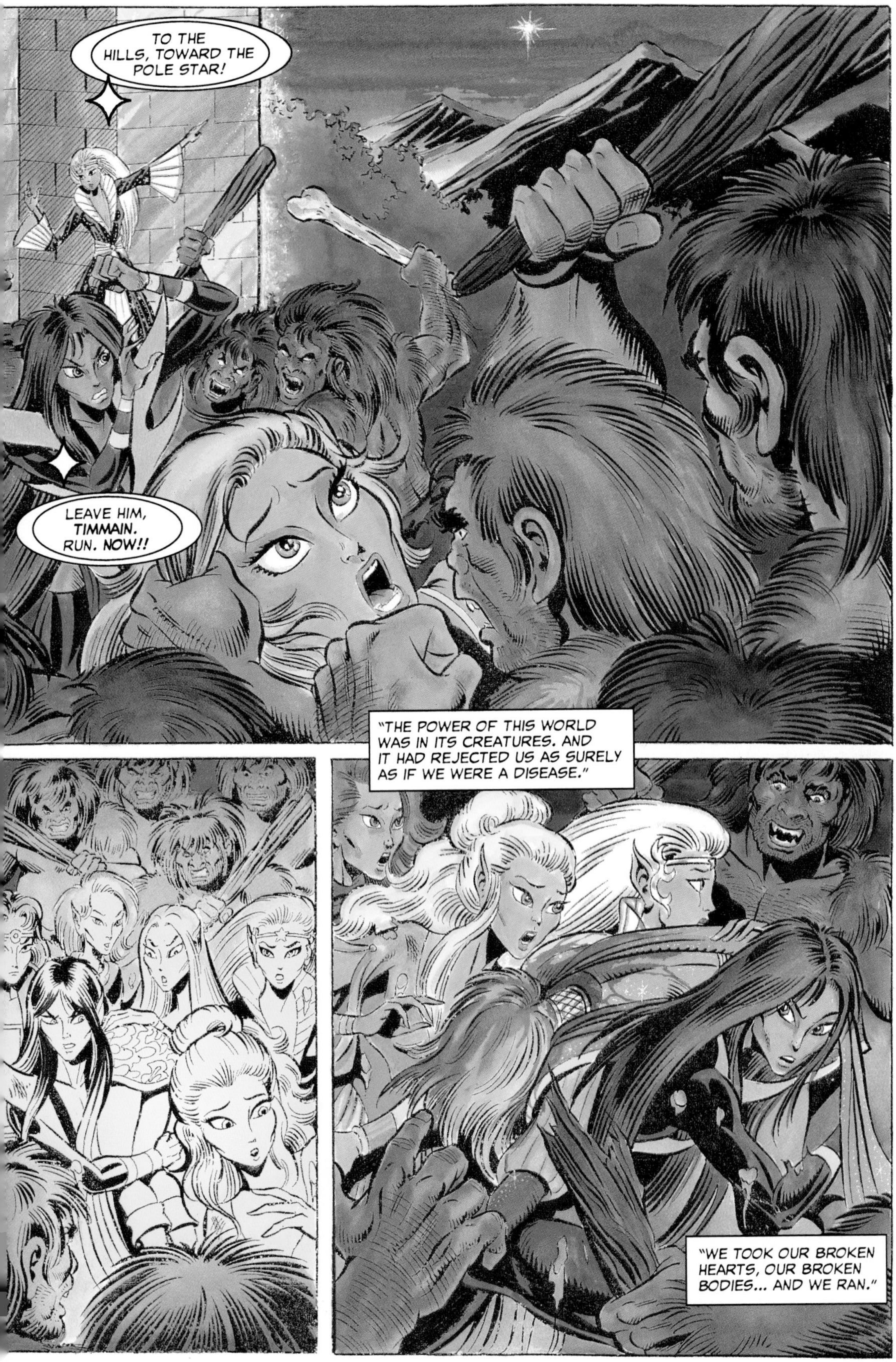
TO THE HILLS, TOWARD THE POLE STAR!
LEAVE HIM, TIMMAIN. RUN. NOW!!
"THE POWER OF THIS WORLD WAS IN ITS CREATURES. AND IT HAD REJECTED US AS SURELY AS IF WE WERE A DISEASE."
"WE TOOK OUR BROKEN HEARTS, OUR BROKEN BODIES... AND WE RAN."

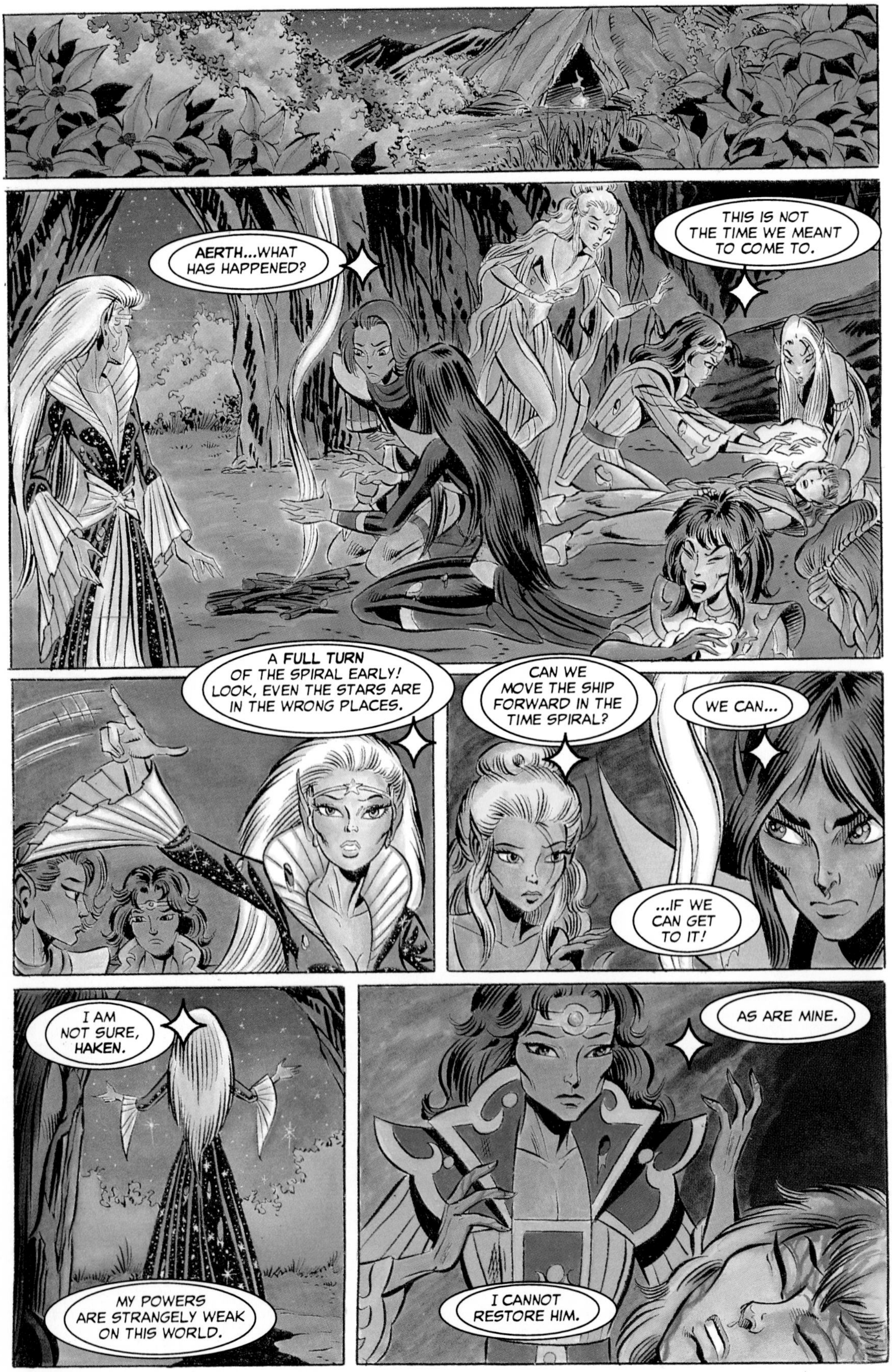

AERTH...WHAT HAS HAPPENED?
THIS IS NOT THE TIME WE MEANT TO COME TO.
A FULL TURN OF THE SPIRAL EARLY! LOOK, EVEN THE STARS ARE IN THE WRONG PLACES.
CAN WE MOVE THE SHIP FORWARD IN THE TIME SPIRAL?
WE CAN...
...IF WE CAN GET TO IT!
I AM NOT SURE, HAKEN.
MY POWERS ARE STRANGELY WEAK ON THIS WORLD.
AS ARE MINE.
I CANNOT RESTORE HIM.

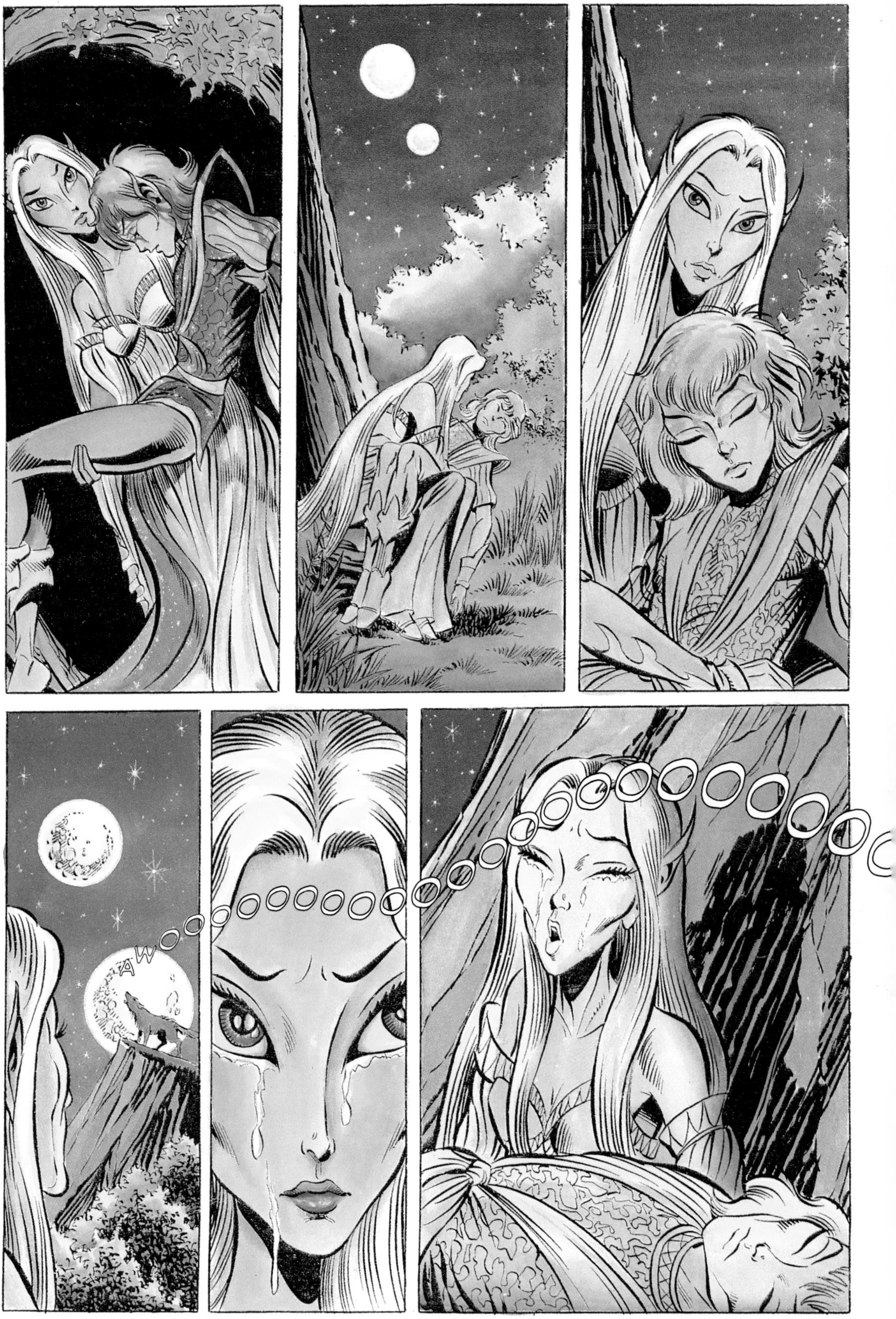
AWOOOOOOOOOOOOOOOOOOOOOOOOOOOO

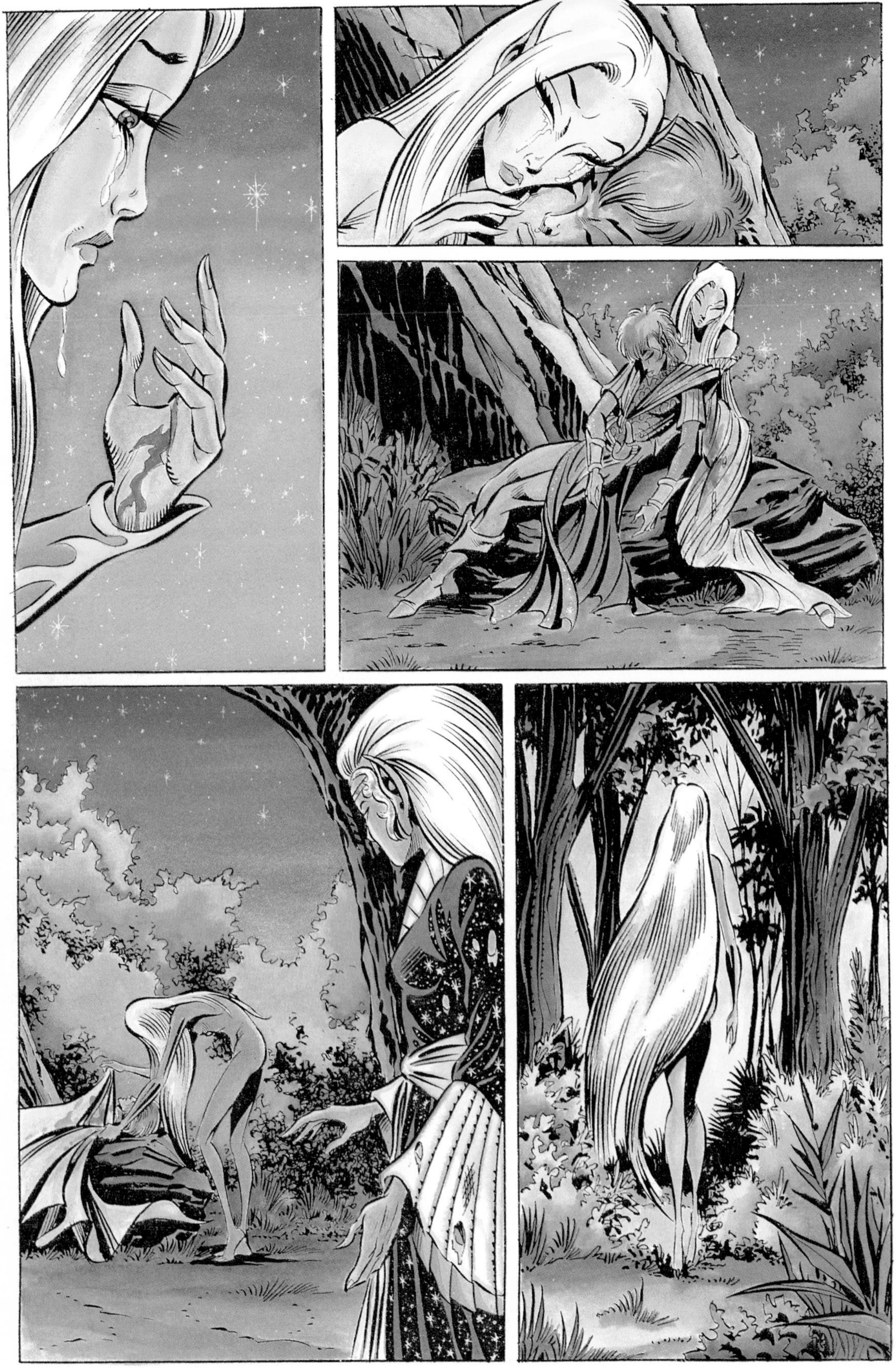

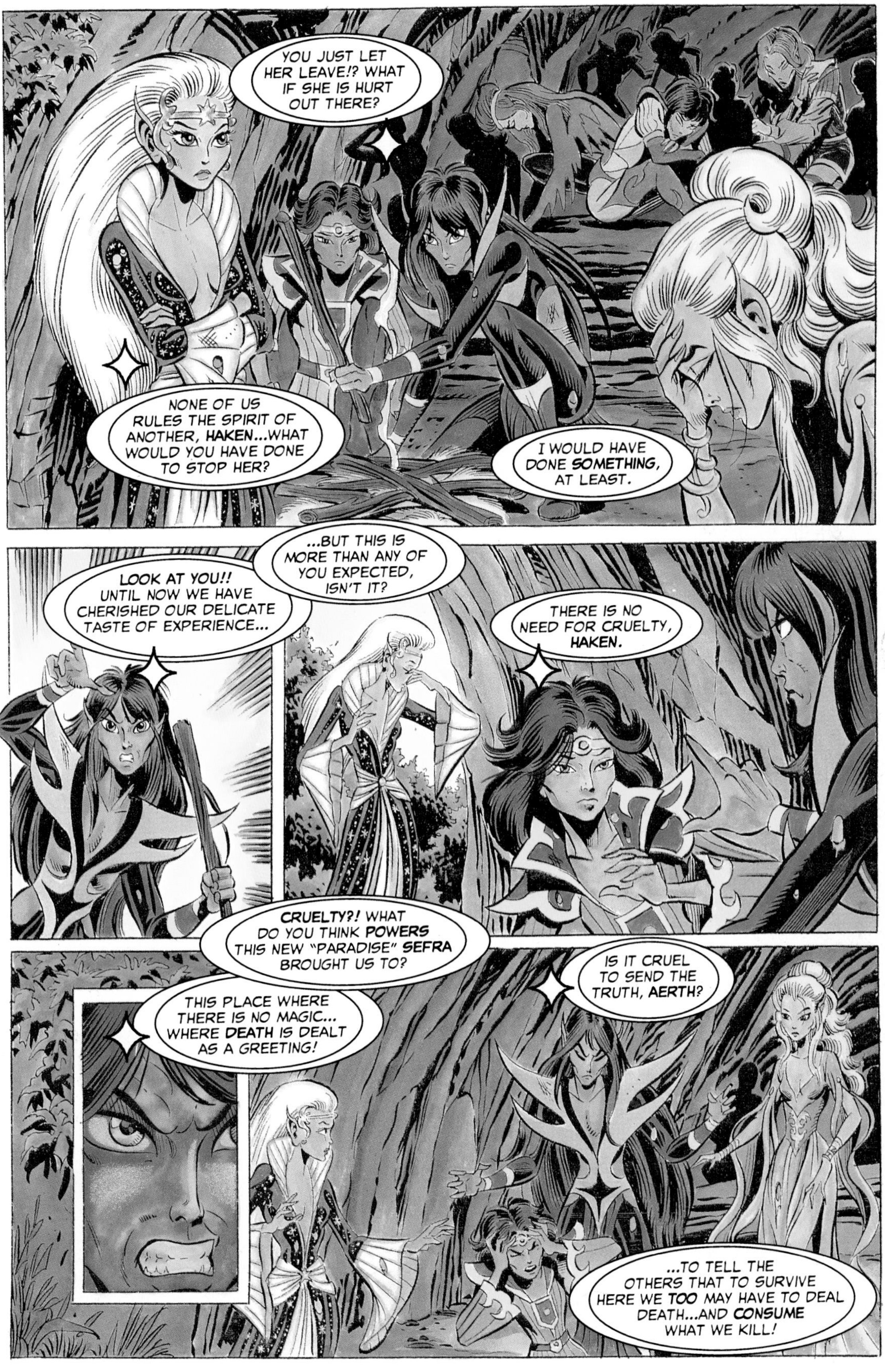
YOU JUST LET HER LEAVE!? WHAT IF SHE IS HURT OUT THERE?
NONE OF US RULES THE SPIRIT OF ANOTHER, **HAKEN**...WHAT WOULD YOU HAVE DONE TO STOP HER?
I WOULD HAVE DONE **SOMETHING**, AT LEAST.
LOOK AT YOU!! UNTIL NOW WE HAVE CHERISHED OUR DELICATE TASTE OF EXPERIENCE...
...BUT THIS IS MORE THAN ANY OF YOU EXPECTED, ISN'T IT?
THERE IS NO NEED FOR CRUELTY, **HAKEN.**
CRUELTY?! WHAT DO YOU THINK **POWERS** THIS NEW "PARADISE" **SEFRA** BROUGHT US TO?
THIS PLACE WHERE THERE IS NO MAGIC... WHERE **DEATH** IS DEALT AS A GREETING!
IS IT CRUEL TO SEND THE TRUTH, **AERTH**?
...TO TELL THE OTHERS THAT TO SURVIVE HERE WE **TOO** MAY HAVE TO DEAL DEATH...AND **CONSUME** WHAT WE KILL!

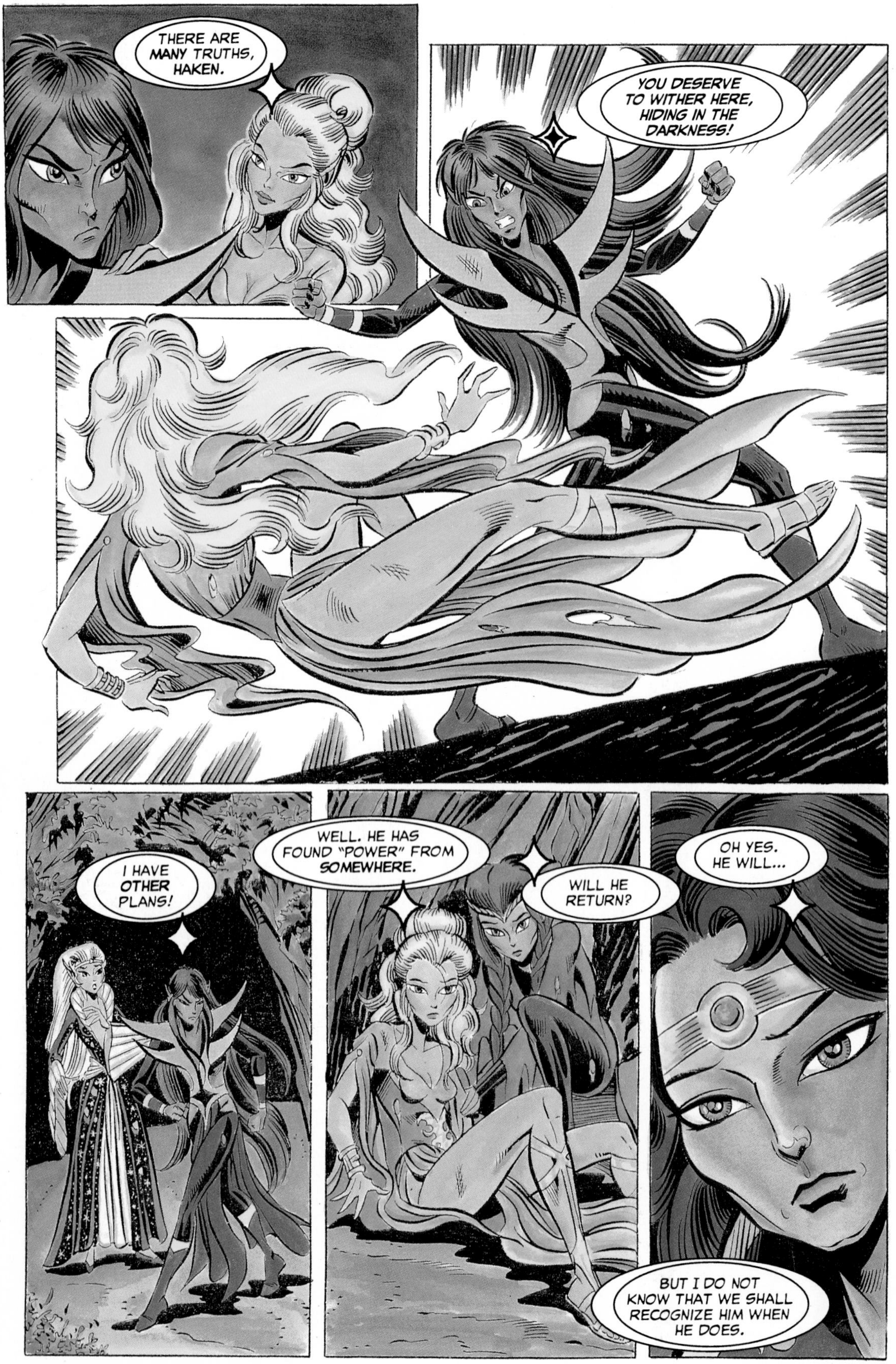
THERE ARE MANY TRUTHS, HAKEN.
YOU DESERVE TO WITHER HERE, HIDING IN THE DARKNESS!
I HAVE OTHER PLANS!
WELL. HE HAS FOUND "POWER" FROM SOMEWHERE.
WILL HE RETURN?
OH YES. HE WILL...
BUT I DO NOT KNOW THAT WE SHALL RECOGNIZE HIM WHEN HE DOES.

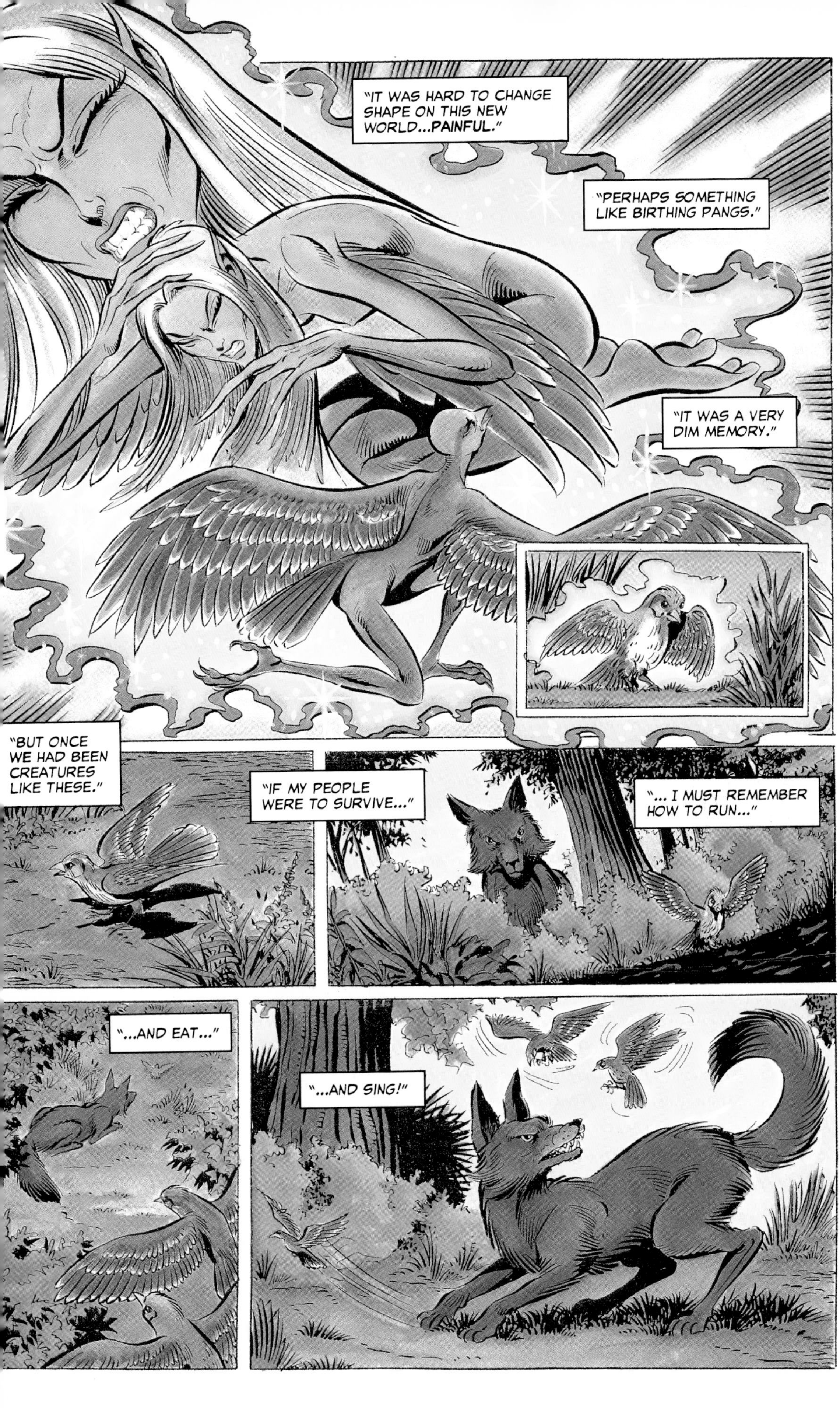
"IT WAS HARD TO CHANGE SHAPE ON THIS NEW WORLD...**PAINFUL.**"
"PERHAPS SOMETHING LIKE BIRTHING PANGS."
"IT WAS A VERY DIM MEMORY."
"BUT ONCE WE HAD BEEN CREATURES LIKE THESE."
"IF MY PEOPLE WERE TO SURVIVE..."
"... I MUST REMEMBER HOW TO RUN..."
"...AND EAT..."
"...AND SING!"

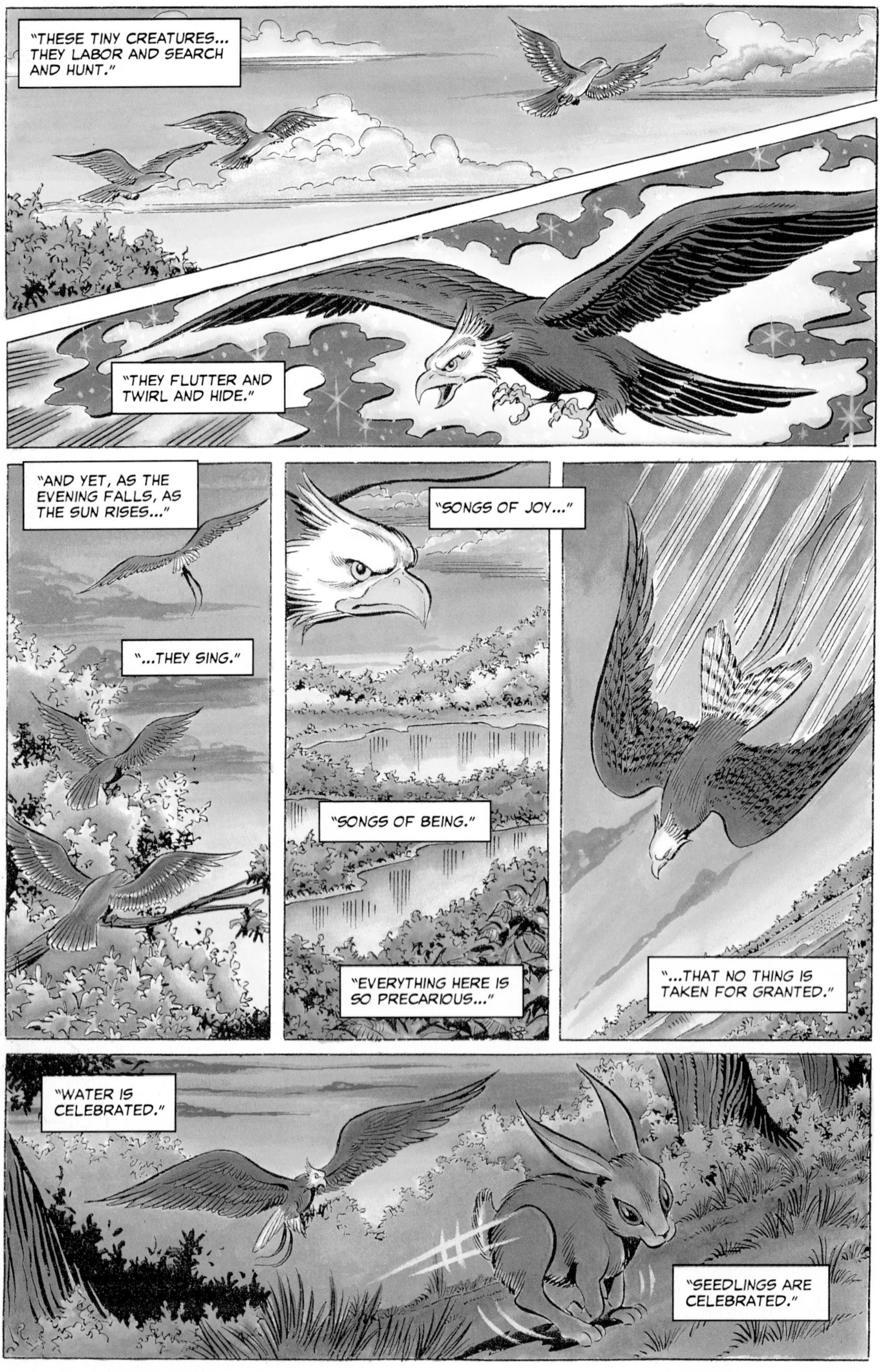
"THESE TINY CREATURES... THEY LABOR AND SEARCH AND HUNT."
"THEY FLUTTER AND TWIRL AND HIDE."
"AND YET, AS THE EVENING FALLS, AS THE SUN RISES..."
"...THEY SING."
"SONGS OF JOY..."
"SONGS OF BEING."
"EVERYTHING HERE IS SO PRECARIOUS..."
"...THAT NO THING IS TAKEN FOR GRANTED."
"WATER IS CELEBRATED."
"SEEDLINGS ARE CELEBRATED."

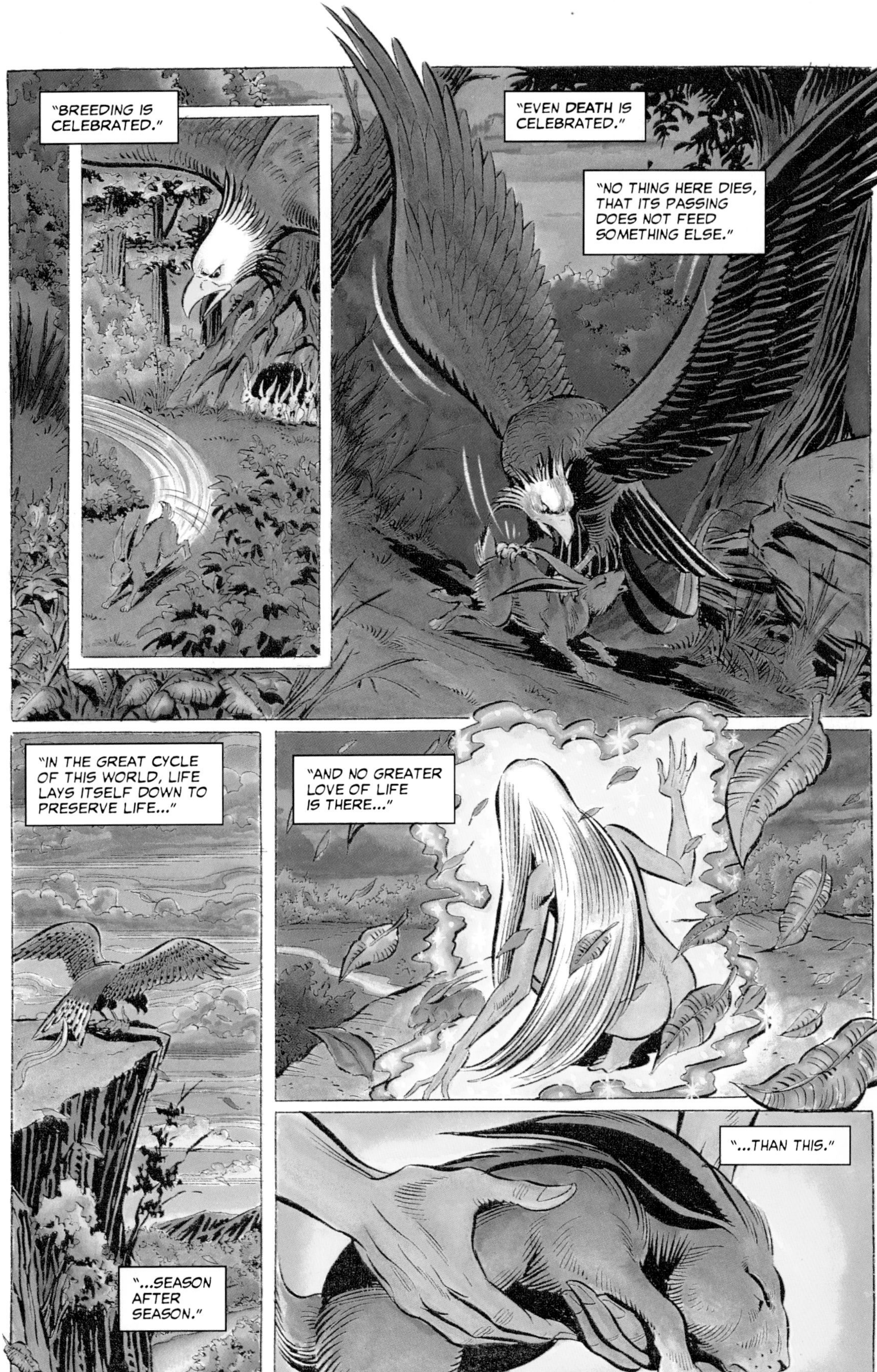
"BREEDING IS CELEBRATED."
"EVEN DEATH IS CELEBRATED."
"NO THING HERE DIES, THAT ITS PASSING DOES NOT FEED SOMETHING ELSE."
"IN THE GREAT CYCLE OF THIS WORLD, LIFE LAYS ITSELF DOWN TO PRESERVE LIFE..."
"...SEASON AFTER SEASON."
"AND NO GREATER LOVE OF LIFE IS THERE..."
"...THAN THIS."

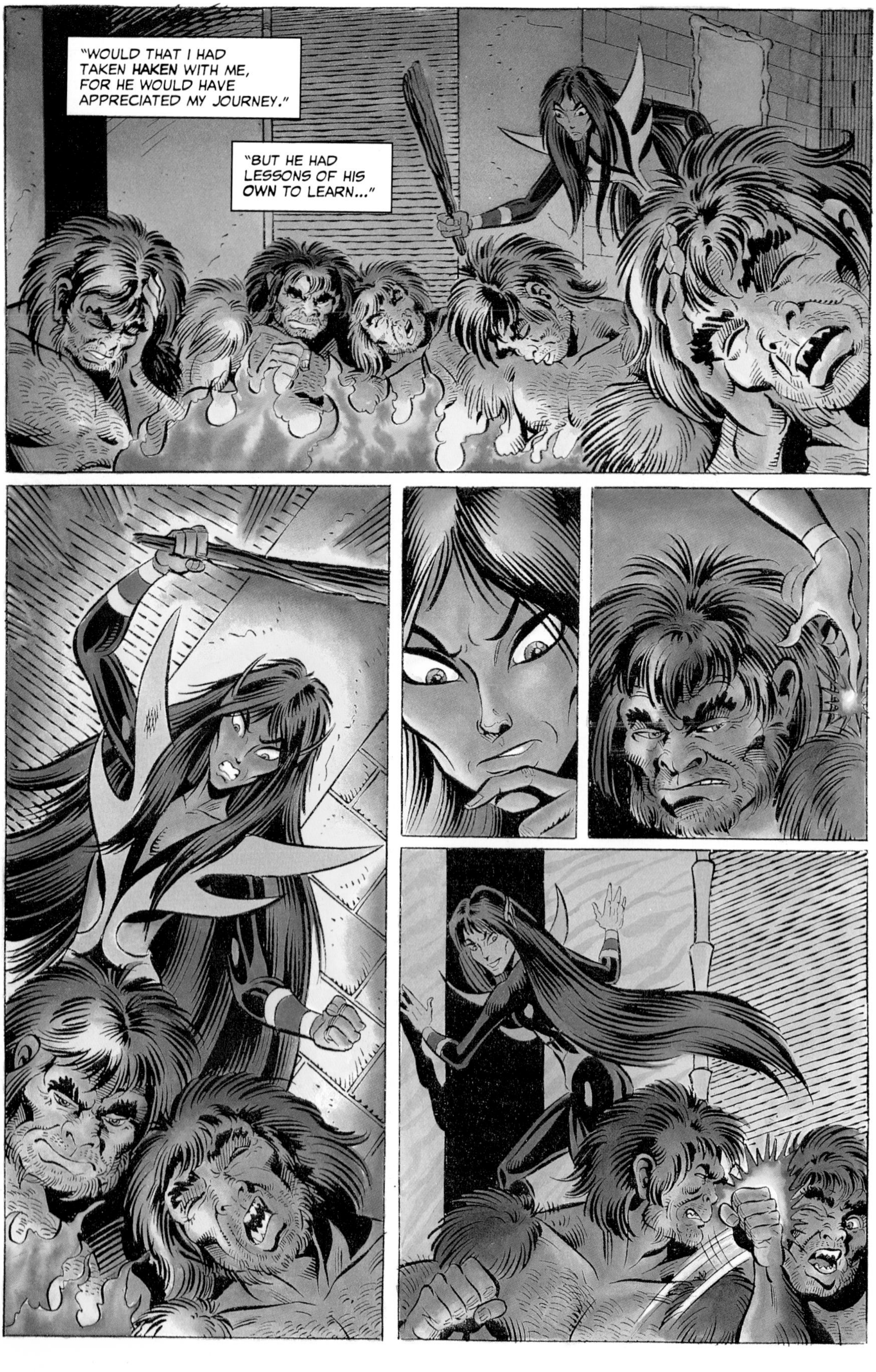
"WOULD THAT I HAD TAKEN HAKEN WITH ME, FOR HE WOULD HAVE APPRECIATED MY JOURNEY."
"BUT HE HAD LESSONS OF HIS OWN TO LEARN..."

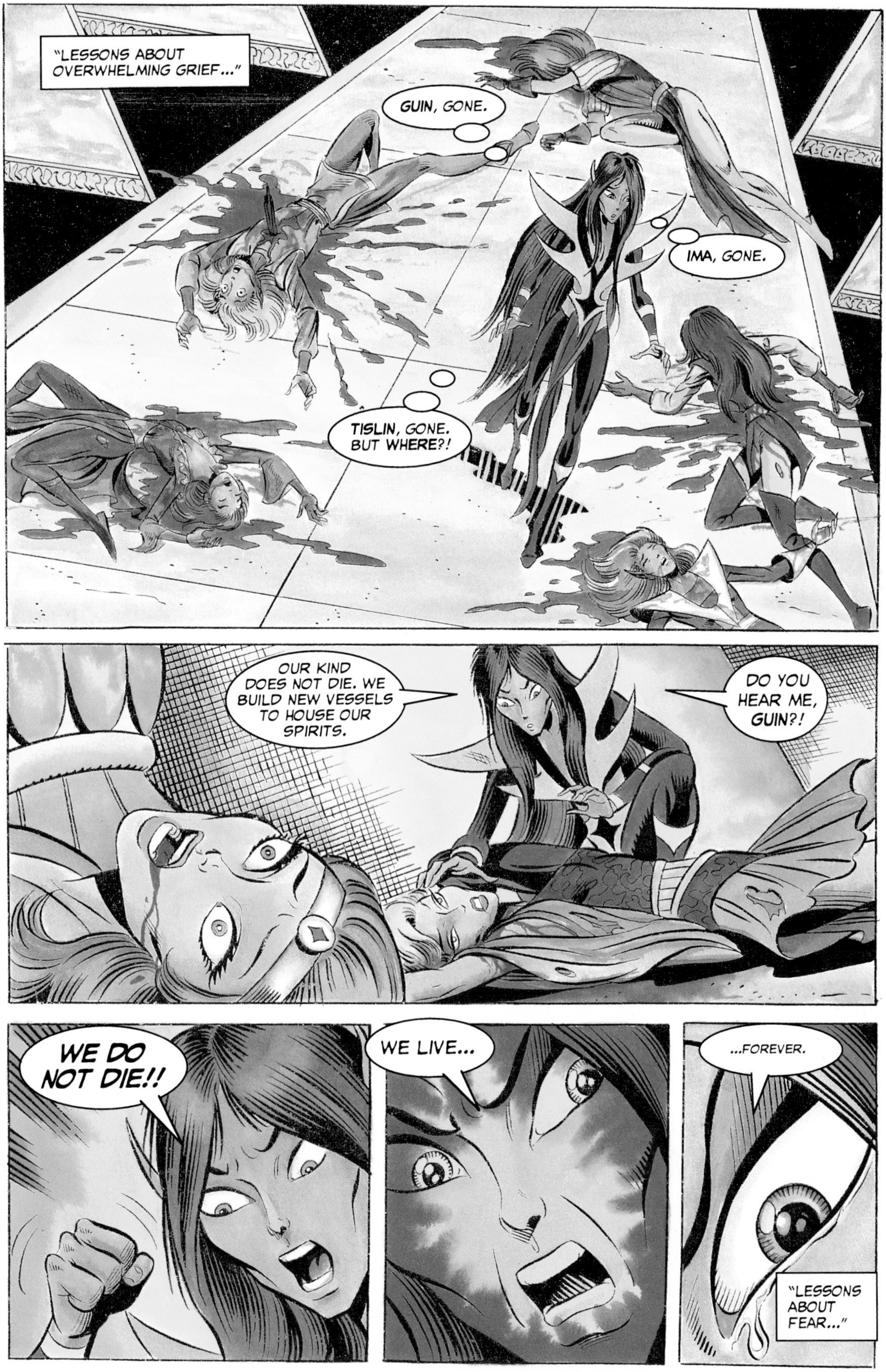
"LESSONS ABOUT OVERWHELMING GRIEF..."
GUIN, GONE.
IMA, GONE.
TISLIN, GONE. BUT WHERE?!
OUR KIND DOES NOT DIE. WE BUILD NEW VESSELS TO HOUSE OUR SPIRITS.
DO YOU HEAR ME, GUIN?!
WE DO NOT DIE!!
WE LIVE...
...FOREVER.
"LESSONS ABOUT FEAR..."

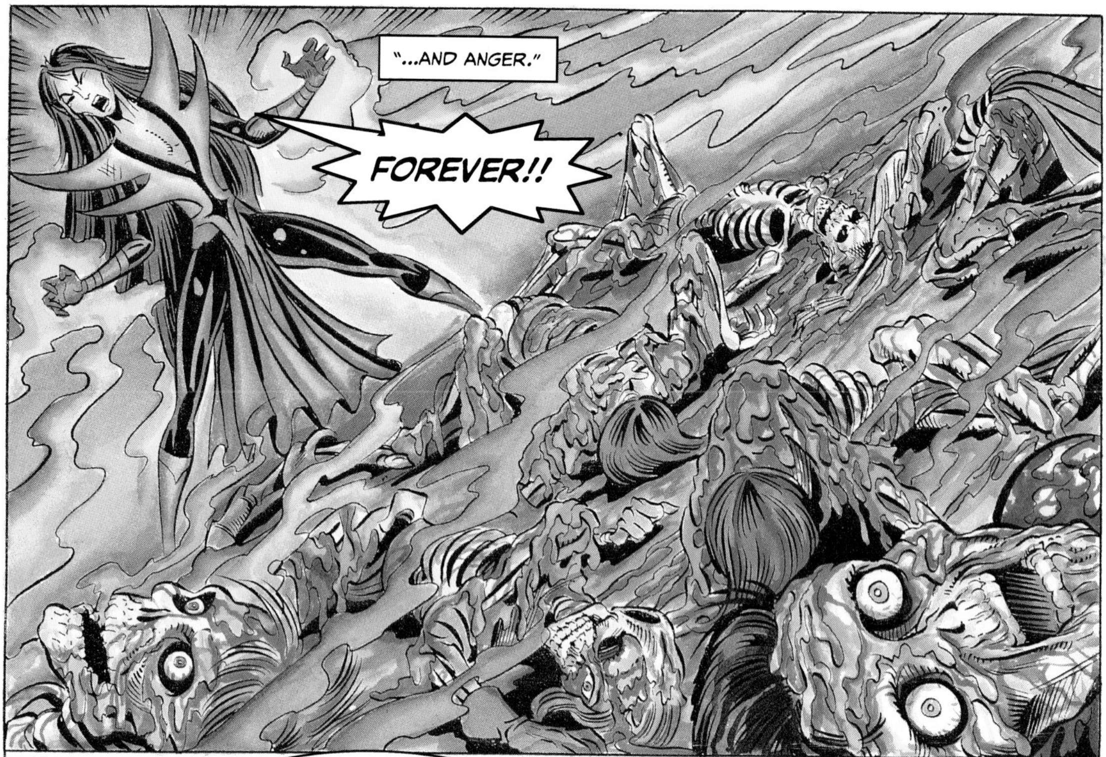
"...AND ANGER."
FOREVER!!

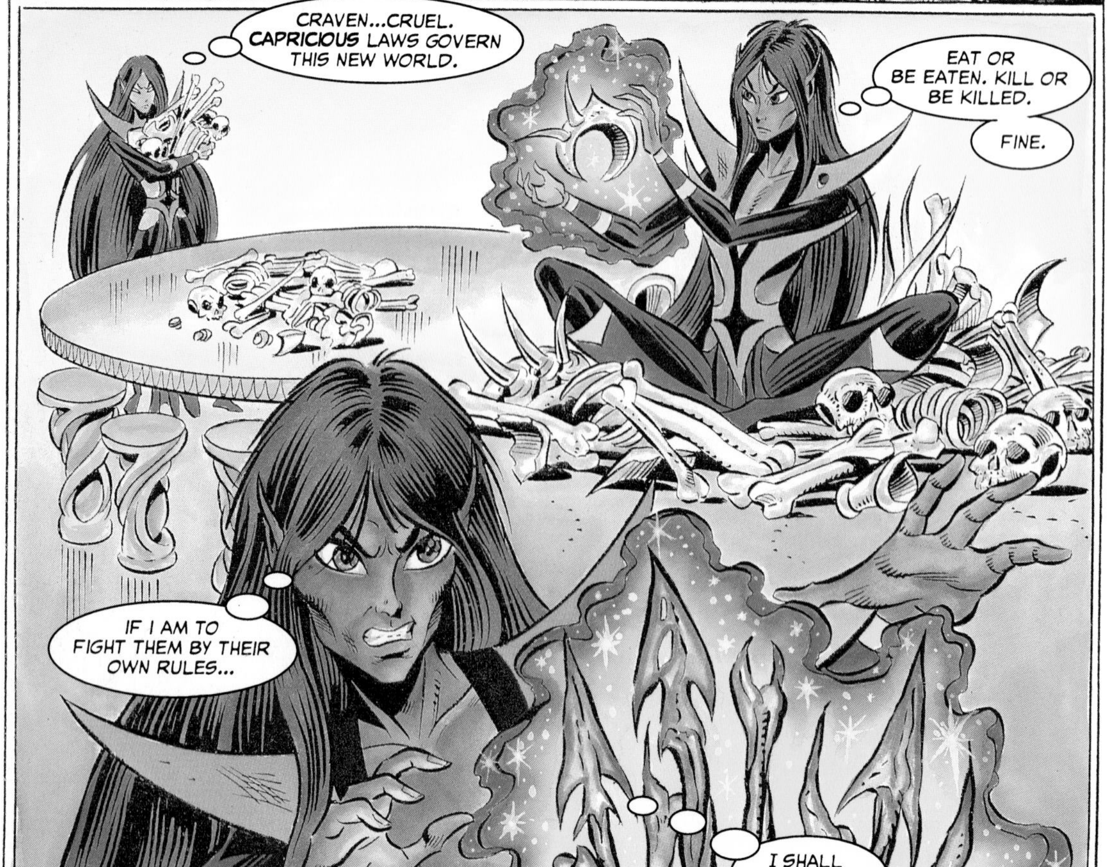
CRAVEN...CRUEL. CAPRICIOUS LAWS GOVERN THIS NEW WORLD.
EAT OR BE EATEN. KILL OR BE KILLED.
FINE.
IF I AM TO FIGHT THEM BY THEIR OWN RULES...
I SHALL DO IT WELL!

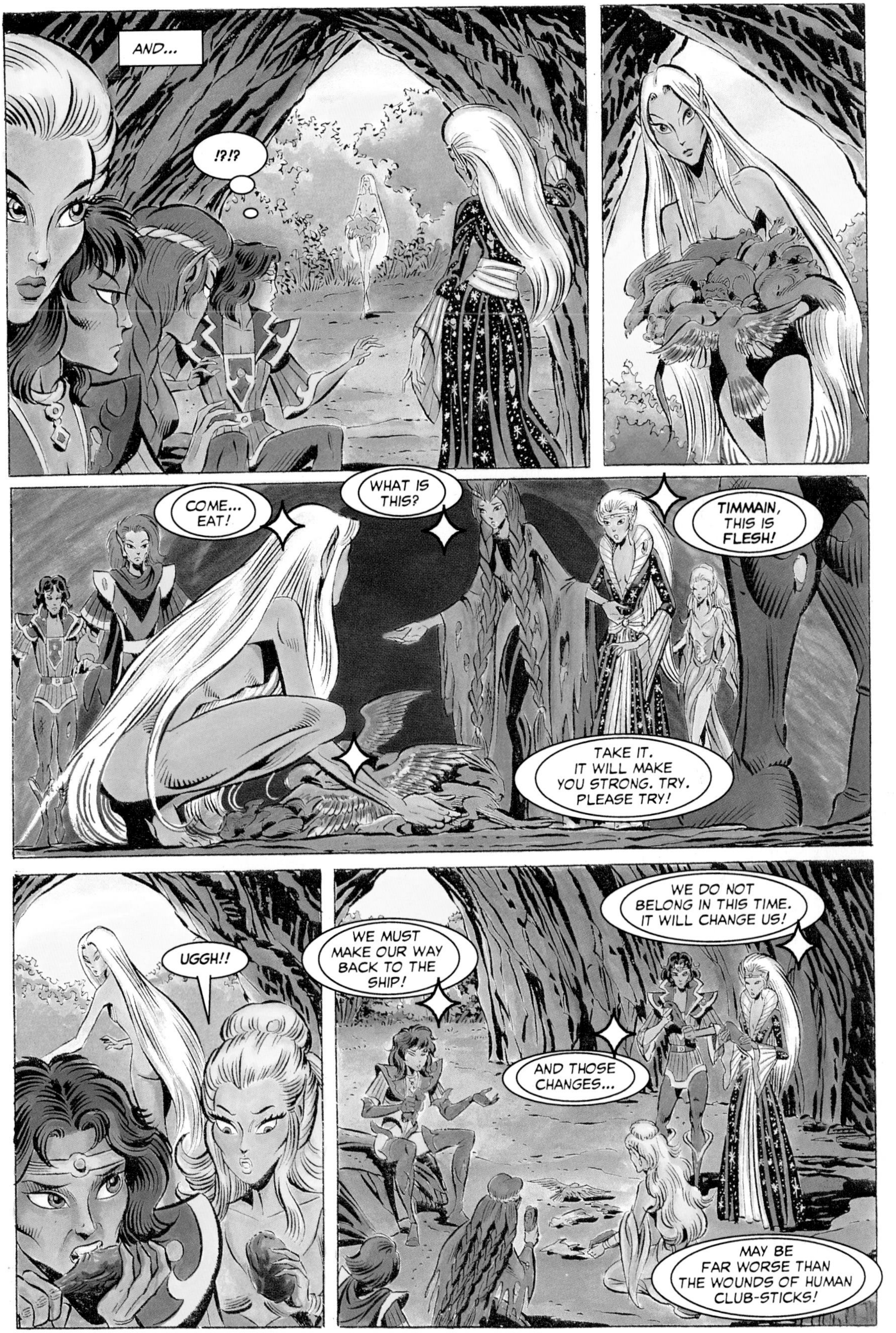
AND...
!?!?
COME... EAT!
WHAT IS THIS?
TIMMAIN, THIS IS FLESH!
TAKE IT. IT WILL MAKE YOU STRONG. TRY. PLEASE TRY!
UGGH!!
WE MUST MAKE OUR WAY BACK TO THE SHIP!
WE DO NOT BELONG IN THIS TIME. IT WILL CHANGE US!
AND THOSE CHANGES...
MAY BE FAR WORSE THAN THE WOUNDS OF HUMAN CLUB-STICKS!

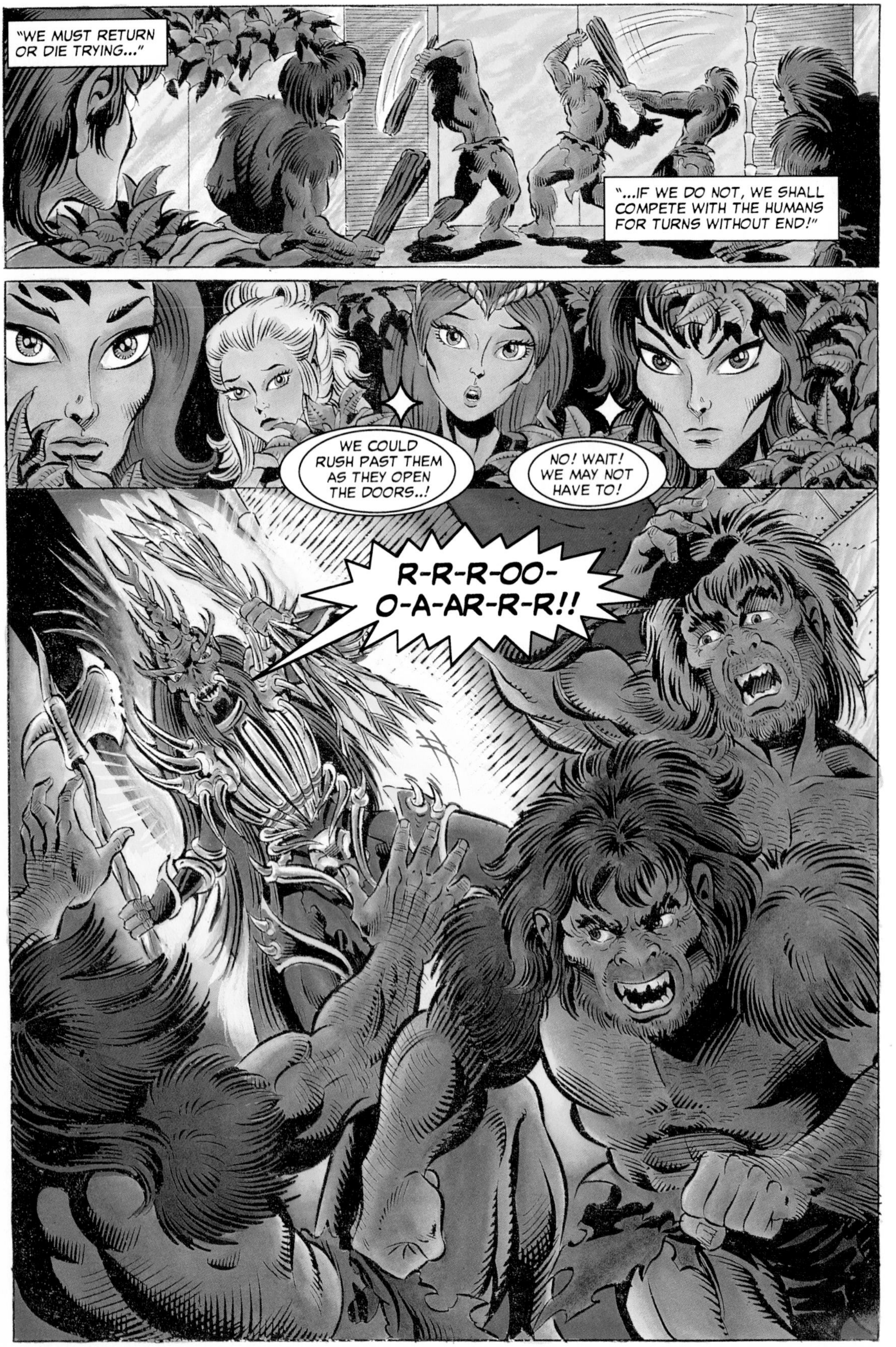
"WE MUST RETURN OR DIE TRYING..."
"...IF WE DO NOT, WE SHALL COMPETE WITH THE HUMANS FOR TURNS WITHOUT END!"
WE COULD RUSH PAST THEM AS THEY OPEN THE DOORS..!
NO! WAIT! WE MAY NOT HAVE TO!
R-R-R-OO-O-A-AR-R-R!!

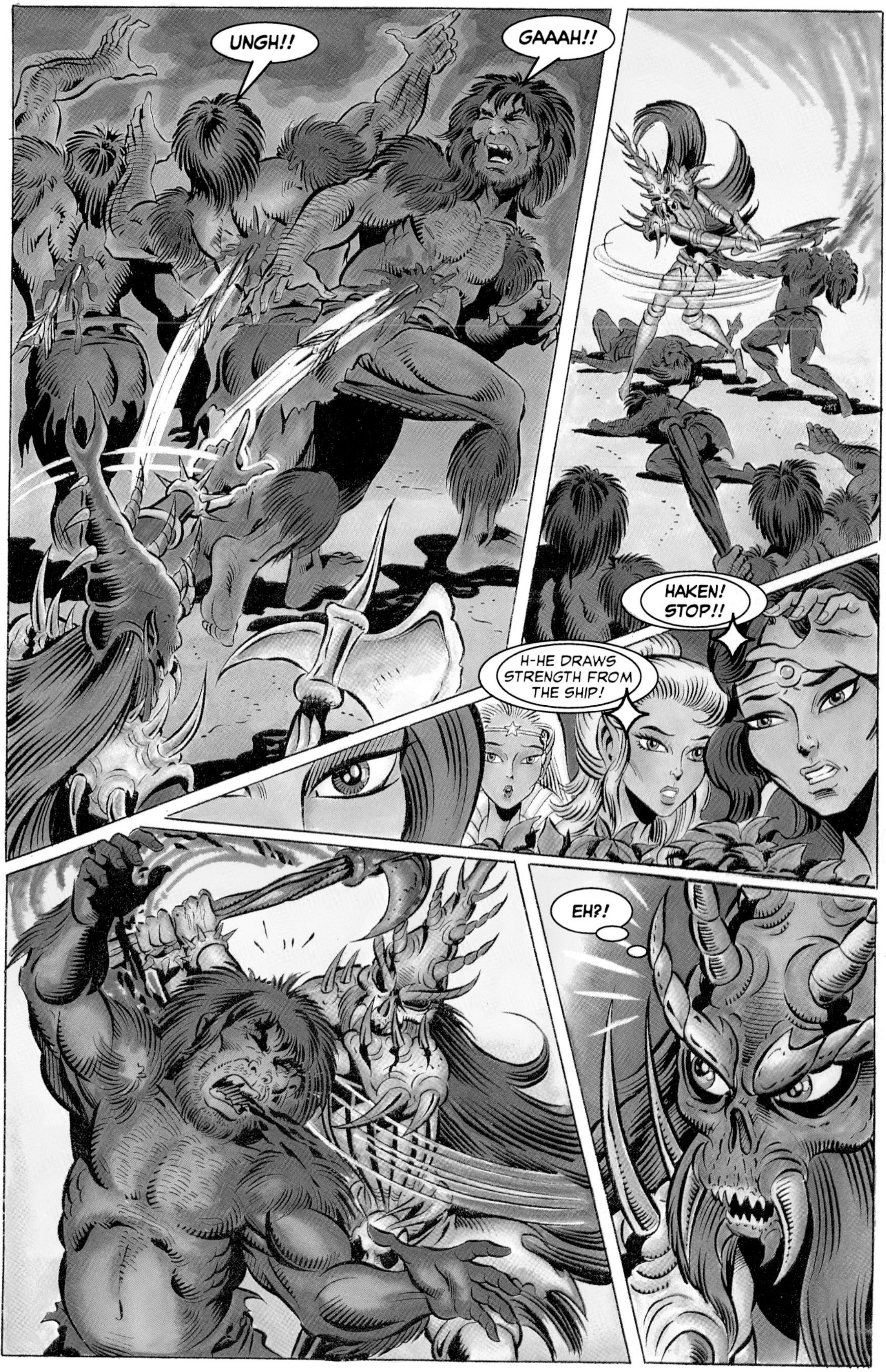
UNGH!!
GAAAH!!
HAKEN! STOP!!
H-HE DRAWS STRENGTH FROM THE SHIP!
EH?!

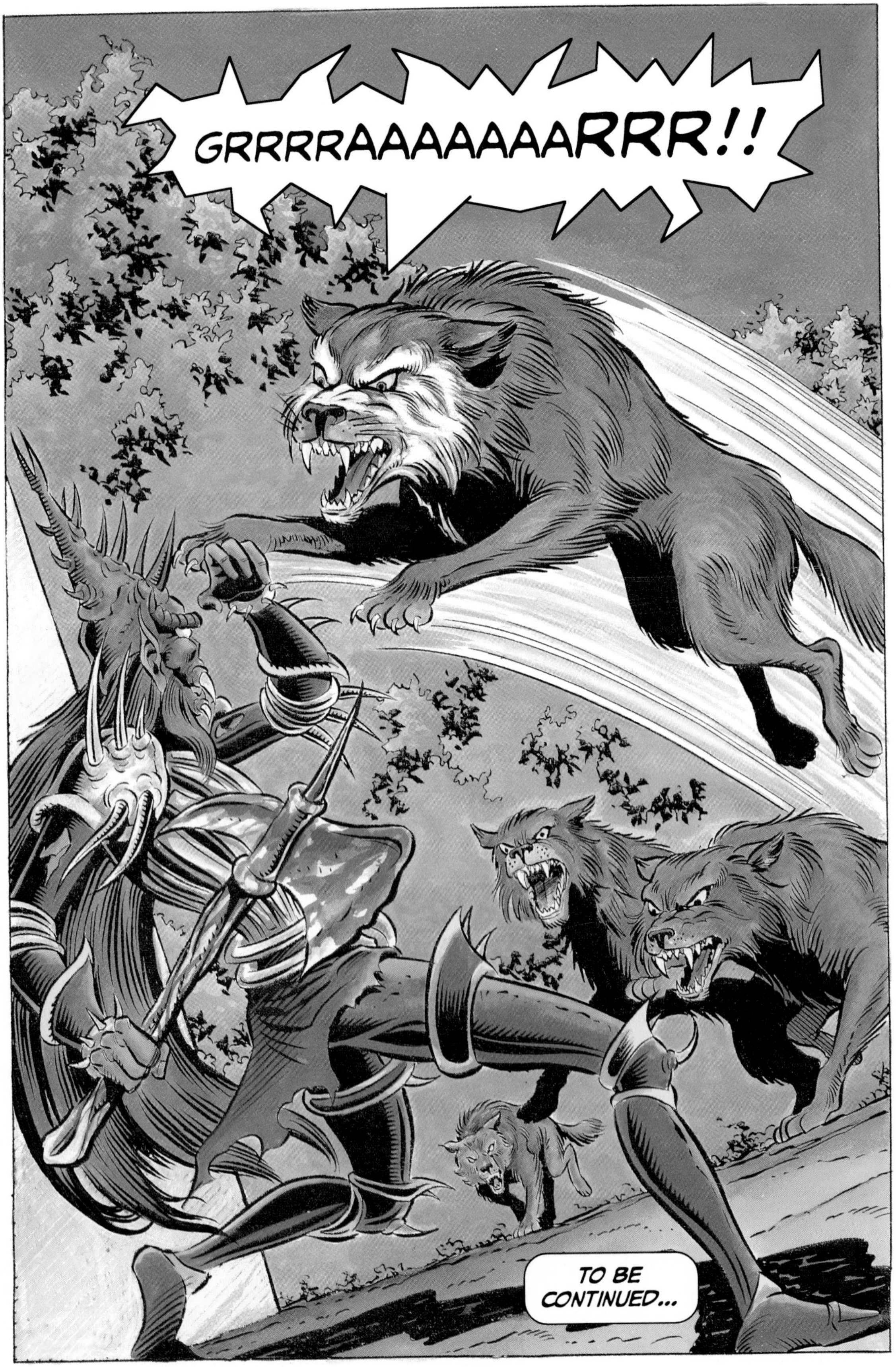
GRRRRAAAAAAAARRR!!
TO BE CONTINUED...

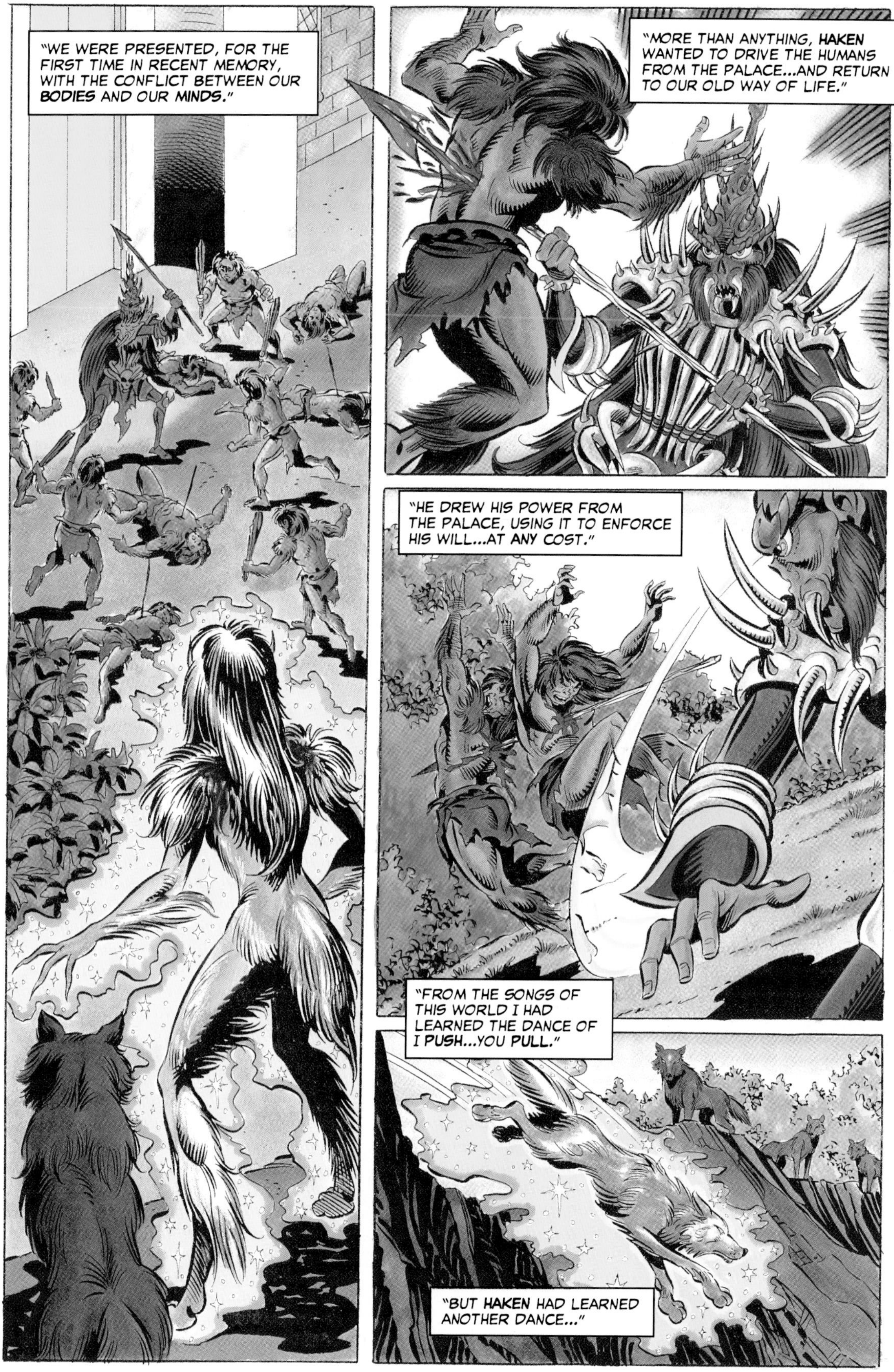
"WE WERE PRESENTED, FOR THE FIRST TIME IN RECENT MEMORY, WITH THE CONFLICT BETWEEN OUR **BODIES** AND OUR **MINDS**."
"MORE THAN ANYTHING, **HAKEN** WANTED TO DRIVE THE HUMANS FROM THE PALACE...AND RETURN TO OUR OLD WAY OF LIFE."
"HE DREW HIS POWER FROM THE PALACE, USING IT TO ENFORCE HIS WILL...AT **ANY COST**."
"FROM THE SONGS OF THIS WORLD I HAD LEARNED THE DANCE OF I **PUSH**...YOU **PULL**."
"BUT **HAKEN** HAD LEARNED ANOTHER DANCE..."

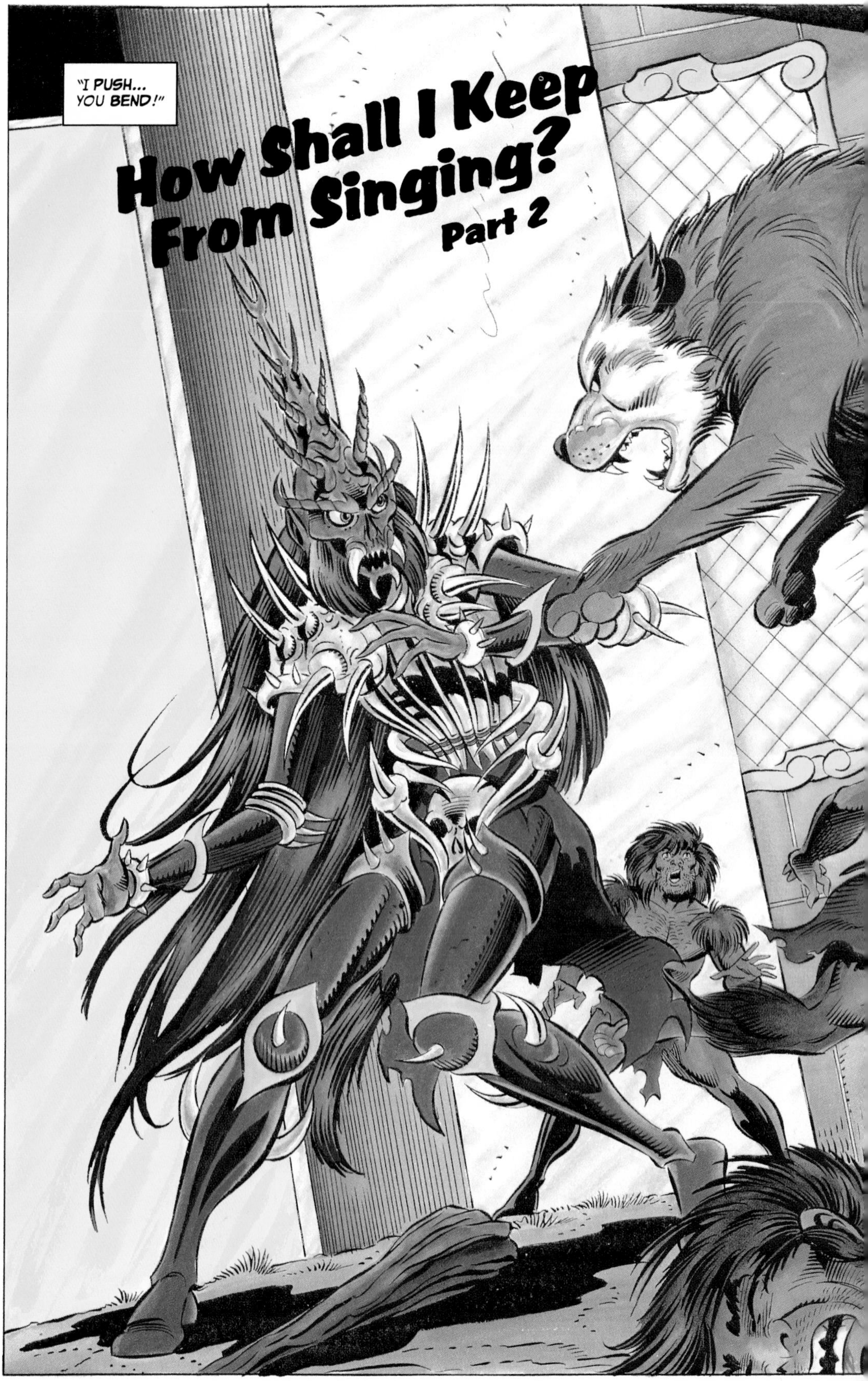
"I PUSH... YOU BEND!"
How Shall I Keep From Singing?
Part 2

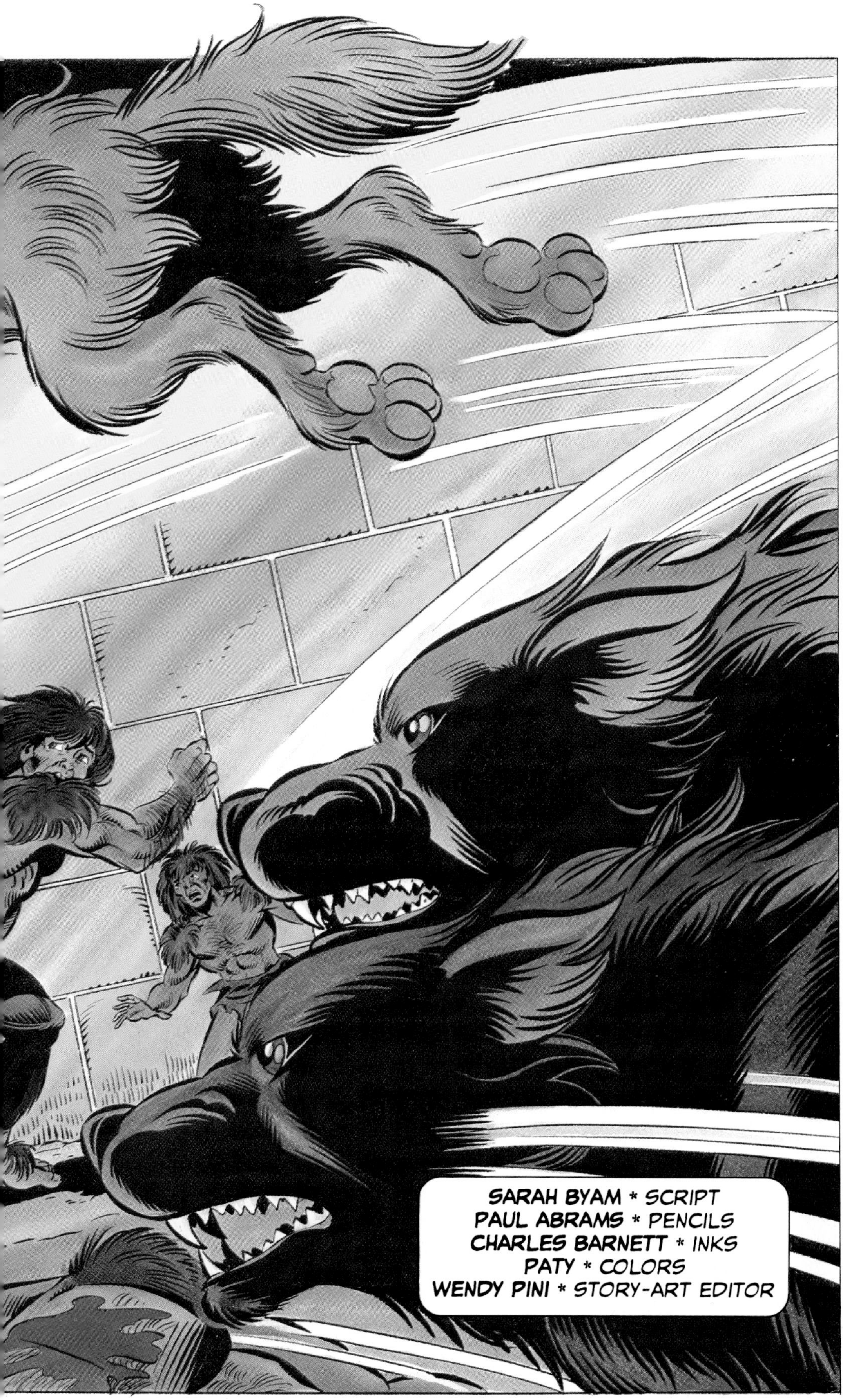
SARAH BYAM * SCRIPT
PAUL ABRAMS * PENCILS
CHARLES BARNETT * INKS
PATY * COLORS
WENDY PINI * STORY-ART EDITOR

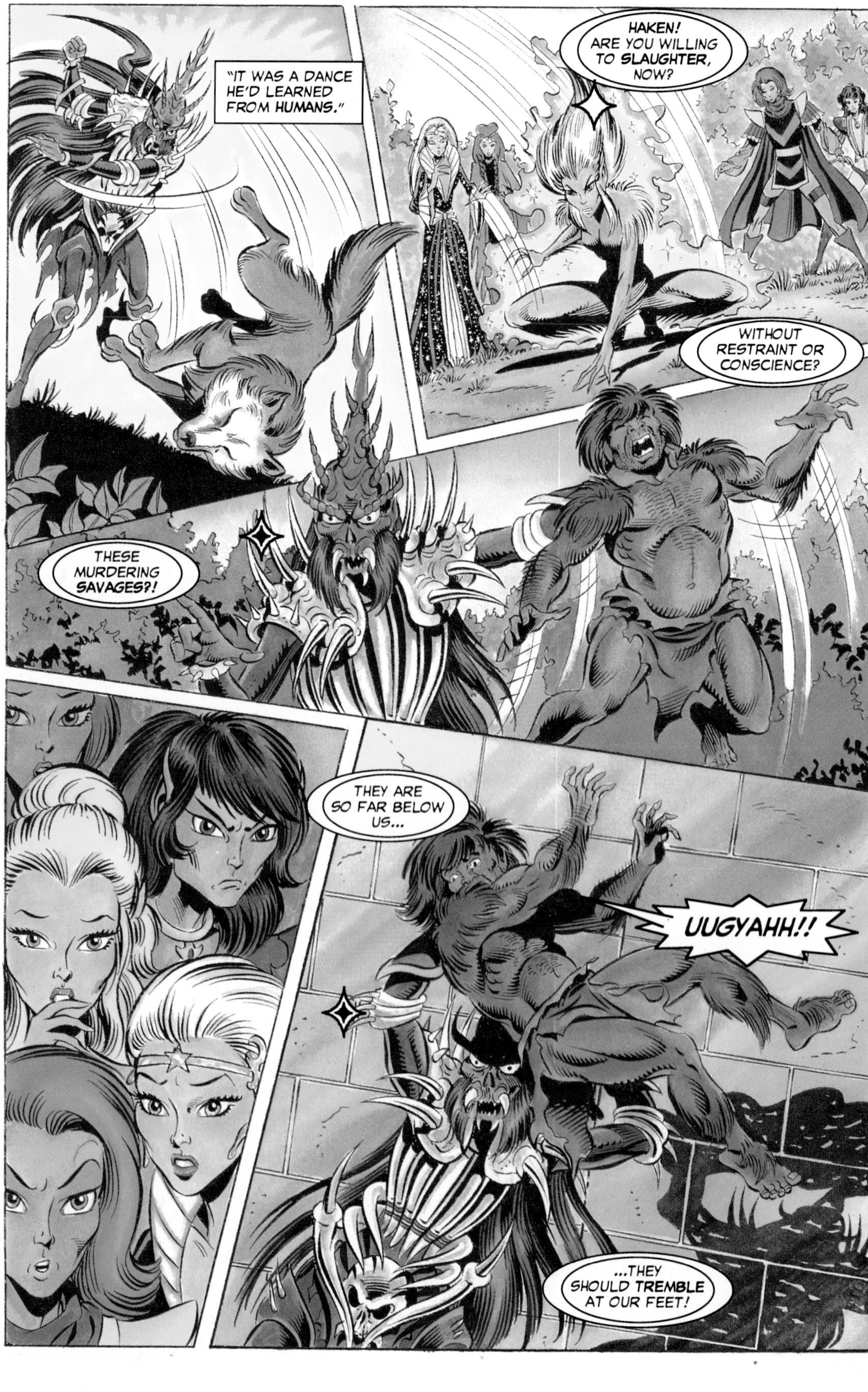
"IT WAS A DANCE HE'D LEARNED FROM HUMANS."
HAKEN! ARE YOU WILLING TO SLAUGHTER, NOW?
WITHOUT RESTRAINT OR CONSCIENCE?
THESE MURDERING SAVAGES?!
THEY ARE SO FAR BELOW US...
UUGYAHH!!
...THEY SHOULD TREMBLE AT OUR FEET!

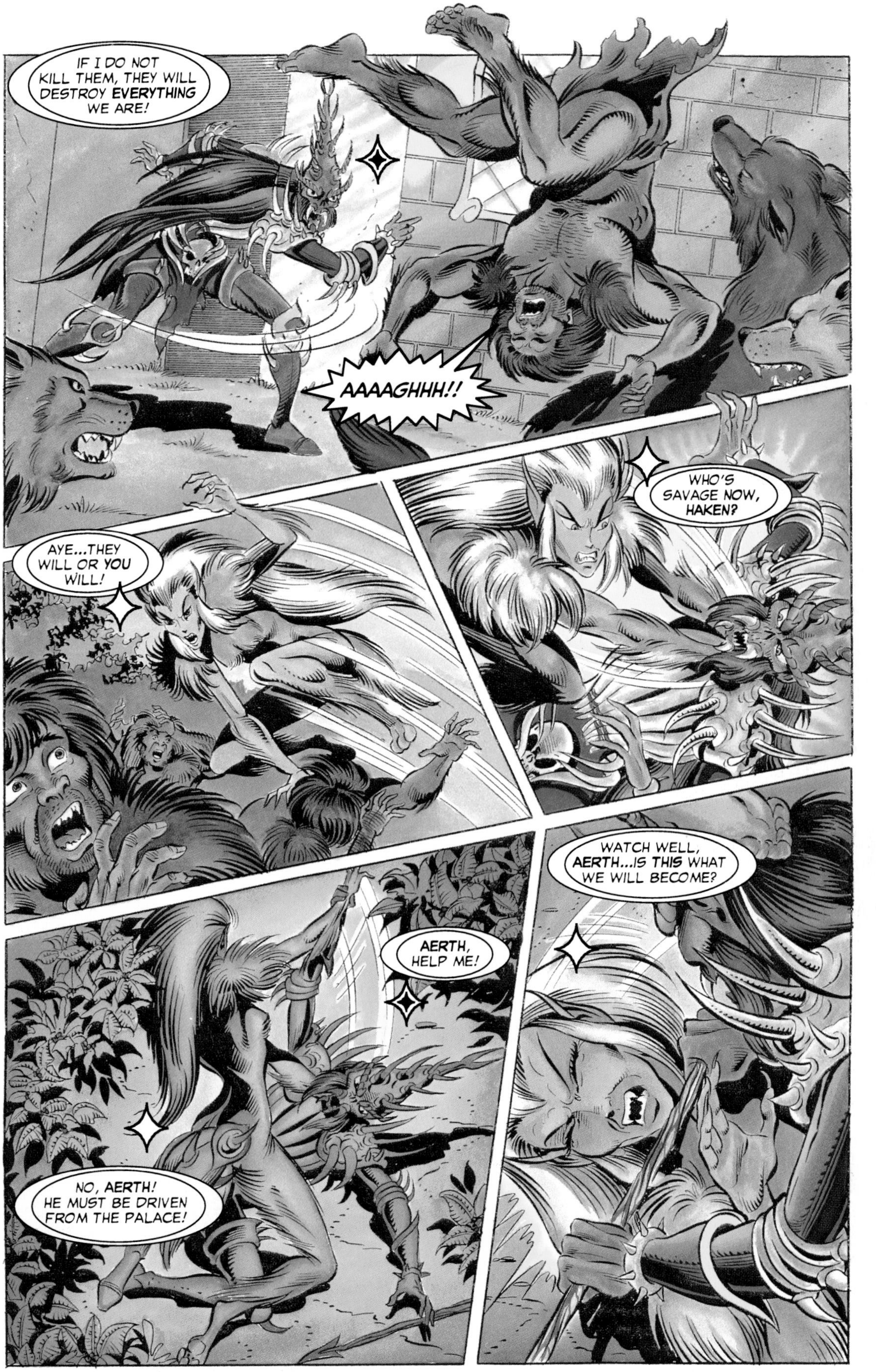
IF I DO NOT KILL THEM, THEY WILL DESTROY EVERYTHING WE ARE!
AAAAGHHH!!
AYE...THEY WILL OR YOU WILL!
WHO'S SAVAGE NOW, HAKEN?
WATCH WELL, AERTH...IS THIS WHAT WE WILL BECOME?
AERTH, HELP ME!
NO, AERTH! HE MUST BE DRIVEN FROM THE PALACE!

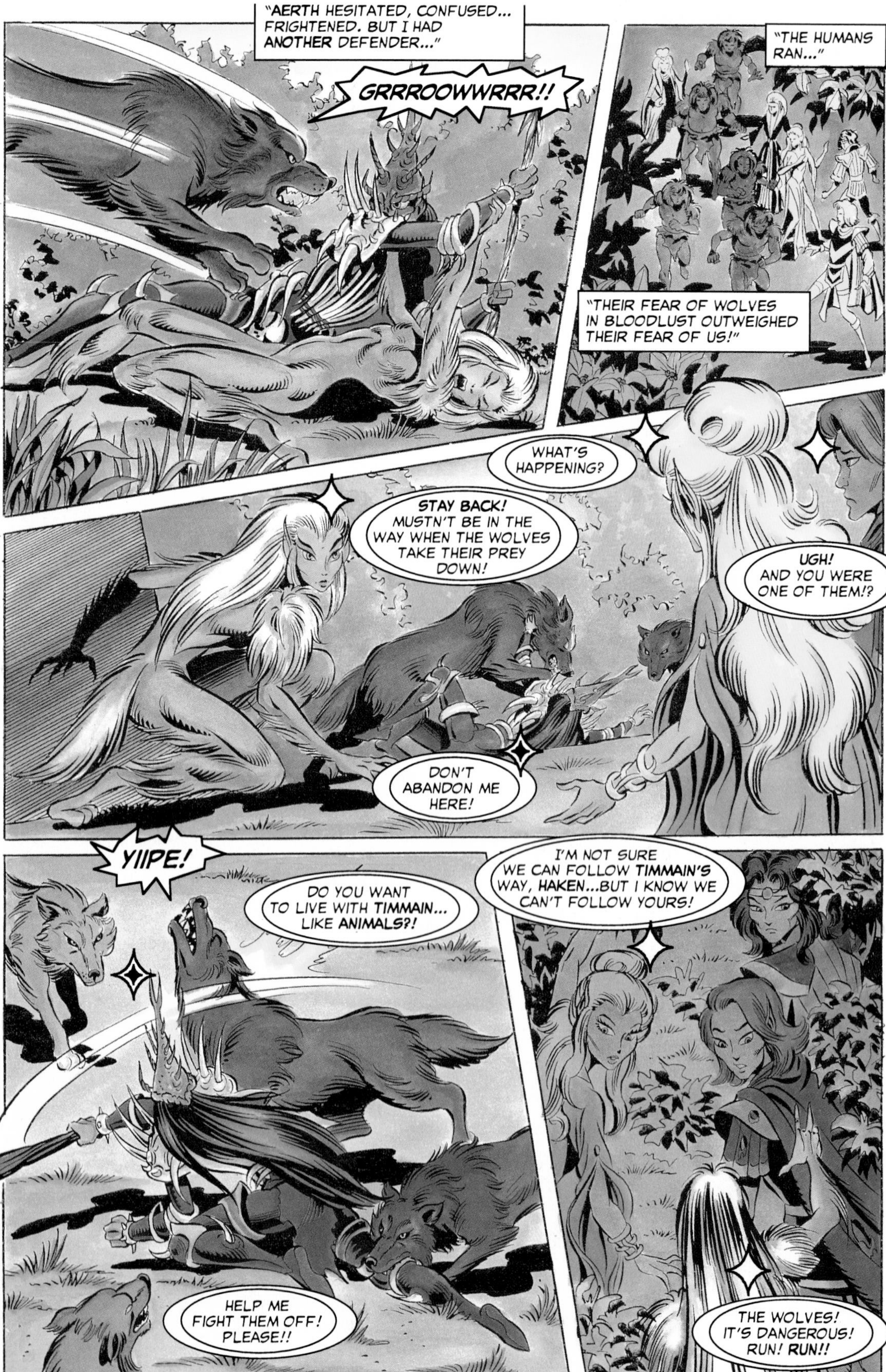
"AERTH HESITATED, CONFUSED... FRIGHTENED. BUT I HAD ANOTHER DEFENDER..."
GRRROOWWRRR!!
"THE HUMANS RAN..."
"THEIR FEAR OF WOLVES IN BLOODLUST OUTWEIGHED THEIR FEAR OF US!"
WHAT'S HAPPENING?
STAY BACK! MUSTN'T BE IN THE WAY WHEN THE WOLVES TAKE THEIR PREY DOWN!
UGH! AND YOU WERE ONE OF THEM!?
DON'T ABANDON ME HERE!
YIIPE!
DO YOU WANT TO LIVE WITH TIMMAIN... LIKE ANIMALS?!
I'M NOT SURE WE CAN FOLLOW TIMMAIN'S WAY, HAKEN...BUT I KNOW WE CAN'T FOLLOW YOURS!
HELP ME FIGHT THEM OFF! PLEASE!!
THE WOLVES! IT'S DANGEROUS! RUN! RUN!!

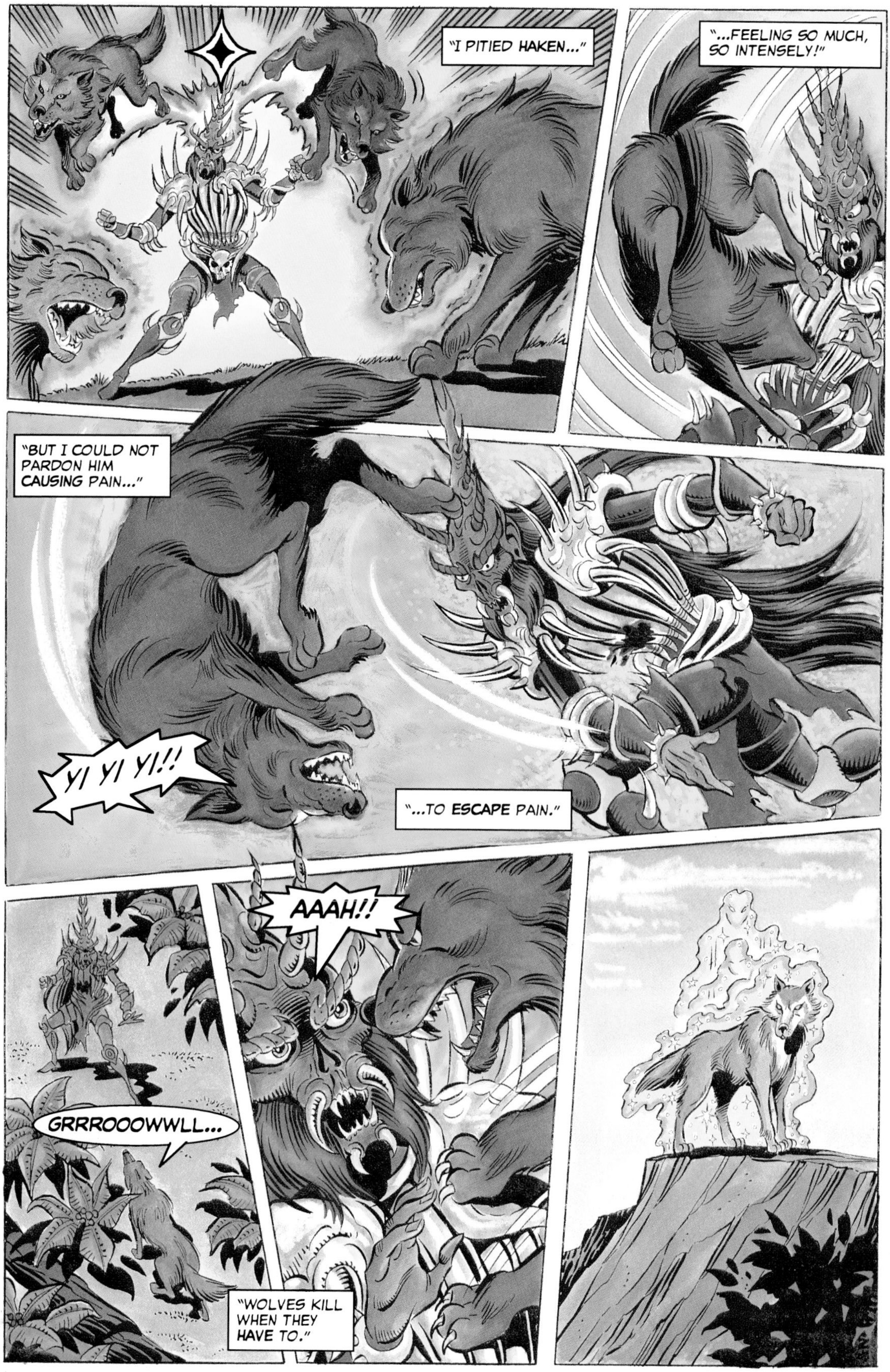
"I PITIED HAKEN..."
"...FEELING SO MUCH, SO INTENSELY!"
"BUT I COULD NOT PARDON HIM CAUSING PAIN..."
YI YI YI!!
"...TO ESCAPE PAIN."
GRRROOOWWLL...
AAAH!!
"WOLVES KILL WHEN THEY HAVE TO."

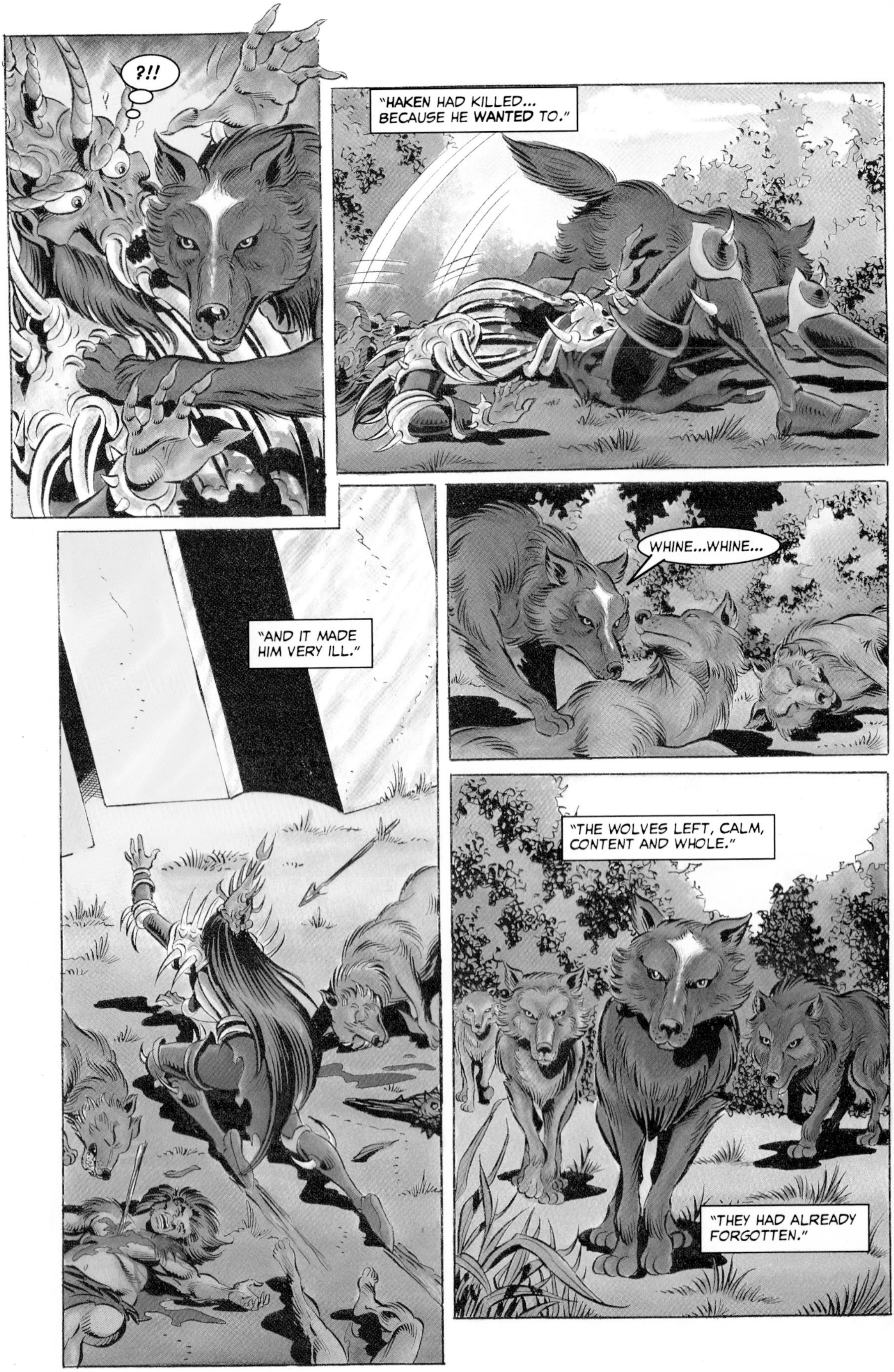
?!!
"HAKEN HAD KILLED... BECAUSE HE WANTED TO."
"AND IT MADE HIM VERY ILL."
WHINE...WHINE...
"THE WOLVES LEFT, CALM, CONTENT AND WHOLE."
"THEY HAD ALREADY FORGOTTEN."

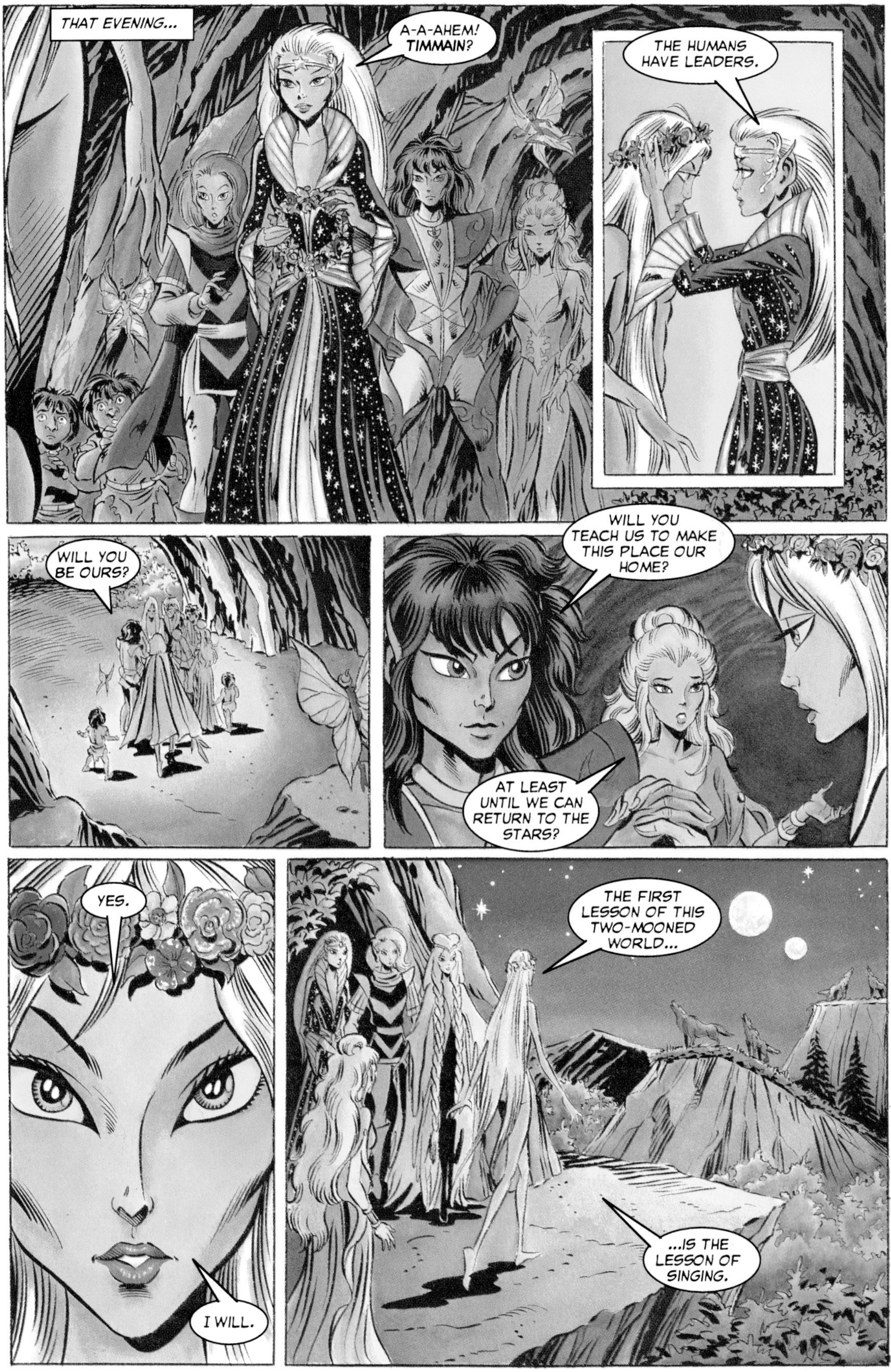
THAT EVENING...
A-A-AHEM! TIMMAIN?
THE HUMANS HAVE LEADERS.
WILL YOU BE OURS?
WILL YOU TEACH US TO MAKE THIS PLACE OUR HOME?
AT LEAST UNTIL WE CAN RETURN TO THE STARS?
YES.
I WILL.
THE FIRST LESSON OF THIS TWO-MOONED WORLD...
...IS THE LESSON OF SINGING.

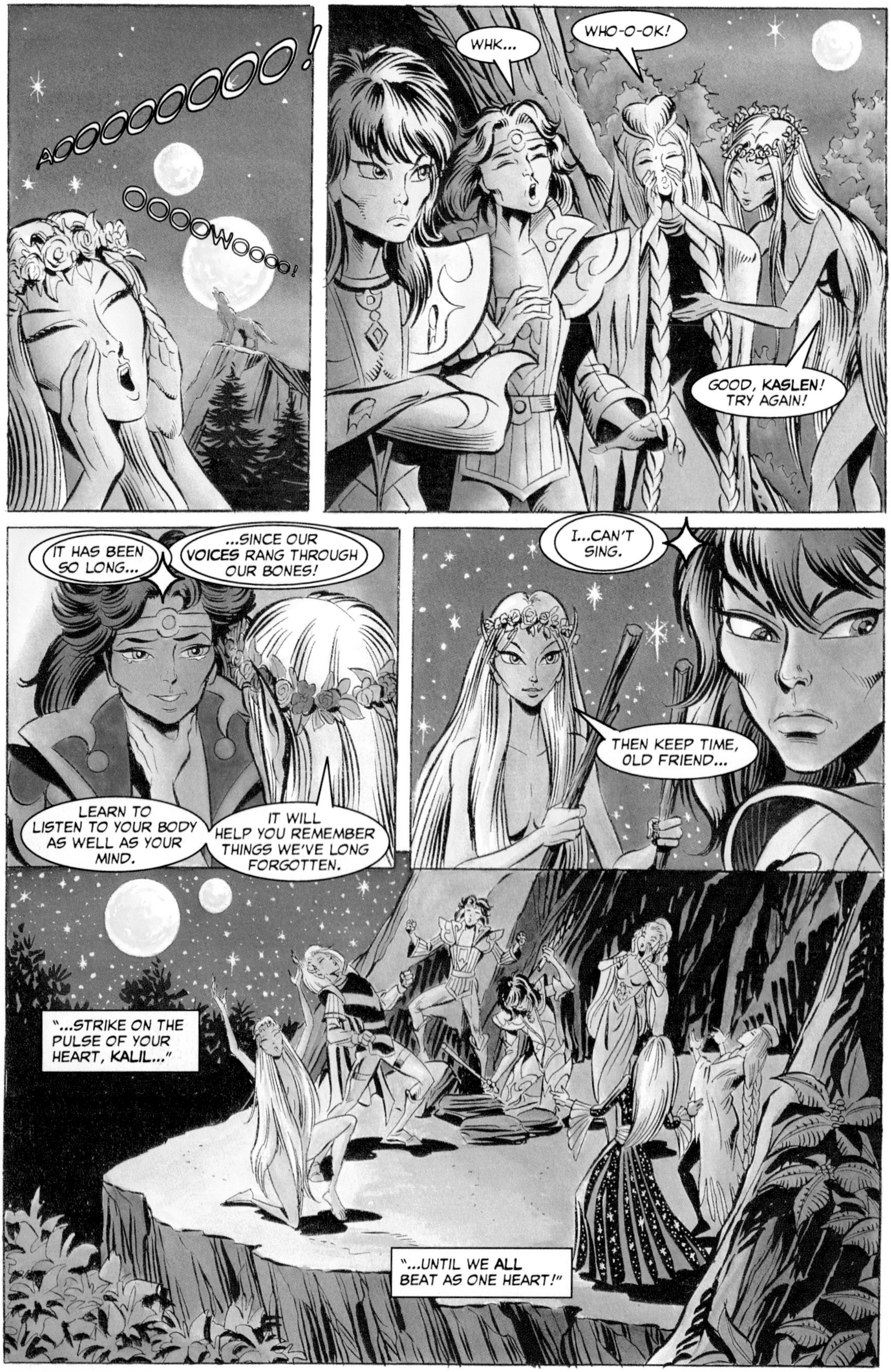
AOOOOOOOOOO!
OOOOWOOOO!
WHK...
WHO-O-OK!
GOOD, KASLEN! TRY AGAIN!
IT HAS BEEN SO LONG...
...SINCE OUR VOICES RANG THROUGH OUR BONES!
LEARN TO LISTEN TO YOUR BODY AS WELL AS YOUR MIND.
IT WILL HELP YOU REMEMBER THINGS WE'VE LONG FORGOTTEN.
I...CAN'T SING.
THEN KEEP TIME, OLD FRIEND...
"...STRIKE ON THE PULSE OF YOUR HEART, KALIL..."
"...UNTIL WE ALL BEAT AS ONE HEART!"

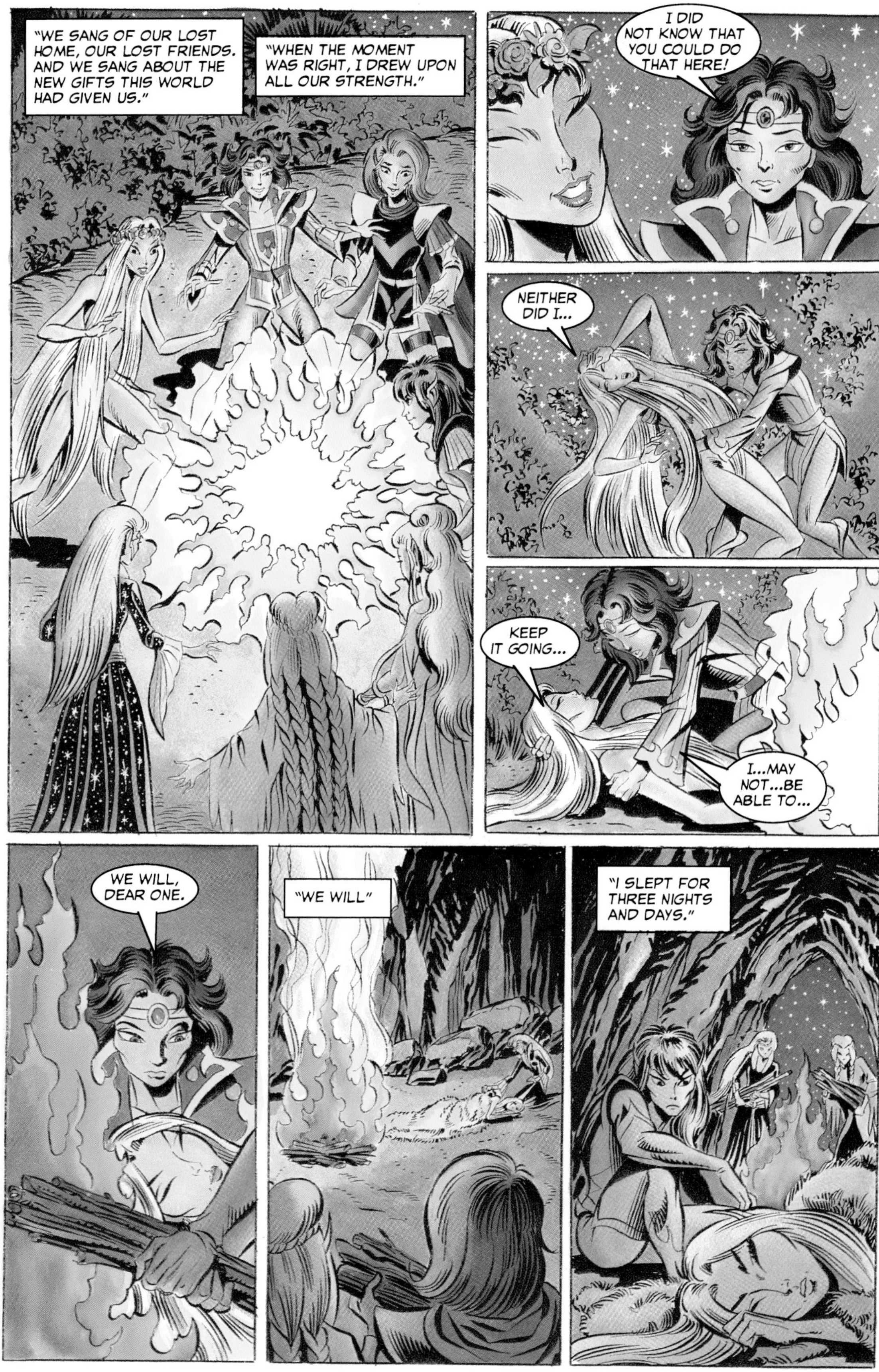
"WE SANG OF OUR LOST HOME, OUR LOST FRIENDS. AND WE SANG ABOUT THE NEW GIFTS THIS WORLD HAD GIVEN US."
"WHEN THE MOMENT WAS RIGHT, I DREW UPON ALL OUR STRENGTH."
I DID NOT KNOW THAT YOU COULD DO THAT HERE!
NEITHER DID I...
KEEP IT GOING...
I...MAY NOT...BE ABLE TO...
WE WILL, DEAR ONE.
"WE WILL"
"I SLEPT FOR THREE NIGHTS AND DAYS."

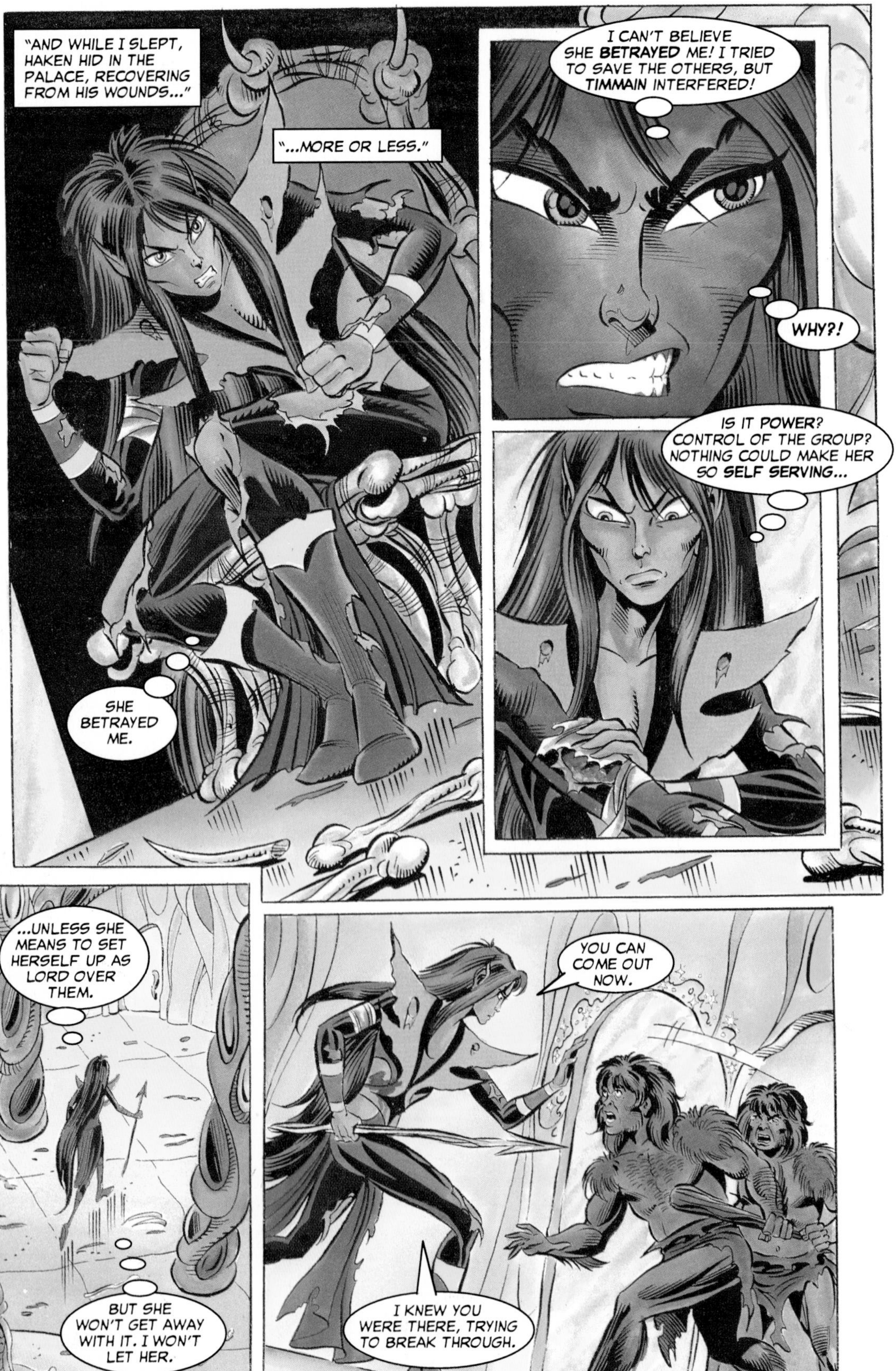
"AND WHILE I SLEPT, HAKEN HID IN THE PALACE, RECOVERING FROM HIS WOUNDS..."
"...MORE OR LESS."
SHE BETRAYED ME.
I CAN'T BELIEVE SHE BETRAYED ME! I TRIED TO SAVE THE OTHERS, BUT TIMMAIN INTERFERED!
WHY?!
IS IT POWER? CONTROL OF THE GROUP? NOTHING COULD MAKE HER SO SELF SERVING...
...UNLESS SHE MEANS TO SET HERSELF UP AS LORD OVER THEM.
BUT SHE WON'T GET AWAY WITH IT. I WON'T LET HER.
YOU CAN COME OUT NOW.
I KNEW YOU WERE THERE, TRYING TO BREAK THROUGH.

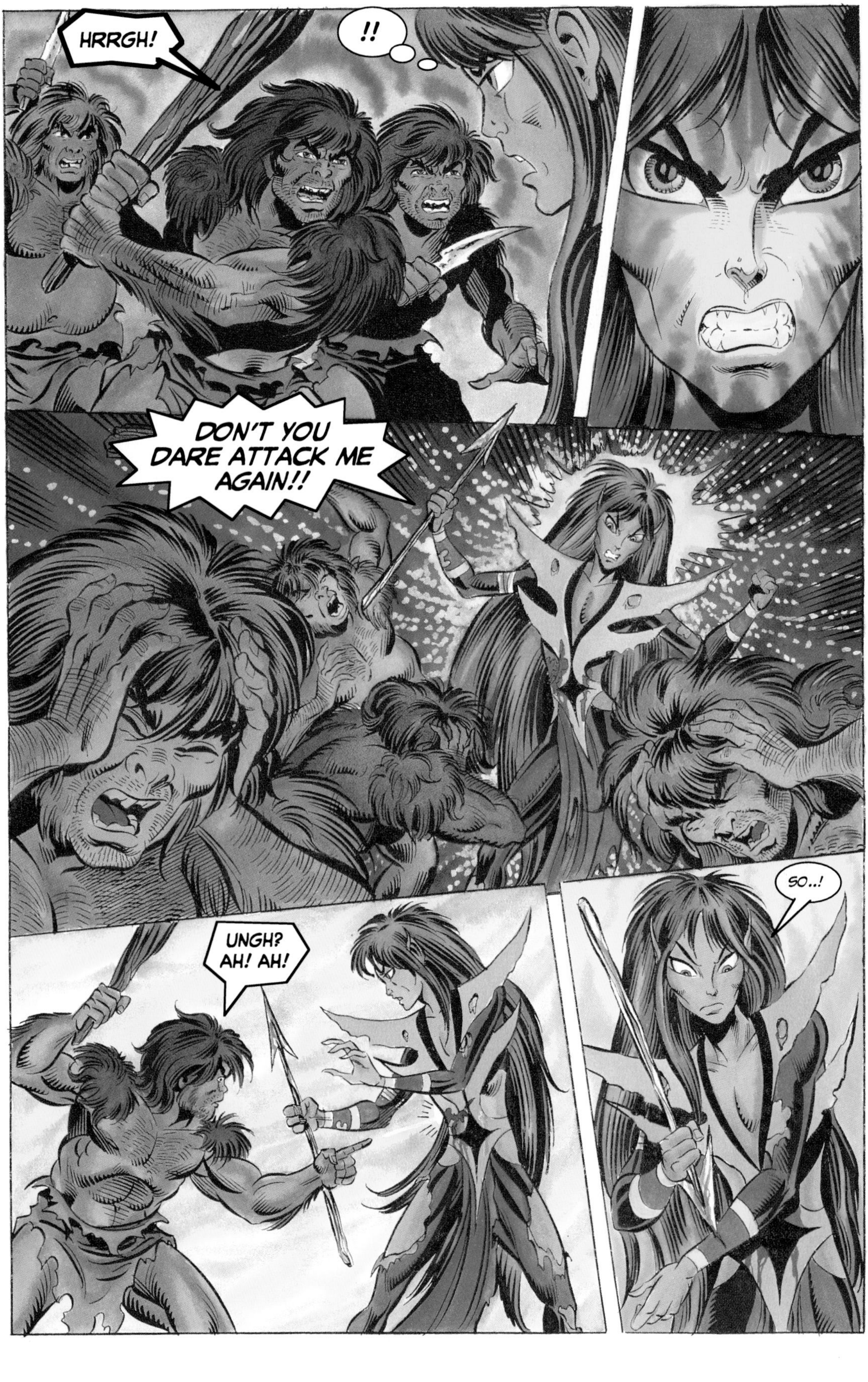
HRRGH!
!!
DON'T YOU DARE ATTACK ME AGAIN!!
UNGH? AH! AH!
SO..!

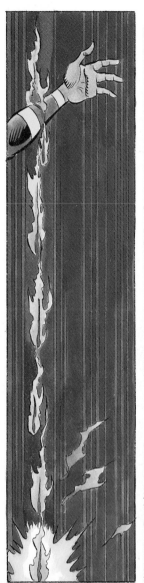

HMPH! I THOUGHT SO. WHAT SAVAGES DON'T UNDERSTAND, YOU EITHER KILL...OR WORSHIP!

ALL RIGHT, THEN, MY CHARMING FOLLOWERS. MY FIRST COMMAND IS...

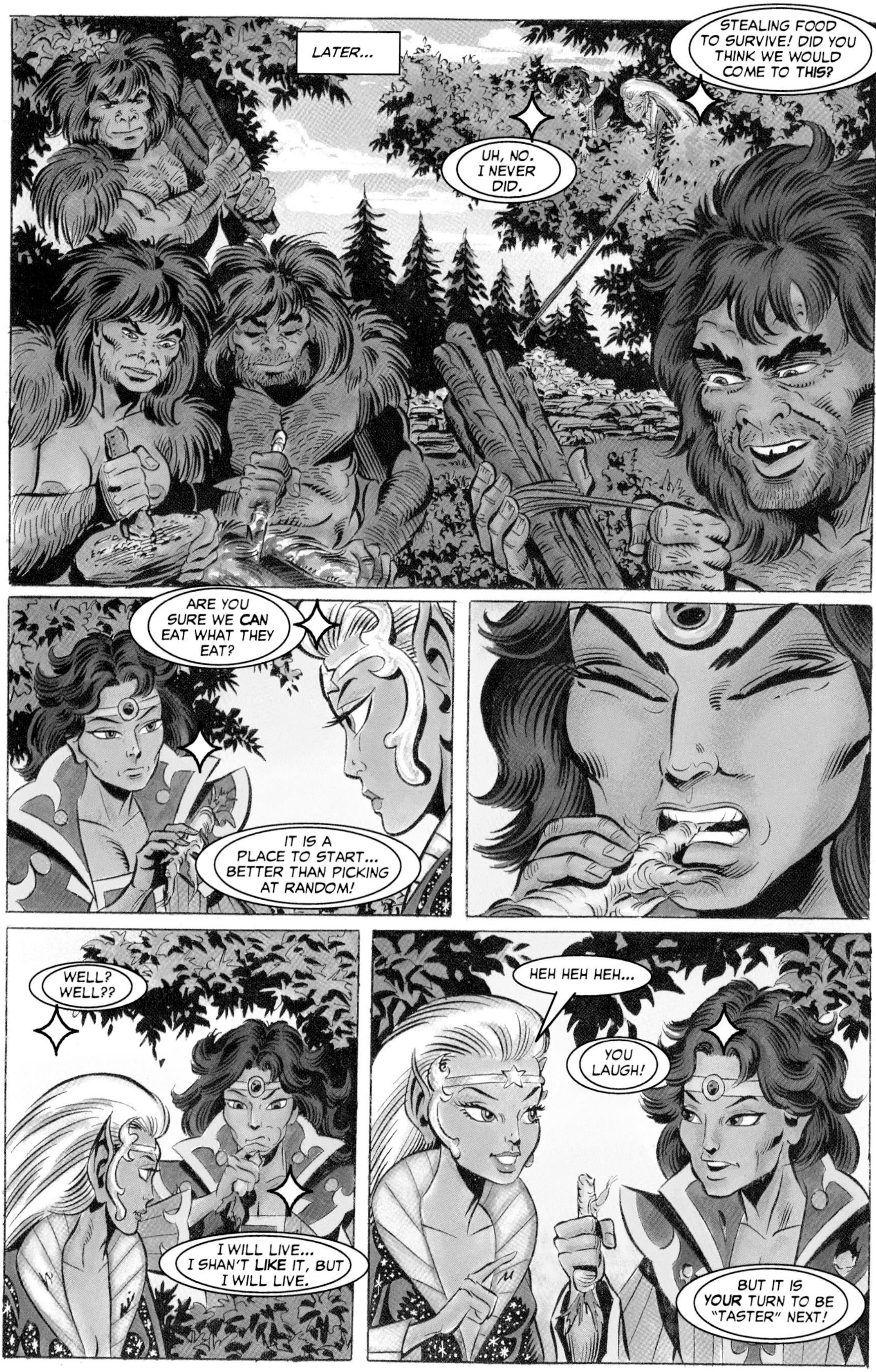
LATER...
STEALING FOOD TO SURVIVE! DID YOU THINK WE WOULD COME TO THIS?
UH, NO. I NEVER DID.
ARE YOU SURE WE CAN EAT WHAT THEY EAT?
IT IS A PLACE TO START... BETTER THAN PICKING AT RANDOM!
WELL? WELL??
I WILL LIVE... I SHAN'T LIKE IT, BUT I WILL LIVE.
HEH HEH HEH...
YOU LAUGH!
BUT IT IS YOUR TURN TO BE "TASTER" NEXT!

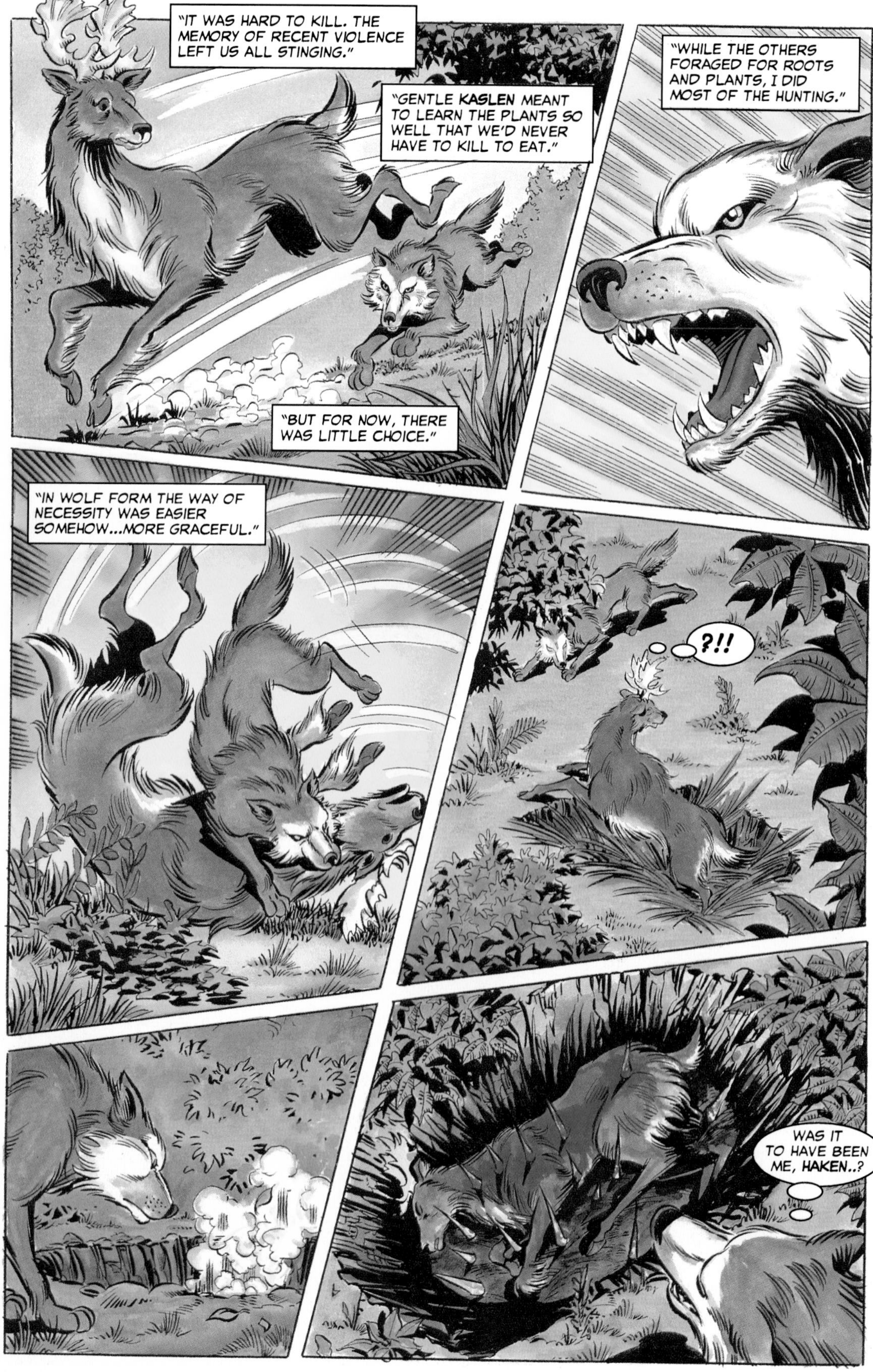
"IT WAS HARD TO KILL. THE MEMORY OF RECENT VIOLENCE LEFT US ALL STINGING."
"GENTLE KASLEN MEANT TO LEARN THE PLANTS SO WELL THAT WE'D NEVER HAVE TO KILL TO EAT."
"BUT FOR NOW, THERE WAS LITTLE CHOICE."
"WHILE THE OTHERS FORAGED FOR ROOTS AND PLANTS, I DID MOST OF THE HUNTING."
"IN WOLF FORM THE WAY OF NECESSITY WAS EASIER SOMEHOW...MORE GRACEFUL."
?!!
WAS IT TO HAVE BEEN ME, HAKEN..?

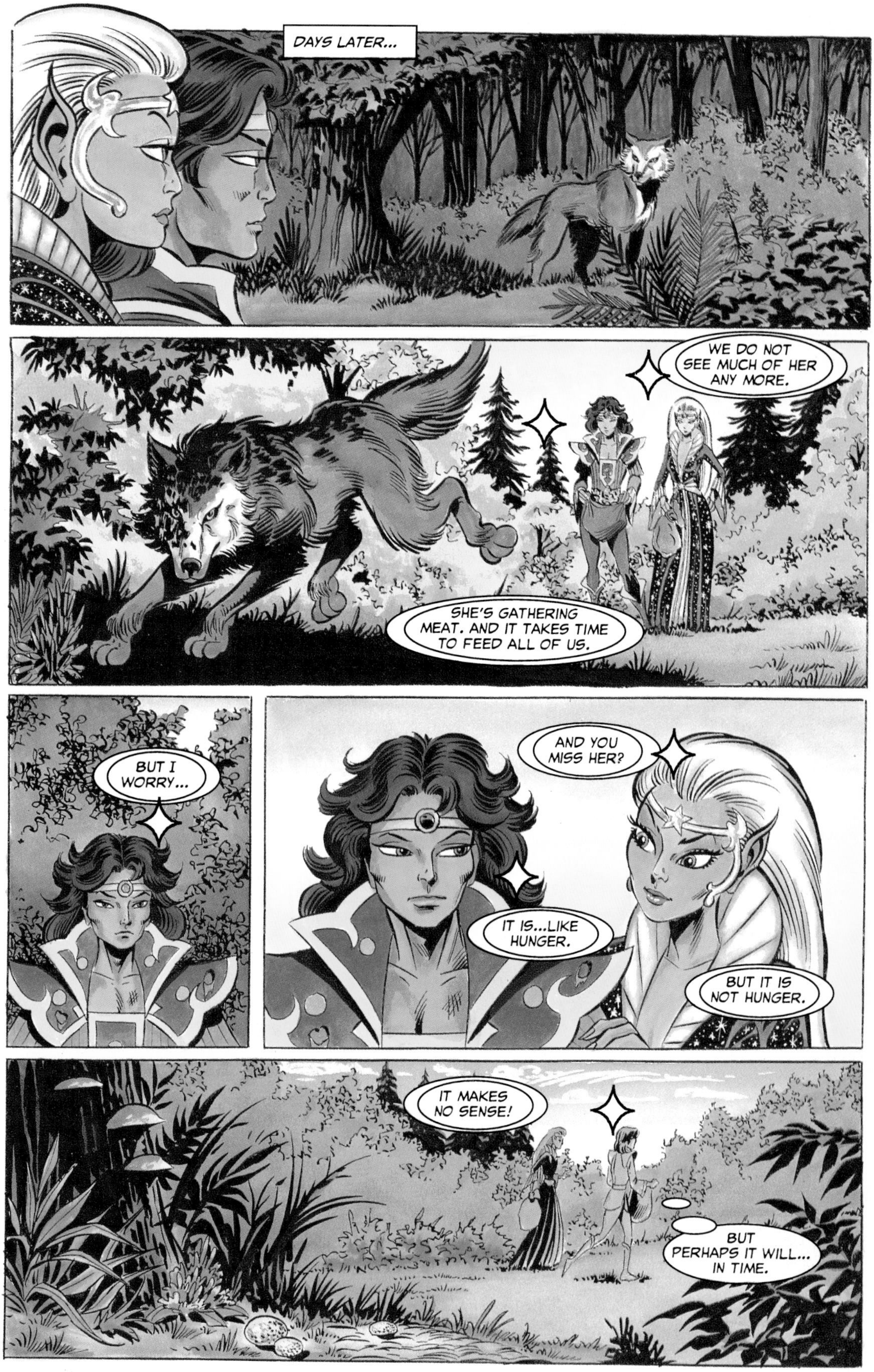
DAYS LATER...
WE DO NOT SEE MUCH OF HER ANY MORE.
SHE'S GATHERING MEAT. AND IT TAKES TIME TO FEED ALL OF US.
BUT I WORRY...
AND YOU MISS HER?
IT IS...LIKE HUNGER.
BUT IT IS NOT HUNGER.
IT MAKES NO SENSE!
BUT PERHAPS IT WILL... IN TIME.

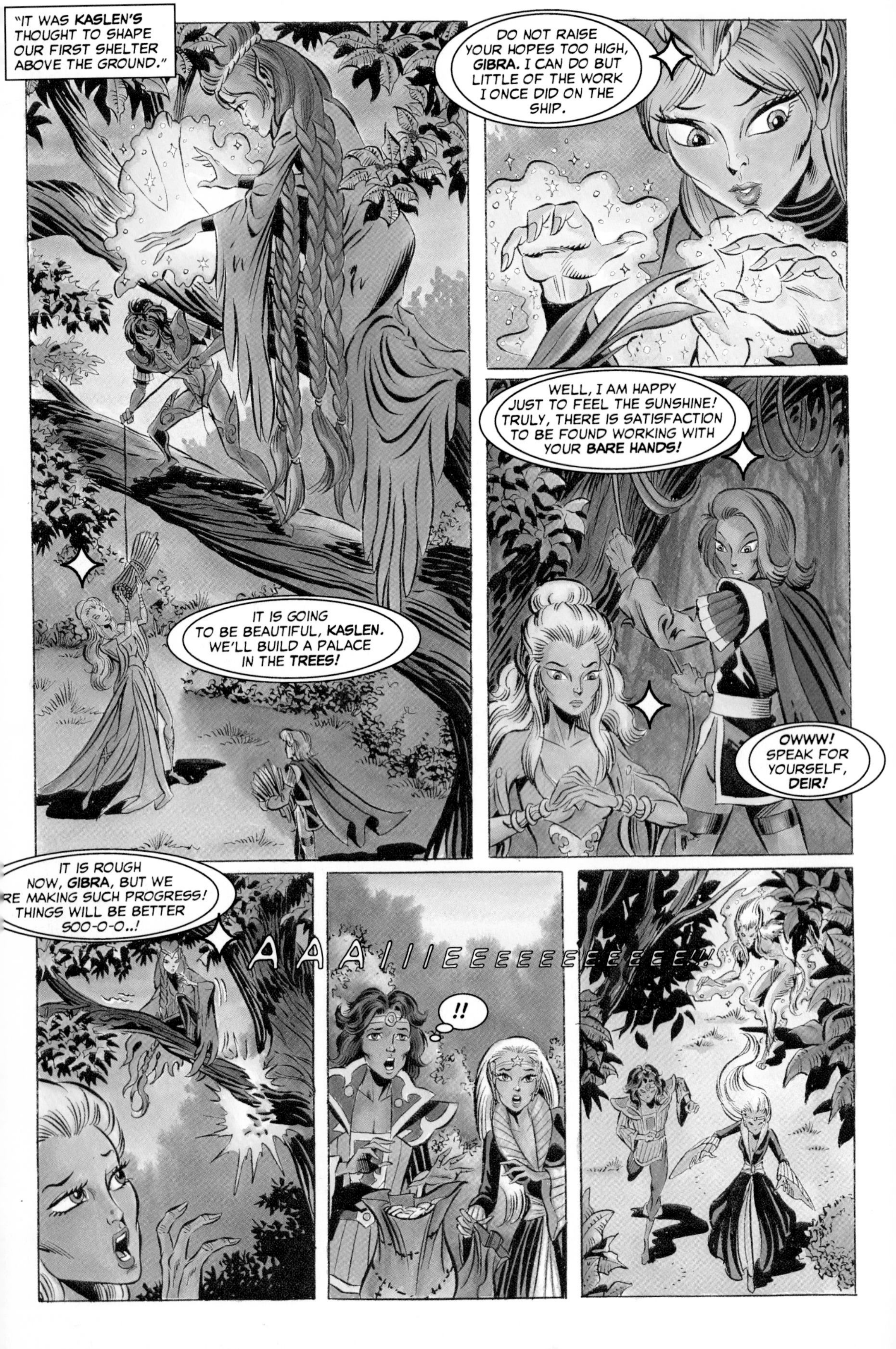
"IT WAS KASLEN'S THOUGHT TO SHAPE OUR FIRST SHELTER ABOVE THE GROUND."
DO NOT RAISE YOUR HOPES TOO HIGH, GIBRA. I CAN DO BUT LITTLE OF THE WORK I ONCE DID ON THE SHIP.
IT IS GOING TO BE BEAUTIFUL, KASLEN. WE'LL BUILD A PALACE IN THE TREES!
WELL, I AM HAPPY JUST TO FEEL THE SUNSHINE! TRULY, THERE IS SATISFACTION TO BE FOUND WORKING WITH YOUR BARE HANDS!
OWWW! SPEAK FOR YOURSELF, DEIR!
IT IS ROUGH NOW, GIBRA, BUT WE RE MAKING SUCH PROGRESS! THINGS WILL BE BETTER SOO-O-O..!
AAAIIIEEEEEEEEEEE!!
!!

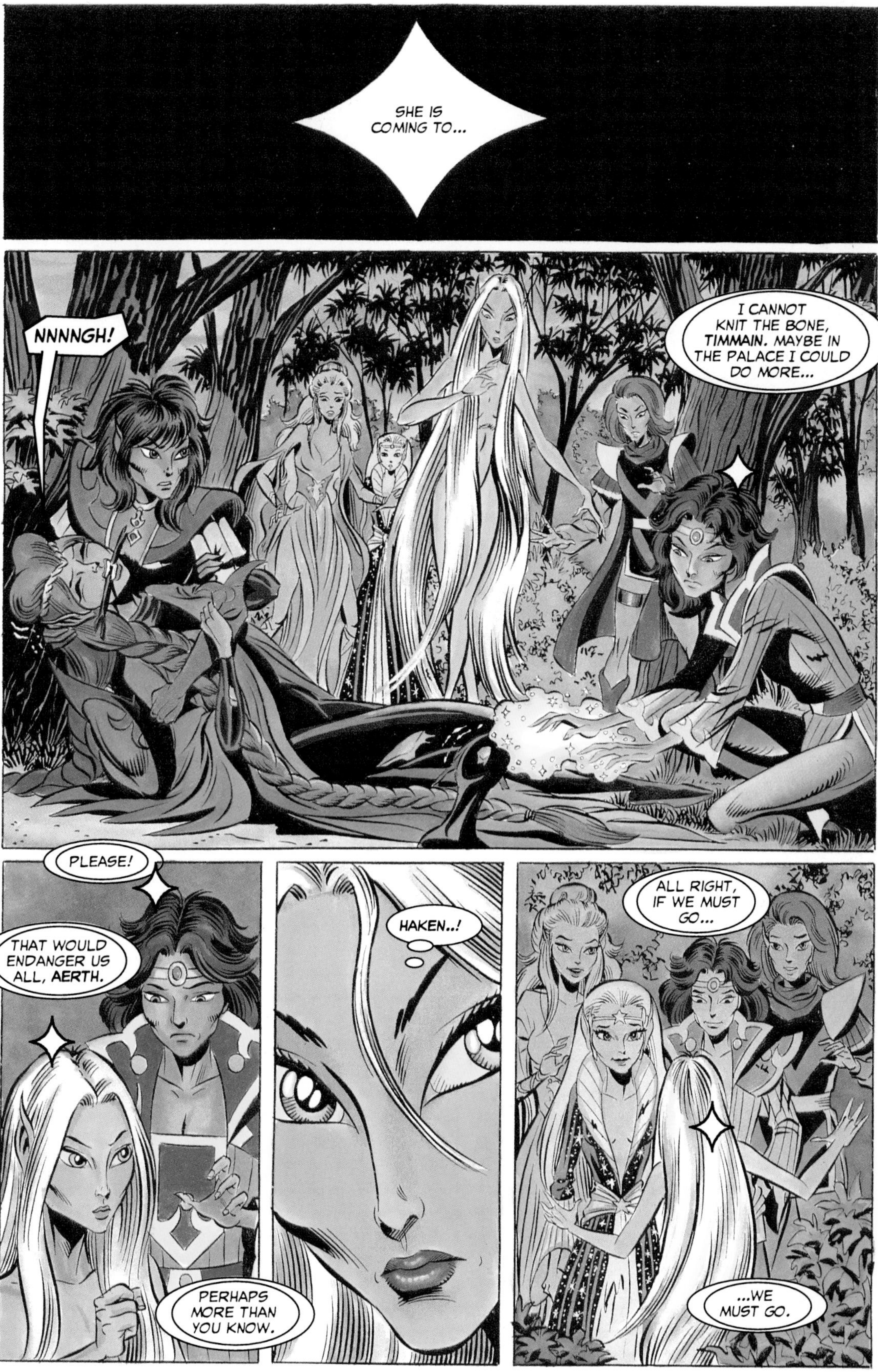
SHE IS COMING TO...
NNNNGH!
I CANNOT KNIT THE BONE, TIMMAIN. MAYBE IN THE PALACE I COULD DO MORE...
PLEASE!
THAT WOULD ENDANGER US ALL, AERTH.
PERHAPS MORE THAN YOU KNOW.
HAKEN..!
ALL RIGHT, IF WE MUST GO...
...WE MUST GO.

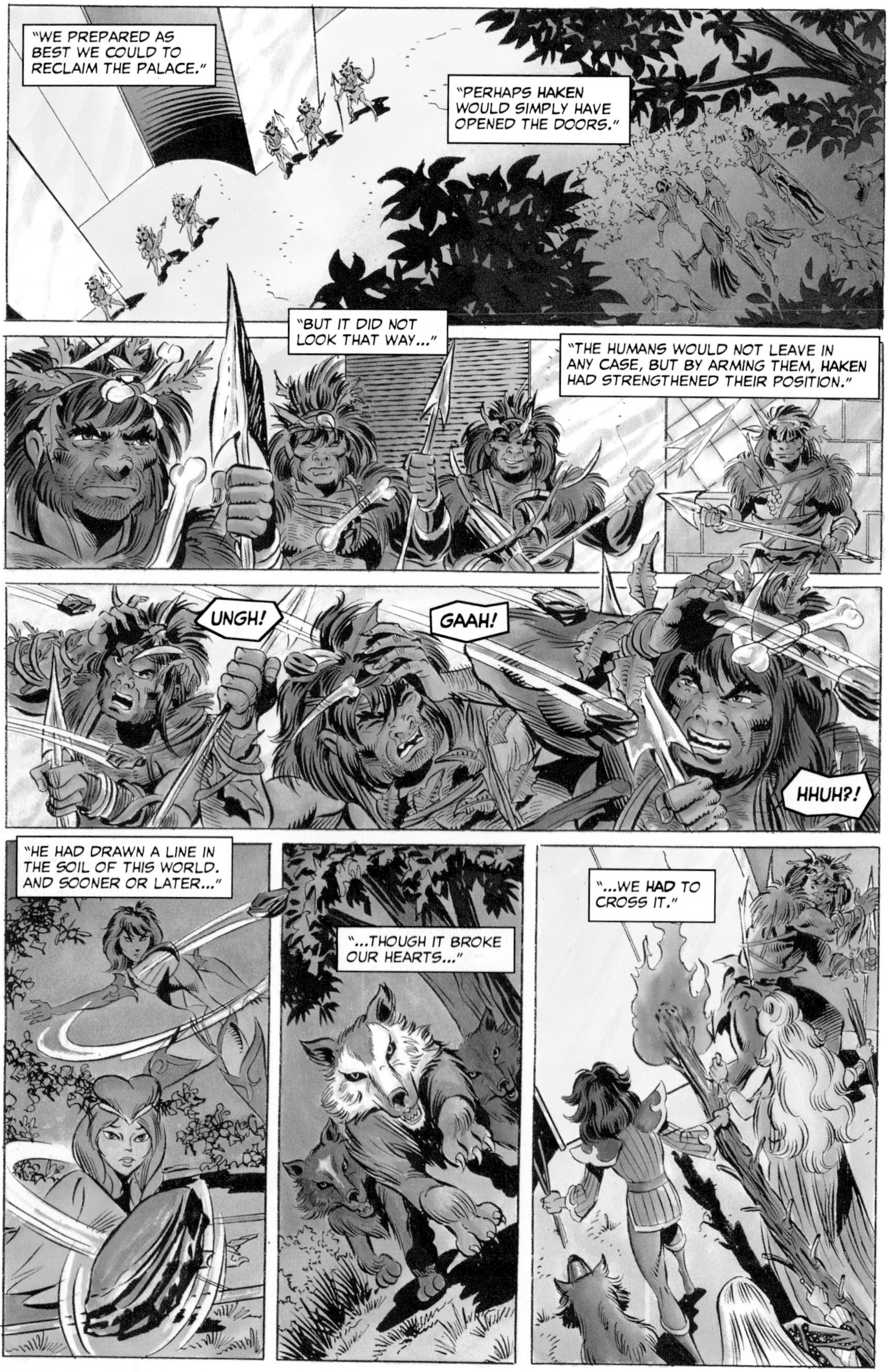
"WE PREPARED AS BEST WE COULD TO RECLAIM THE PALACE."
"PERHAPS HAKEN WOULD SIMPLY HAVE OPENED THE DOORS."
"BUT IT DID NOT LOOK THAT WAY..."
"THE HUMANS WOULD NOT LEAVE IN ANY CASE, BUT BY ARMING THEM, HAKEN HAD STRENGTHENED THEIR POSITION."
UNGH!
GAAH!
HHUH?!
"HE HAD DRAWN A LINE IN THE SOIL OF THIS WORLD. AND SOONER OR LATER..."
"...THOUGH IT BROKE OUR HEARTS..."
"...WE HAD TO CROSS IT."

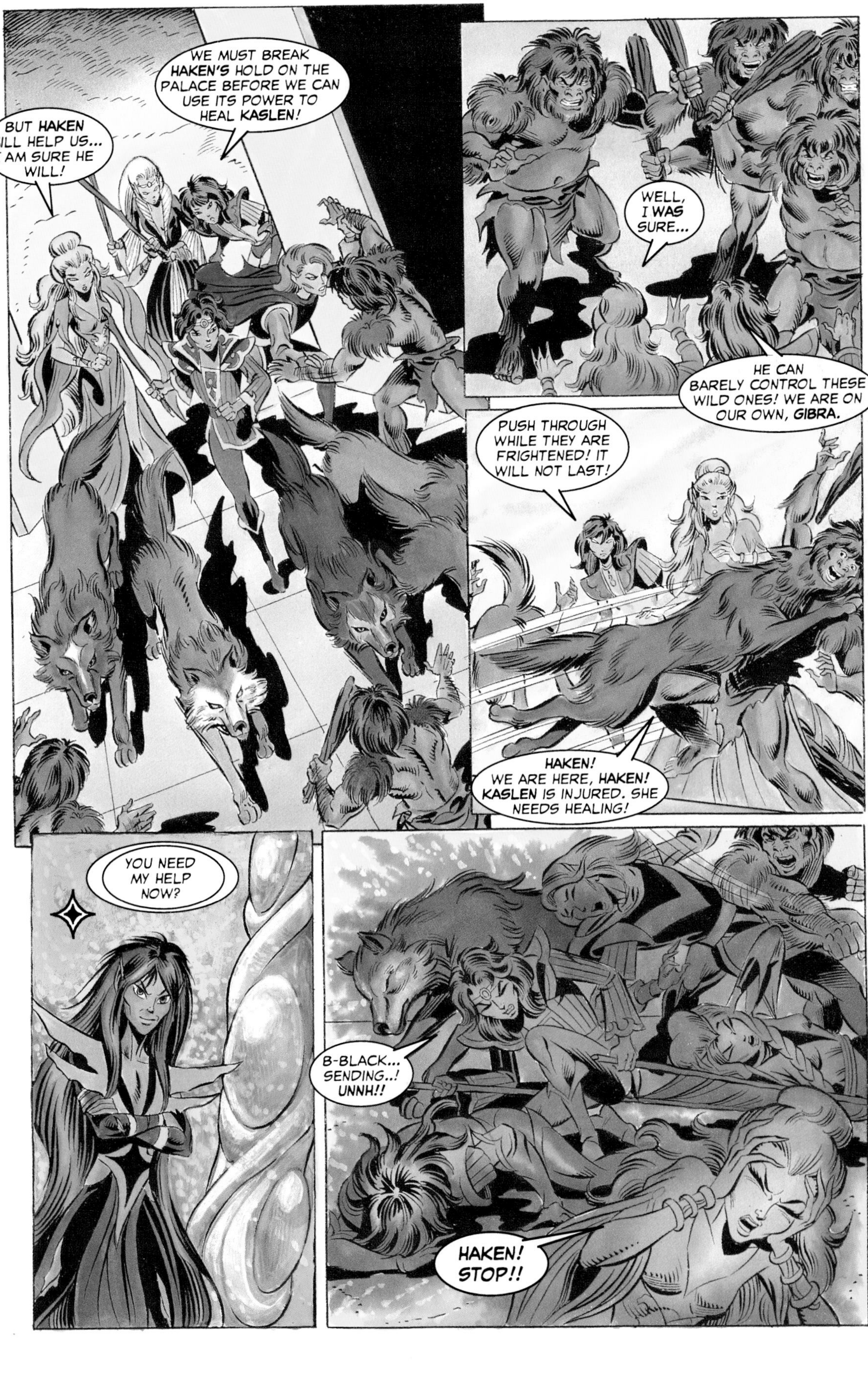

WE MUST BREAK HAKEN'S HOLD ON THE PALACE BEFORE WE CAN USE ITS POWER TO HEAL KASLEN!
BUT HAKEN ILL HELP US... AM SURE HE WILL!
WELL, I WAS SURE...
HE CAN BARELY CONTROL THESE WILD ONES! WE ARE ON OUR OWN, GIBRA.
PUSH THROUGH WHILE THEY ARE FRIGHTENED! IT WILL NOT LAST!
HAKEN! WE ARE HERE, HAKEN! KASLEN IS INJURED. SHE NEEDS HEALING!
YOU NEED MY HELP NOW?
B-BLACK... SENDING..! UNNH!!
HAKEN! STOP!!

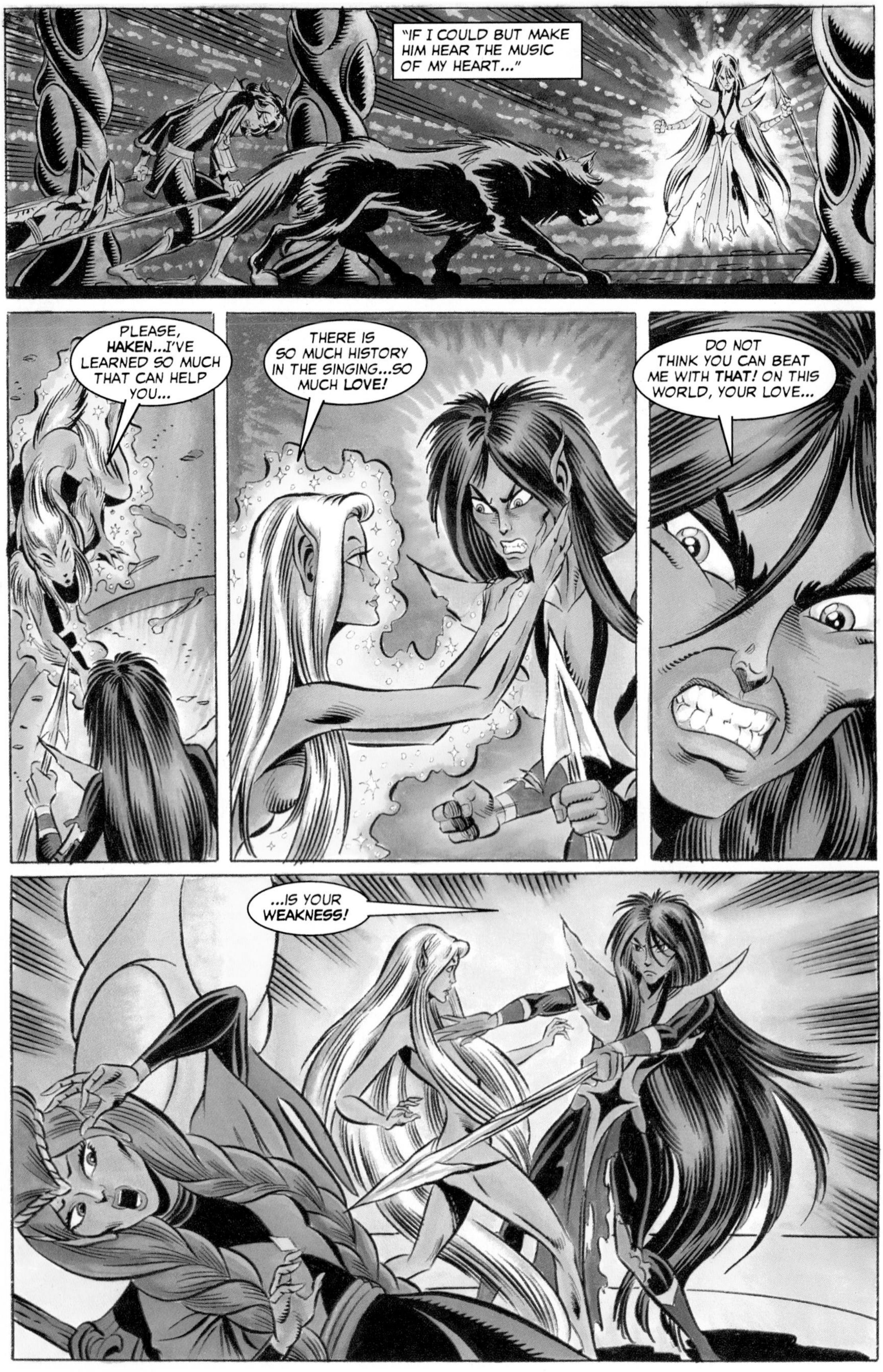
"IF I COULD BUT MAKE HIM HEAR THE MUSIC OF MY HEART..."
PLEASE, **HAKEN**..I'VE LEARNED SO MUCH THAT CAN HELP YOU...
THERE IS SO MUCH HISTORY IN THE SINGING...SO MUCH **LOVE!**
DO NOT THINK YOU CAN BEAT ME WITH **THAT!** ON THIS WORLD, YOUR LOVE...
...IS YOUR **WEAKNESS!**

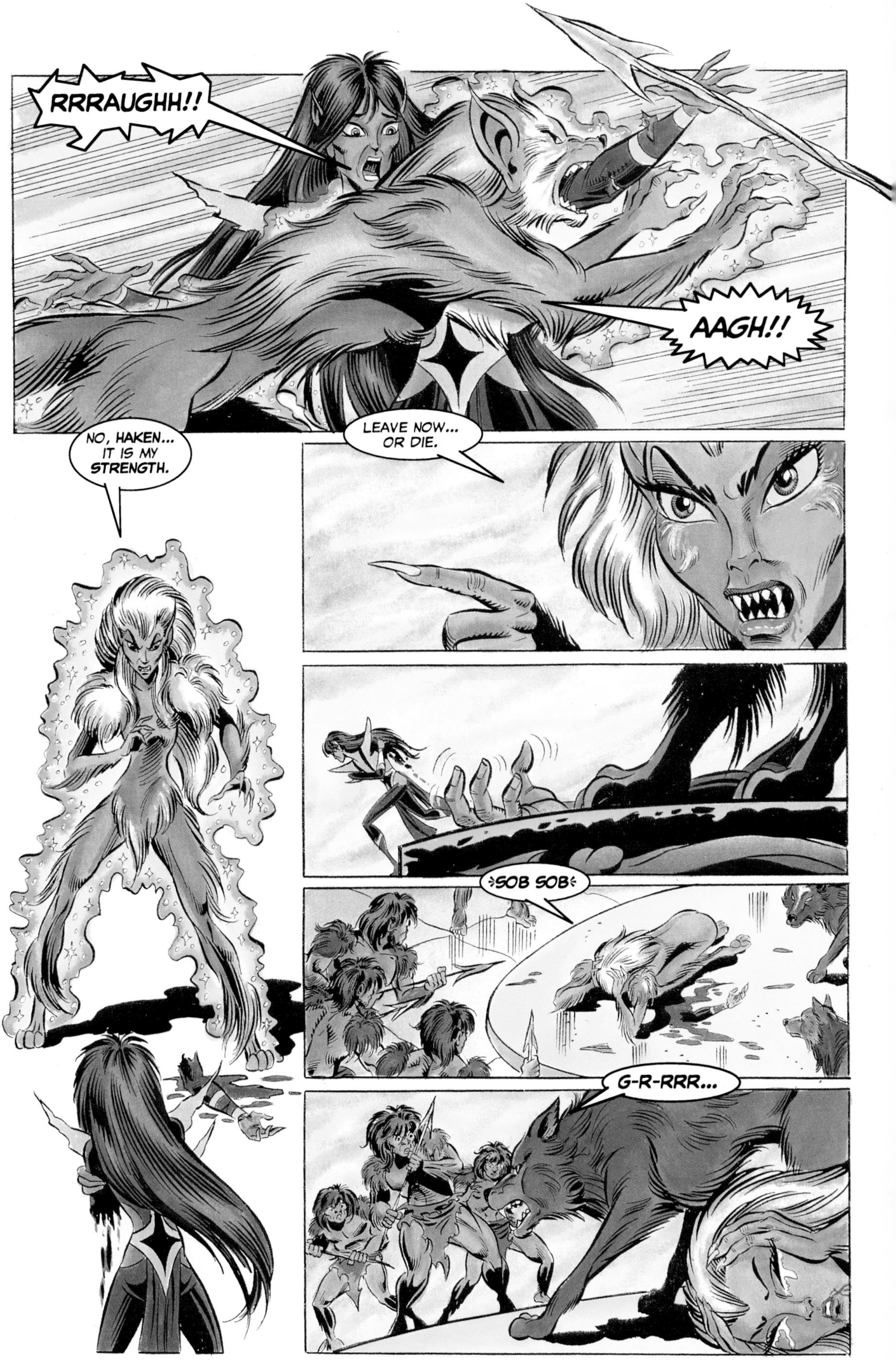
RRRAUGHH!!
AAGH!!
NO, HAKEN... IT IS MY STRENGTH.
LEAVE NOW... OR DIE.
SOB SOB
G-R-RRR...

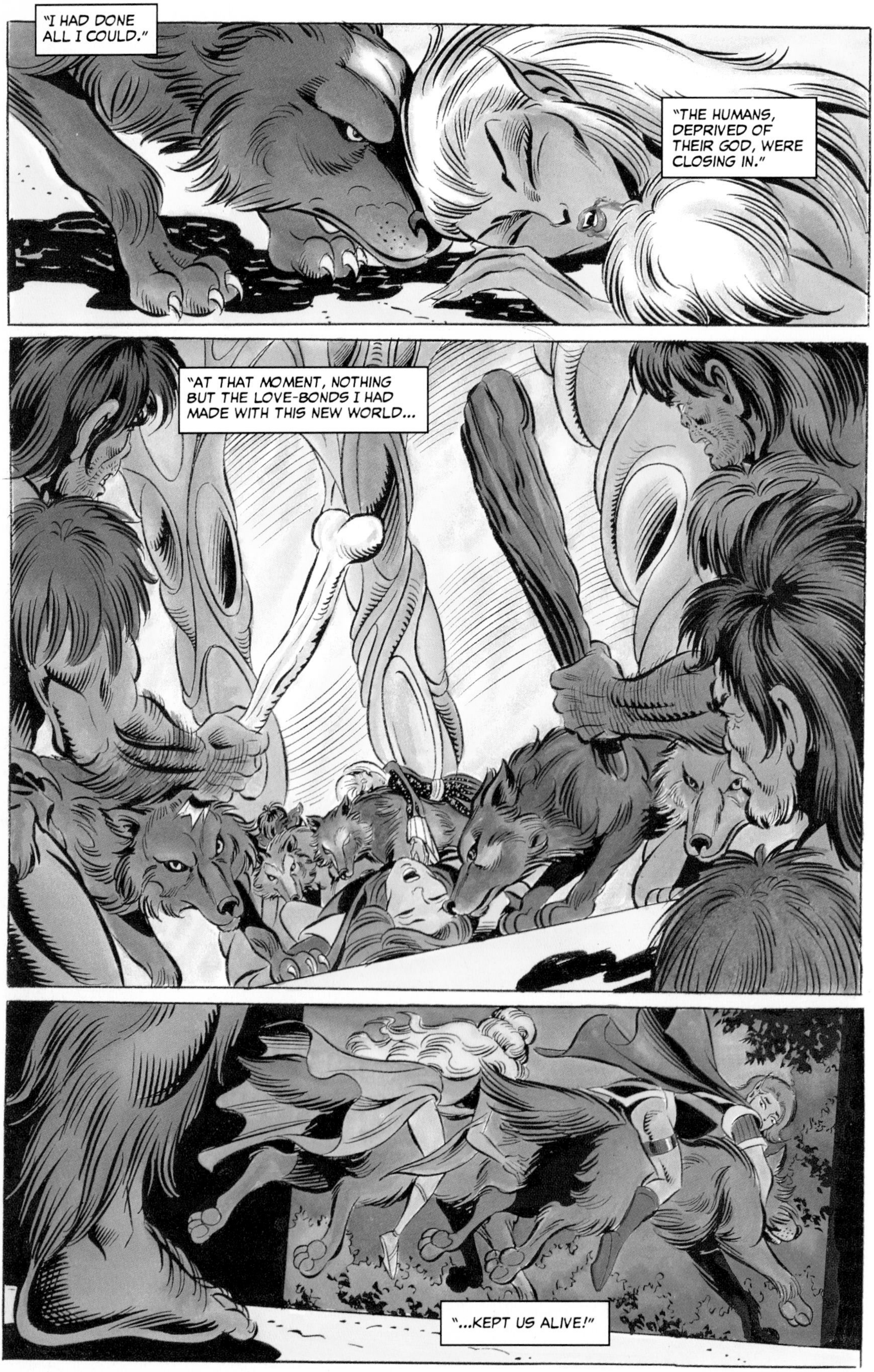
"I HAD DONE ALL I COULD."
"THE HUMANS, DEPRIVED OF THEIR GOD, WERE CLOSING IN."
"AT THAT MOMENT, NOTHING BUT THE LOVE-BONDS I HAD MADE WITH THIS NEW WORLD...
"...KEPT US ALIVE!"

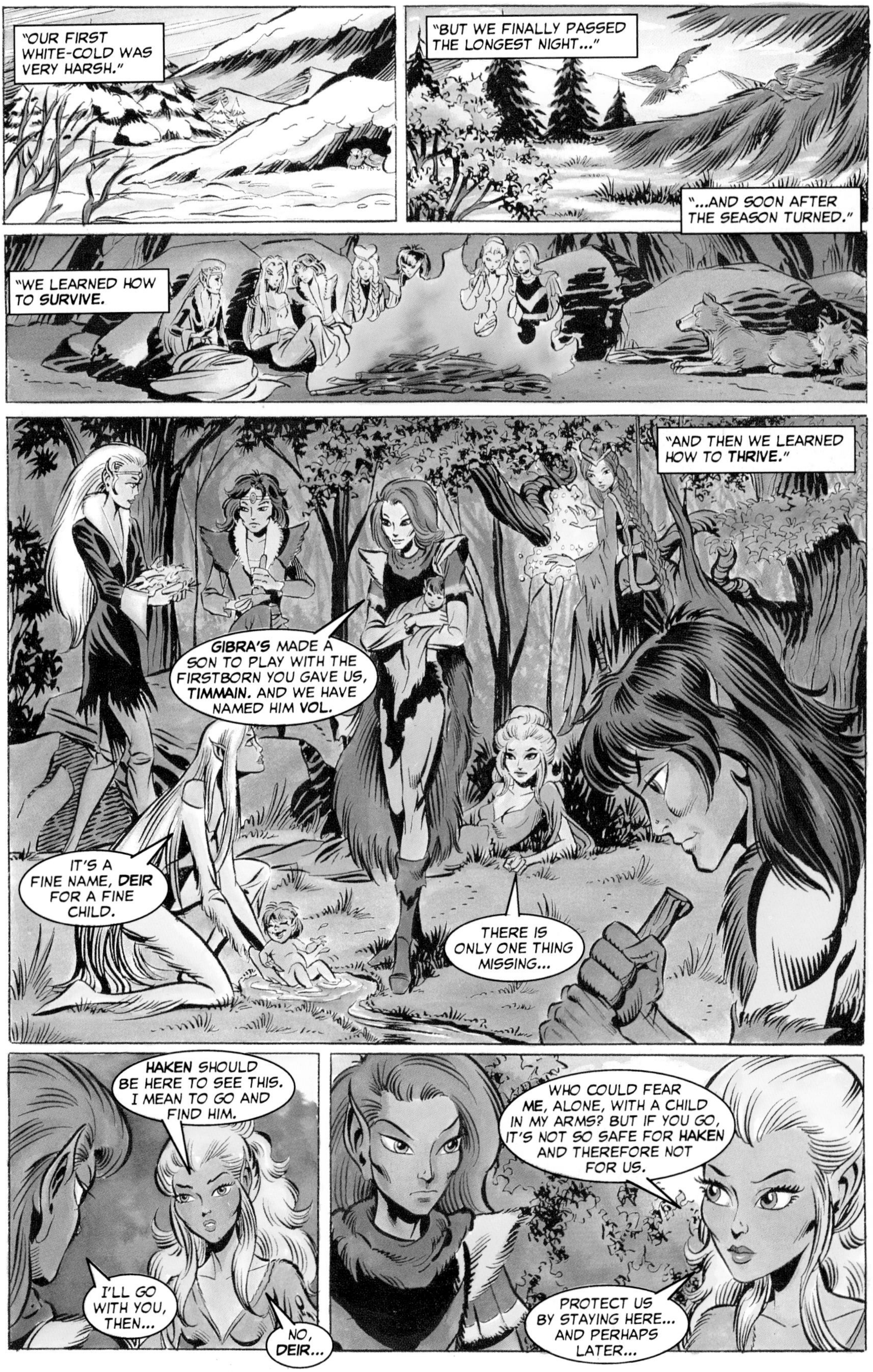
"OUR FIRST WHITE-COLD WAS VERY HARSH."
"BUT WE FINALLY PASSED THE LONGEST NIGHT..."
"...AND SOON AFTER THE SEASON TURNED."
"WE LEARNED HOW TO SURVIVE.
"AND THEN WE LEARNED HOW TO THRIVE."
GIBRA'S MADE A SON TO PLAY WITH THE FIRSTBORN YOU GAVE US, TIMMAIN. AND WE HAVE NAMED HIM VOL.
IT'S A FINE NAME, DEIR FOR A FINE CHILD.
THERE IS ONLY ONE THING MISSING...
HAKEN SHOULD BE HERE TO SEE THIS. I MEAN TO GO AND FIND HIM.
I'LL GO WITH YOU, THEN...
NO, DEIR...
WHO COULD FEAR ME, ALONE, WITH A CHILD IN MY ARMS? BUT IF YOU GO, IT'S NOT SO SAFE FOR HAKEN AND THEREFORE NOT FOR US.
PROTECT US BY STAYING HERE... AND PERHAPS LATER...

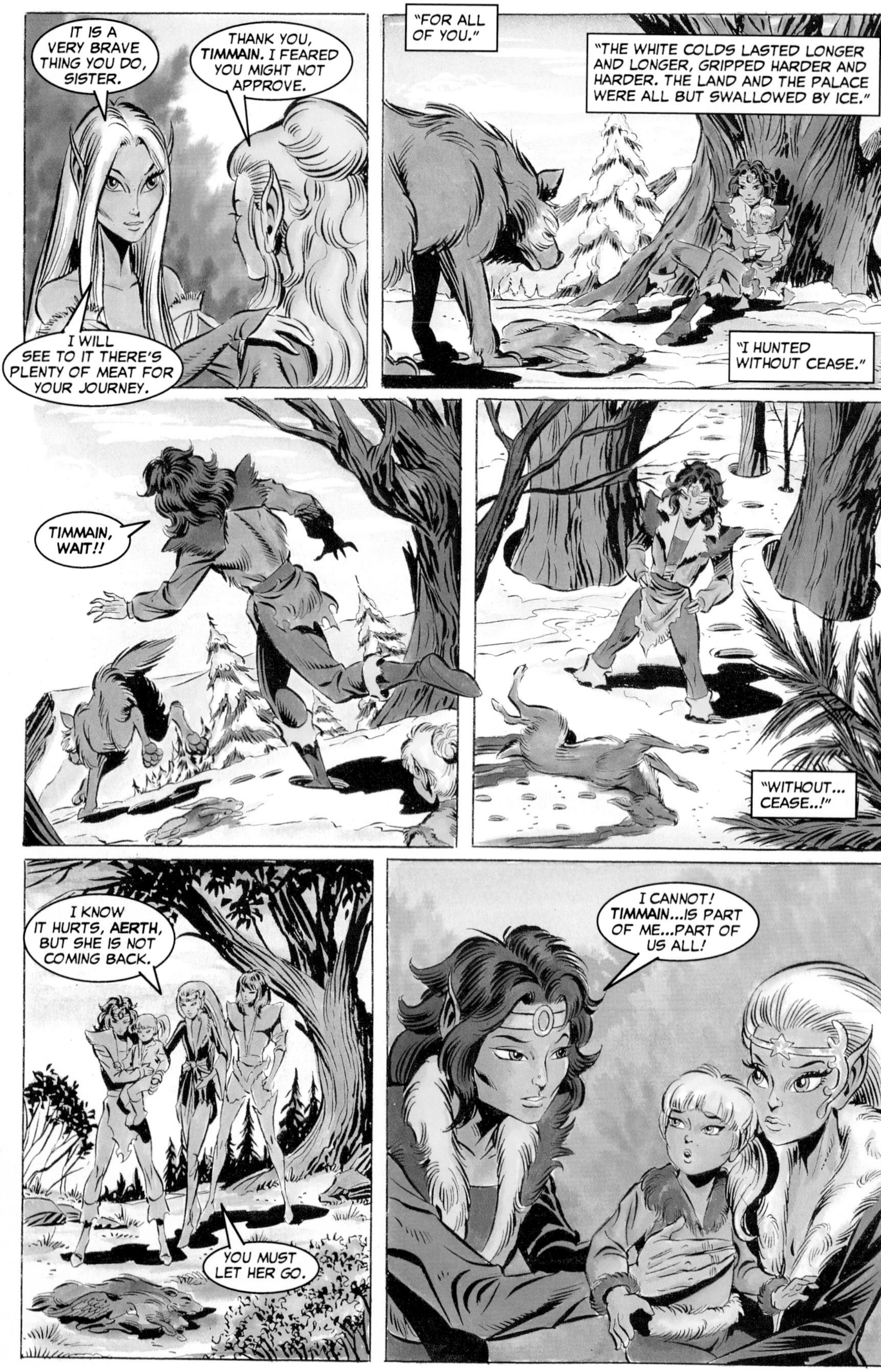
IT IS A VERY BRAVE THING YOU DO, SISTER.
THANK YOU, TIMMAIN. I FEARED YOU MIGHT NOT APPROVE.
I WILL SEE TO IT THERE'S PLENTY OF MEAT FOR YOUR JOURNEY.
"FOR ALL OF YOU."
"THE WHITE COLDS LASTED LONGER AND LONGER, GRIPPED HARDER AND HARDER. THE LAND AND THE PALACE WERE ALL BUT SWALLOWED BY ICE."
"I HUNTED WITHOUT CEASE."
TIMMAIN, WAIT!!
"WITHOUT... CEASE..!"
I KNOW IT HURTS, AERTH, BUT SHE IS NOT COMING BACK.
YOU MUST LET HER GO.
I CANNOT! TIMMAIN...IS PART OF ME...PART OF US ALL!

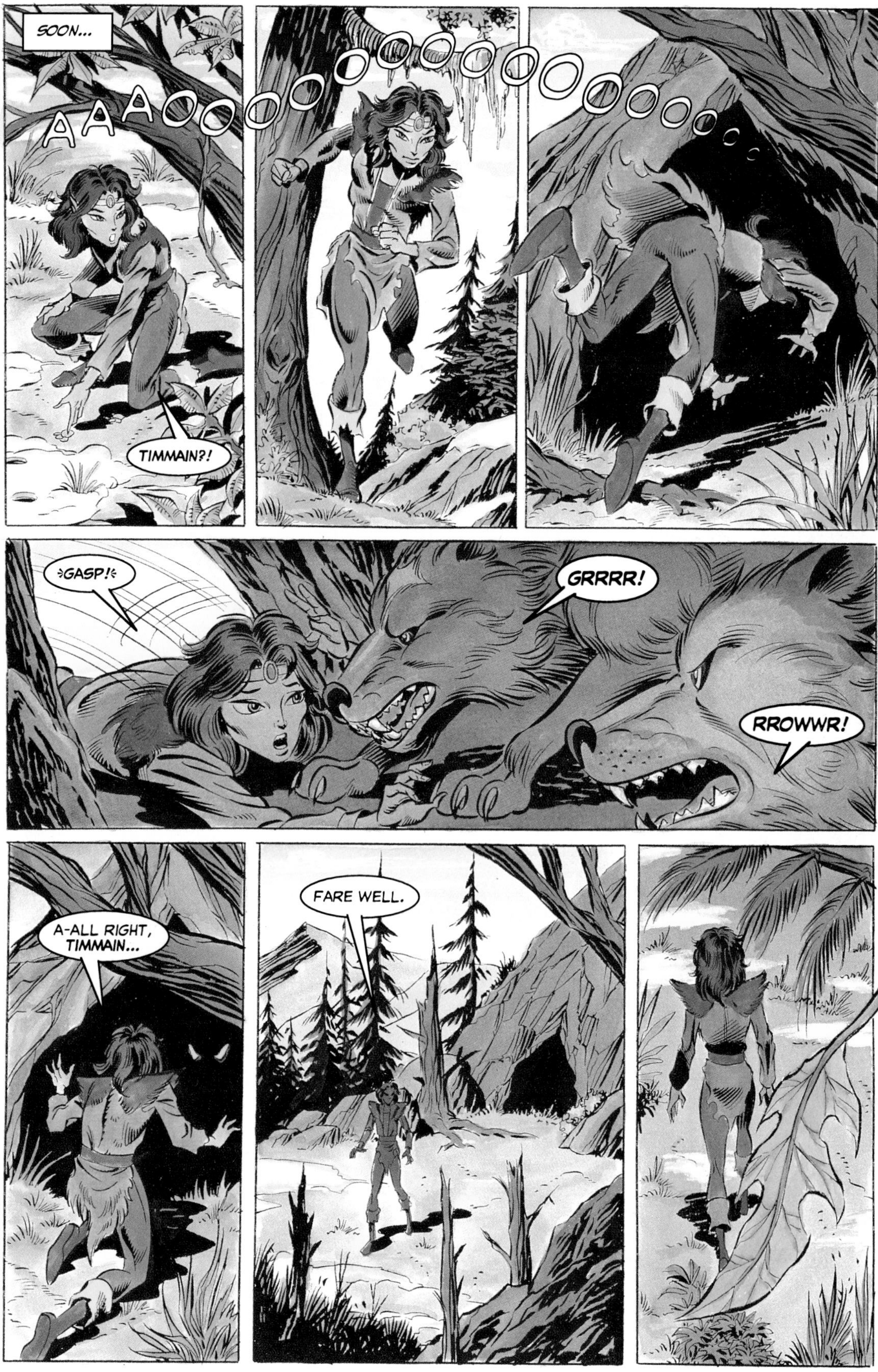
SOON...
AAAOOOOOOOOOOOOOOOOOO
TIMMAIN?!
GASP!
GRRRR!
RROWWR!
A-ALL RIGHT, TIMMAIN...
FARE WELL.

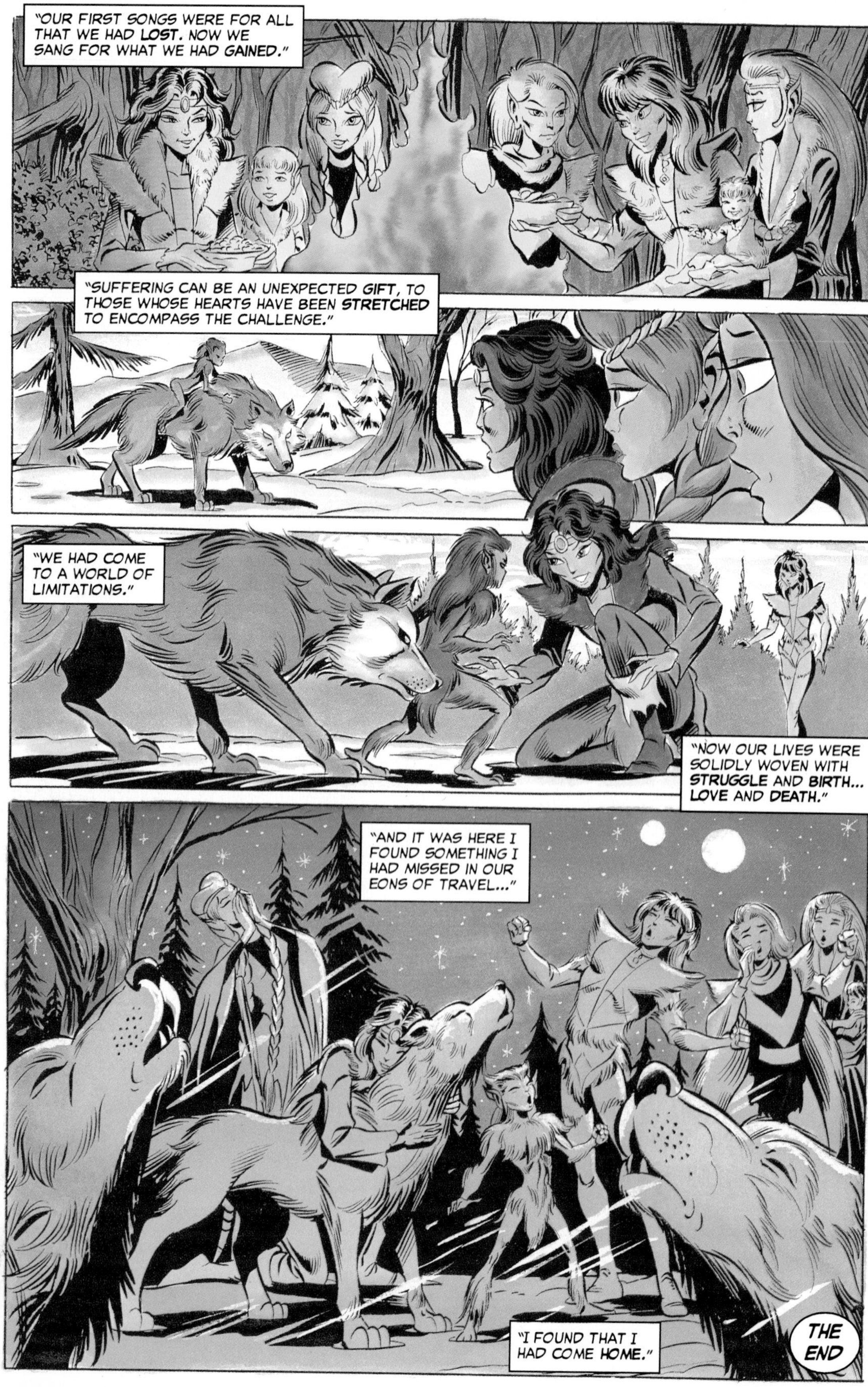
"OUR FIRST SONGS WERE FOR ALL THAT WE HAD LOST. NOW WE SANG FOR WHAT WE HAD GAINED."
"SUFFERING CAN BE AN UNEXPECTED GIFT, TO THOSE WHOSE HEARTS HAVE BEEN STRETCHED TO ENCOMPASS THE CHALLENGE."
"WE HAD COME TO A WORLD OF LIMITATIONS."
"NOW OUR LIVES WERE SOLIDLY WOVEN WITH STRUGGLE AND BIRTH... LOVE AND DEATH."
"AND IT WAS HERE I FOUND SOMETHING I HAD MISSED IN OUR EONS OF TRAVEL..."
"I FOUND THAT I HAD COME HOME."
THE END

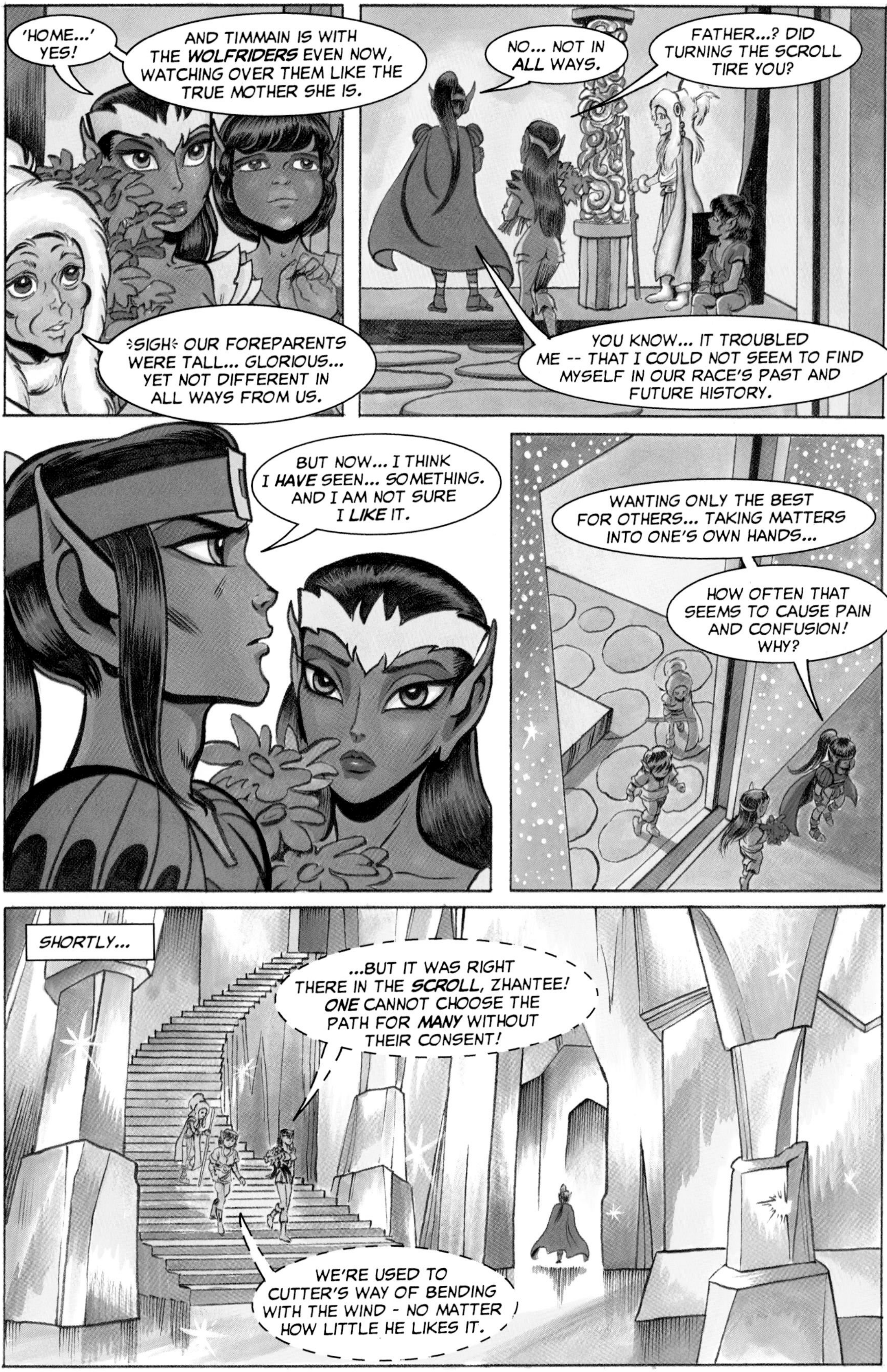
'HOME...' YES!
AND TIMMAIN IS WITH THE WOLFRIDERS EVEN NOW, WATCHING OVER THEM LIKE THE TRUE MOTHER SHE IS.
SIGH OUR FOREPARENTS WERE TALL... GLORIOUS... YET NOT DIFFERENT IN ALL WAYS FROM US.
NO... NOT IN ALL WAYS.
FATHER...? DID TURNING THE SCROLL TIRE YOU?
YOU KNOW... IT TROUBLED ME -- THAT I COULD NOT SEEM TO FIND MYSELF IN OUR RACE'S PAST AND FUTURE HISTORY.
BUT NOW... I THINK I HAVE SEEN... SOMETHING. AND I AM NOT SURE I LIKE IT.
WANTING ONLY THE BEST FOR OTHERS... TAKING MATTERS INTO ONE'S OWN HANDS...
HOW OFTEN THAT SEEMS TO CAUSE PAIN AND CONFUSION! WHY?
SHORTLY...
...BUT IT WAS RIGHT THERE IN THE SCROLL, ZHANTEE! ONE CANNOT CHOOSE THE PATH FOR MANY WITHOUT THEIR CONSENT!
WE'RE USED TO CUTTER'S WAY OF BENDING WITH THE WIND - NO MATTER HOW LITTLE HE LIKES IT.

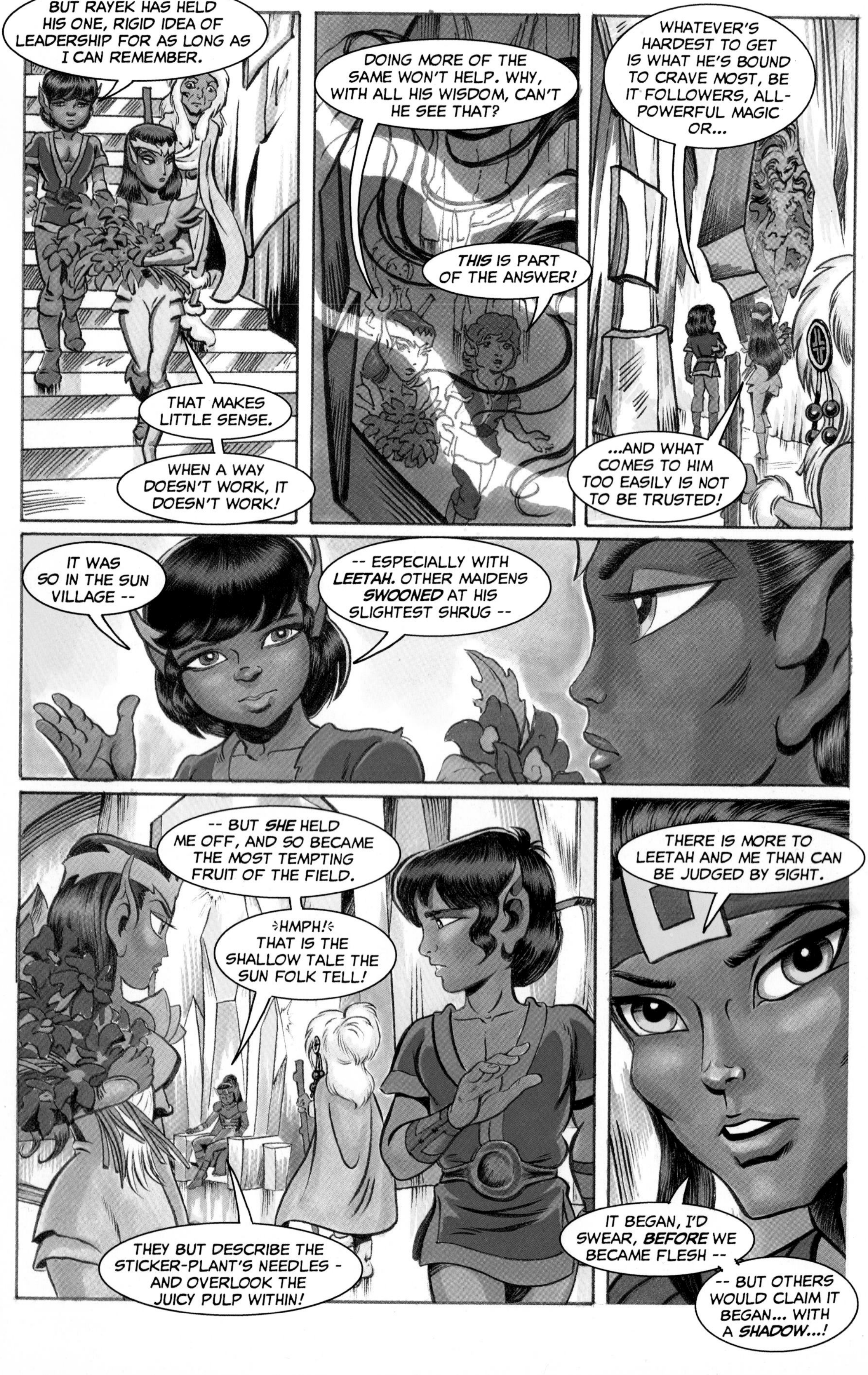
BUT RAYEK HAS HELD HIS ONE, RIGID IDEA OF LEADERSHIP FOR AS LONG AS I CAN REMEMBER.
THAT MAKES LITTLE SENSE.
WHEN A WAY DOESN'T WORK, IT DOESN'T WORK!
DOING MORE OF THE SAME WON'T HELP. WHY, WITH ALL HIS WISDOM, CAN'T HE SEE THAT?
THIS IS PART OF THE ANSWER!
WHATEVER'S HARDEST TO GET IS WHAT HE'S BOUND TO CRAVE MOST, BE IT FOLLOWERS, ALL-POWERFUL MAGIC OR...
...AND WHAT COMES TO HIM TOO EASILY IS NOT TO BE TRUSTED!
IT WAS SO IN THE SUN VILLAGE --
-- ESPECIALLY WITH LEETAH. OTHER MAIDENS SWOONED AT HIS SLIGHTEST SHRUG --
-- BUT SHE HELD ME OFF, AND SO BECAME THE MOST TEMPTING FRUIT OF THE FIELD.
HMPH! THAT IS THE SHALLOW TALE THE SUN FOLK TELL!
THEY BUT DESCRIBE THE STICKER-PLANT'S NEEDLES - AND OVERLOOK THE JUICY PULP WITHIN!
THERE IS MORE TO LEETAH AND ME THAN CAN BE JUDGED BY SIGHT.
IT BEGAN, I'D SWEAR, BEFORE WE BECAME FLESH --
-- BUT OTHERS WOULD CLAIM IT BEGAN... WITH A SHADOW...!

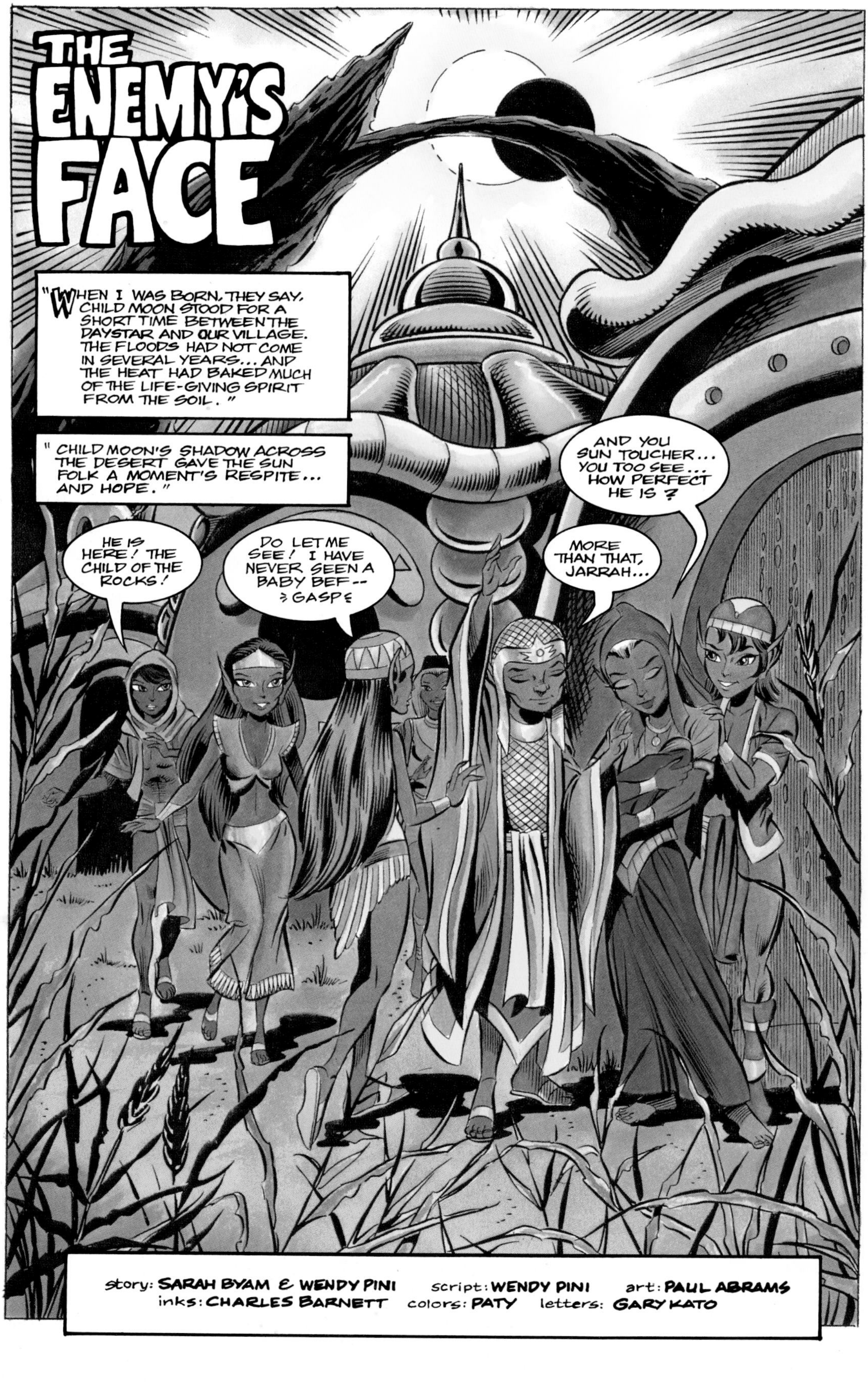
THE ENEMY'S FACE
"WHEN I WAS BORN, THEY SAY, CHILD MOON STOOD FOR A SHORT TIME BETWEEN THE DAYSTAR AND OUR VILLAGE. THE FLOODS HAD NOT COME IN SEVERAL YEARS... AND THE HEAT HAD BAKED MUCH OF THE LIFE-GIVING SPIRIT FROM THE SOIL."
"CHILD MOON'S SHADOW ACROSS THE DESERT GAVE THE SUN FOLK A MOMENT'S RESPITE... AND HOPE."
HE IS HERE! THE CHILD OF THE ROCKS!
DO LET ME SEE! I HAVE NEVER SEEN A BABY BEF-- GASP
AND YOU SUN TOUCHER... YOU TOO SEE... HOW PERFECT HE IS?
MORE THAN THAT, JARRAH...
story: SARAH BYAM & WENDY PINI script: WENDY PINI art: PAUL ABRAMS
inks: CHARLES BARNETT colors: PATY letters: GARY KATO

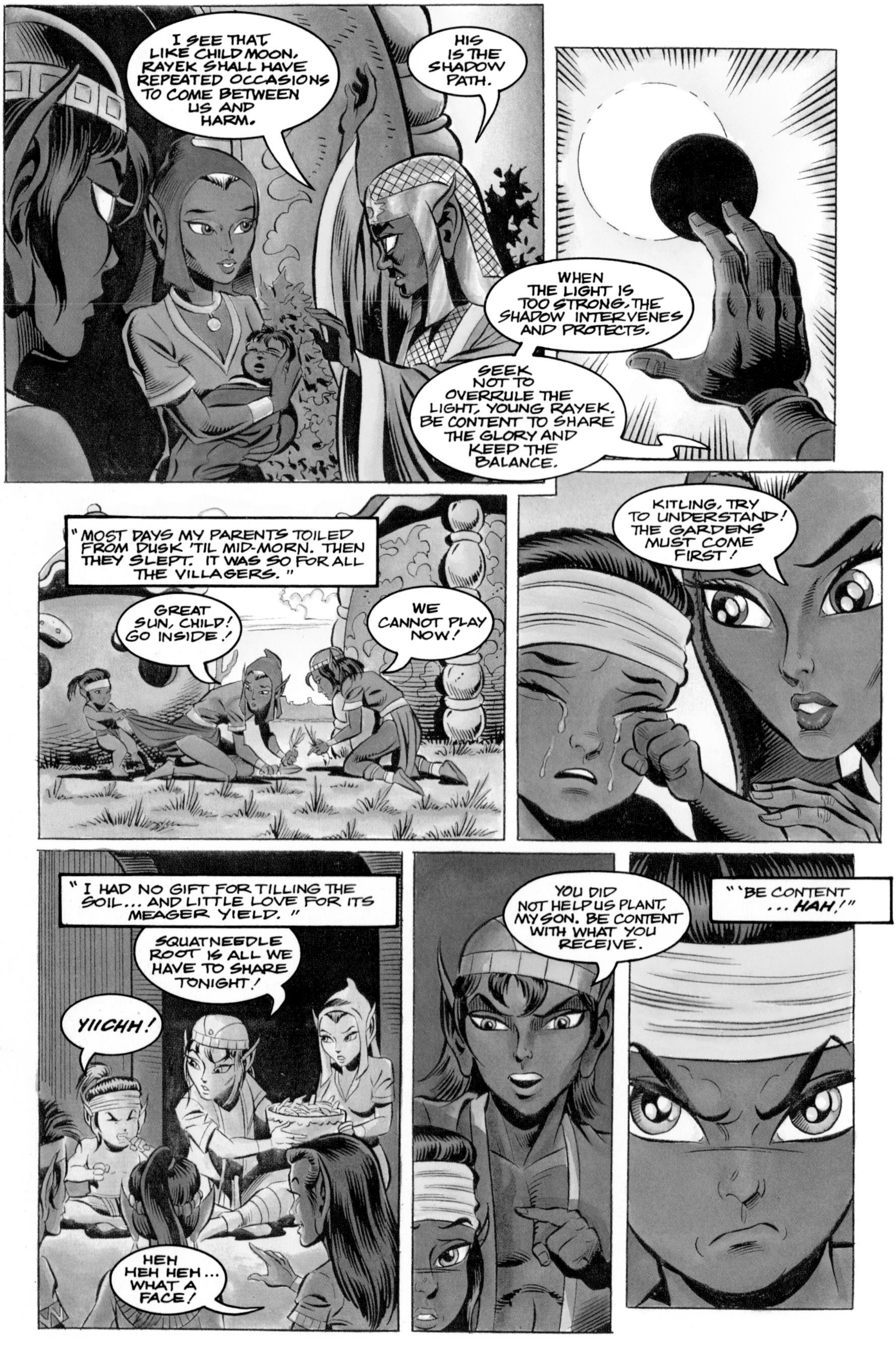
I SEE THAT LIKE CHILD MOON, RAYEK SHALL HAVE REPEATED OCCASIONS TO COME BETWEEN US AND HARM.
HIS IS THE SHADOW PATH.
WHEN THE LIGHT IS TOO STRONG, THE SHADOW INTERVENES AND PROTECTS.
SEEK NOT TO OVERRULE THE LIGHT, YOUNG RAYEK. BE CONTENT TO SHARE THE GLORY AND KEEP THE BALANCE.
"MOST DAYS MY PARENTS TOILED FROM DUSK 'TIL MID-MORN. THEN THEY SLEPT. IT WAS SO FOR ALL THE VILLAGERS."
GREAT SUN, CHILD! GO INSIDE!
WE CANNOT PLAY NOW!
KITLING, TRY TO UNDERSTAND! THE GARDENS MUST COME FIRST!
"I HAD NO GIFT FOR TILLING THE SOIL... AND LITTLE LOVE FOR ITS MEAGER YIELD."
SQUATNEEDLE ROOT IS ALL WE HAVE TO SHARE TONIGHT!
YIICHH!
HEH HEH HEH... WHAT A FACE!
YOU DID NOT HELP US PLANT, MY SON. BE CONTENT WITH WHAT YOU RECEIVE.
"'BE CONTENT ...HAH!'"

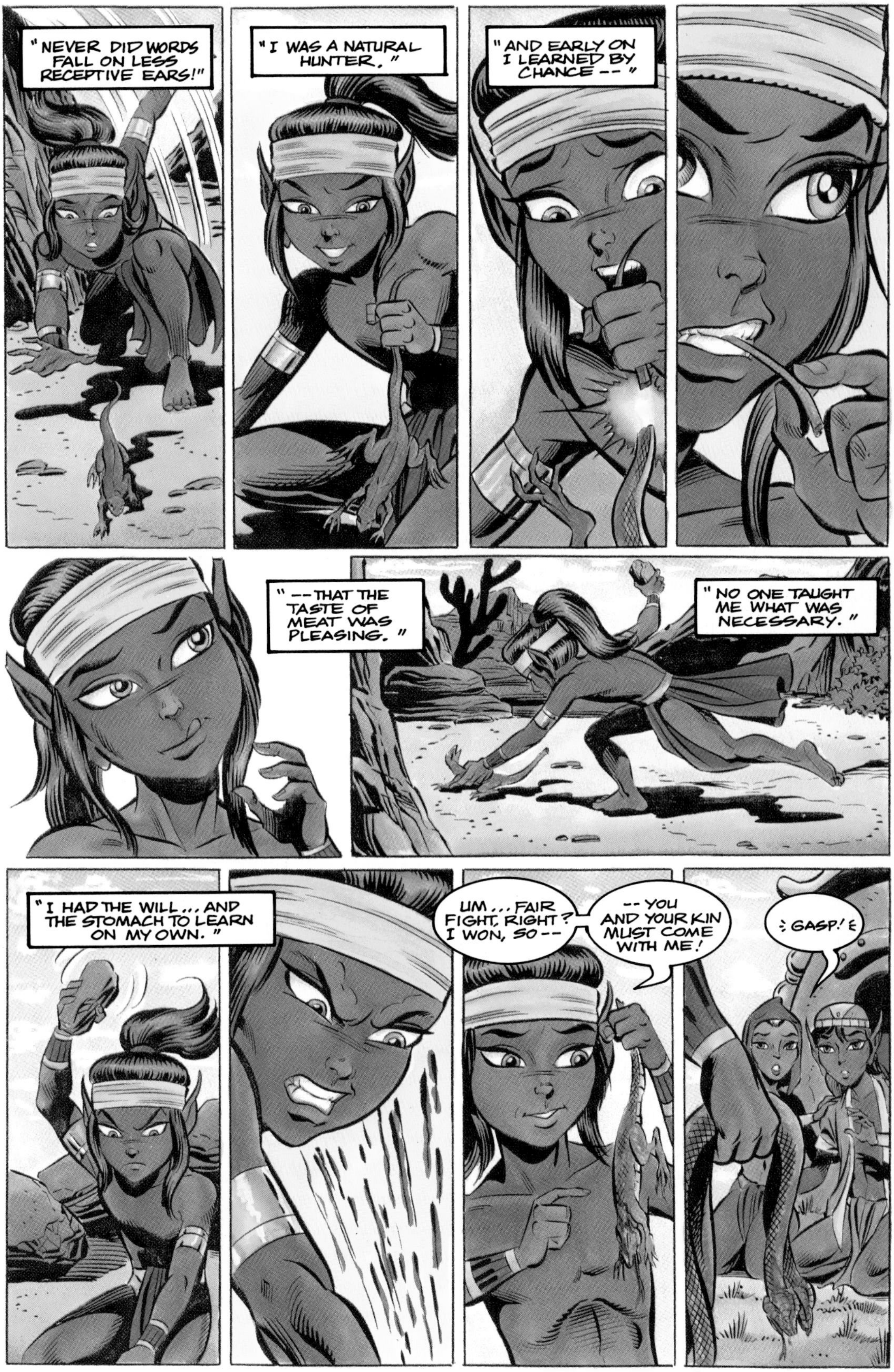
"NEVER DID WORDS FALL ON LESS RECEPTIVE EARS!"
"I WAS A NATURAL HUNTER."
"AND EARLY ON I LEARNED BY CHANCE --"
"--THAT THE TASTE OF MEAT WAS PLEASING."
"NO ONE TAUGHT ME WHAT WAS NECESSARY."
"I HAD THE WILL... AND THE STOMACH TO LEARN ON MY OWN."
UM... FAIR FIGHT, RIGHT? I WON, SO --
-- YOU AND YOUR KIN MUST COME WITH ME!
GASP!

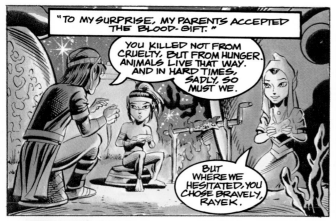

"TO MY SURPRISE, MY PARENTS ACCEPTED THE BLOOD-GIFT."

YOU KILLED NOT FROM CRUELTY, BUT FROM HUNGER. ANIMALS LIVE THAT WAY, AND IN HARD TIMES, SADLY, SO MUST WE.

BUT WHERE WE HESITATED, YOU CHOSE BRAVELY, RAYEK.

"THEIR PRAISE FELT GOOD. I WISHED TO GO ON FEELING GOOD."

"TRUE TO MY NAME, I FELT MORE AT HOME AMONG THE SAND-SMOOTHED LEDGES AND CRAGS THAN IN MY FAMILY HUT."

"AS FOR HUNTING, MY PREY AT FIRST WAS SMALL - THE SMALLER, THE CRAFTIER."

"BUT ONE DAY THE BATTLE OF WITS BECAME--"

"--A BATTLE OF NATURAL WEAPONS!"

"TINY TEETH AND CLAWS AGAINST --"

AAAOOOWWWW

"--WHAT?!"

≥GASP!≤ LOOK!

SO MAN?

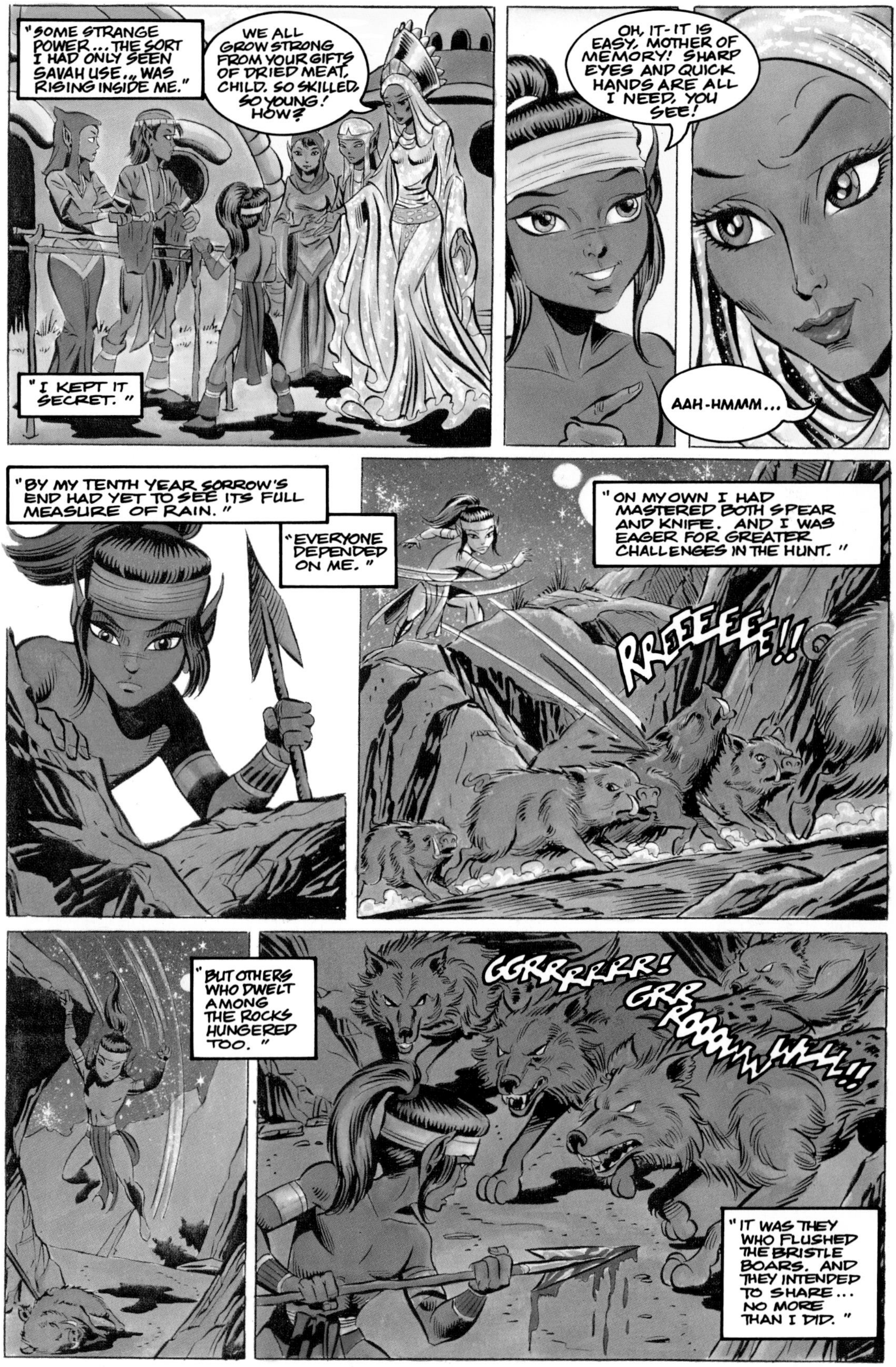
"SOME STRANGE POWER... THE SORT I HAD ONLY SEEN SAVAH USE... WAS RISING INSIDE ME."
WE ALL GROW STRONG FROM YOUR GIFTS OF DRIED MEAT, CHILD. SO SKILLED, SO YOUNG! HOW?
"I KEPT IT SECRET."
OH, IT-IT IS EASY, MOTHER OF MEMORY! SHARP EYES AND QUICK HANDS ARE ALL I NEED, YOU SEE!
AAH-HMMM...
"BY MY TENTH YEAR SORROW'S END HAD YET TO SEE ITS FULL MEASURE OF RAIN."
"EVERYONE DEPENDED ON ME."
"ON MY OWN I HAD MASTERED BOTH SPEAR AND KNIFE. AND I WAS EAGER FOR GREATER CHALLENGES IN THE HUNT."
RREEEEEE!!
"BUT OTHERS WHO DWELT AMONG THE ROCKS HUNGERED TOO."
GGRRRRRRR!
GRR ROOOWWLL!!
"IT WAS THEY WHO FLUSHED THE BRISTLE BOARS. AND THEY INTENDED TO SHARE... NO MORE THAN I DID."

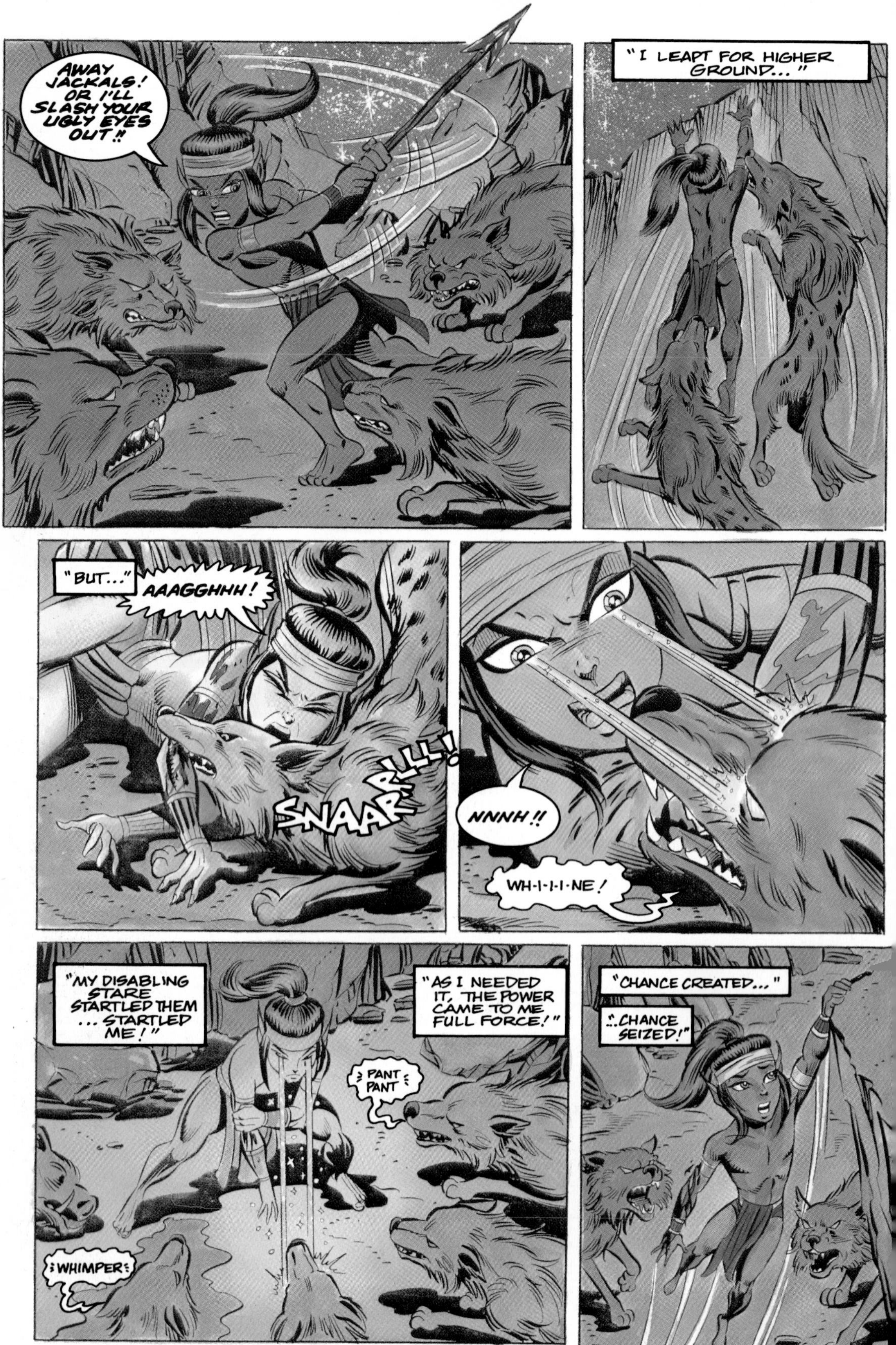
AWAY JACKALS! OR I'LL SLASH YOUR UGLY EYES OUT!!
"I LEAPT FOR HIGHER GROUND..."
"BUT..."
AAAGGHHH!
SNAARRLLL!
NNNH!!
WH-I-I-I-NE!
"MY DISABLING STARE STARTLED THEM ... STARTLED ME!"
"AS I NEEDED IT, THE POWER CAME TO ME FULL FORCE!"
PANT PANT
WHIMPER
"CHANCE CREATED..."
"...CHANCE SEIZED!"

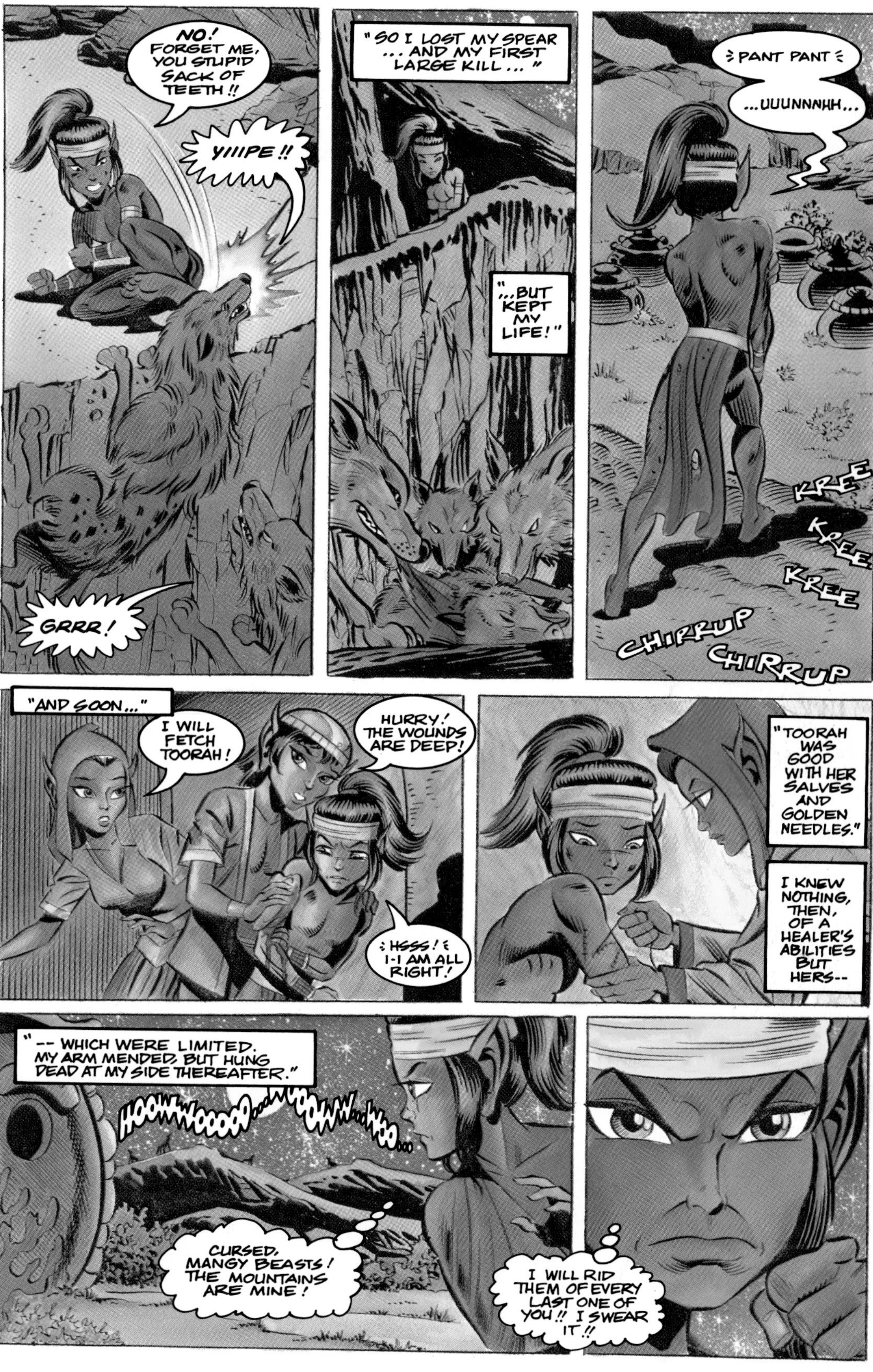
NO! FORGET ME, YOU STUPID SACK OF TEETH!!
YIIIPE!!
GRRR!
"SO I LOST MY SPEAR ... AND MY FIRST LARGE KILL ..."
"...BUT KEPT MY LIFE!"
PANT PANT
...UUUNNNHH...
KREE
KREE
KREE
CHIRRUP
CHIRRUP
"AND SOON..."
I WILL FETCH TOORAH!
HURRY! THE WOUNDS ARE DEEP!
HSSS! I-I AM ALL RIGHT!
"TOORAH WAS GOOD WITH HER SALVES AND GOLDEN NEEDLES."
I KNEW NOTHING, THEN, OF A HEALER'S ABILITIES BUT HERS--
"-- WHICH WERE LIMITED. MY ARM MENDED, BUT HUNG DEAD AT MY SIDE THEREAFTER."
HOOWHOOOOO...OOOWH...HOO...
CURSED, MANGY BEASTS! THE MOUNTAINS ARE MINE!
I WILL RID THEM OF EVERY LAST ONE OF YOU!! I SWEAR IT!!

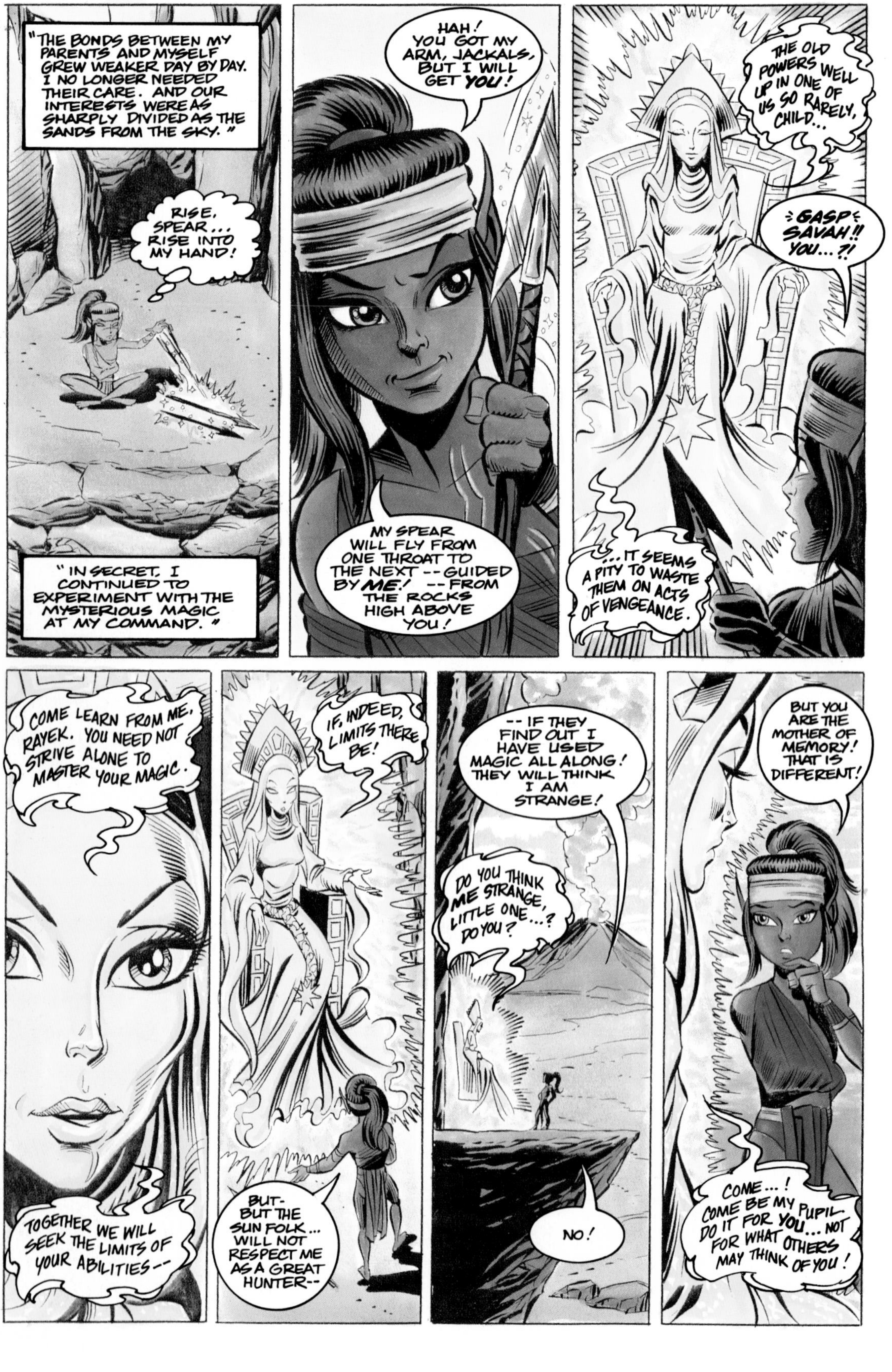
"THE BONDS BETWEEN MY PARENTS AND MYSELF GREW WEAKER DAY BY DAY. I NO LONGER NEEDED THEIR CARE. AND OUR INTERESTS WERE AS SHARPLY DIVIDED AS THE SANDS FROM THE SKY."
RISE, SPEAR... RISE INTO MY HAND!
"IN SECRET, I CONTINUED TO EXPERIMENT WITH THE MYSTERIOUS MAGIC AT MY COMMAND."
HAH! YOU GOT MY ARM, JACKALS, BUT I WILL GET YOU!
MY SPEAR WILL FLY FROM ONE THROAT TO THE NEXT -- GUIDED BY ME! -- FROM THE ROCKS HIGH ABOVE YOU!
THE OLD POWERS WELL UP IN ONE OF US SO RARELY, CHILD...
:GASP: SAVAH!! YOU...?!
...IT SEEMS A PITY TO WASTE THEM ON ACTS OF VENGEANCE.
COME LEARN FROM ME, RAYEK. YOU NEED NOT STRIVE ALONE TO MASTER YOUR MAGIC.
TOGETHER WE WILL SEEK THE LIMITS OF YOUR ABILITIES --
IF, INDEED, LIMITS THERE BE!
BUT- BUT THE SUN FOLK... WILL NOT RESPECT ME AS A GREAT HUNTER--
-- IF THEY FIND OUT I HAVE USED MAGIC ALL ALONG! THEY WILL THINK I AM STRANGE!
DO YOU THINK ME STRANGE, LITTLE ONE...? DO YOU?
NO!
BUT YOU ARE THE MOTHER OF MEMORY! THAT IS DIFFERENT!
COME...! COME BE MY PUPIL. DO IT FOR YOU... NOT FOR WHAT OTHERS MAY THINK OF YOU!

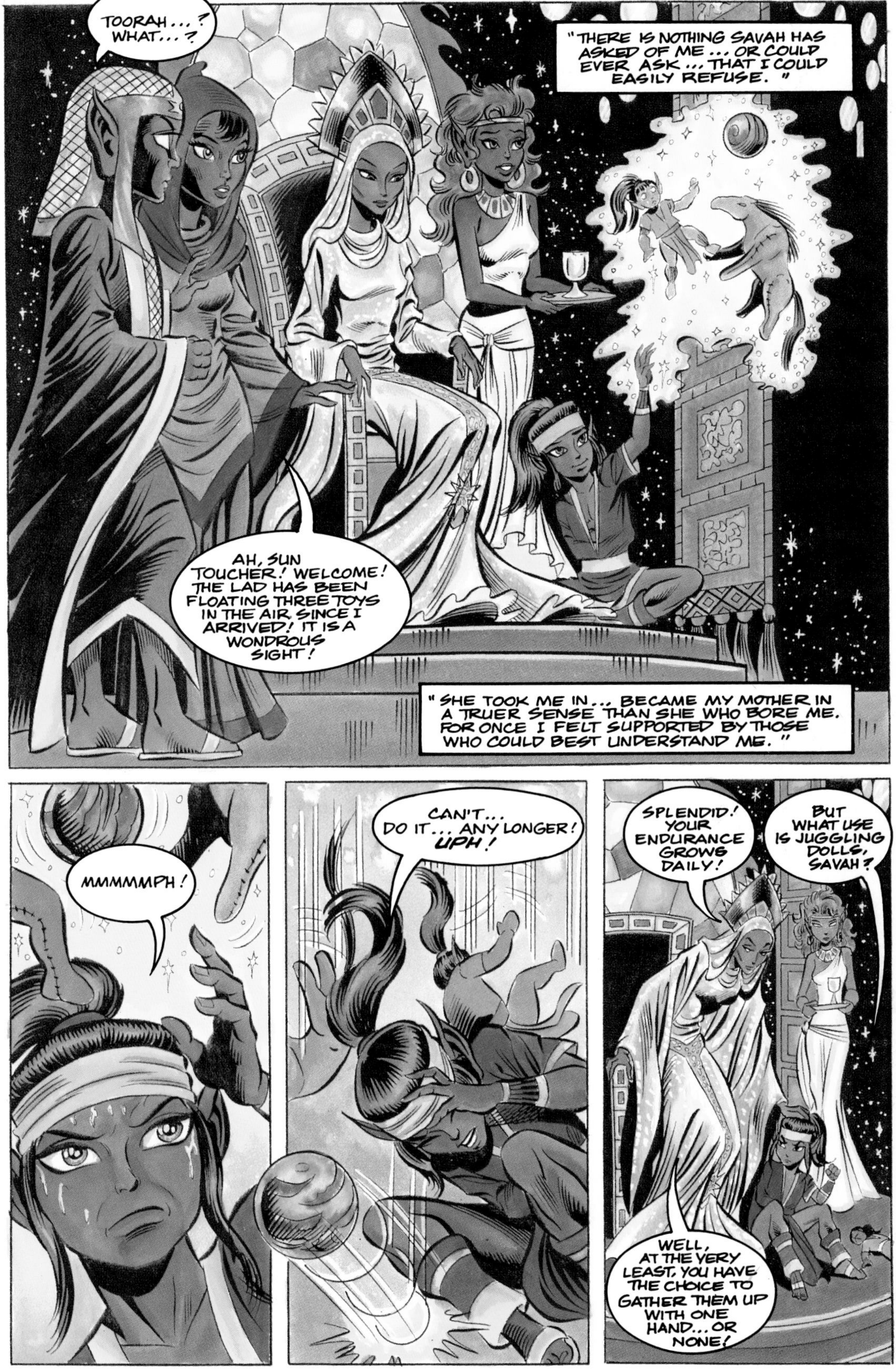
TOORAH...? WHAT...?
"THERE IS NOTHING SAVAH HAS ASKED OF ME... OR COULD EVER ASK... THAT I COULD EASILY REFUSE."
AH, SUN TOUCHER! WELCOME! THE LAD HAS BEEN FLOATING THREE TOYS IN THE AIR SINCE I ARRIVED! IT IS A WONDROUS SIGHT!
"SHE TOOK ME IN... BECAME MY MOTHER IN A TRUER SENSE THAN SHE WHO BORE ME. FOR ONCE I FELT SUPPORTED BY THOSE WHO COULD BEST UNDERSTAND ME."
MMMMMPH!
CAN'T... DO IT... ANY LONGER! UPH!
SPLENDID! YOUR ENDURANCE GROWS DAILY!
BUT WHAT USE IS JUGGLING DOLLS, SAVAH?
WELL, AT THE VERY LEAST, YOU HAVE THE CHOICE TO GATHER THEM UP WITH ONE HAND... OR NONE!

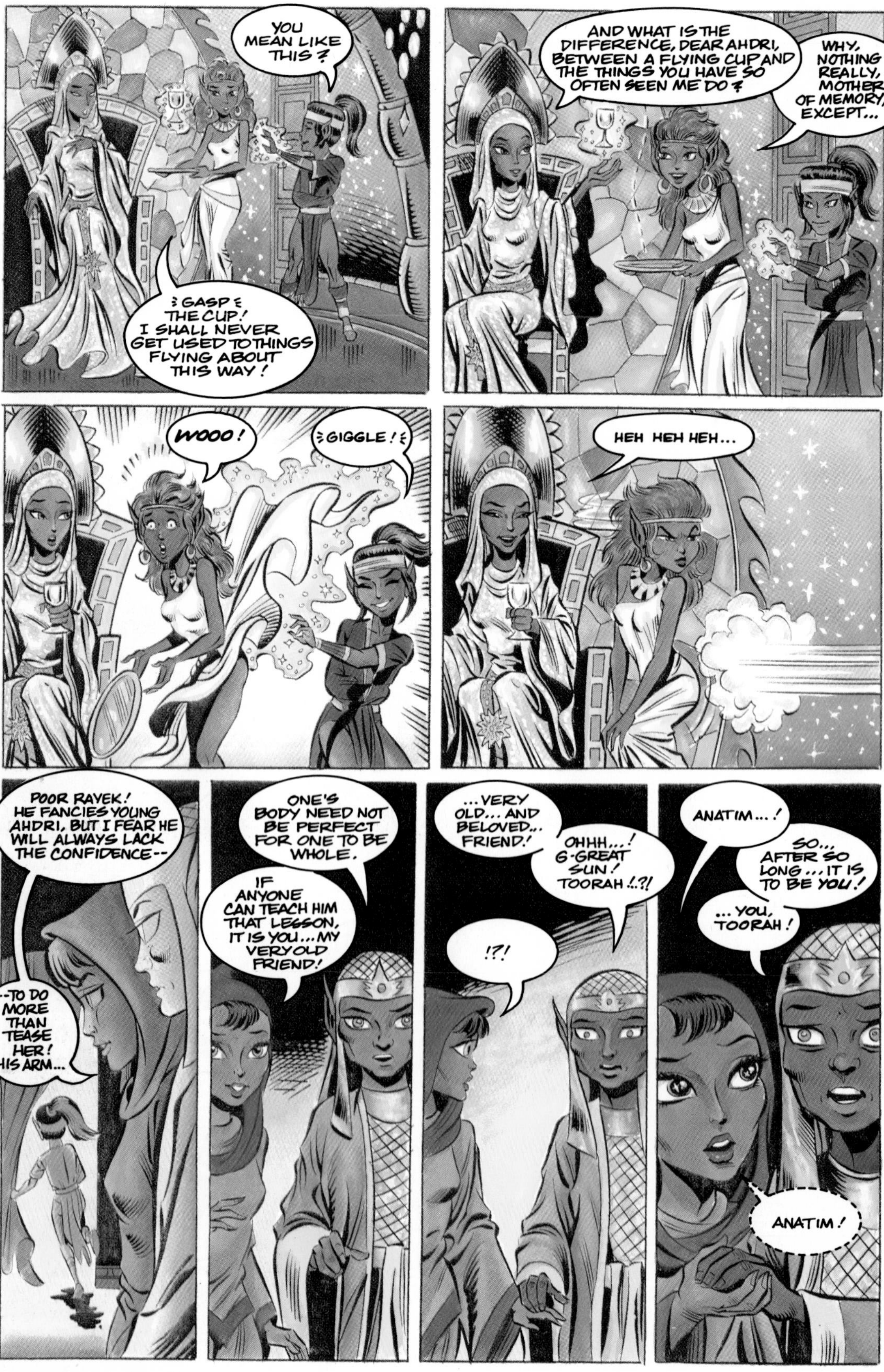
YOU MEAN LIKE THIS?
GASP THE CUP! I SHALL NEVER GET USED TO THINGS FLYING ABOUT THIS WAY!
AND WHAT IS THE DIFFERENCE, DEAR AHDRI, BETWEEN A FLYING CUP AND THE THINGS YOU HAVE SO OFTEN SEEN ME DO?
WHY, NOTHING REALLY, MOTHER OF MEMORY, EXCEPT...
WOOO!
GIGGLE!
HEH HEH HEH...
POOR RAYEK! HE FANCIES YOUNG AHDRI, BUT I FEAR HE WILL ALWAYS LACK THE CONFIDENCE--
--TO DO MORE THAN TEASE HER! HIS ARM...
ONE'S BODY NEED NOT BE PERFECT FOR ONE TO BE WHOLE.
IF ANYONE CAN TEACH HIM THAT LESSON, IT IS YOU... MY VERY OLD FRIEND!
...VERY OLD... AND BELOVED... FRIEND!
OHHH...! G-GREAT SUN! TOORAH!.?!
!?!
ANATIM...!
SO... AFTER SO LONG... IT IS TO BE YOU!
...YOU, TOORAH!
ANATIM!

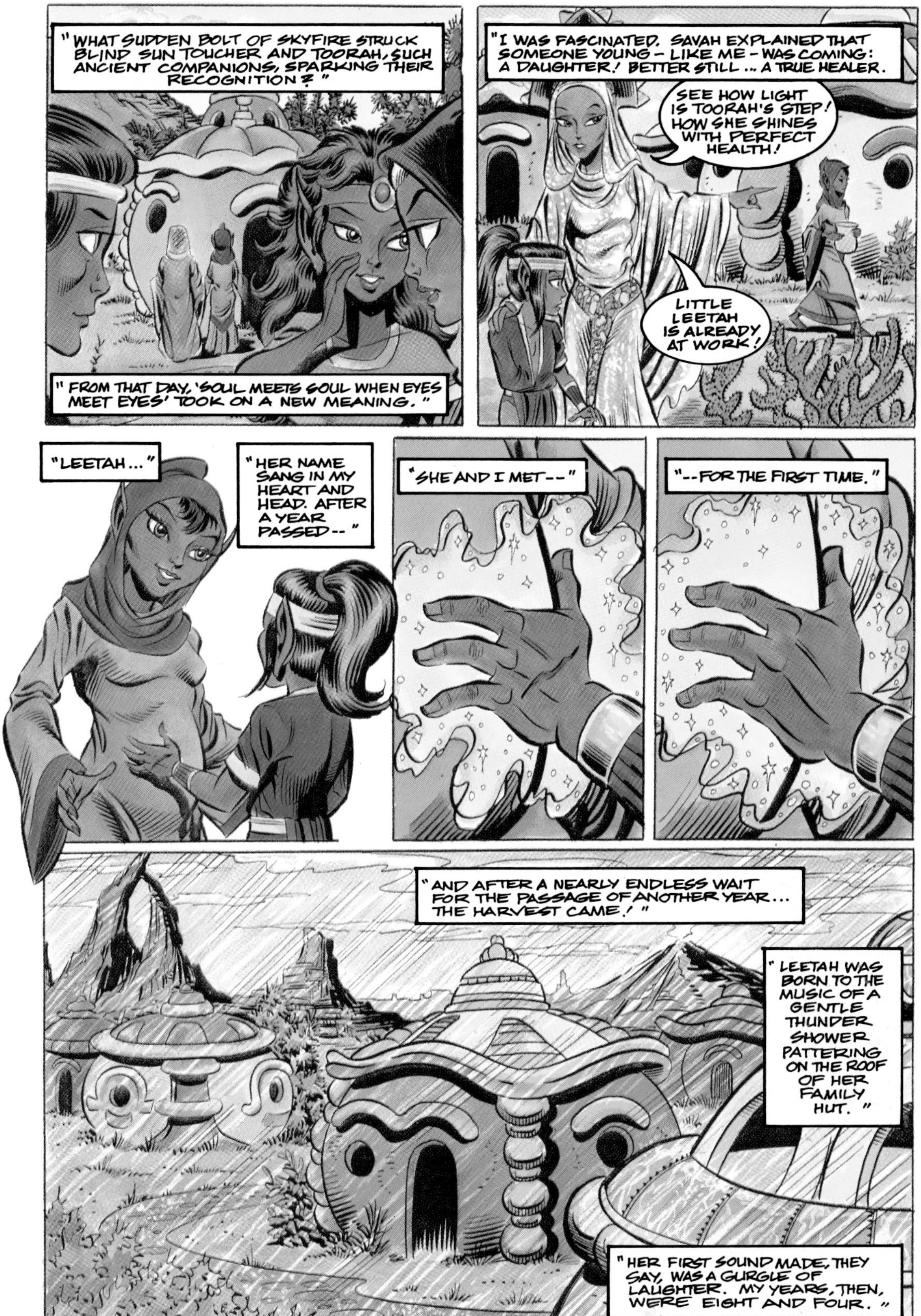

"WHAT SUDDEN BOLT OF SKYFIRE STRUCK BLIND SUN TOUCHER AND TOORAH, SUCH ANCIENT COMPANIONS, SPARKING THEIR RECOGNITION?"
"FROM THAT DAY, 'SOUL MEETS SOUL WHEN EYES MEET EYES' TOOK ON A NEW MEANING."
"I WAS FASCINATED. SAVAH EXPLAINED THAT SOMEONE YOUNG - LIKE ME - WAS COMING: A DAUGHTER! BETTER STILL ... A TRUE HEALER.
SEE HOW LIGHT IS TOORAH'S STEP! HOW SHE SHINES WITH PERFECT HEALTH!
LITTLE LEETAH IS ALREADY AT WORK!
"LEETAH..."
"HER NAME SANG IN MY HEART AND HEAD. AFTER A YEAR PASSED--"
"SHE AND I MET--"
"--FOR THE FIRST TIME."
"AND AFTER A NEARLY ENDLESS WAIT FOR THE PASSAGE OF ANOTHER YEAR... THE HARVEST CAME!"
"LEETAH WAS BORN TO THE MUSIC OF A GENTLE THUNDER SHOWER PATTERING ON THE ROOF OF HER FAMILY HUT."
"HER FIRST SOUND MADE, THEY SAY, WAS A GURGLE OF LAUGHTER. MY YEARS, THEN, WERE EIGHT AND FOUR."

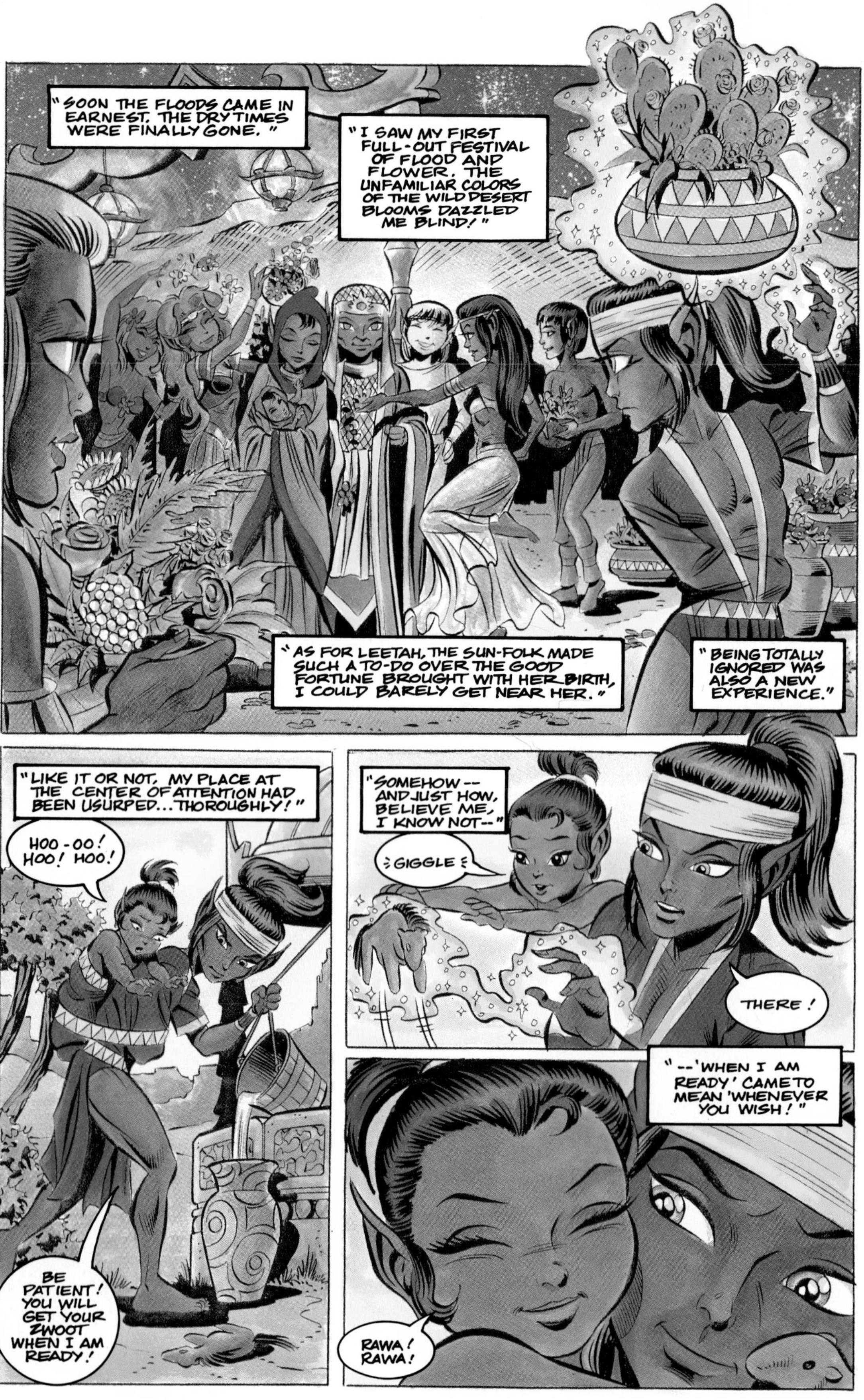
"SOON THE FLOODS CAME IN EARNEST. THE DRY TIMES WERE FINALLY GONE."
"I SAW MY FIRST FULL-OUT FESTIVAL OF FLOOD AND FLOWER. THE UNFAMILIAR COLORS OF THE WILD DESERT BLOOMS DAZZLED ME BLIND!"
"AS FOR LEETAH, THE SUN-FOLK MADE SUCH A TO-DO OVER THE GOOD FORTUNE BROUGHT WITH HER BIRTH, I COULD BARELY GET NEAR HER."
"BEING TOTALLY IGNORED WAS ALSO A NEW EXPERIENCE."
"LIKE IT OR NOT, MY PLACE AT THE CENTER OF ATTENTION HAD BEEN USURPED... THOROUGHLY!"
HOO-OO! HOO! HOO!
BE PATIENT! YOU WILL GET YOUR ZWOOT WHEN I AM READY!
"SOMEHOW -- AND JUST HOW, BELIEVE ME, I KNOW NOT--"
GIGGLE
THERE!
"--'WHEN I AM READY' CAME TO MEAN 'WHENEVER YOU WISH!'"
RAWA! RAWA!

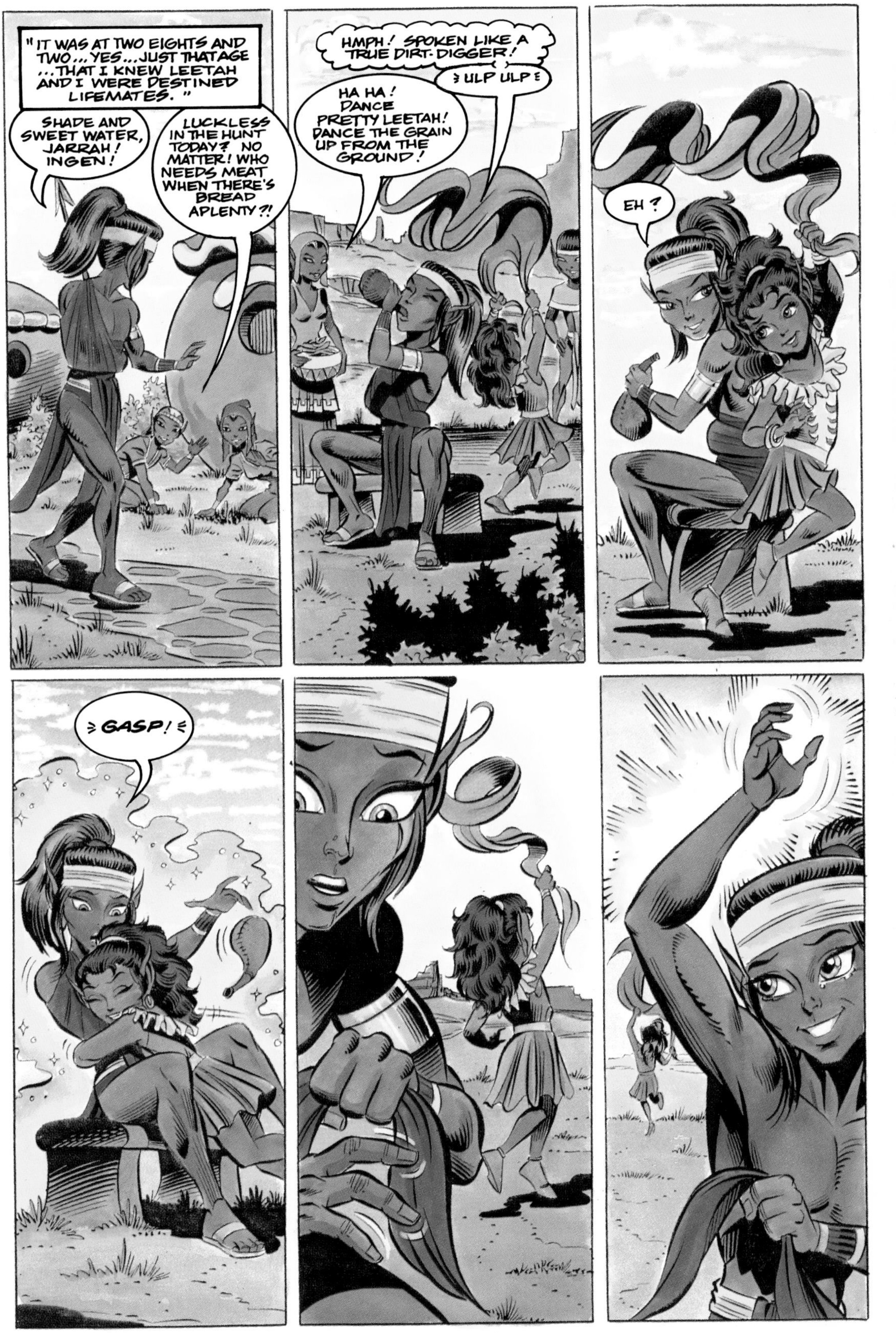
"IT WAS AT TWO EIGHTS AND TWO... YES... JUST THAT AGE ...THAT I KNEW LEETAH AND I WERE DESTINED LIFEMATES."
SHADE AND SWEET WATER, JARRAH! INGEN!
LUCKLESS IN THE HUNT TODAY? NO MATTER! WHO NEEDS MEAT WHEN THERE'S BREAD APLENTY?!
HMPH! SPOKEN LIKE A TRUE DIRT-DIGGER!
ULP ULP
HA HA! DANCE PRETTY LEETAH! DANCE THE GRAIN UP FROM THE GROUND!
EH?
GASP!

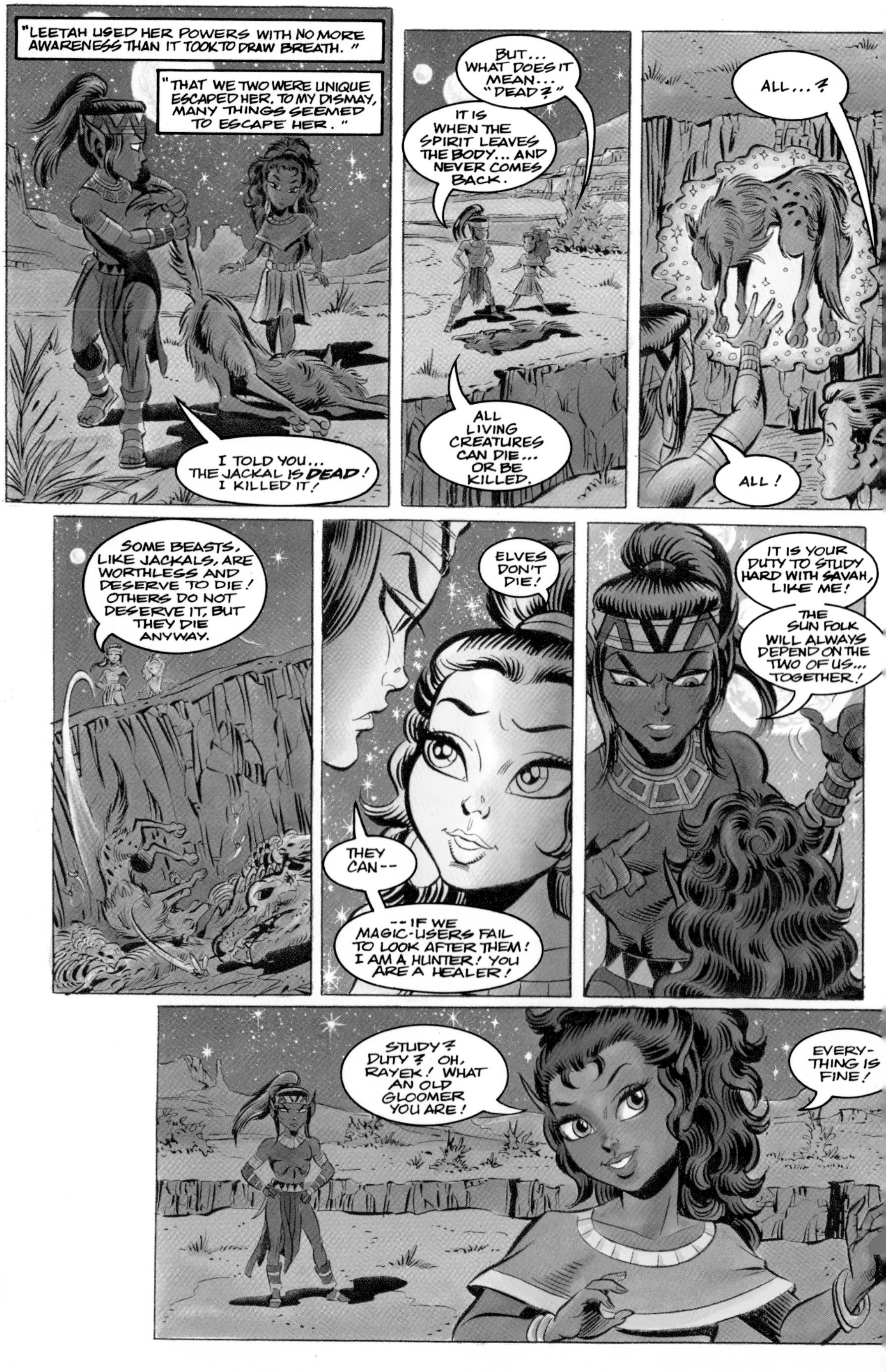
"LEETAH USED HER POWERS WITH NO MORE AWARENESS THAN IT TOOK TO DRAW BREATH."
"THAT WE TWO WERE UNIQUE ESCAPED HER. TO MY DISMAY, MANY THINGS SEEMED TO ESCAPE HER."
I TOLD YOU... THE JACKAL IS DEAD! I KILLED IT!
BUT... WHAT DOES IT MEAN... "DEAD?"
IT IS WHEN THE SPIRIT LEAVES THE BODY... AND NEVER COMES BACK.
ALL LIVING CREATURES CAN DIE... OR BE KILLED.
ALL...?
ALL!
SOME BEASTS, LIKE JACKALS, ARE WORTHLESS AND DESERVE TO DIE! OTHERS DO NOT DESERVE IT, BUT THEY DIE ANYWAY.
ELVES DON'T DIE!
THEY CAN--
--IF WE MAGIC-USERS FAIL TO LOOK AFTER THEM! I AM A HUNTER! YOU ARE A HEALER!
IT IS YOUR DUTY TO STUDY HARD WITH SAVAH, LIKE ME!
THE SUN FOLK WILL ALWAYS DEPEND ON THE TWO OF US... TOGETHER!
STUDY? DUTY? OH, RAYEK! WHAT AN OLD GLOOMER YOU ARE!
EVERYTHING IS FINE!

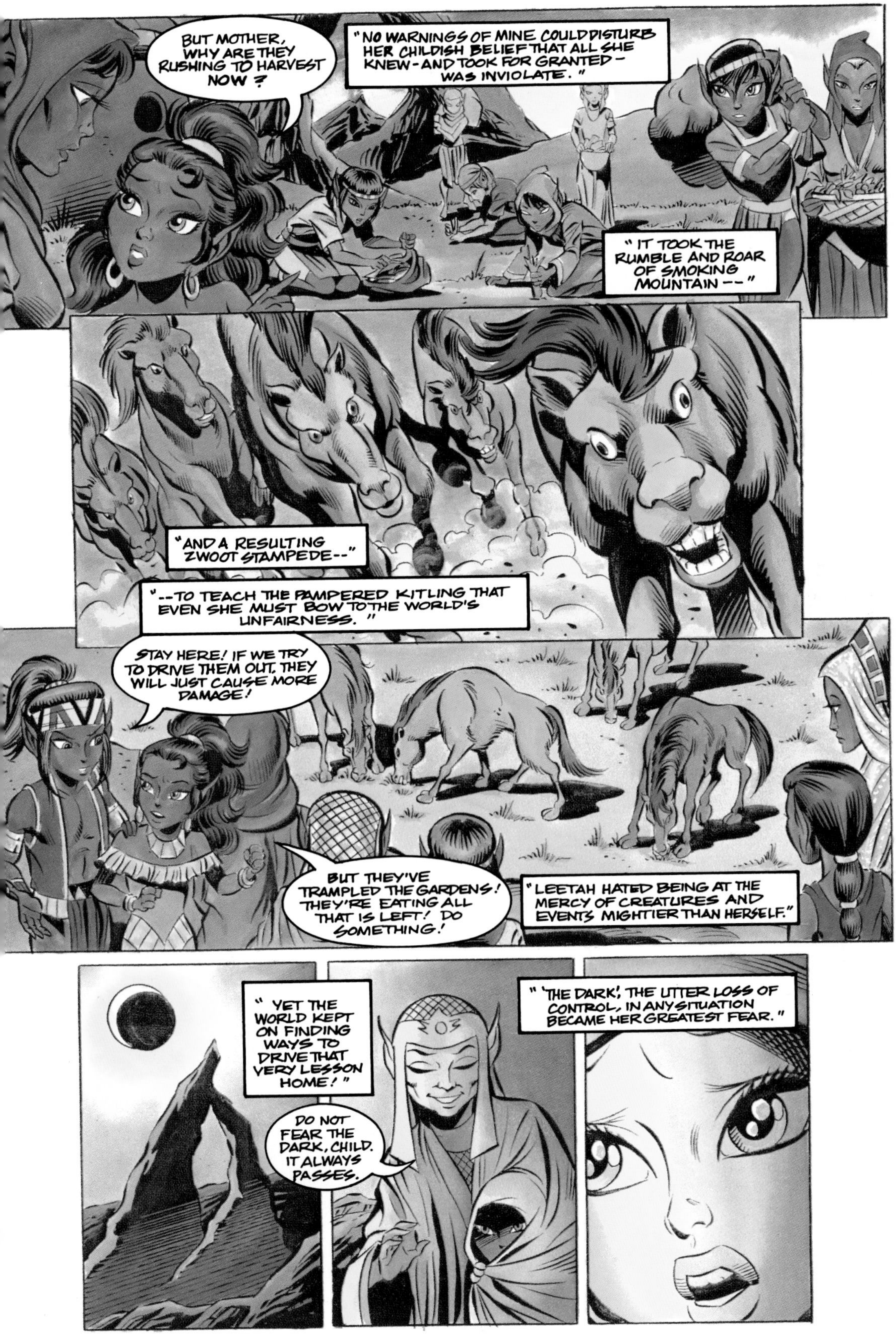
BUT MOTHER, WHY ARE THEY RUSHING TO HARVEST NOW ?
"NO WARNINGS OF MINE COULD DISTURB HER CHILDISH BELIEF THAT ALL SHE KNEW - AND TOOK FOR GRANTED - WAS INVIOLATE."
"IT TOOK THE RUMBLE AND ROAR OF SMOKING MOUNTAIN --"
"AND A RESULTING ZWOOT STAMPEDE--"
"--TO TEACH THE PAMPERED KITLING THAT EVEN SHE MUST BOW TO THE WORLD'S UNFAIRNESS."
STAY HERE! IF WE TRY TO DRIVE THEM OUT, THEY WILL JUST CAUSE MORE DAMAGE!
BUT THEY'VE TRAMPLED THE GARDENS! THEY'RE EATING ALL THAT IS LEFT! DO SOMETHING!
"LEETAH HATED BEING AT THE MERCY OF CREATURES AND EVENTS MIGHTIER THAN HERSELF."
"YET THE WORLD KEPT ON FINDING WAYS TO DRIVE THAT VERY LESSON HOME!"
DO NOT FEAR THE DARK, CHILD. IT ALWAYS PASSES.
"'THE DARK,' THE UTTER LOSS OF CONTROL, IN ANY SITUATION BECAME HER GREATEST FEAR."

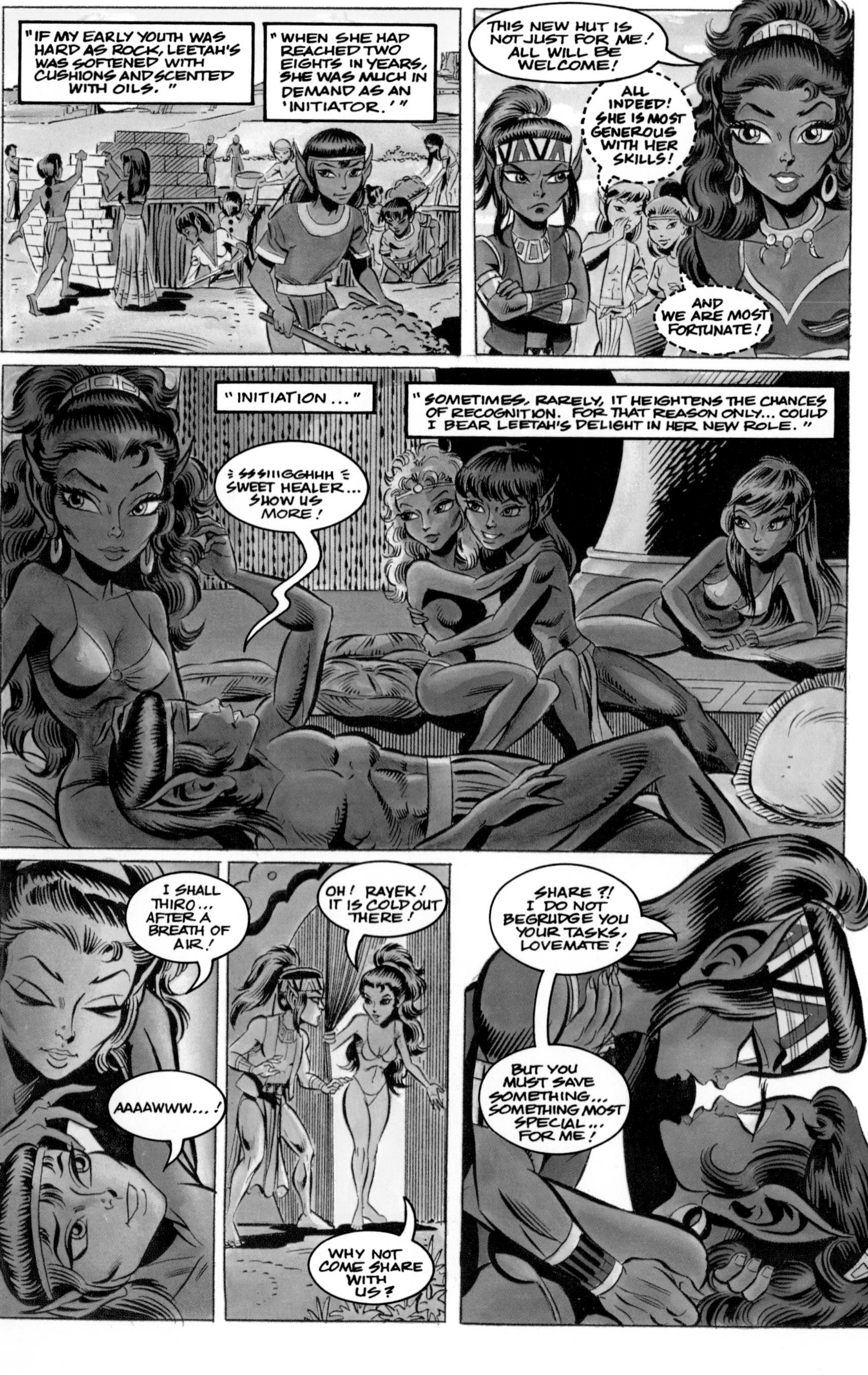
"IF MY EARLY YOUTH WAS HARD AS ROCK, LEETAH'S WAS SOFTENED WITH CUSHIONS AND SCENTED WITH OILS."
"WHEN SHE HAD REACHED TWO EIGHTS IN YEARS, SHE WAS MUCH IN DEMAND AS AN 'INITIATOR.'"
THIS NEW HUT IS NOT JUST FOR ME! ALL WILL BE WELCOME!
ALL INDEED! SHE IS MOST GENEROUS WITH HER SKILLS!
AND WE ARE MOST FORTUNATE!
"INITIATION ..."
"SOMETIMES, RARELY, IT HEIGHTENS THE CHANCES OF RECOGNITION. FOR THAT REASON ONLY... COULD I BEAR LEETAH'S DELIGHT IN HER NEW ROLE."
≡SSSIIIGGHHH≡ SWEET HEALER... SHOW US MORE!
I SHALL THIRD... AFTER A BREATH OF AIR!
AAAAWWW...!
OH! RAYEK! IT IS COLD OUT THERE!
WHY NOT COME SHARE WITH US?
SHARE?! I DO NOT BEGRUDGE YOU YOUR TASKS, LOVEMATE!
BUT YOU MUST SAVE SOMETHING... SOMETHING MOST SPECIAL... FOR ME!

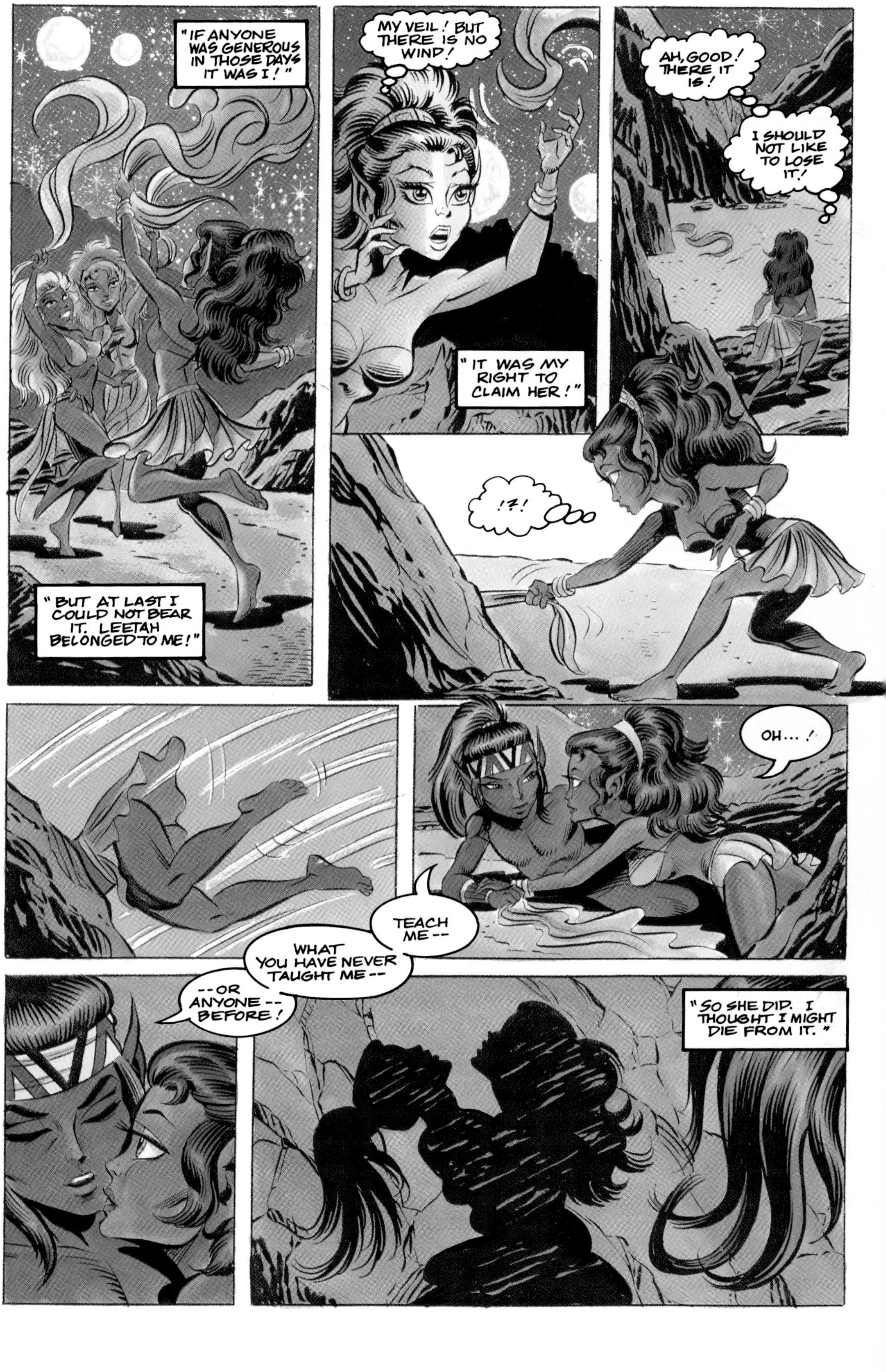
"IF ANYONE WAS GENEROUS IN THOSE DAYS IT WAS I!"
"BUT AT LAST I COULD NOT BEAR IT. LEETAH BELONGED TO ME!"
MY VEIL! BUT THERE IS NO WIND!
"IT WAS MY RIGHT TO CLAIM HER!"
AH, GOOD! THERE IT IS!
I SHOULD NOT LIKE TO LOSE IT!
!?!
OH... !
TEACH ME--
WHAT YOU HAVE NEVER TAUGHT ME--
--OR ANYONE--BEFORE!
"SO SHE DID. I THOUGHT I MIGHT DIE FROM IT."

"BUT MORE... I HOPED TO LIVE!"
...r-recog...nition...!
Let it be now...! I beg you! NOW!
WHY?! WHY DO YOU HOLD BACK?? I WANT ALL OF YOU!
YOU ARE MINE!!!
...n-no...!
SO... IT IS TO BE A HUNT, THEN!
PANT PANT PANT
IF THAT IS WHAT RECOGNITION MUST COST ME -- NO! NONE BUT I SHALL DECIDE WHEN... AND WITH WHOM!
"TIME PASSED. I WAS FORCED TO ACQUIRE SOMETHING AKIN TO PATIENCE."

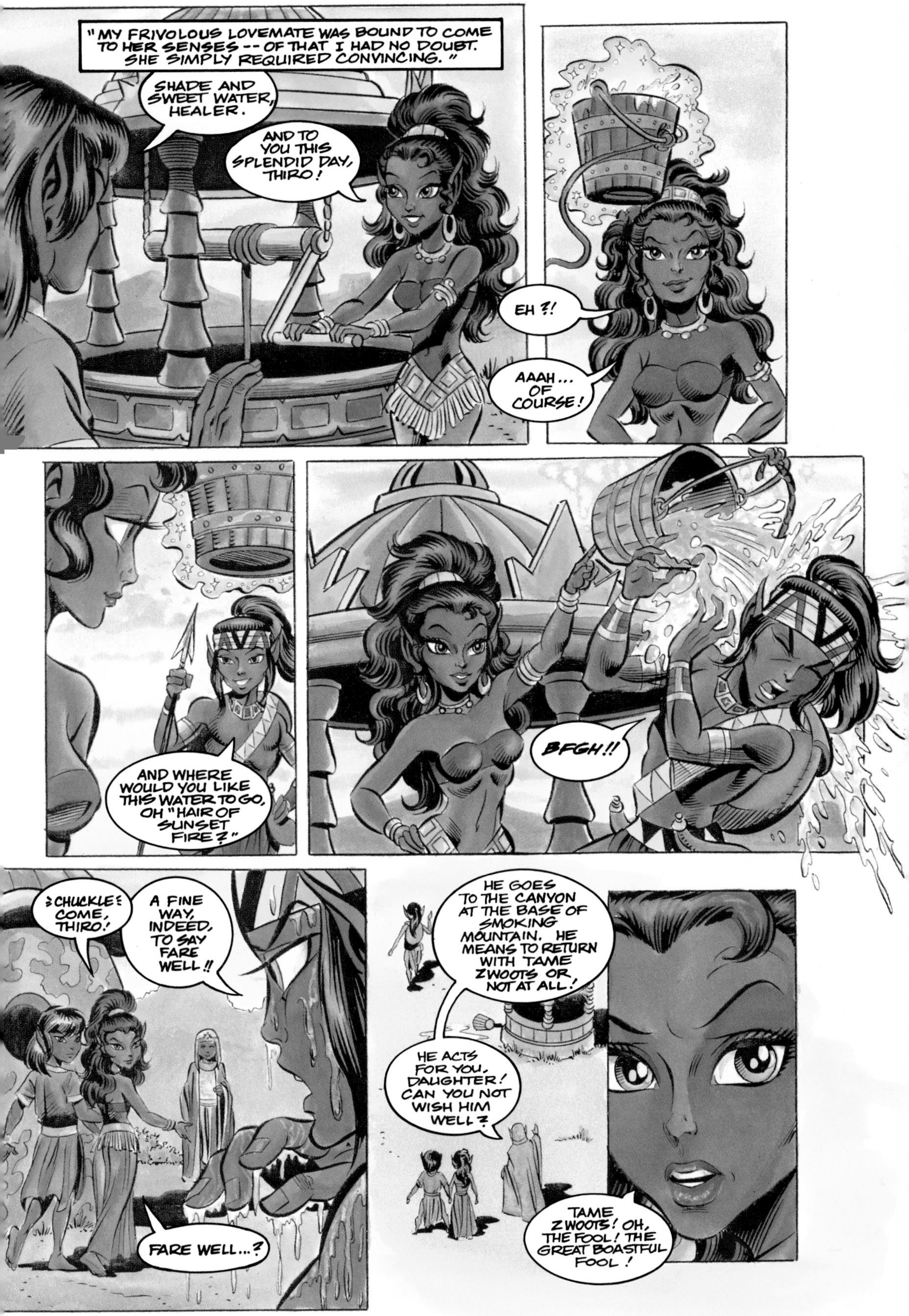
"MY FRIVOLOUS LOVEMATE WAS BOUND TO COME TO HER SENSES -- OF THAT I HAD NO DOUBT. SHE SIMPLY REQUIRED CONVINCING."
SHADE AND SWEET WATER, HEALER.
AND TO YOU THIS SPLENDID DAY, THIRO!
EH ?!
AAAH... OF COURSE!
AND WHERE WOULD YOU LIKE THIS WATER TO GO, OH "HAIR OF SUNSET FIRE?"
BFGH!!
CHUCKLE COME, THIRO!
A FINE WAY, INDEED, TO SAY FARE WELL!!
FARE WELL...?
HE GOES TO THE CANYON AT THE BASE OF SMOKING MOUNTAIN. HE MEANS TO RETURN WITH TAME ZWOOTS OR NOT AT ALL!
HE ACTS FOR YOU, DAUGHTER! CAN YOU NOT WISH HIM WELL?
TAME ZWOOTS! OH, THE FOOL! THE GREAT BOASTFUL FOOL!

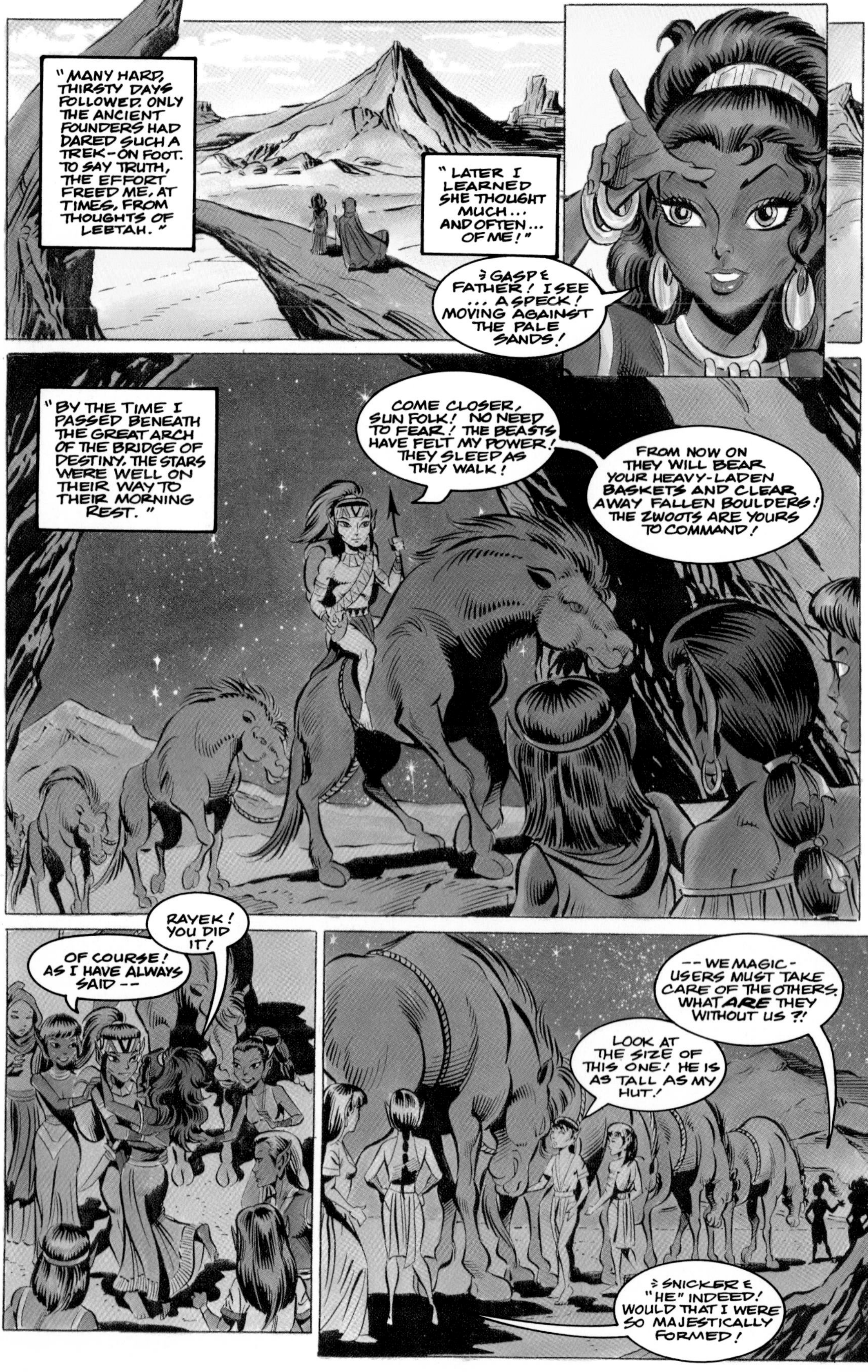
"MANY HARD, THIRSTY DAYS FOLLOWED. ONLY THE ANCIENT FOUNDERS HAD DARED SUCH A TREK-ON FOOT. TO SAY TRUTH, THE EFFORT FREED ME, AT TIMES, FROM THOUGHTS OF LEETAH."
"LATER I LEARNED SHE THOUGHT MUCH... AND OFTEN... OF ME!"
≥GASP≤ FATHER! I SEE ... A SPECK! MOVING AGAINST THE PALE SANDS!
"BY THE TIME I PASSED BENEATH THE GREAT ARCH OF THE BRIDGE OF DESTINY, THE STARS WERE WELL ON THEIR WAY TO THEIR MORNING REST."
COME CLOSER, SUN FOLK! NO NEED TO FEAR! THE BEASTS HAVE FELT MY POWER! THEY SLEEP AS THEY WALK!
FROM NOW ON THEY WILL BEAR YOUR HEAVY-LADEN BASKETS AND CLEAR AWAY FALLEN BOULDERS! THE ZWOOTS ARE YOURS TO COMMAND!
RAYEK! YOU DID IT!
OF COURSE! AS I HAVE ALWAYS SAID --
-- WE MAGIC-USERS MUST TAKE CARE OF THE OTHERS. WHAT ARE THEY WITHOUT US ?!
LOOK AT THE SIZE OF THIS ONE! HE IS AS TALL AS MY HUT!
≥SNICKER≤ "HE" INDEED! WOULD THAT I WERE SO MAJESTICALLY FORMED!

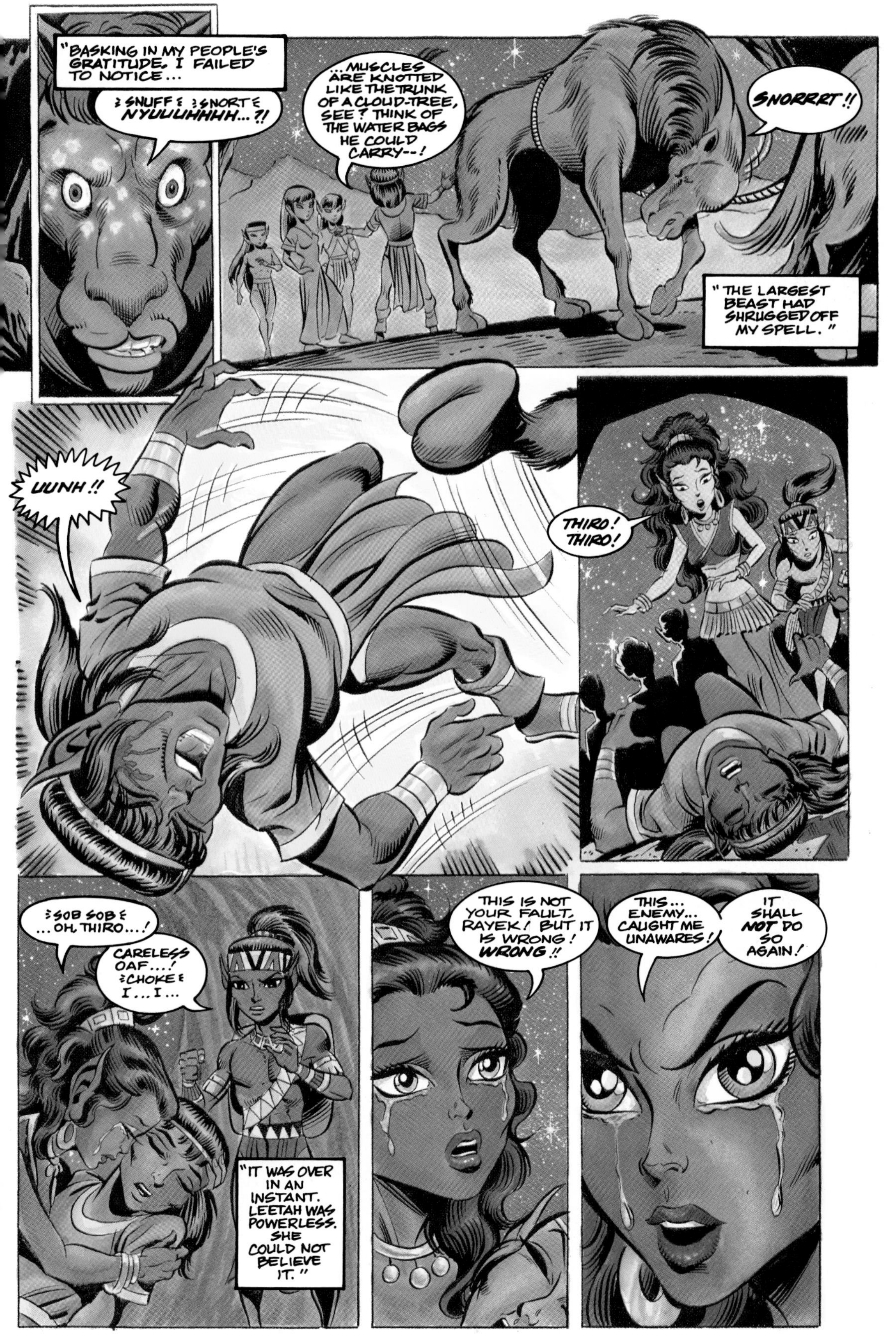
"BASKING IN MY PEOPLE'S GRATITUDE, I FAILED TO NOTICE...
≷SNUFF≷ ≷SNORT≷ NYUUUHHHH...?!
...MUSCLES ARE KNOTTED LIKE THE TRUNK OF A CLOUD-TREE, SEE? THINK OF THE WATER BAGS HE COULD CARRY--!
SNORRRT!!
"THE LARGEST BEAST HAD SHRUGGED OFF MY SPELL."
UUNH!!
THIRO! THIRO!
≷SOB SOB≷ ...OH, THIRO...!
CARELESS OAF...! ≷CHOKE≷ I...I...
"IT WAS OVER IN AN INSTANT. LEETAH WAS POWERLESS. SHE COULD NOT BELIEVE IT."
THIS IS NOT YOUR FAULT, RAYEK! BUT IT IS WRONG! WRONG!!
THIS... ENEMY... CAUGHT ME UNAWARES!
IT SHALL NOT DO SO AGAIN!

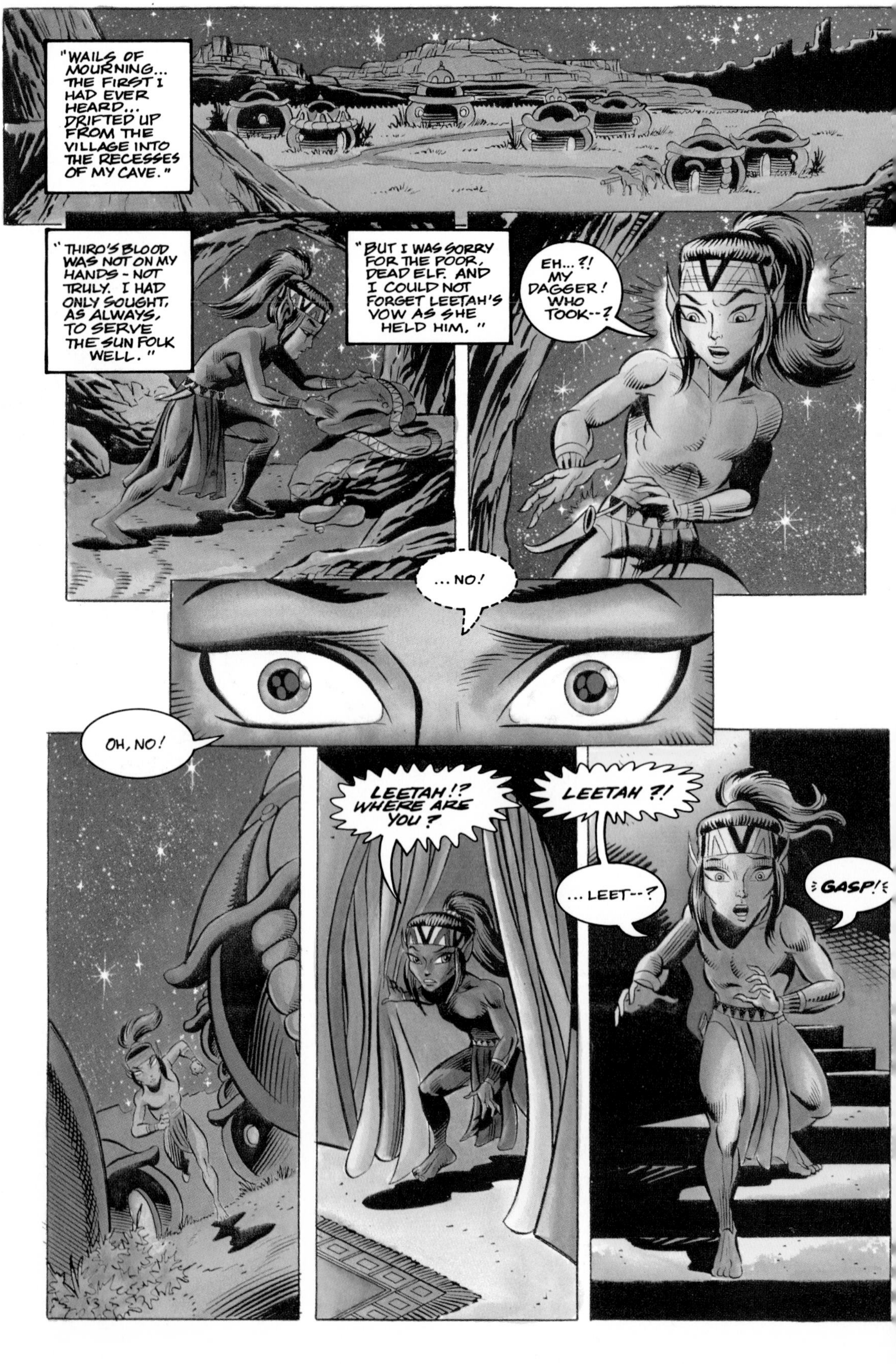
"WAILS OF MOURNING... THE FIRST I HAD EVER HEARD... DRIFTED UP FROM THE VILLAGE INTO THE RECESSES OF MY CAVE."
"THIRO'S BLOOD WAS NOT ON MY HANDS - NOT TRULY. I HAD ONLY SOUGHT, AS ALWAYS, TO SERVE THE SUN FOLK WELL."
"BUT I WAS SORRY FOR THE POOR, DEAD ELF. AND I COULD NOT FORGET LEETAH'S VOW AS SHE HELD HIM."
EH...?! MY DAGGER! WHO TOOK--?
...NO!
OH, NO!
LEETAH!? WHERE ARE YOU?
LEETAH?!
...LEET--?
GASP!

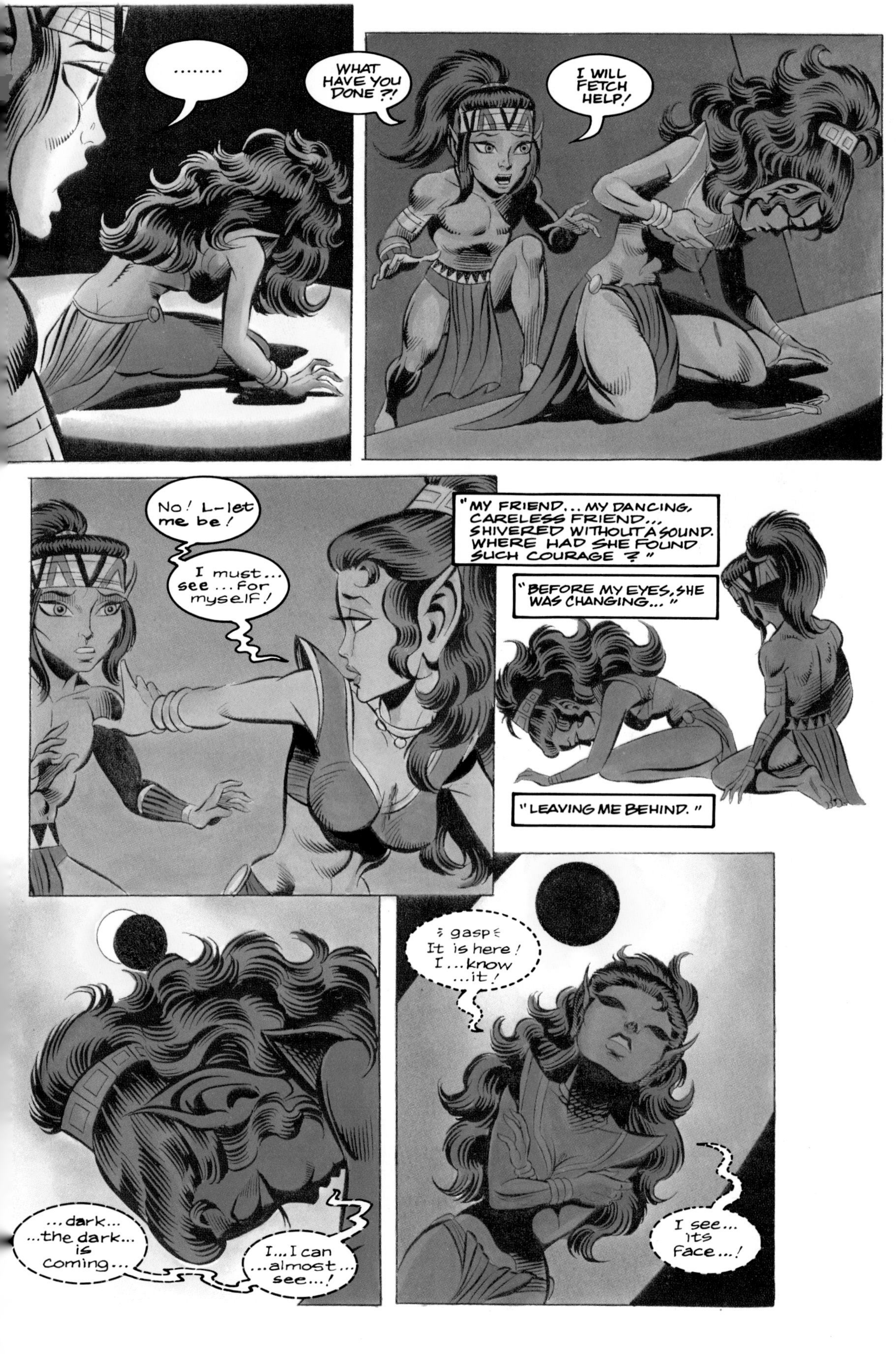
....
WHAT HAVE YOU DONE ?!
I WILL FETCH HELP!
No! L-let me be!
I must... see... for myself!
"MY FRIEND... MY DANCING, CARELESS FRIEND... SHIVERED WITHOUT A SOUND. WHERE HAD SHE FOUND SUCH COURAGE ?"
"BEFORE MY EYES, SHE WAS CHANGING..."
"LEAVING ME BEHIND."
...dark... ...the dark... is coming...
I... I can ...almost... see...!
gasp
It is here! I... know ...it!
I see... its face...!

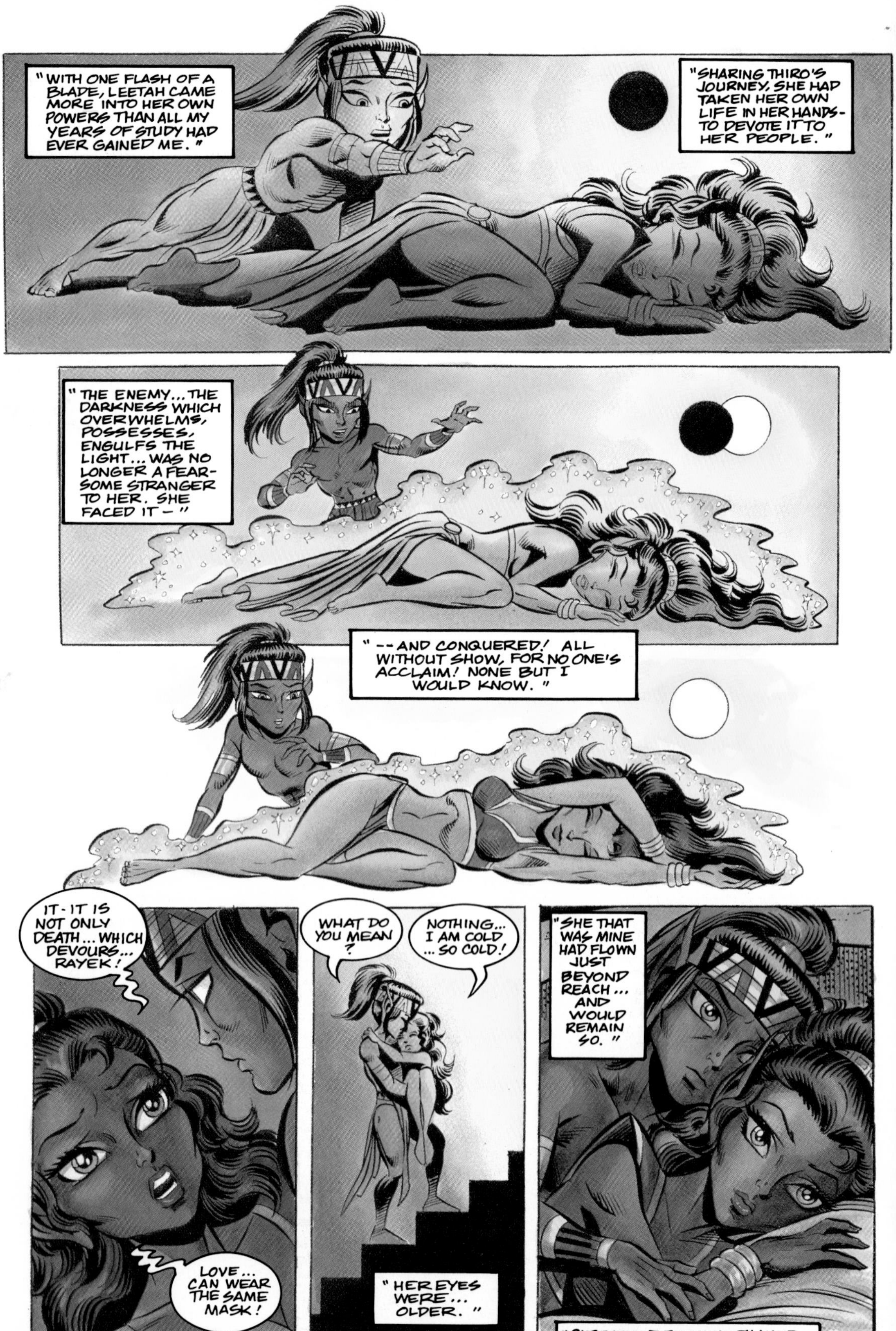
"WITH ONE FLASH OF A BLADE, LEETAH CAME MORE INTO HER OWN POWERS THAN ALL MY YEARS OF STUDY HAD EVER GAINED ME."
"SHARING THIRO'S JOURNEY, SHE HAD TAKEN HER OWN LIFE IN HER HANDS- TO DEVOTE IT TO HER PEOPLE."
"THE ENEMY... THE DARKNESS WHICH OVERWHELMS, POSSESSES, ENGULFS THE LIGHT... WAS NO LONGER A FEAR-SOME STRANGER TO HER. SHE FACED IT -"
"--AND CONQUERED! ALL WITHOUT SHOW, FOR NO ONE'S ACCLAIM! NONE BUT I WOULD KNOW."
IT- IT IS NOT ONLY DEATH... WHICH DEVOURS... RAYEK!
LOVE... CAN WEAR THE SAME MASK!
WHAT DO YOU MEAN ?
NOTHING... I AM COLD ... SO COLD!
"HER EYES WERE... OLDER."
"SHE THAT WAS MINE HAD FLOWN JUST BEYOND REACH... AND WOULD REMAIN SO."
"BUT I WOULD FOLLOW WITH HAND OUTSTRETCHED. I ALWAYS SHALL.
end

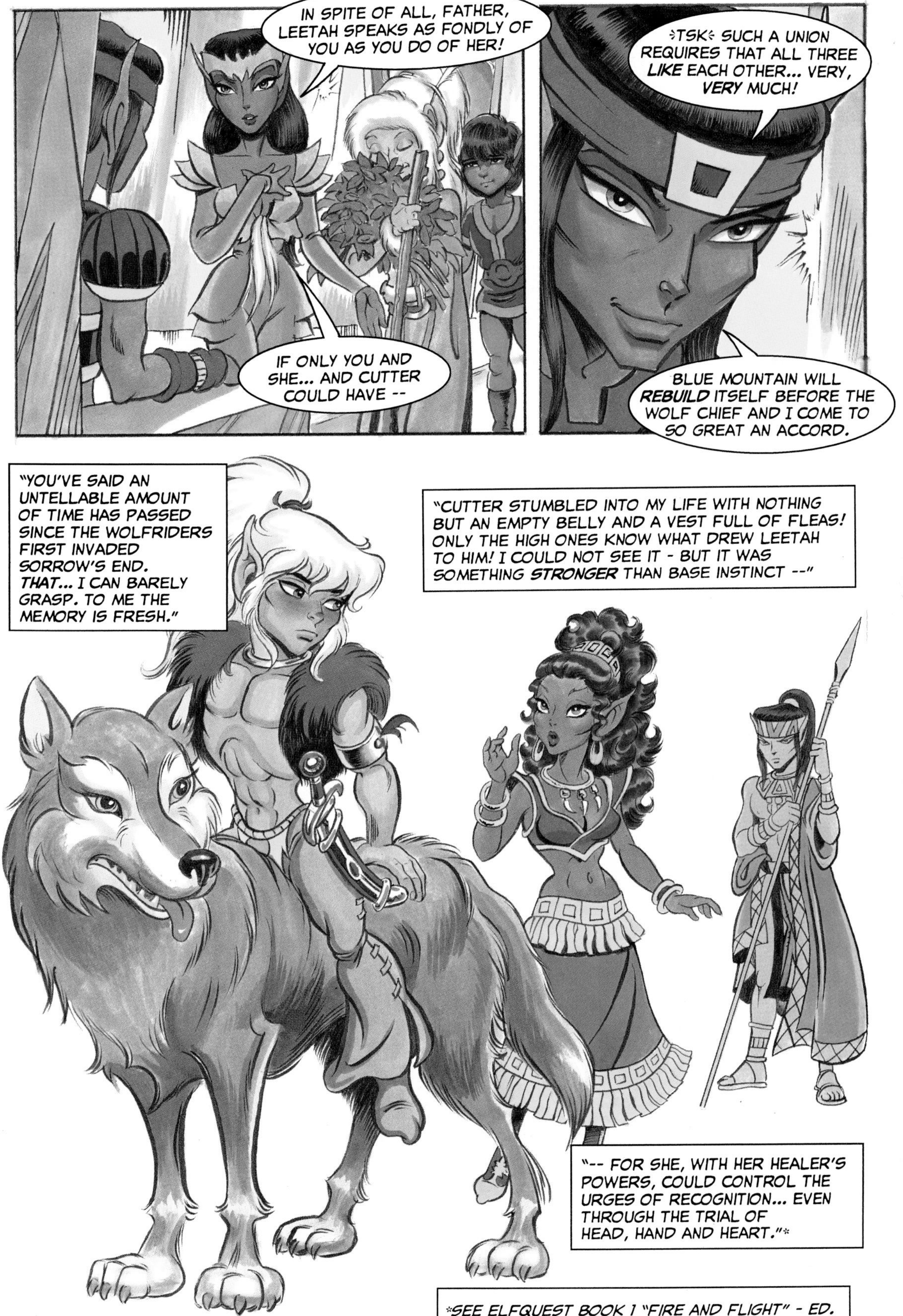
IN SPITE OF ALL, FATHER, LEETAH SPEAKS AS FONDLY OF YOU AS YOU DO OF HER!
IF ONLY YOU AND SHE... AND CUTTER COULD HAVE --
TSK SUCH A UNION REQUIRES THAT ALL THREE LIKE EACH OTHER... VERY, VERY MUCH!
BLUE MOUNTAIN WILL REBUILD ITSELF BEFORE THE WOLF CHIEF AND I COME TO SO GREAT AN ACCORD.
"YOU'VE SAID AN UNTELLABLE AMOUNT OF TIME HAS PASSED SINCE THE WOLFRIDERS FIRST INVADED SORROW'S END. THAT... I CAN BARELY GRASP. TO ME THE MEMORY IS FRESH."
"CUTTER STUMBLED INTO MY LIFE WITH NOTHING BUT AN EMPTY BELLY AND A VEST FULL OF FLEAS! ONLY THE HIGH ONES KNOW WHAT DREW LEETAH TO HIM! I COULD NOT SEE IT - BUT IT WAS SOMETHING STRONGER THAN BASE INSTINCT --"
"-- FOR SHE, WITH HER HEALER'S POWERS, COULD CONTROL THE URGES OF RECOGNITION... EVEN THROUGH THE TRIAL OF HEAD, HAND AND HEART."*
*SEE ELFQUEST BOOK 1 "FIRE AND FLIGHT" - ED.

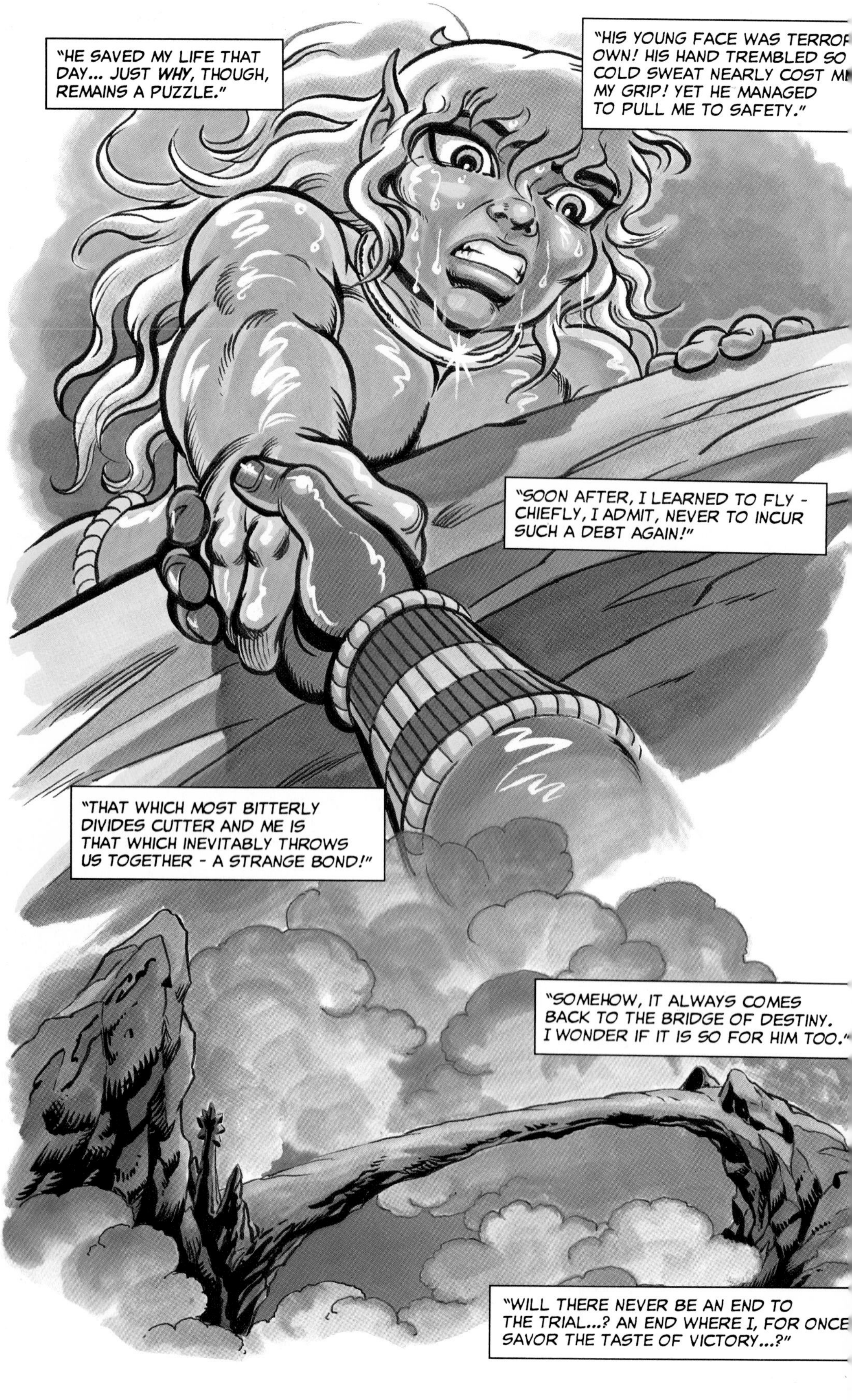
"HE SAVED MY LIFE THAT DAY... JUST WHY, THOUGH, REMAINS A PUZZLE."
"HIS YOUNG FACE WAS TERRO OWN! HIS HAND TREMBLED SO COLD SWEAT NEARLY COST M MY GRIP! YET HE MANAGED TO PULL ME TO SAFETY."
"SOON AFTER, I LEARNED TO FLY - CHIEFLY, I ADMIT, NEVER TO INCUR SUCH A DEBT AGAIN!"
"THAT WHICH MOST BITTERLY DIVIDES CUTTER AND ME IS THAT WHICH INEVITABLY THROWS US TOGETHER - A STRANGE BOND!"
"SOMEHOW, IT ALWAYS COMES BACK TO THE BRIDGE OF DESTINY. I WONDER IF IT IS SO FOR HIM TOO."
"WILL THERE NEVER BE AN END TO THE TRIAL...? AN END WHERE I, FOR ONCE SAVOR THE TASTE OF VICTORY...?"

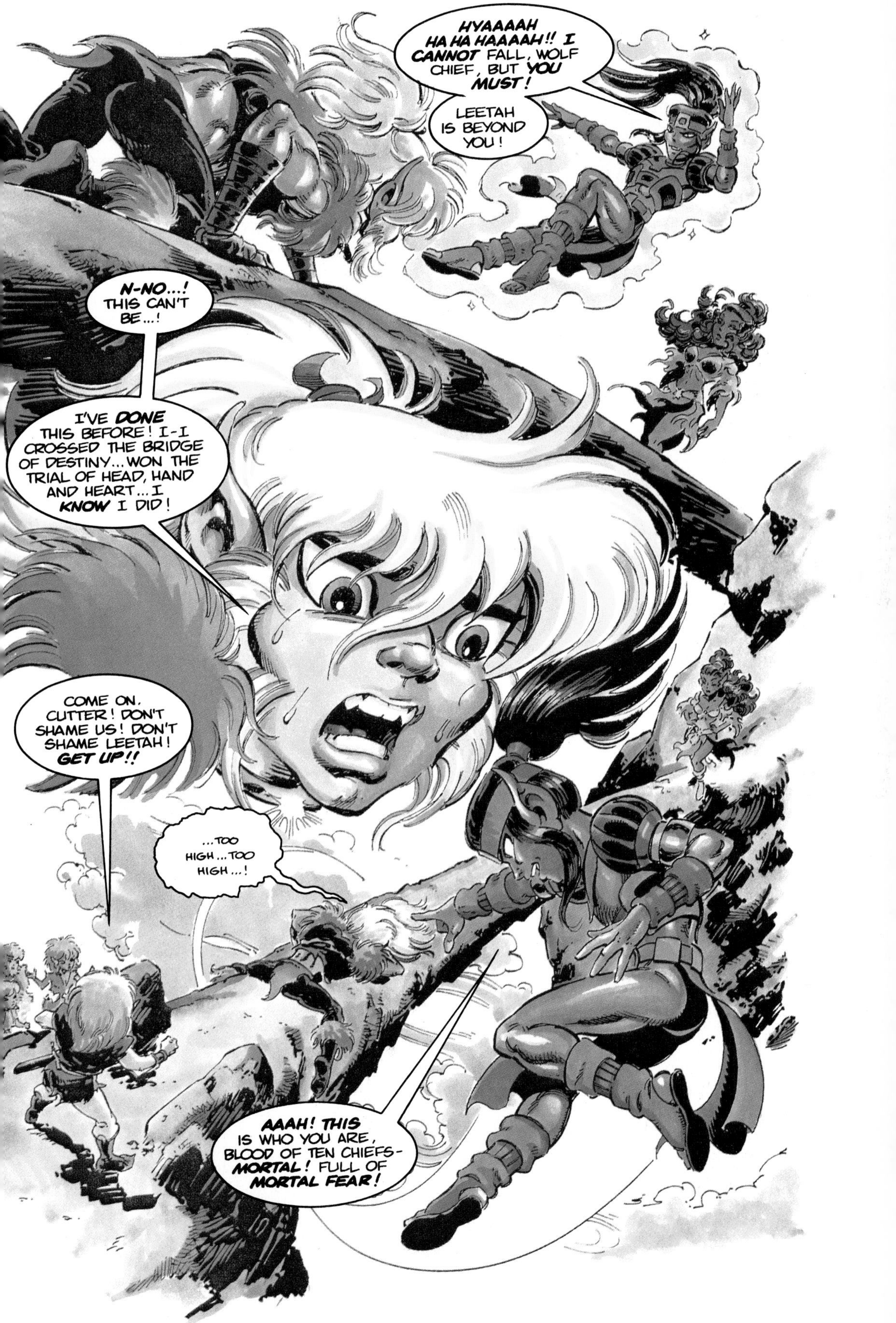
HYAAAAH HA HA HAAAAH!! I CANNOT FALL, WOLF CHIEF, BUT YOU MUST!
LEETAH IS BEYOND YOU!
N-NO...! THIS CAN'T BE...!
I'VE DONE THIS BEFORE! I-I CROSSED THE BRIDGE OF DESTINY...WON THE TRIAL OF HEAD, HAND AND HEART...I KNOW I DID!
COME ON, CUTTER! DON'T SHAME US! DON'T SHAME LEETAH! GET UP!!
...TOO HIGH...TOO HIGH...!
AAAH! THIS IS WHO YOU ARE, BLOOD OF TEN CHIEFS- MORTAL! FULL OF MORTAL FEAR!

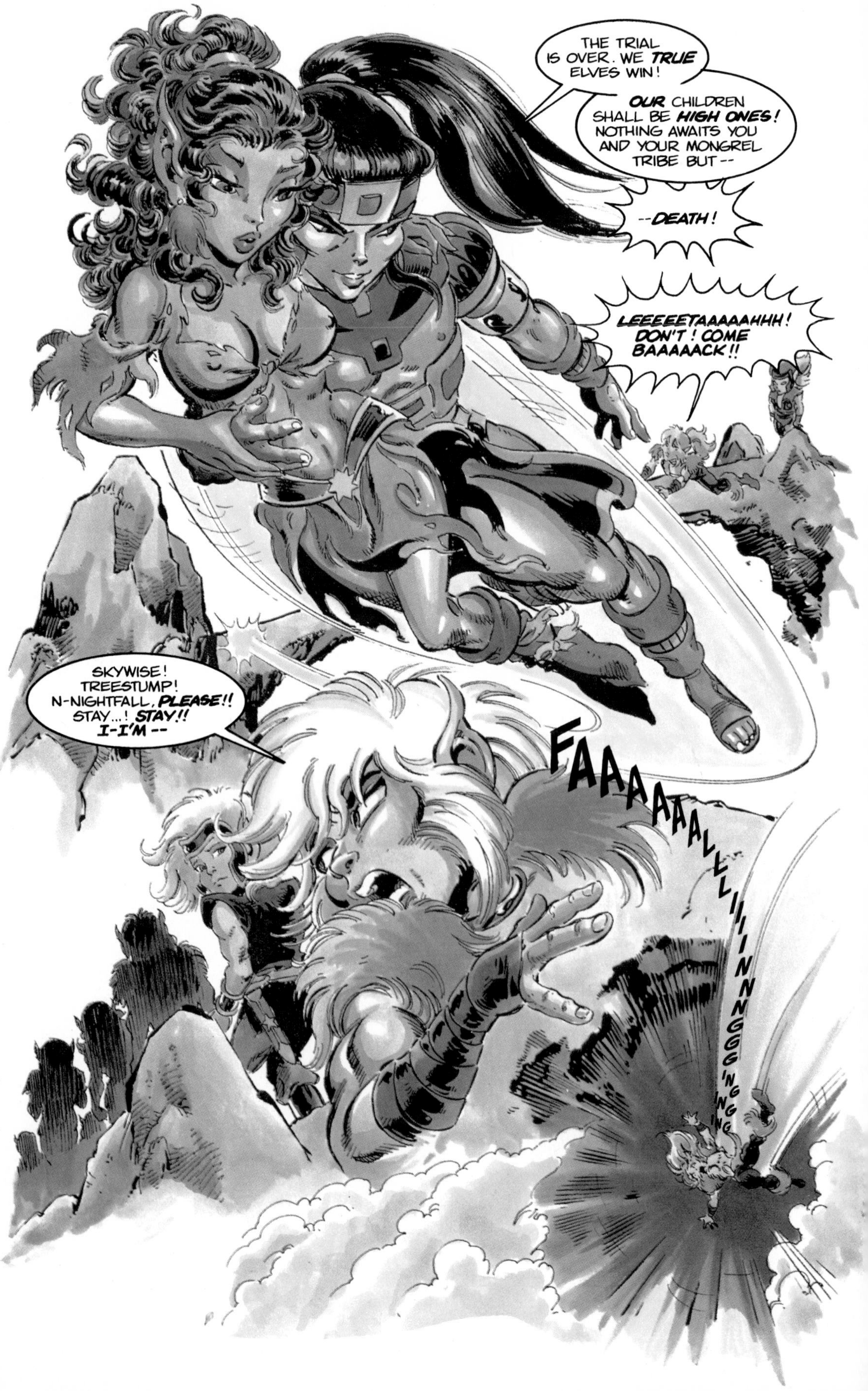
THE TRIAL IS OVER. WE TRUE ELVES WIN!
OUR CHILDREN SHALL BE HIGH ONES! NOTHING AWAITS YOU AND YOUR MONGREL TRIBE BUT --
--DEATH!
LEEEEETAAAAAHHH! DON'T! COME BAAAAACK!!
SKYWISE! TREESTUMP! N-NIGHTFALL, PLEASE!! STAY...! STAY!! I-I'M --
FAAAAAALLIIIINNNGGGinging

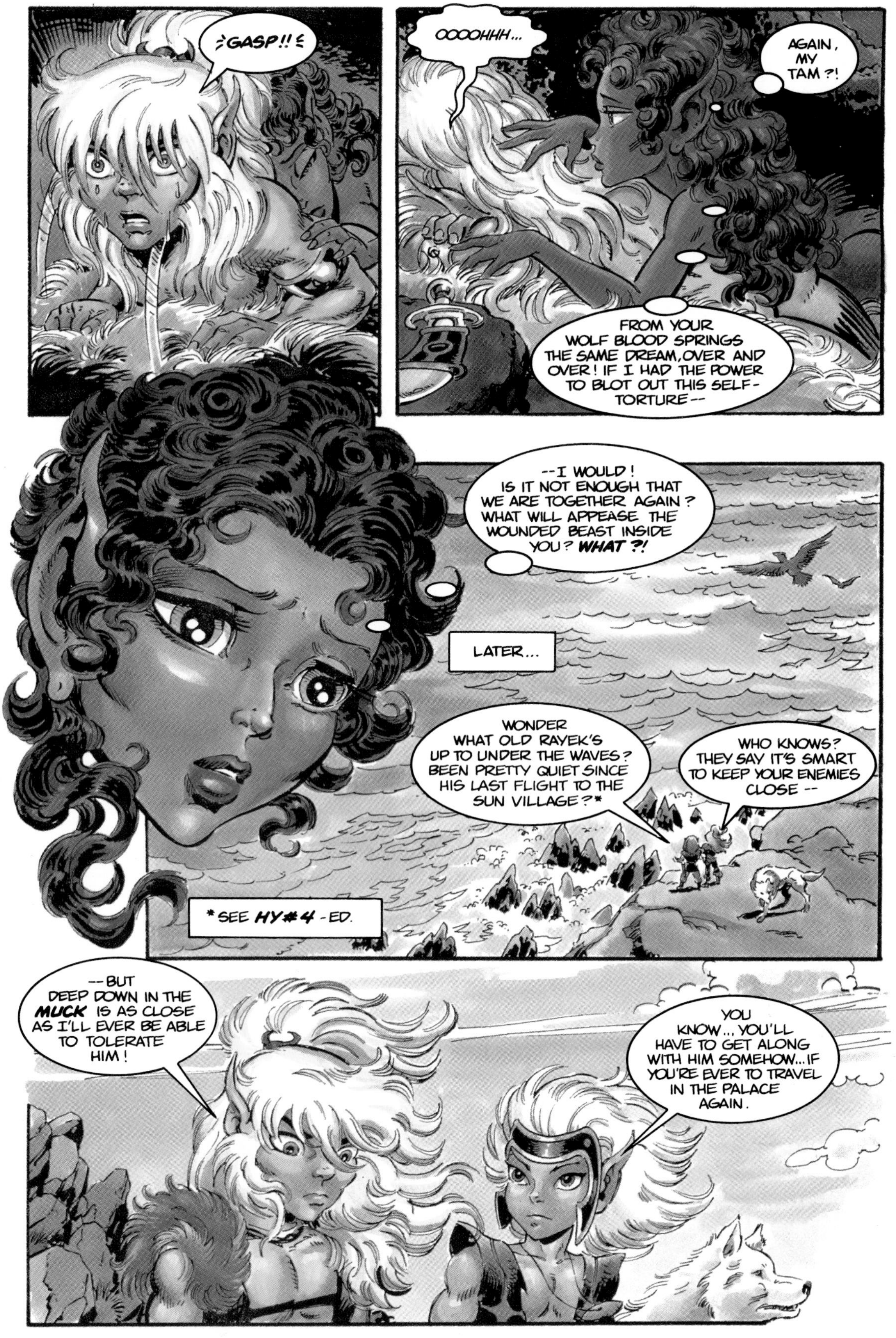

GASP!!
OOOOHHH...
AGAIN, MY TAM ?!
FROM YOUR WOLF BLOOD SPRINGS THE SAME DREAM, OVER AND OVER! IF I HAD THE POWER TO BLOT OUT THIS SELF-TORTURE--
--I WOULD! IS IT NOT ENOUGH THAT WE ARE TOGETHER AGAIN? WHAT WILL APPEASE THE WOUNDED BEAST INSIDE YOU? WHAT ?!
LATER...
WONDER WHAT OLD RAYEK'S UP TO UNDER THE WAVES? BEEN PRETTY QUIET SINCE HIS LAST FLIGHT TO THE SUN VILLAGE?*
WHO KNOWS? THEY SAY IT'S SMART TO KEEP YOUR ENEMIES CLOSE --
*SEE HY#4 -ED.
--BUT DEEP DOWN IN THE MUCK IS AS CLOSE AS I'LL EVER BE ABLE TO TOLERATE HIM!
YOU KNOW..., YOU'LL HAVE TO GET ALONG WITH HIM SOMEHOW...IF YOU'RE EVER TO TRAVEL IN THE PALACE AGAIN.

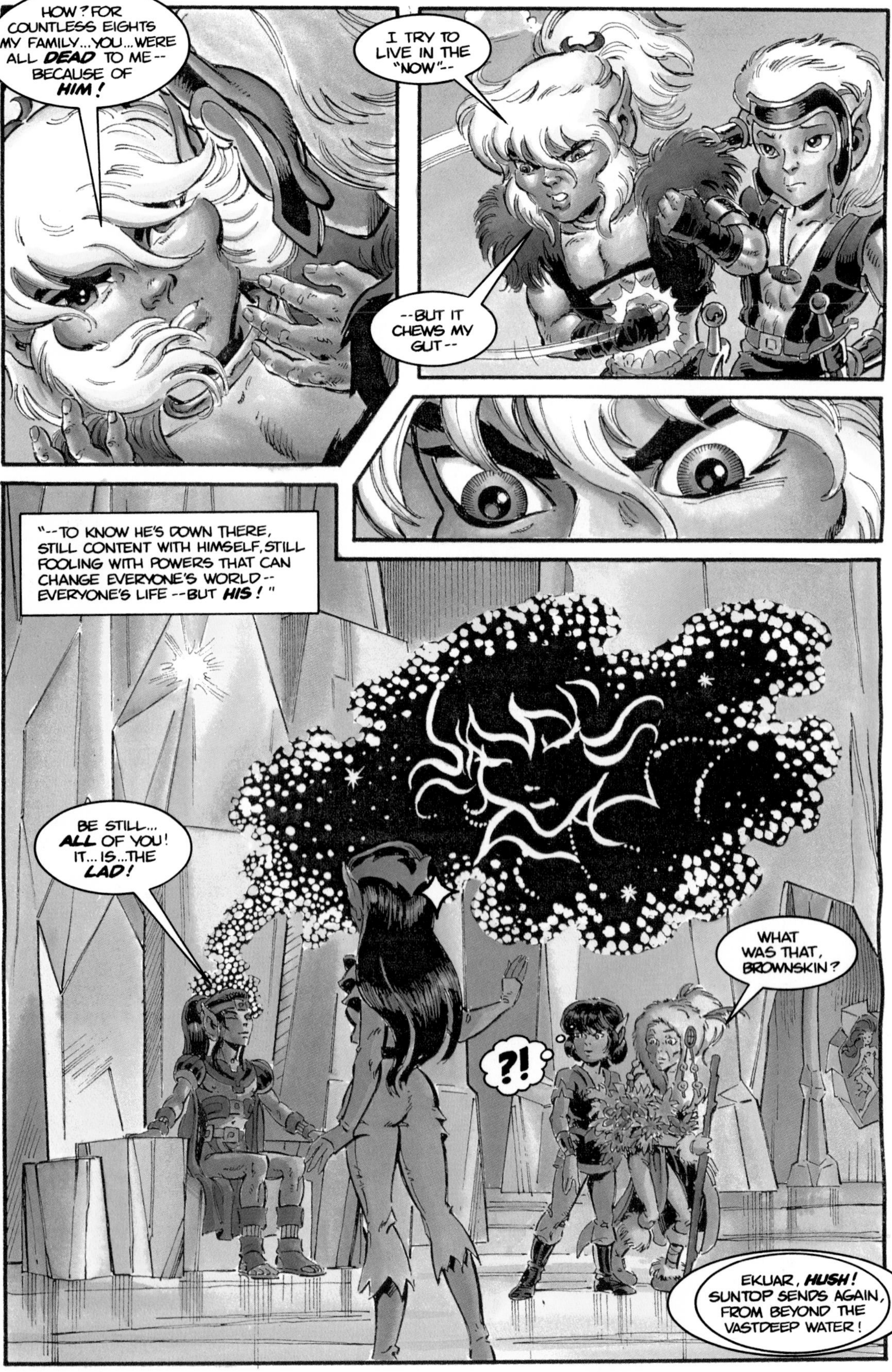
HOW? FOR COUNTLESS EIGHTS MY FAMILY... YOU... WERE ALL DEAD TO ME-- BECAUSE OF HIM!
I TRY TO LIVE IN THE "NOW"--
--BUT IT CHEWS MY GUT--
"--TO KNOW HE'S DOWN THERE, STILL CONTENT WITH HIMSELF, STILL FOOLING WITH POWERS THAT CAN CHANGE EVERYONE'S WORLD-- EVERYONE'S LIFE --BUT HIS!"
BE STILL... ALL OF YOU! IT... IS... THE LAD!
?!
WHAT WAS THAT, BROWNSKIN?
EKUAR, HUSH! SUNTOP SENDS AGAIN, FROM BEYOND THE VASTDEEP WATER!

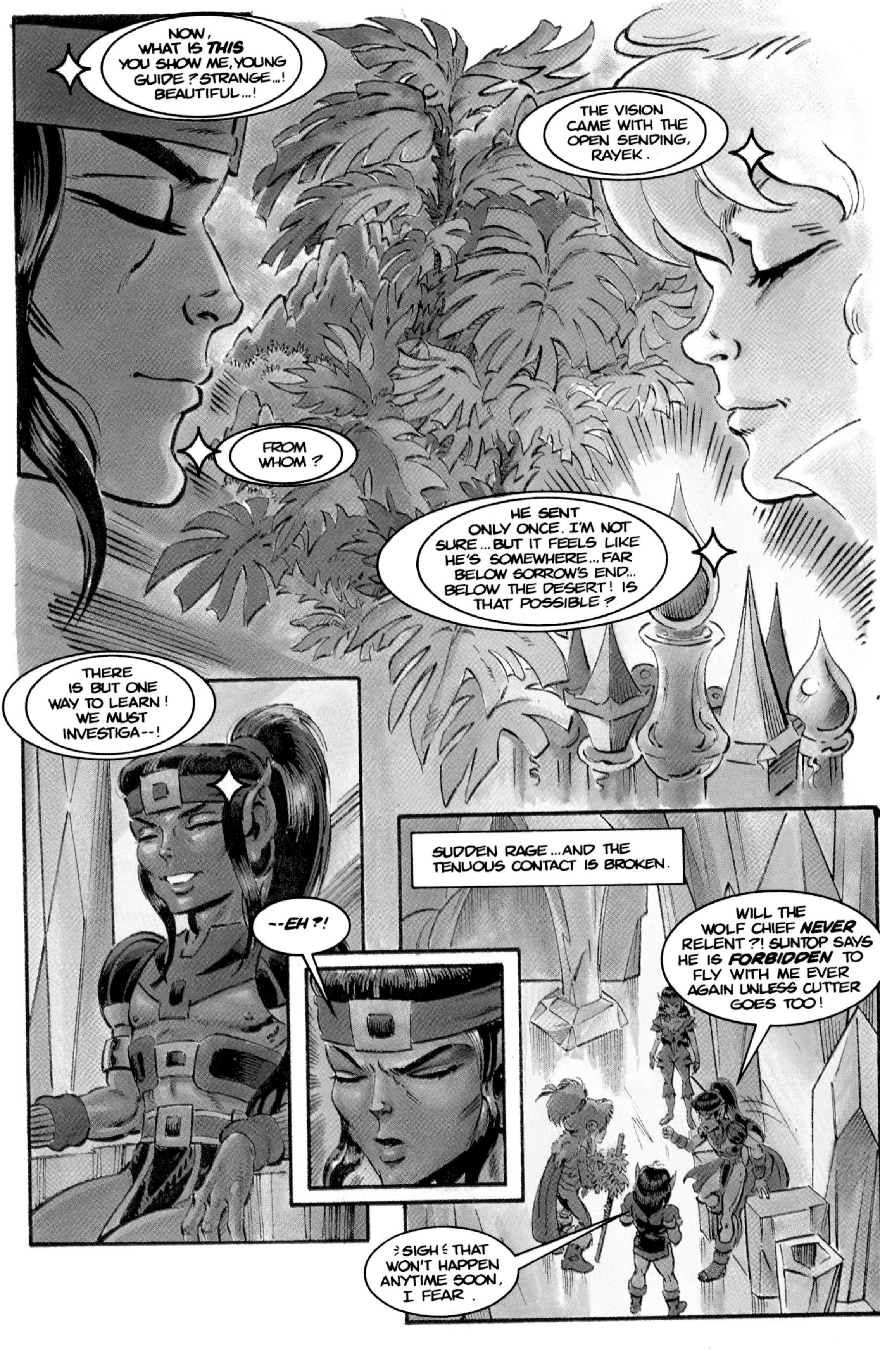
NOW, WHAT IS THIS YOU SHOW ME, YOUNG GUIDE? STRANGE...! BEAUTIFUL...!
THE VISION CAME WITH THE OPEN SENDING, RAYEK.
FROM WHOM?
HE SENT ONLY ONCE. I'M NOT SURE... BUT IT FEELS LIKE HE'S SOMEWHERE... FAR BELOW SORROW'S END... BELOW THE DESERT! IS THAT POSSIBLE?
THERE IS BUT ONE WAY TO LEARN! WE MUST INVESTIGA--!
--EH?!
SUDDEN RAGE... AND THE TENUOUS CONTACT IS BROKEN.
WILL THE WOLF CHIEF NEVER RELENT?! SUNTOP SAYS HE IS FORBIDDEN TO FLY WITH ME EVER AGAIN UNLESS CUTTER GOES TOO!
SIGH THAT WON'T HAPPEN ANYTIME SOON, I FEAR.

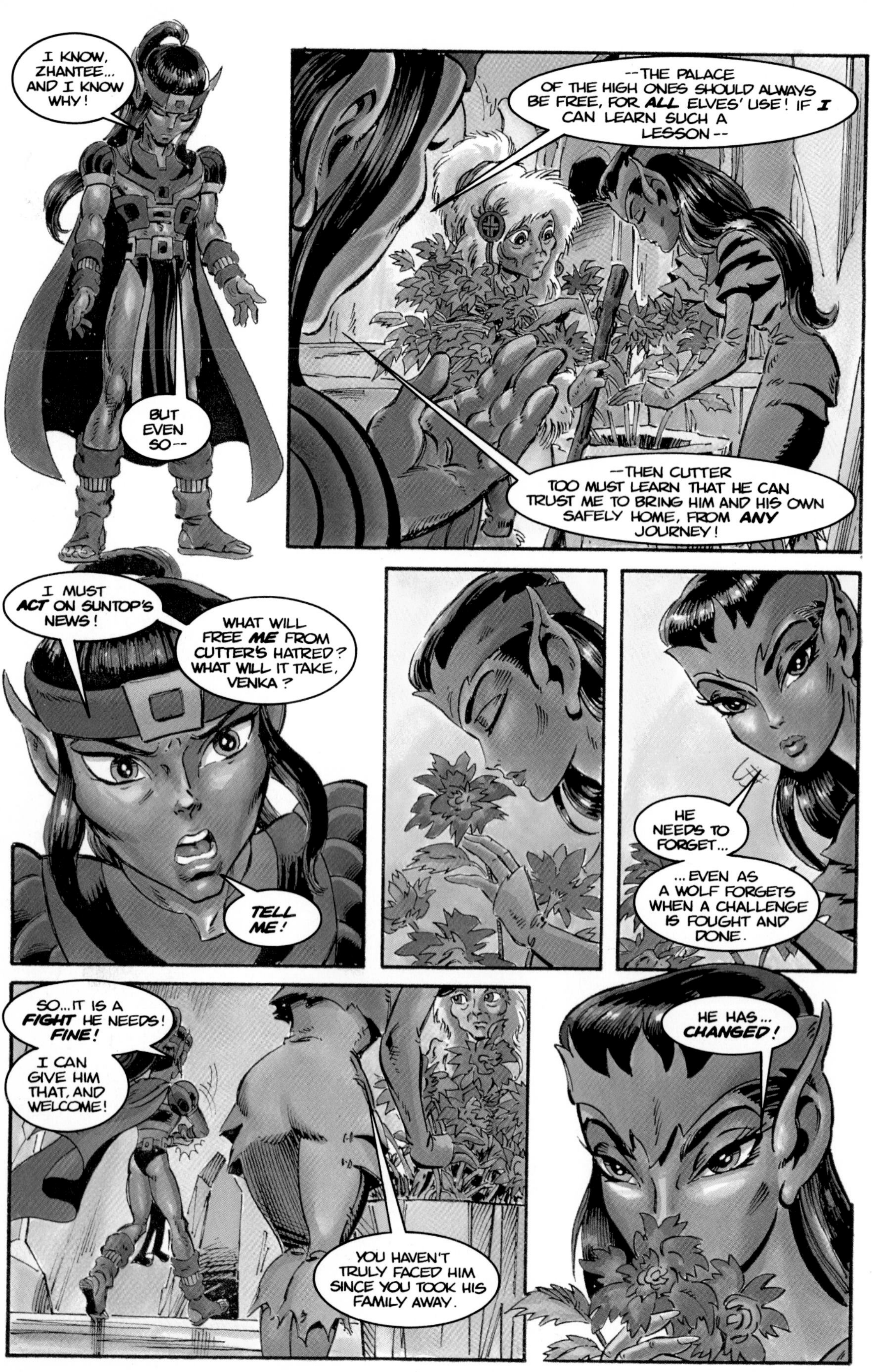
I KNOW, ZHANTEE... AND I KNOW WHY!
BUT EVEN SO--
--THE PALACE OF THE HIGH ONES SHOULD ALWAYS BE FREE, FOR ALL ELVES' USE! IF I CAN LEARN SUCH A LESSON--
--THEN CUTTER TOO MUST LEARN THAT HE CAN TRUST ME TO BRING HIM AND HIS OWN SAFELY HOME, FROM ANY JOURNEY!
I MUST ACT ON SUNTOP'S NEWS!
WHAT WILL FREE ME FROM CUTTER'S HATRED? WHAT WILL IT TAKE, VENKA?
TELL ME!
HE NEEDS TO FORGET...
...EVEN AS A WOLF FORGETS WHEN A CHALLENGE IS FOUGHT AND DONE.
SO...IT IS A FIGHT HE NEEDS! FINE!
I CAN GIVE HIM THAT, AND WELCOME!
YOU HAVEN'T TRULY FACED HIM SINCE YOU TOOK HIS FAMILY AWAY.
HE HAS... CHANGED!

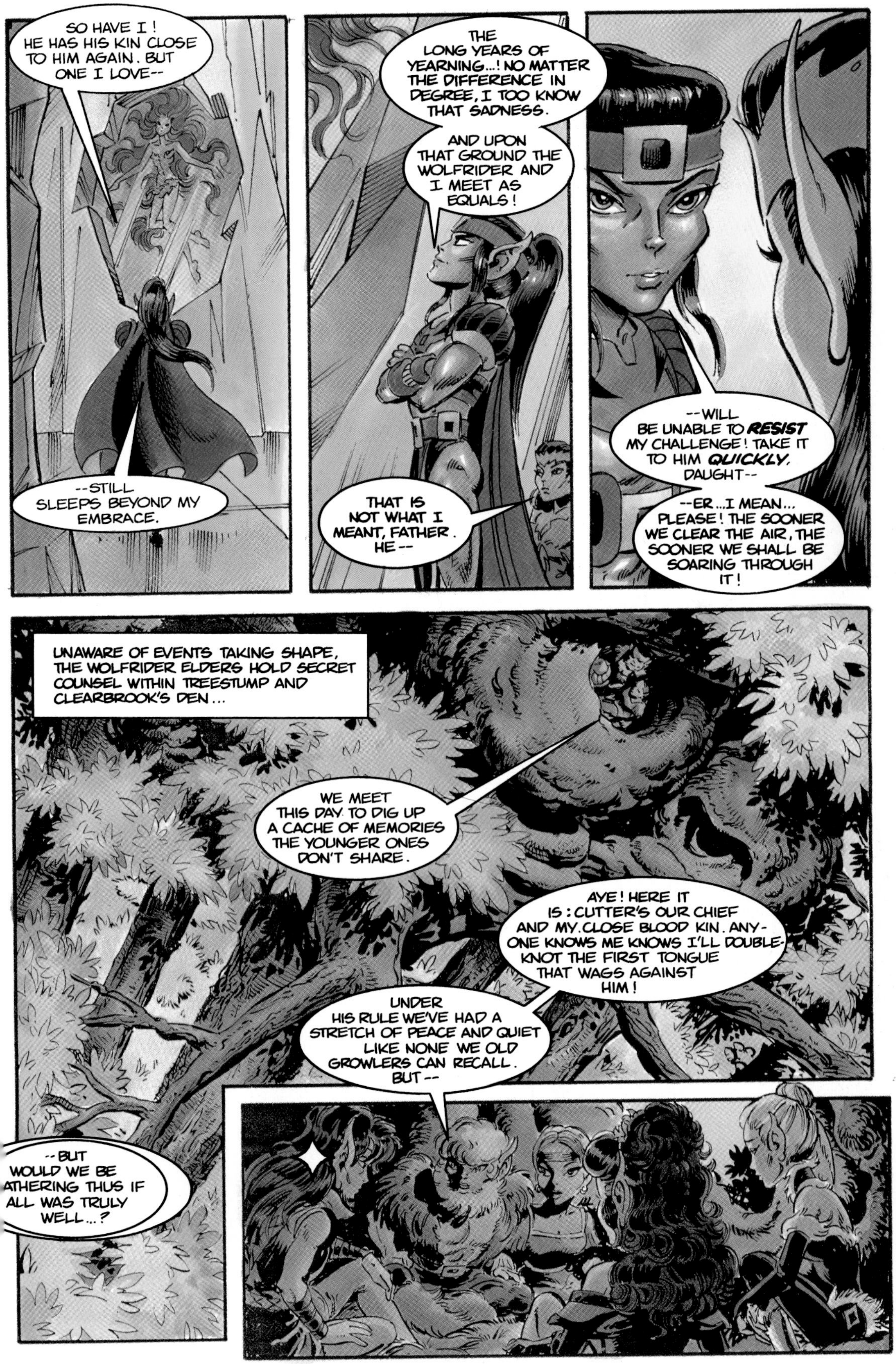
SO HAVE I! HE HAS HIS KIN CLOSE TO HIM AGAIN. BUT ONE I LOVE--
--STILL SLEEPS BEYOND MY EMBRACE.
THE LONG YEARS OF YEARNING...! NO MATTER THE DIFFERENCE IN DEGREE, I TOO KNOW THAT SADNESS.
AND UPON THAT GROUND THE WOLFRIDER AND I MEET AS EQUALS!
THAT IS NOT WHAT I MEANT, FATHER. HE--
--WILL BE UNABLE TO RESIST MY CHALLENGE! TAKE IT TO HIM QUICKLY, DAUGHT--
--ER...I MEAN... PLEASE! THE SOONER WE CLEAR THE AIR, THE SOONER WE SHALL BE SOARING THROUGH IT!
UNAWARE OF EVENTS TAKING SHAPE, THE WOLFRIDER ELDERS HOLD SECRET COUNSEL WITHIN TREESTUMP AND CLEARBROOK'S DEN...
WE MEET THIS DAY TO DIG UP A CACHE OF MEMORIES THE YOUNGER ONES DON'T SHARE.
AYE! HERE IT IS: CUTTER'S OUR CHIEF AND MY CLOSE BLOOD KIN. ANY-ONE KNOWS ME KNOWS I'LL DOUBLE-KNOT THE FIRST TONGUE THAT WAGS AGAINST HIM!
UNDER HIS RULE WE'VE HAD A STRETCH OF PEACE AND QUIET LIKE NONE WE OLD GROWLERS CAN RECALL. BUT--
--BUT WOULD WE BE ATHERING THUS IF ALL WAS TRULY WELL...?

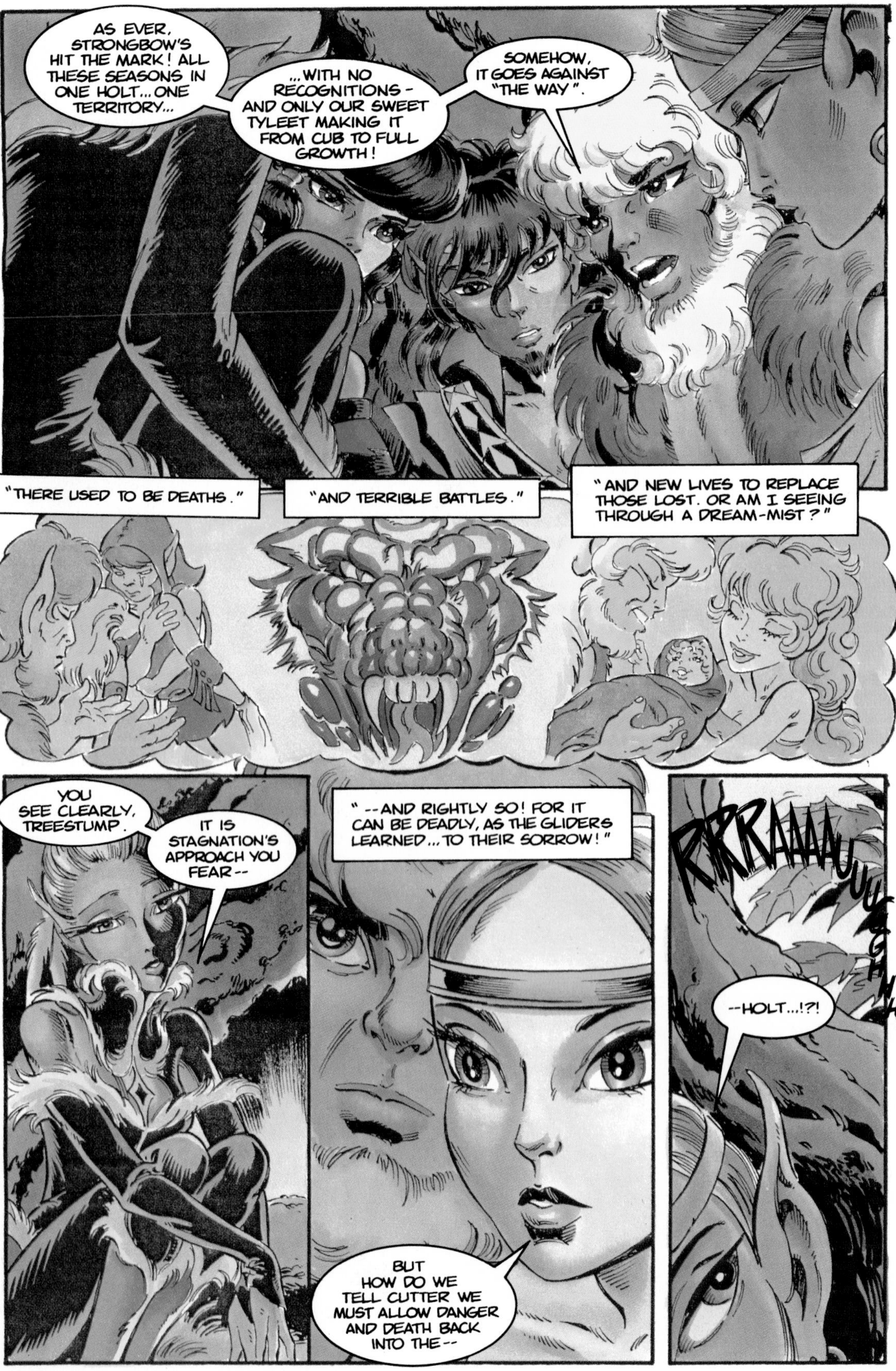
AS EVER, STRONGBOW'S HIT THE MARK! ALL THESE SEASONS IN ONE HOLT... ONE TERRITORY...
...WITH NO RECOGNITIONS - AND ONLY OUR SWEET TYLEET MAKING IT FROM CUB TO FULL GROWTH!
SOMEHOW, IT GOES AGAINST "THE WAY".
"THERE USED TO BE DEATHS."
"AND TERRIBLE BATTLES."
"AND NEW LIVES TO REPLACE THOSE LOST. OR AM I SEEING THROUGH A DREAM-MIST?"
YOU SEE CLEARLY, TREESTUMP.
IT IS STAGNATION'S APPROACH YOU FEAR--
" --AND RIGHTLY SO! FOR IT CAN BE DEADLY, AS THE GLIDERS LEARNED... TO THEIR SORROW!"
BUT HOW DO WE TELL CUTTER WE MUST ALLOW DANGER AND DEATH BACK INTO THE--
RRRRAAAAUUUGHHH!!
--HOLT...!?!

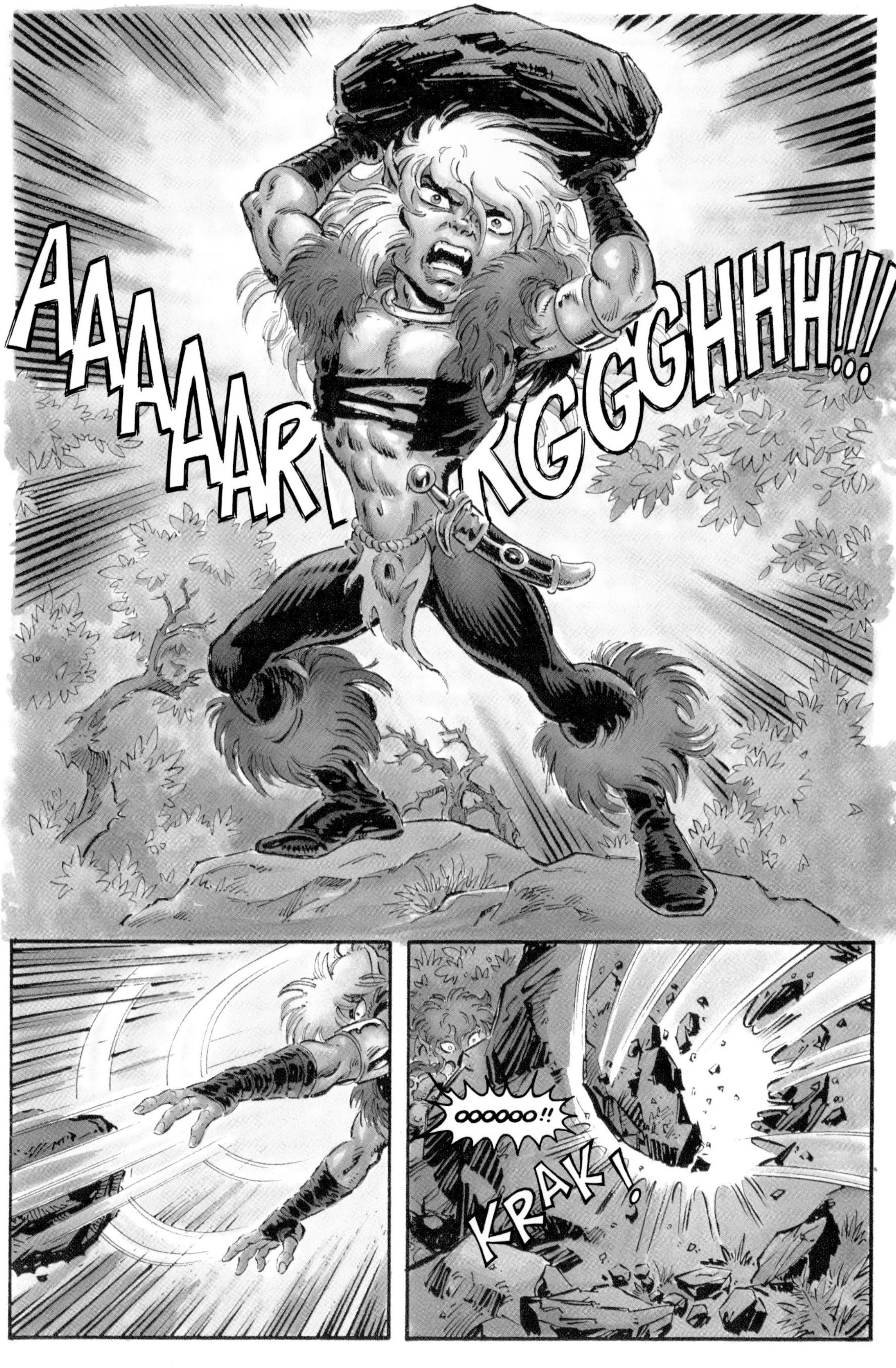
AAAAARRRGGGHHH!!!
OOOOOO!!
KRAK!

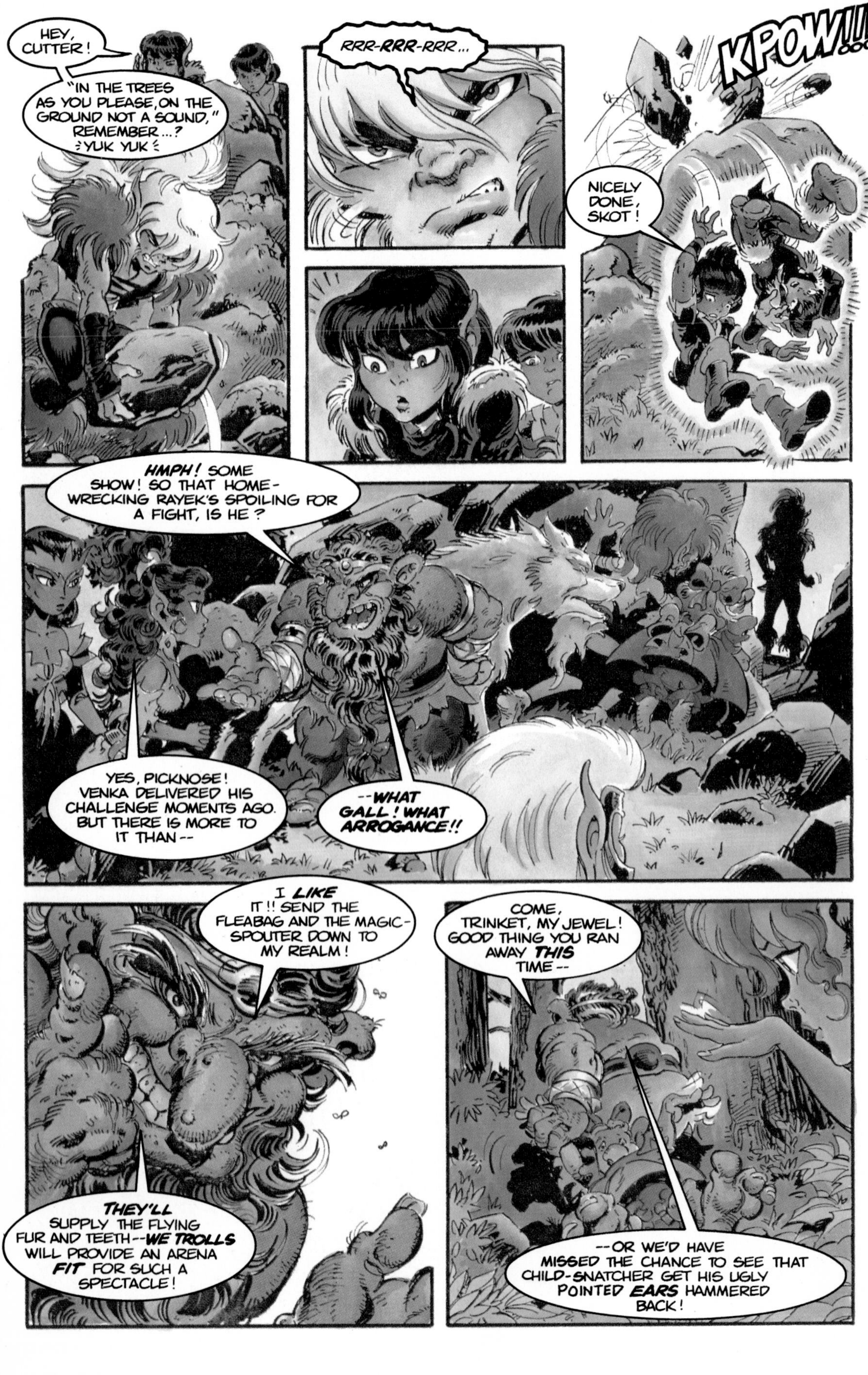
HEY, CUTTER!
"IN THE TREES AS YOU PLEASE, ON THE GROUND NOT A SOUND," REMEMBER...? YUK YUK
RRR-RRR-RRR...
KPOW!!!!
NICELY DONE, SKOT!
HMPH! SOME SHOW! SO THAT HOME-WRECKING RAYEK'S SPOILING FOR A FIGHT, IS HE?
YES, PICKNOSE! VENKA DELIVERED HIS CHALLENGE MOMENTS AGO. BUT THERE IS MORE TO IT THAN--
--WHAT GALL! WHAT ARROGANCE!!
I LIKE IT!! SEND THE FLEABAG AND THE MAGIC-SPOUTER DOWN TO MY REALM!
THEY'LL SUPPLY THE FLYING FUR AND TEETH--WE TROLLS WILL PROVIDE AN ARENA FIT FOR SUCH A SPECTACLE!
COME, TRINKET, MY JEWEL! GOOD THING YOU RAN AWAY THIS TIME--
--OR WE'D HAVE MISSED THE CHANCE TO SEE THAT CHILD-SNATCHER GET HIS UGLY POINTED EARS HAMMERED BACK!

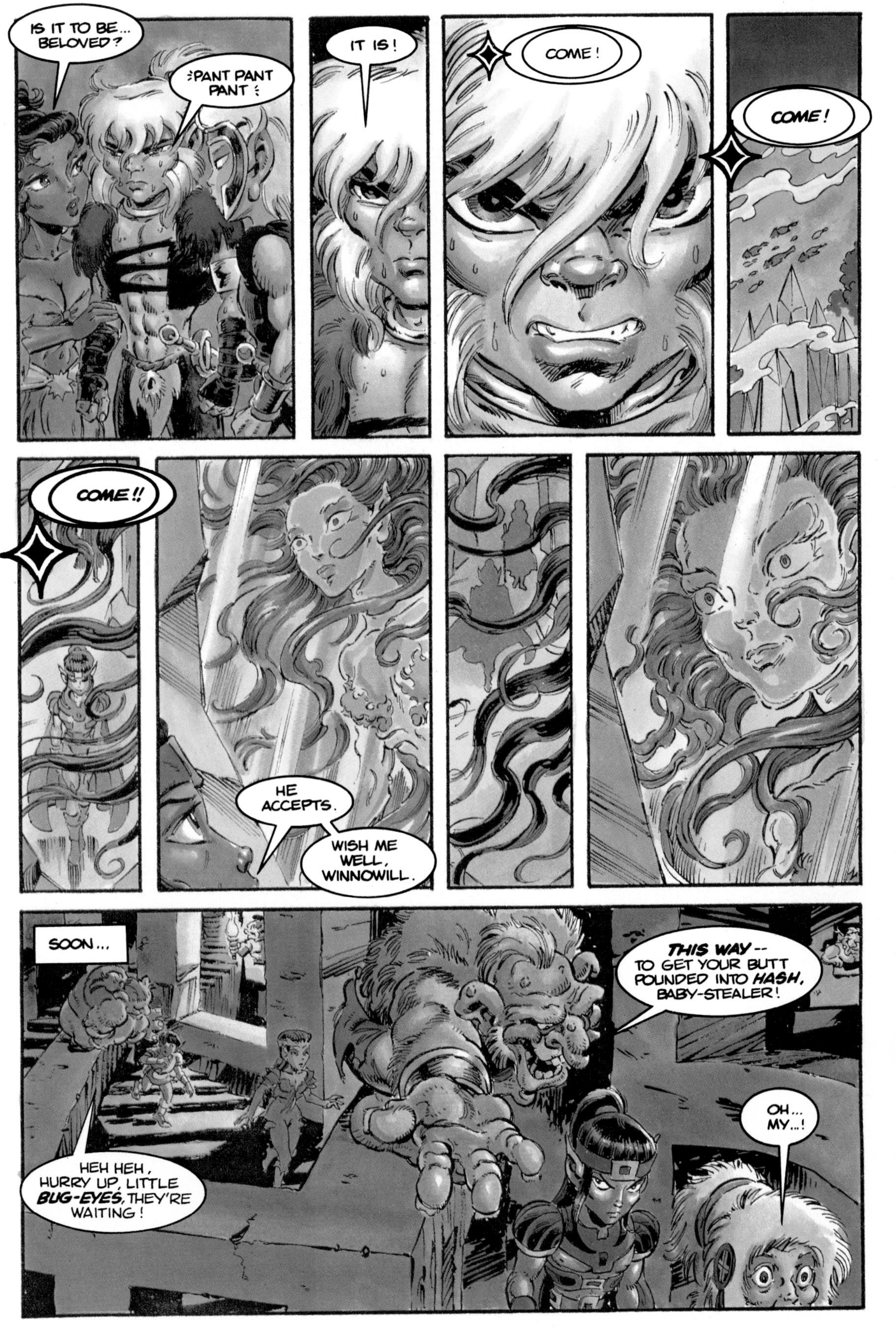

IS IT TO BE... BELOVED?
PANT PANT PANT
IT IS!
COME!
COME!
COME!!
HE ACCEPTS.
WISH ME WELL, WINNOWILL.
SOON...
THIS WAY -- TO GET YOUR BUTT POUNDED INTO HASH, BABY-STEALER!
HEH HEH, HURRY UP, LITTLE BUG-EYES, THEY'RE WAITING!
OH... MY...!

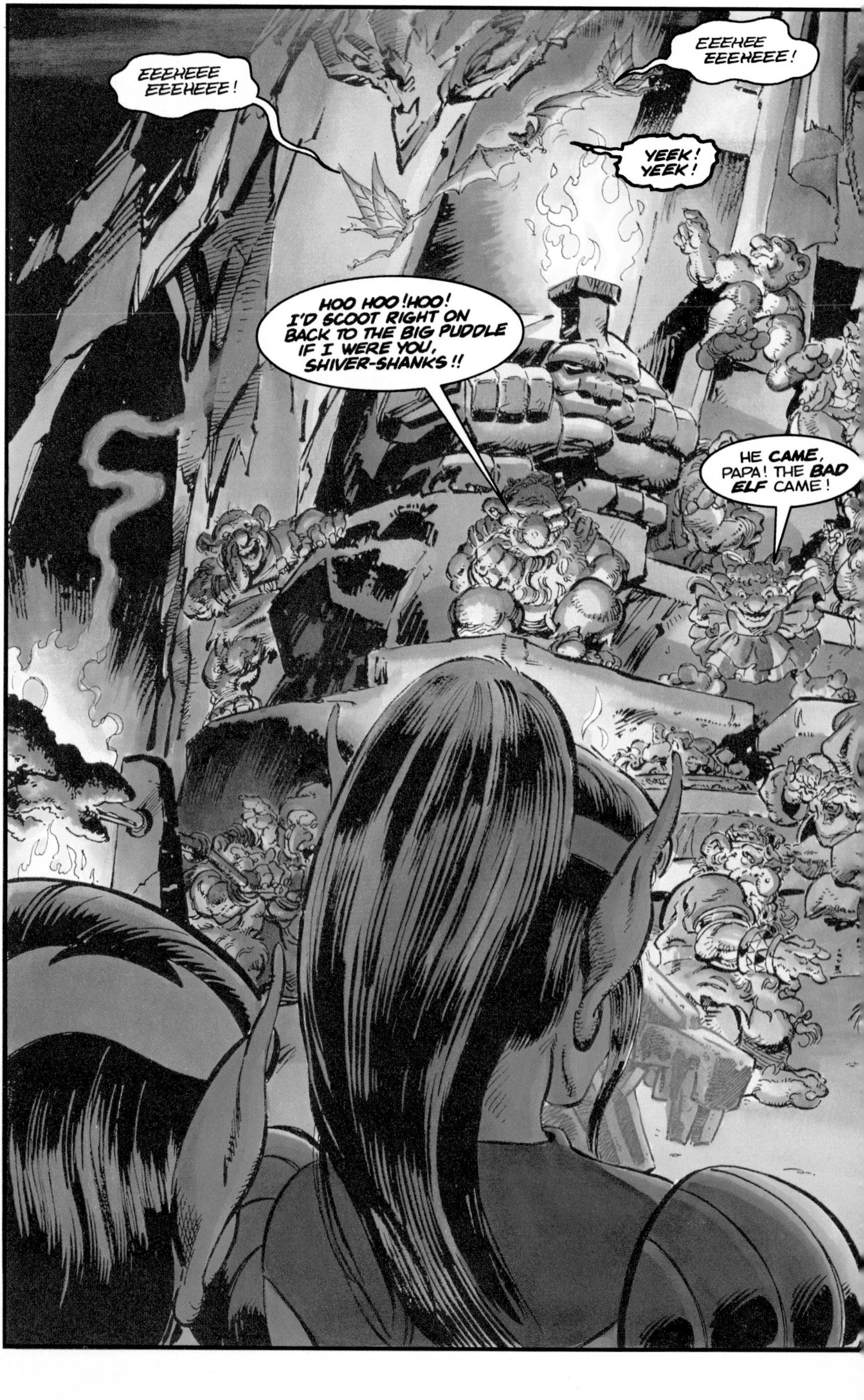
EEEHEEE EEEHEEE!
EEEHEE EEEHEEE!
YEEK! YEEK!
HOO HOO! HOO! I'D SCOOT RIGHT ON BACK TO THE BIG PUDDLE IF I WERE YOU, SHIVER-SHANKS!!
HE CAME, PAPA! THE BAD ELF CAME!

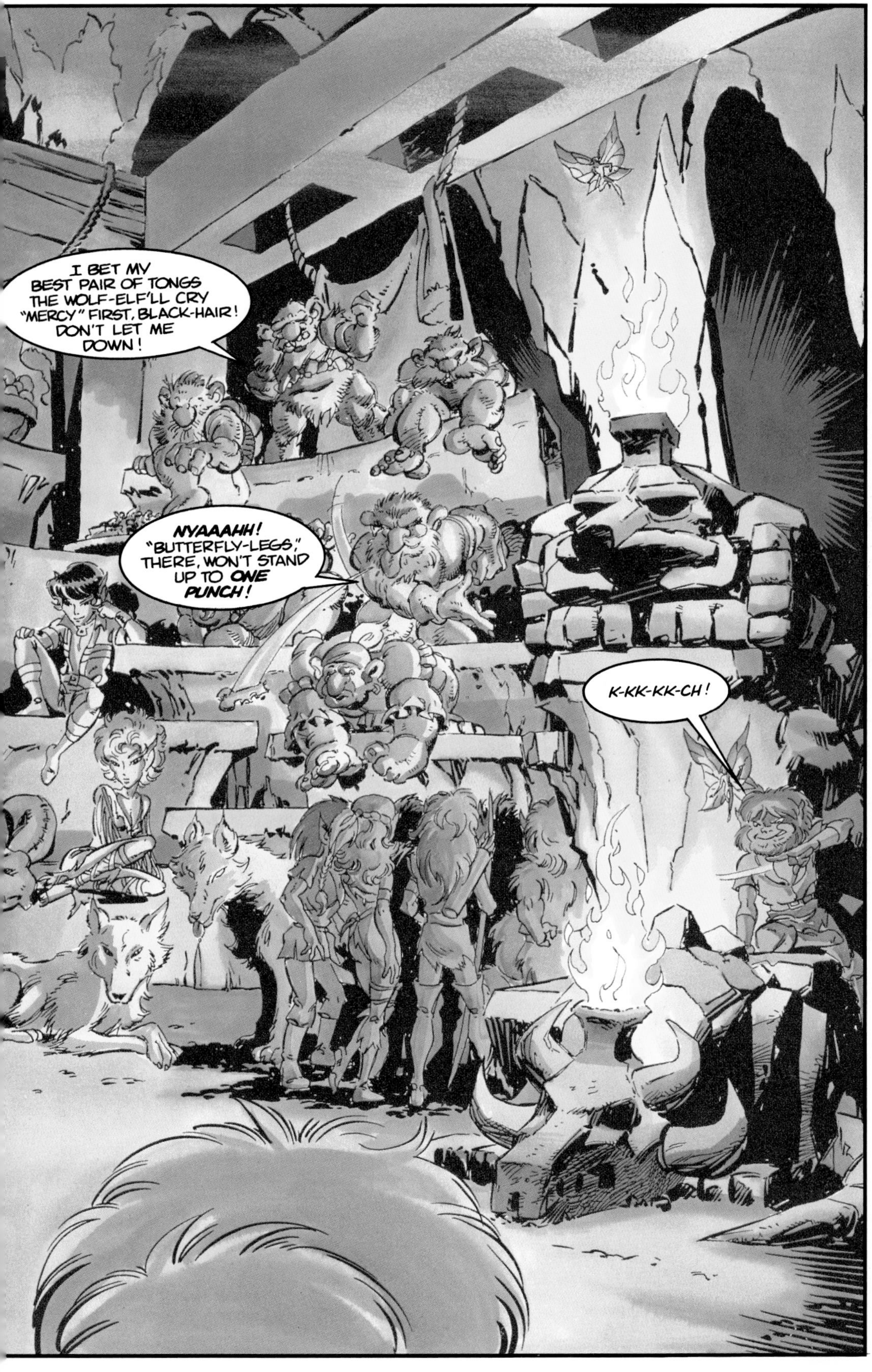
I BET MY BEST PAIR OF TONGS THE WOLF-ELF'LL CRY "MERCY" FIRST, BLACK-HAIR! DON'T LET ME DOWN!
NYAAAHH! "BUTTERFLY-LEGS," THERE, WON'T STAND UP TO ONE PUNCH!
K-KK-KK-CH!

THE WOLFRIDERS... EVEN THEIR WOLVES ARE HERE --

"-- BUT WHERE IS...?"

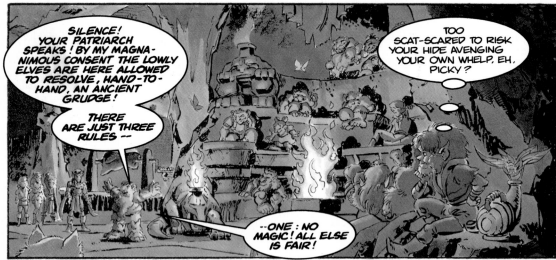

SILENCE! YOUR PATRIARCH SPEAKS! BY MY MAGNANIMOUS CONSENT THE LOWLY ELVES ARE HERE ALLOWED TO RESOLVE, HAND-TO-HAND, AN ANCIENT GRUDGE!

THERE ARE JUST THREE RULES --

TOO SCAT-SCARED TO RISK YOUR HIDE AVENGING YOUR OWN WHELP, EH, PICKY?

--ONE: NO MAGIC! ALL ELSE IS FAIR!

TWO: NO DYING TO SAVE FACE! BOTH MUST SURVIVE!

THREE: HE THAT FIRST CALLS FOR HEALING --LOSES! AND ONE MUST CALL!

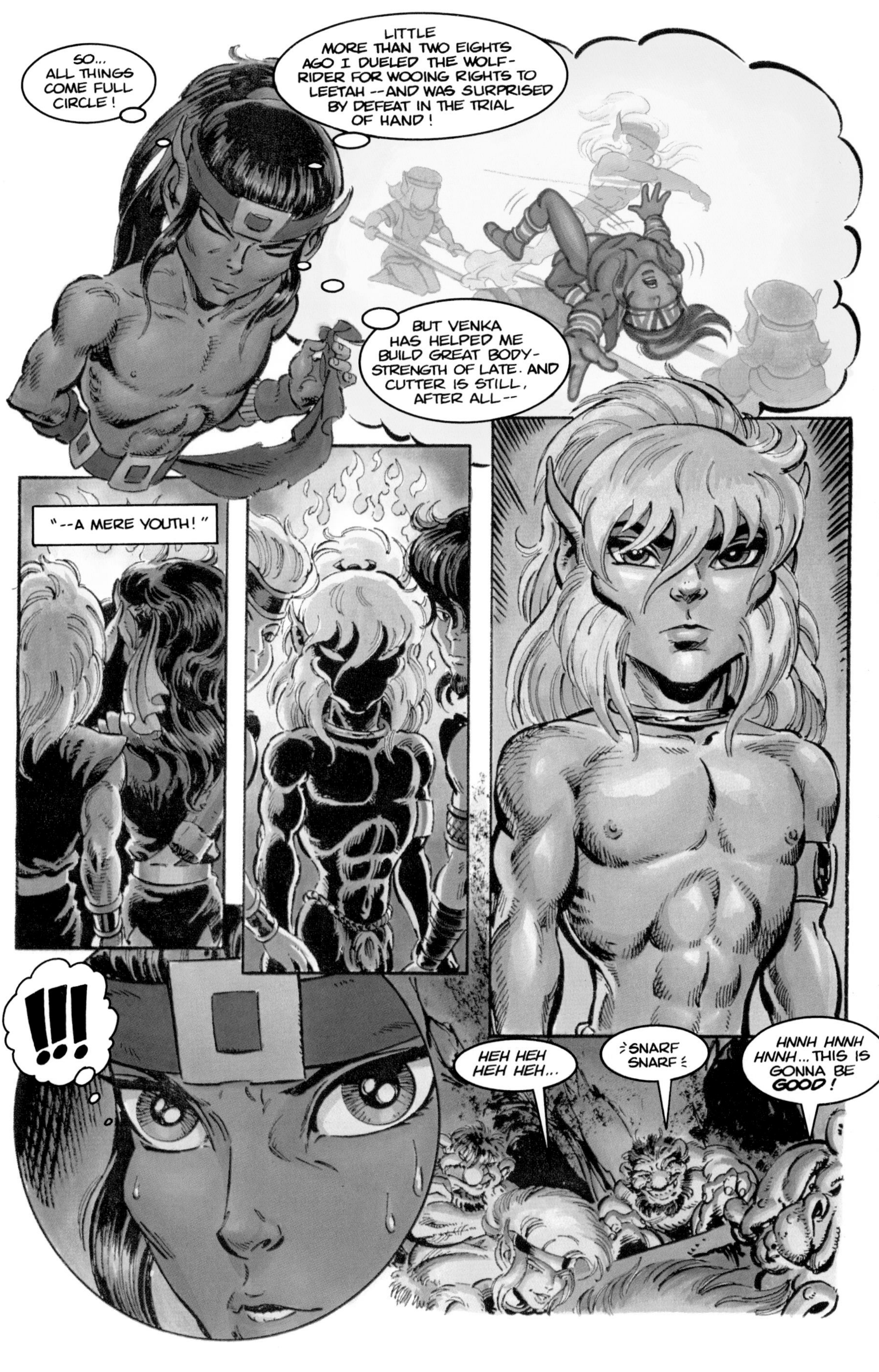
SO... ALL THINGS COME FULL CIRCLE!
LITTLE MORE THAN TWO EIGHTS AGO I DUELED THE WOLF-RIDER FOR WOOING RIGHTS TO LEETAH --AND WAS SURPRISED BY DEFEAT IN THE TRIAL OF HAND!
BUT VENKA HAS HELPED ME BUILD GREAT BODY-STRENGTH OF LATE. AND CUTTER IS STILL, AFTER ALL--
"--A MERE YOUTH!"
!!!
HEH HEH HEH HEH...
SNARF SNARF
HNNH HNNH HNNH... THIS IS GONNA BE GOOD!

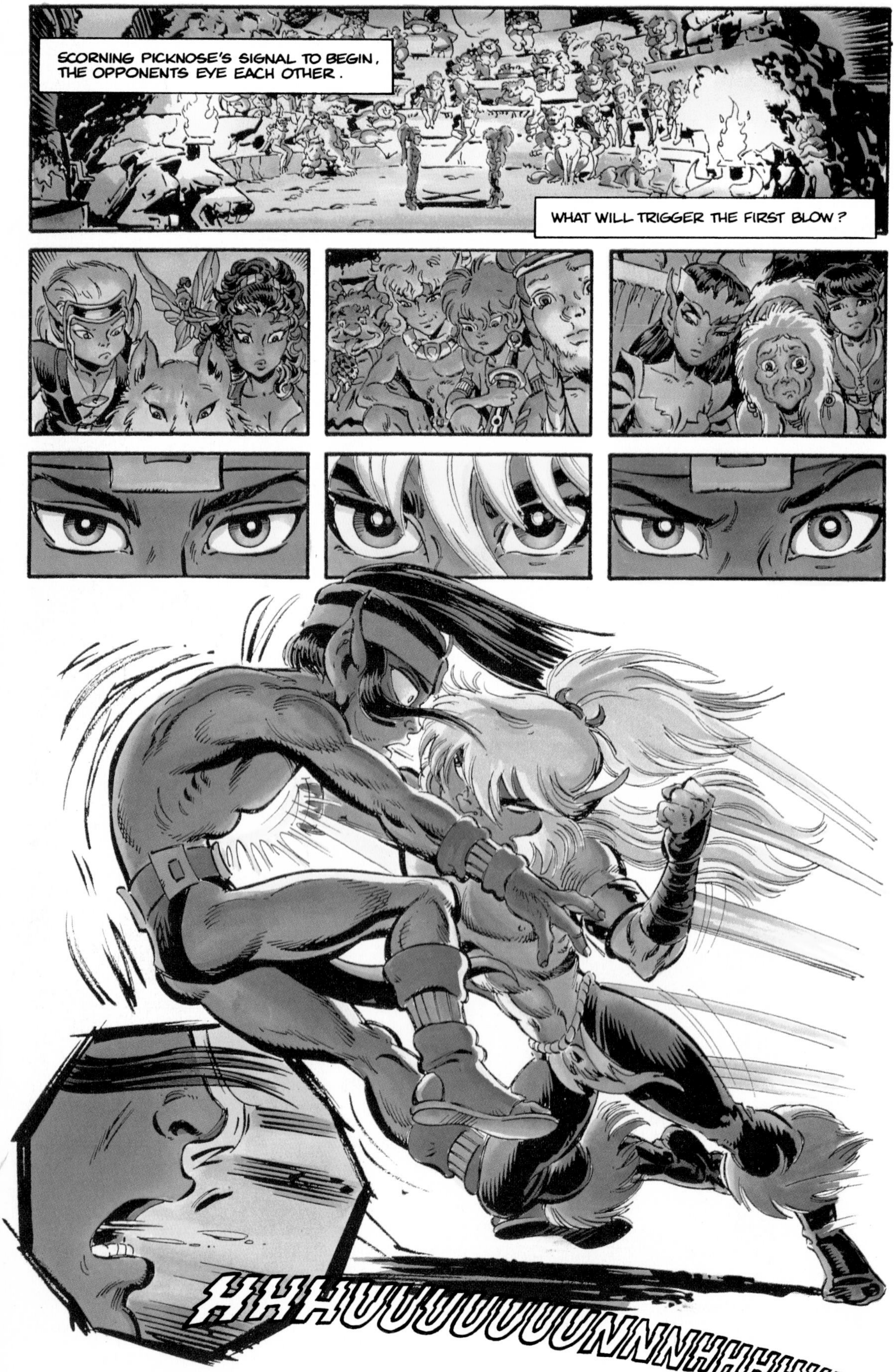
SCORNING PICKNOSE'S SIGNAL TO BEGIN, THE OPPONENTS EYE EACH OTHER.
WHAT WILL TRIGGER THE FIRST BLOW?
HHHUUUUUUUUNNNHHHHHH!!!

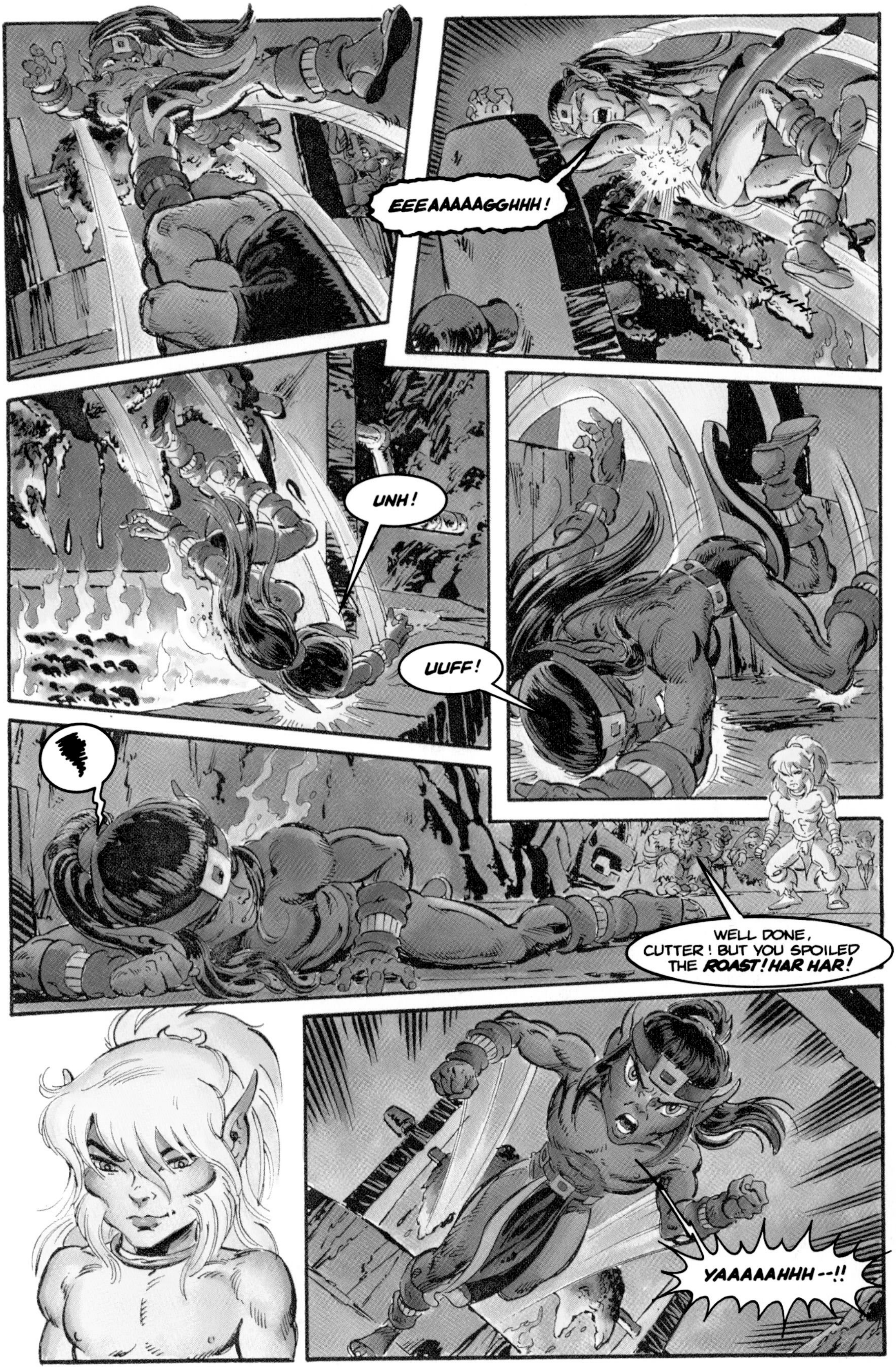
EEEAAAAAGGHHH!
UNH!
UUFF!
WELL DONE, CUTTER! BUT YOU SPOILED THE ROAST! HAR HAR!
YAAAAAHHH--!!

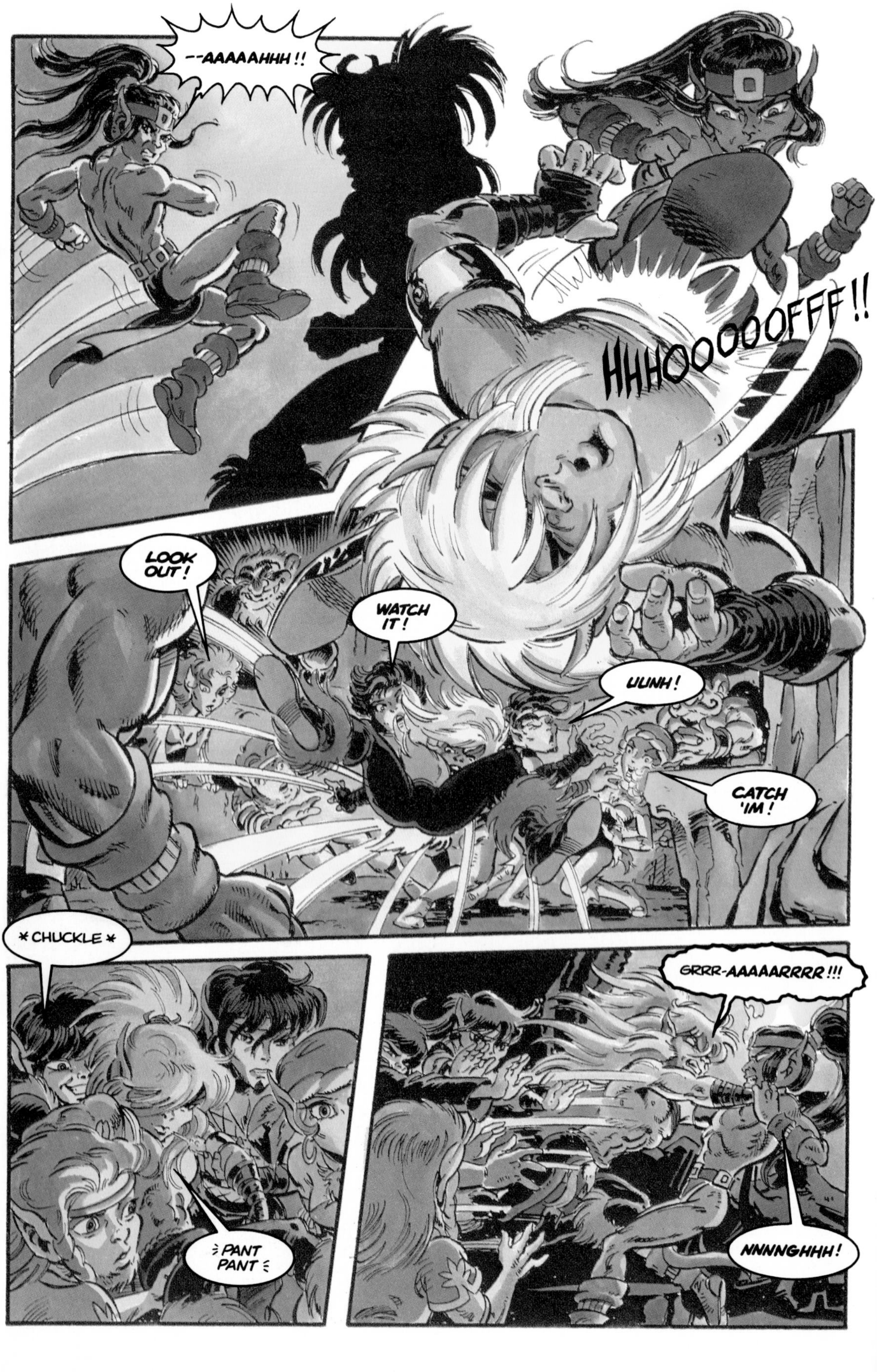
--AAAAAHHH!!
HHHOOOOOOFFF!!
LOOK OUT!
WATCH IT!
UUNH!
CATCH 'IM!
CHUCKLE
PANT PANT
GRRR-AAAAARRRR!!!
NNNNGHHH!

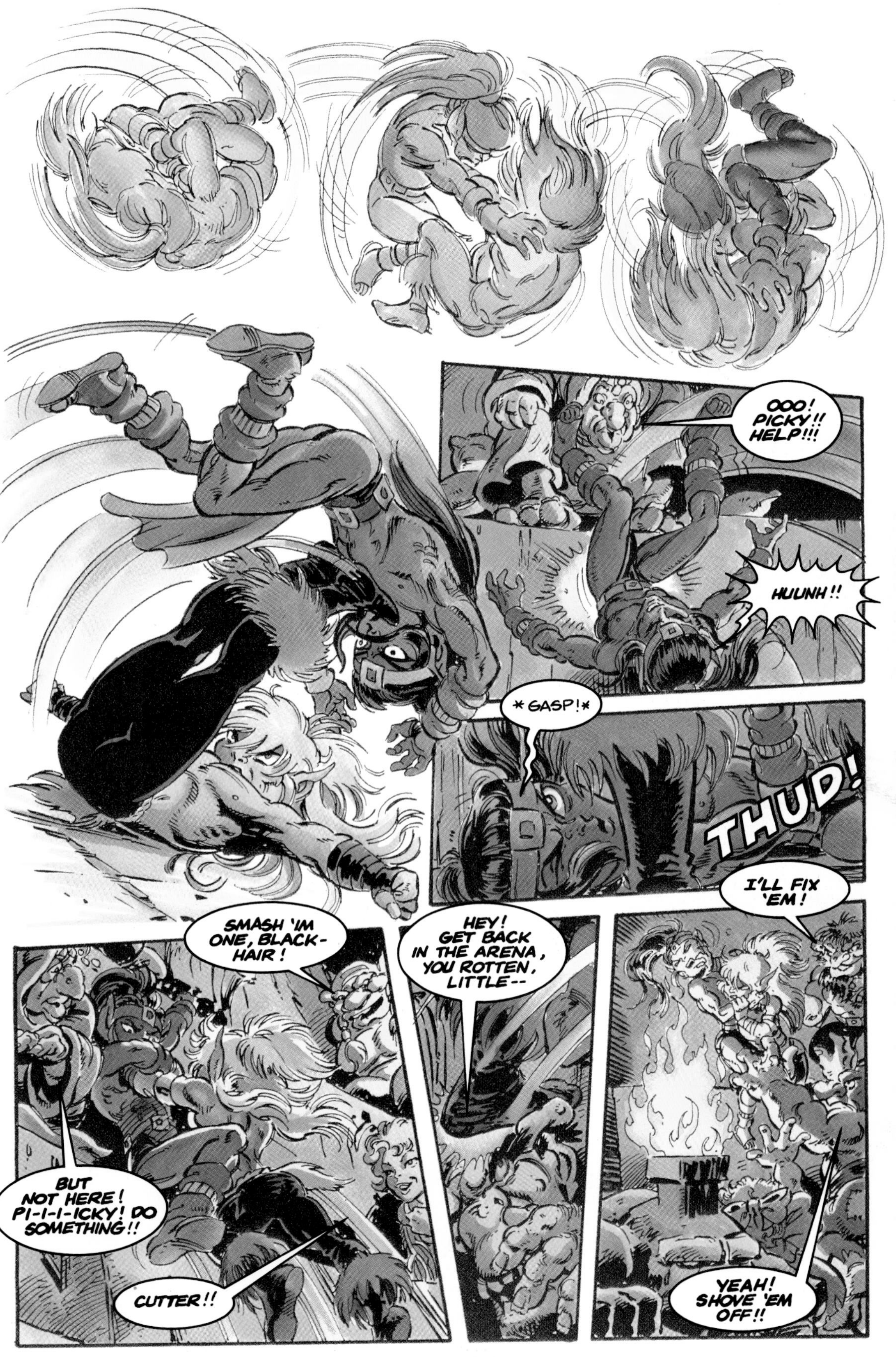
OOO! PICKY!! HELP!!!
HUUNH!!
GASP!
THUD!
SMASH 'IM ONE, BLACK-HAIR!
BUT NOT HERE! PI-I-I-ICKY! DO SOMETHING!!
CUTTER!!
HEY! GET BACK IN THE ARENA, YOU ROTTEN, LITTLE--
I'LL FIX 'EM!
YEAH! SHOVE 'EM OFF!!

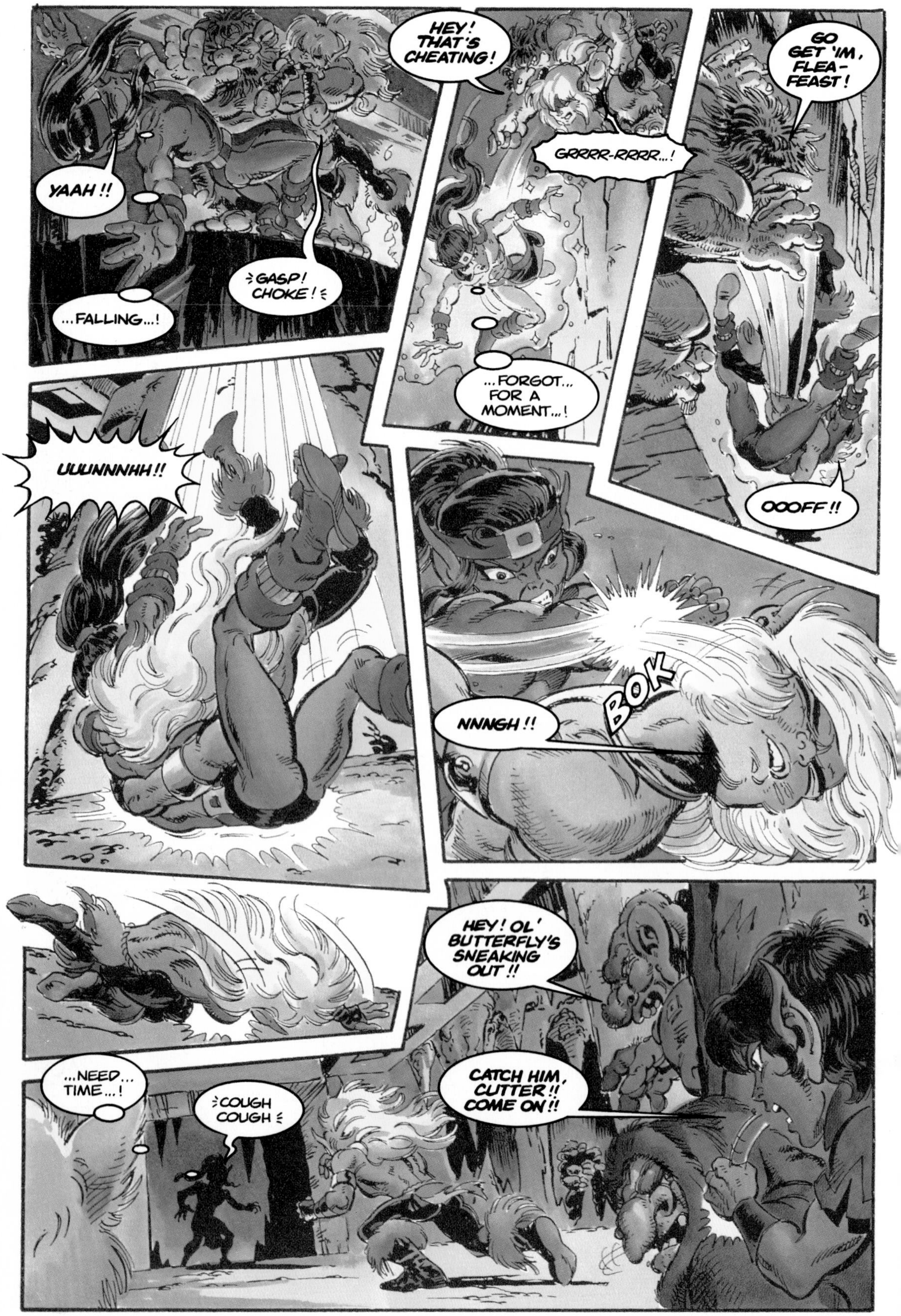
YAAH!!
...FALLING...!
GASP! CHOKE!
HEY! THAT'S CHEATING!
GRRRR-RRRR...!
...FORGOT... FOR A MOMENT...!
GO GET 'IM, FLEA-FEAST!
OOOFF!!
UUUNNNHH!!
BOK
NNNGH!!
HEY! OL' BUTTERFLY'S SNEAKING OUT!!
...NEED... TIME...!
COUGH COUGH
CATCH HIM, CUTTER!! COME ON!!

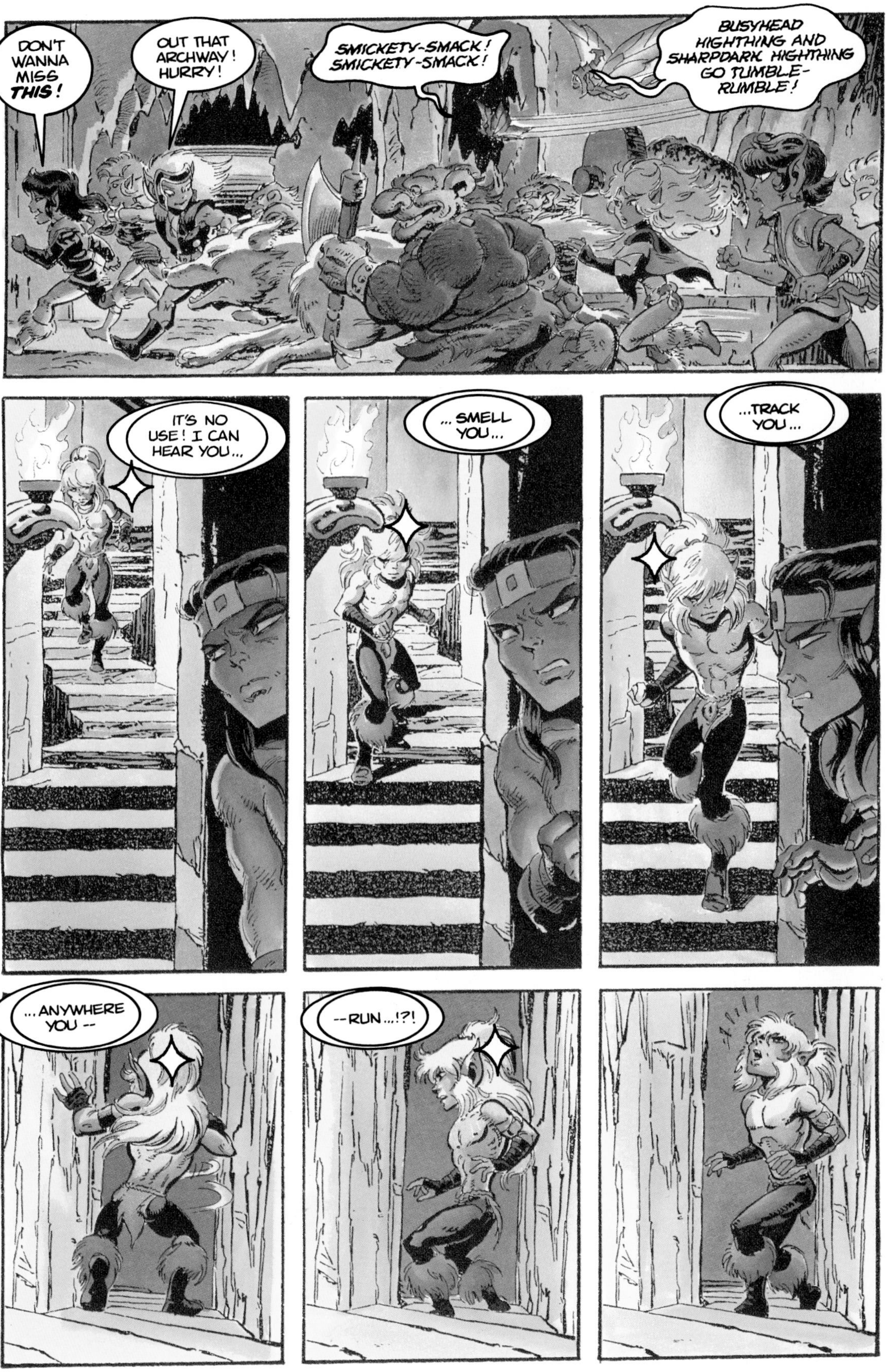

DON'T WANNA MISS THIS!
OUT THAT ARCHWAY! HURRY!
SMICKETY-SMACK! SMICKETY-SMACK!
BUSYHEAD HIGHTHING AND SHARPDARK HIGHTHING GO TUMBLE-RUMBLE!
IT'S NO USE! I CAN HEAR YOU...
... SMELL YOU...
...TRACK YOU...
... ANYWHERE YOU --
--RUN...!?!

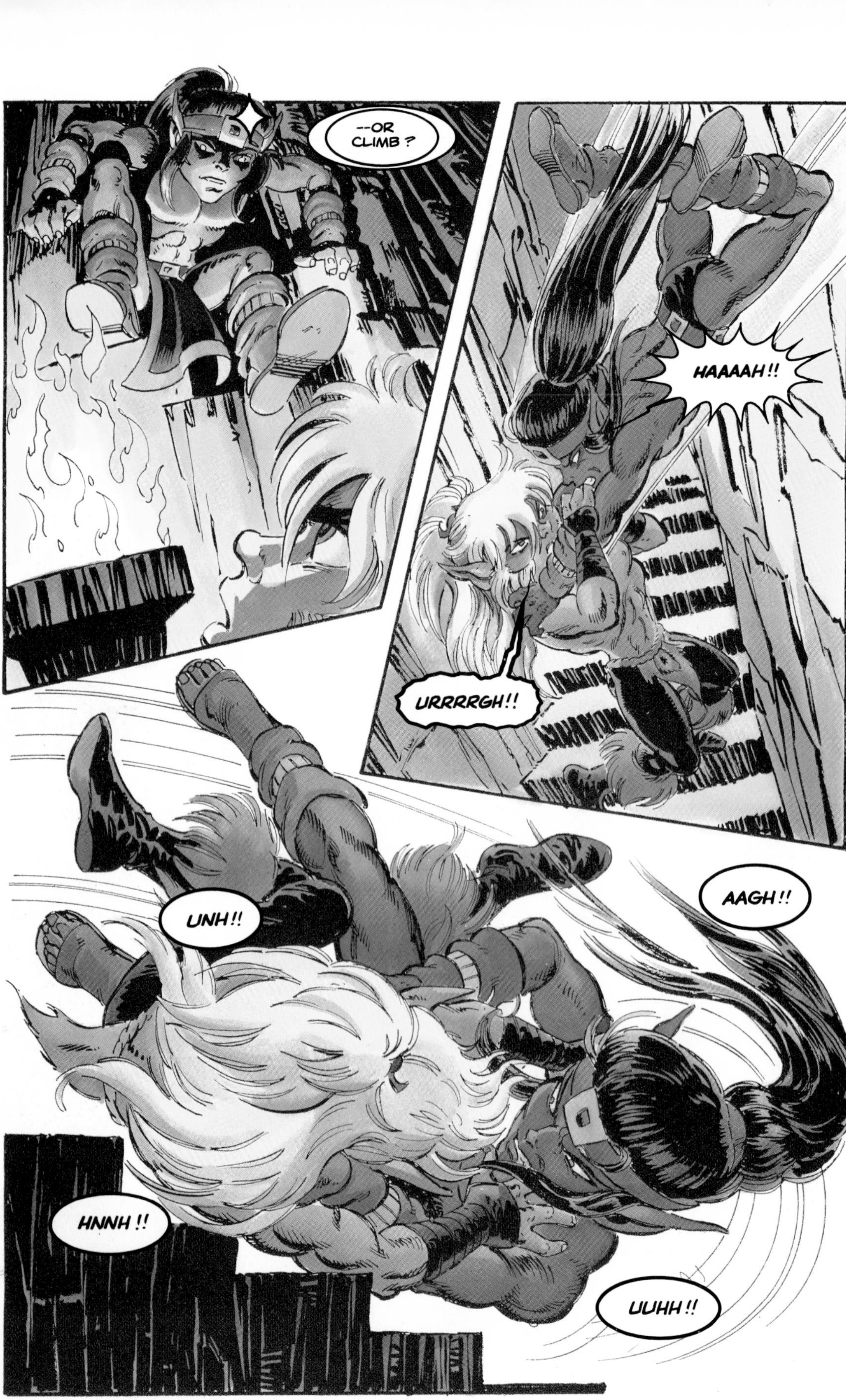
--OR CLIMB?
HAAAAH!!
URRRRGH!!
AAGH!!
UNH!!
HNNH!!
UUHH!!

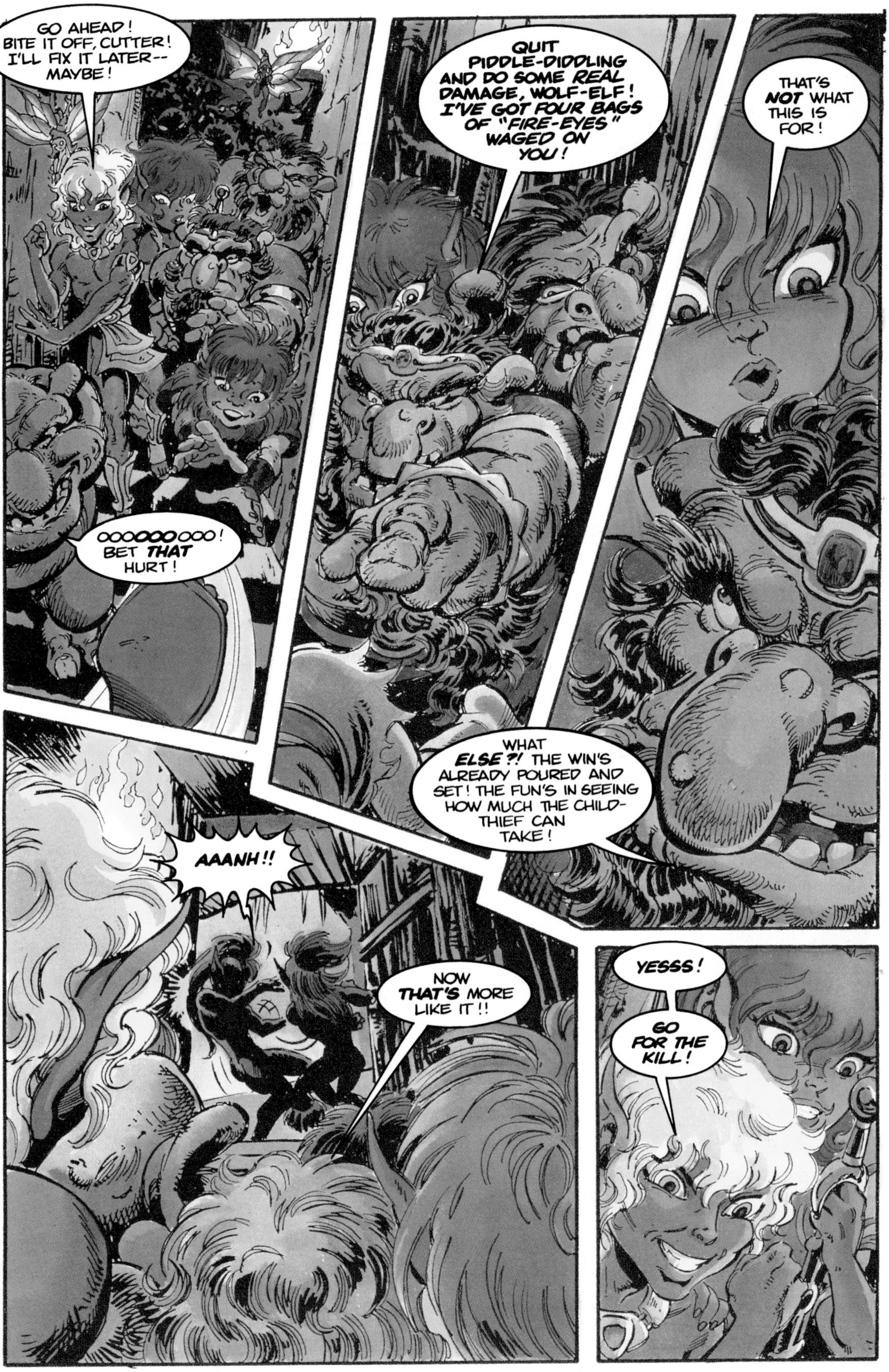
GO AHEAD! BITE IT OFF, CUTTER! I'LL FIX IT LATER-- MAYBE!
OOOOOOOOO! BET THAT HURT!
QUIT PIDDLE-DIDDLING AND DO SOME REAL DAMAGE, WOLF-ELF! I'VE GOT FOUR BAGS OF "FIRE-EYES" WAGED ON YOU!
THAT'S NOT WHAT THIS IS FOR!
WHAT ELSE?! THE WIN'S ALREADY POURED AND SET! THE FUN'S IN SEEING HOW MUCH THE CHILD-THIEF CAN TAKE!
AAANH!!
NOW THAT'S MORE LIKE IT!!
YESSS!
GO FOR THE KILL!

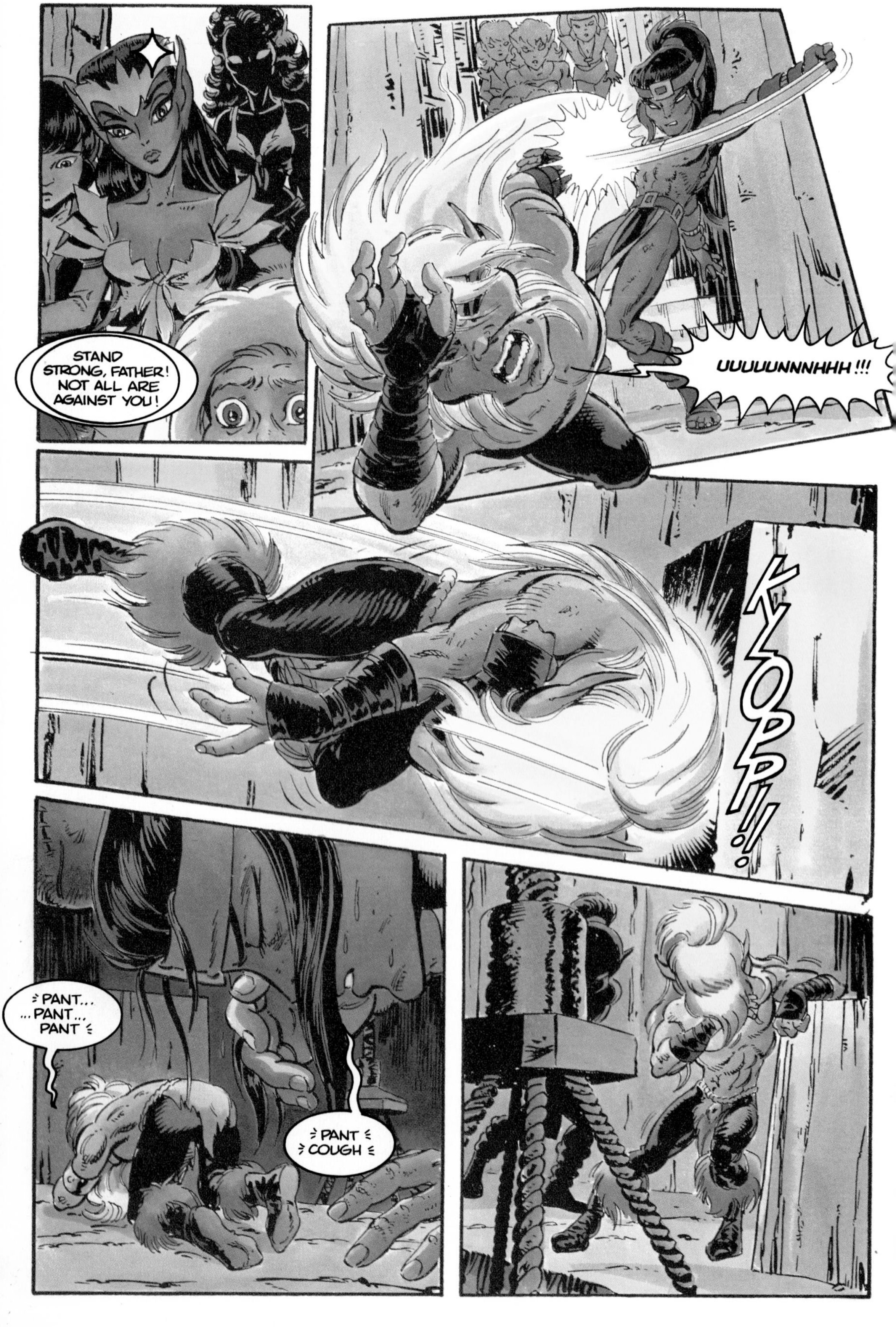
STAND STRONG, FATHER! NOT ALL ARE AGAINST YOU!
UUUUUNNNHHH!!!
KLOPP!!!
PANT... ...PANT..., PANT
PANT COUGH

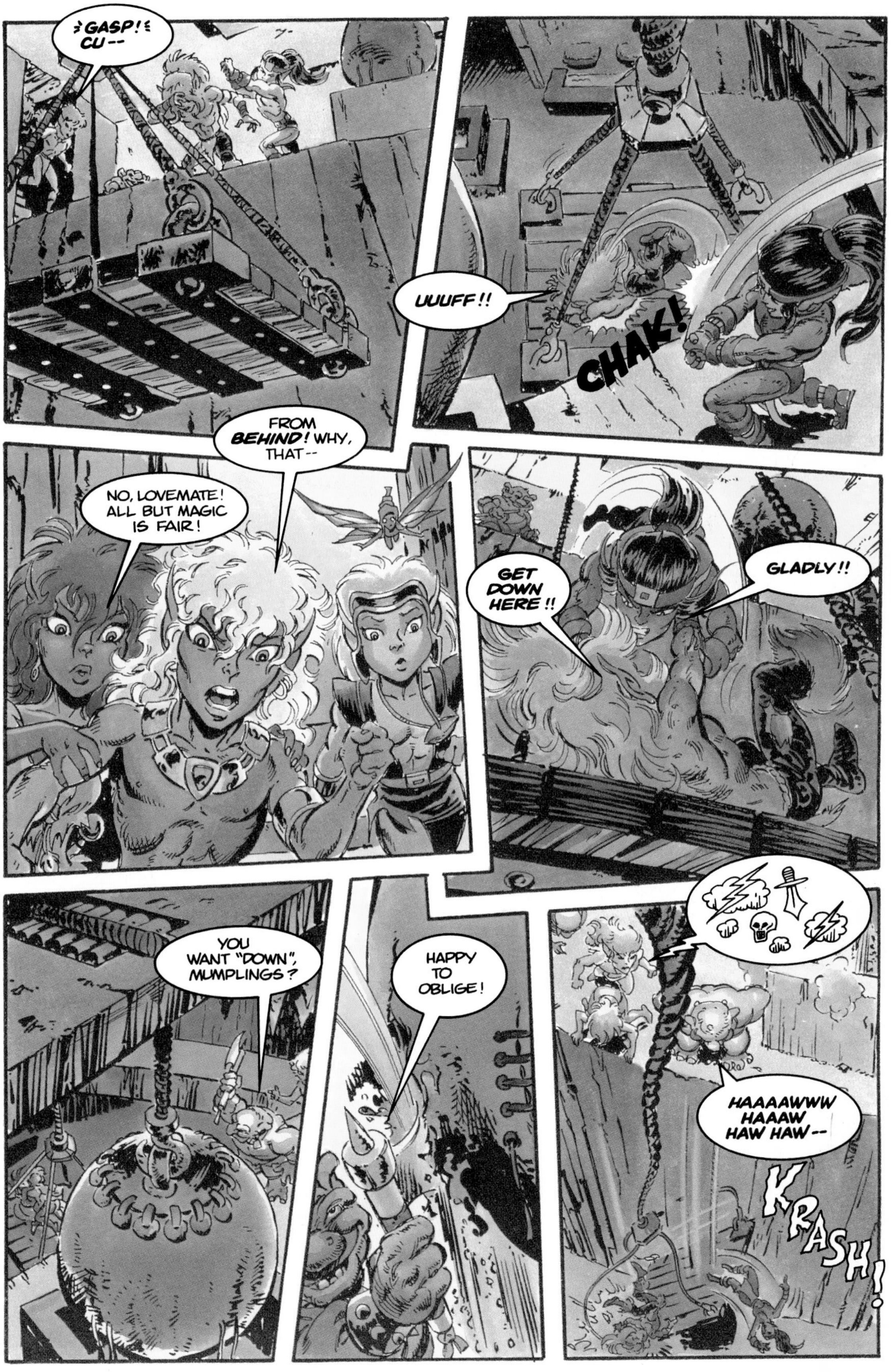
GASP! CU--
UUUFF!!
CHAK!
FROM BEHIND! WHY, THAT--
NO, LOVEMATE! ALL BUT MAGIC IS FAIR!
GET DOWN HERE!!
GLADLY!!
YOU WANT "DOWN", MUMPLINGS?
HAPPY TO OBLIGE!
HAAAAWWW HAAAW HAW HAW--
KRASH!

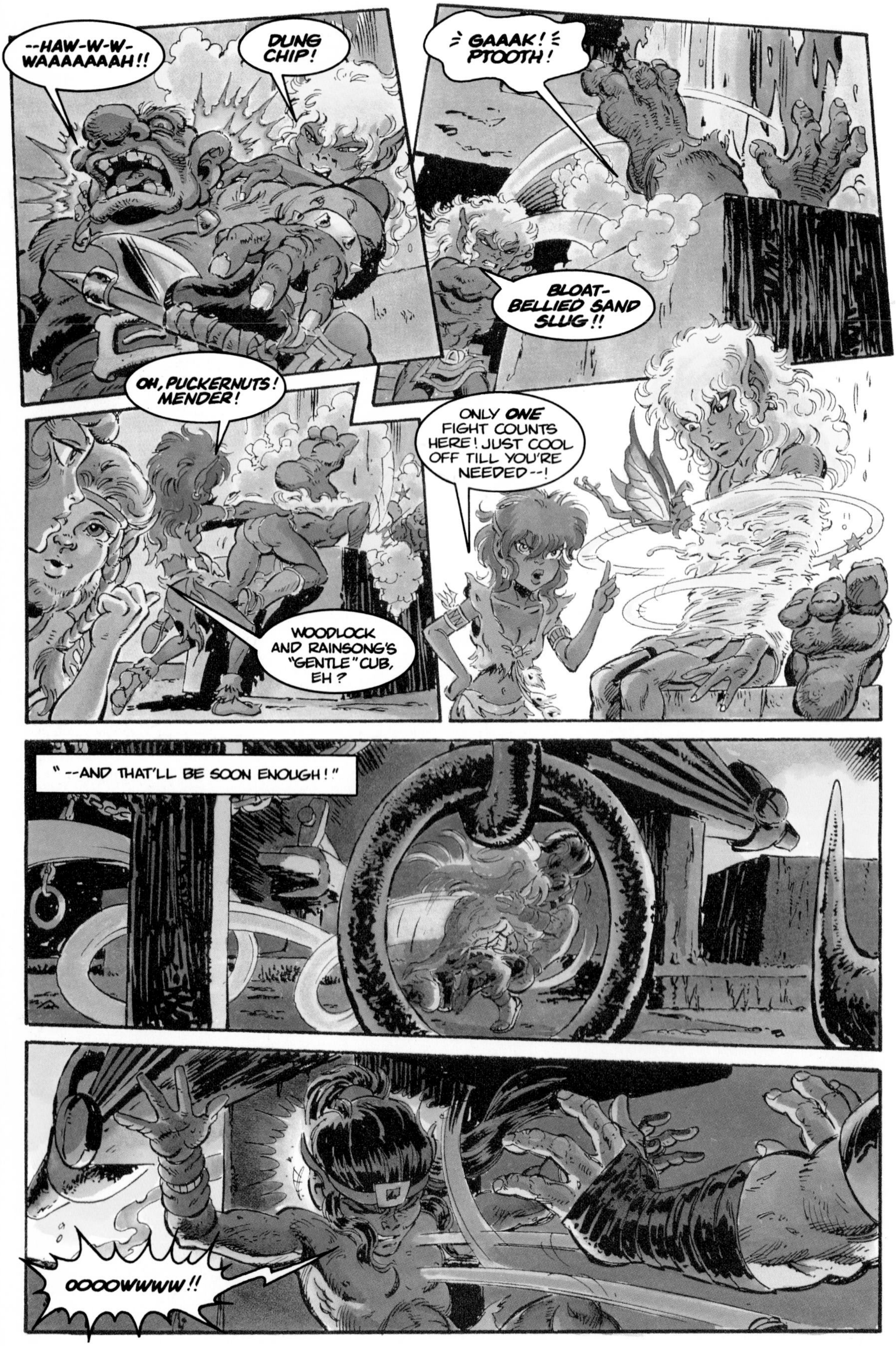
--HAW-W-W-WAAAAAAAH!!
DUNG CHIP!
GAAAK! PTOOTH!
BLOAT-BELLIED SAND SLUG!!
OH, PUCKERNUTS! MENDER!
WOODLOCK AND RAINSONG'S "GENTLE" CUB, EH?
ONLY ONE FIGHT COUNTS HERE! JUST COOL OFF TILL YOU'RE NEEDED--!
"--AND THAT'LL BE SOON ENOUGH!"
OOOOWWWW!!

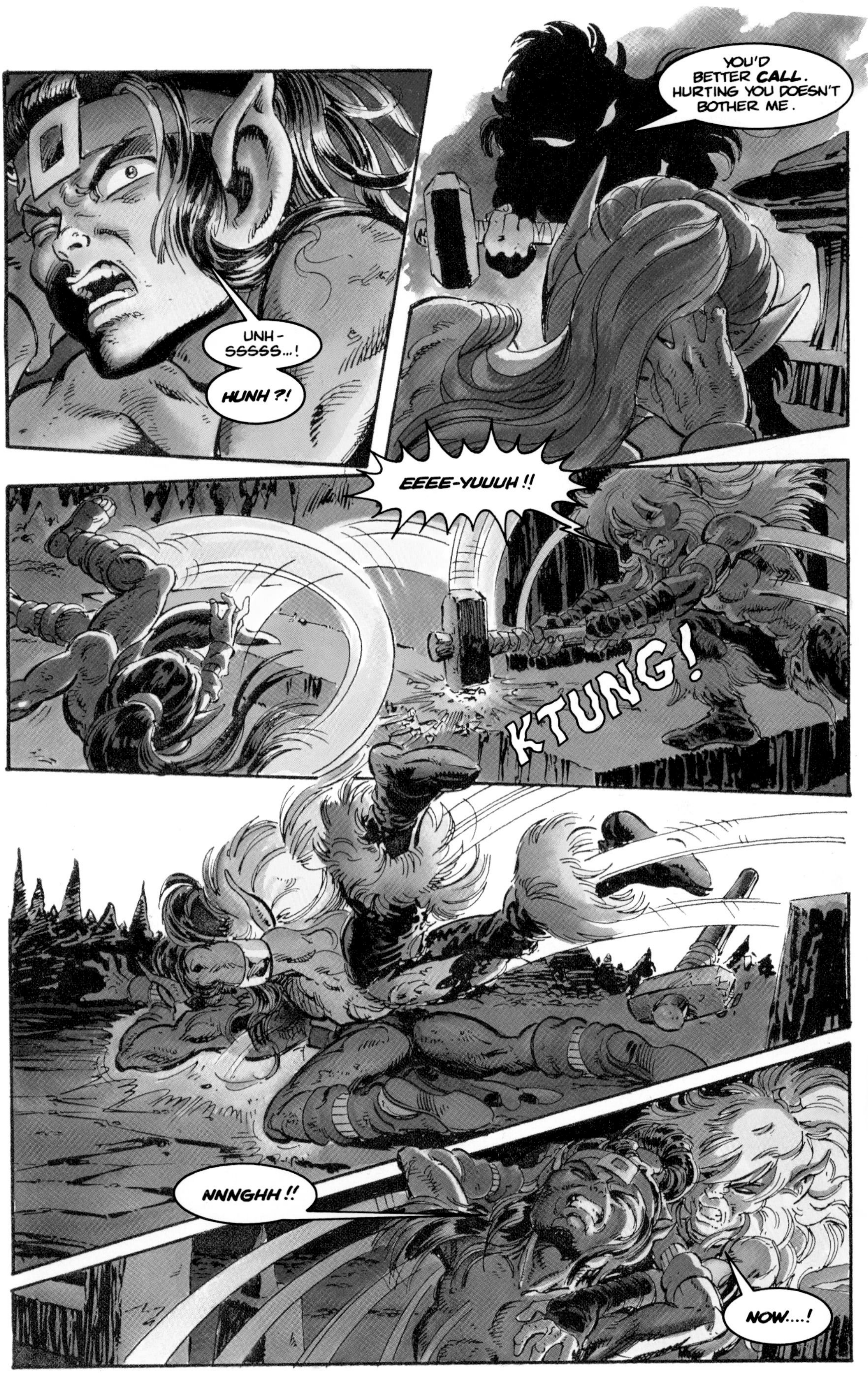
YOU'D BETTER CALL. HURTING YOU DOESN'T BOTHER ME.
UNH-SSSSS...!
HUNH?!
EEEE-YUUUH!!
KTUNG!
NNNGHH!!
NOW....!

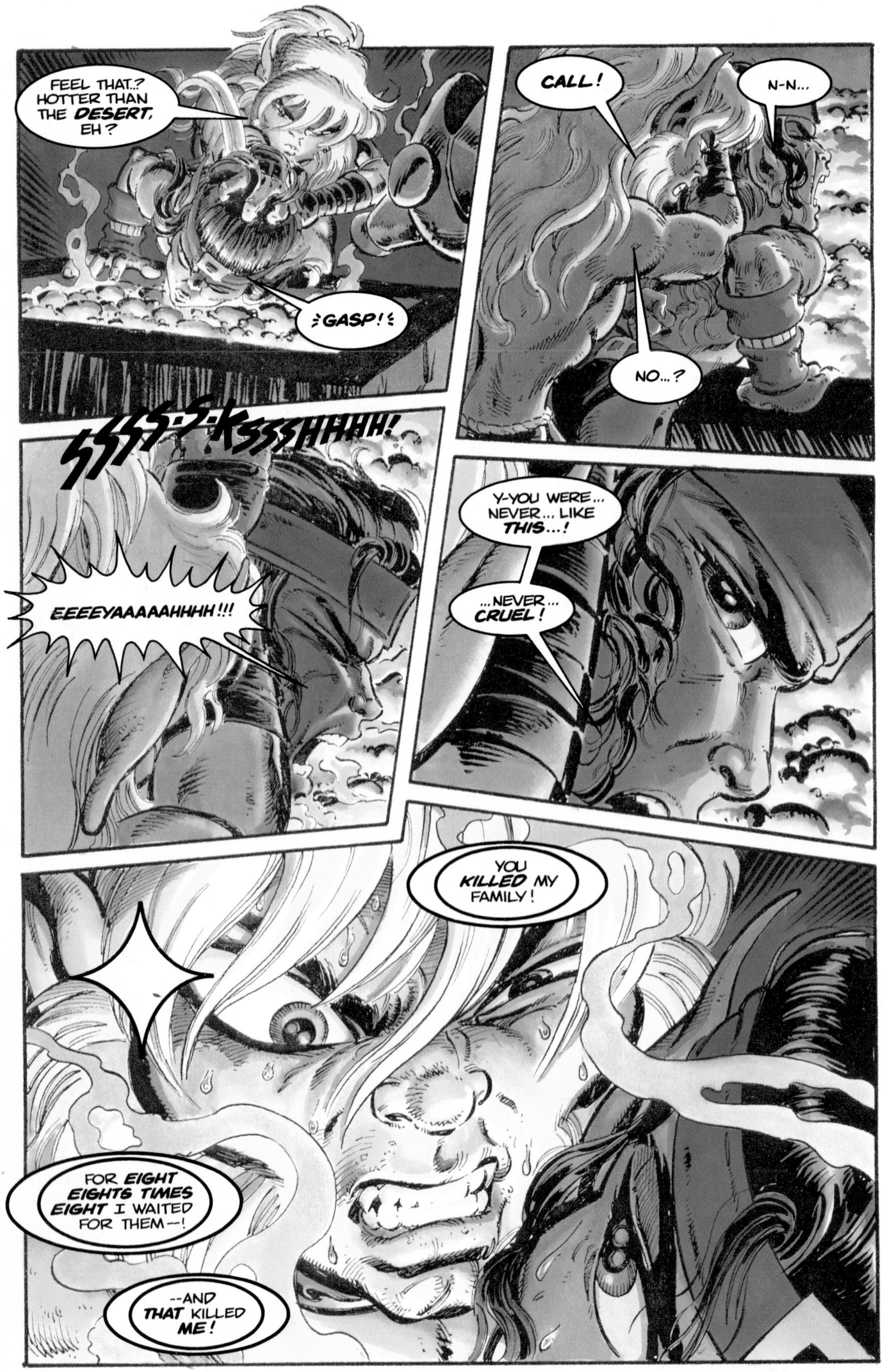
FEEL THAT..? HOTTER THAN THE DESERT, EH?
GASP!
CALL!
N-N...
NO...?
SSSS-S-KSSSHHHH!
EEEEYAAAAAHHHH!!!
Y-YOU WERE... NEVER... LIKE THIS...!
...NEVER... CRUEL!
YOU KILLED MY FAMILY!
FOR EIGHT EIGHTS TIMES EIGHT I WAITED FOR THEM--!
--AND THAT KILLED ME!

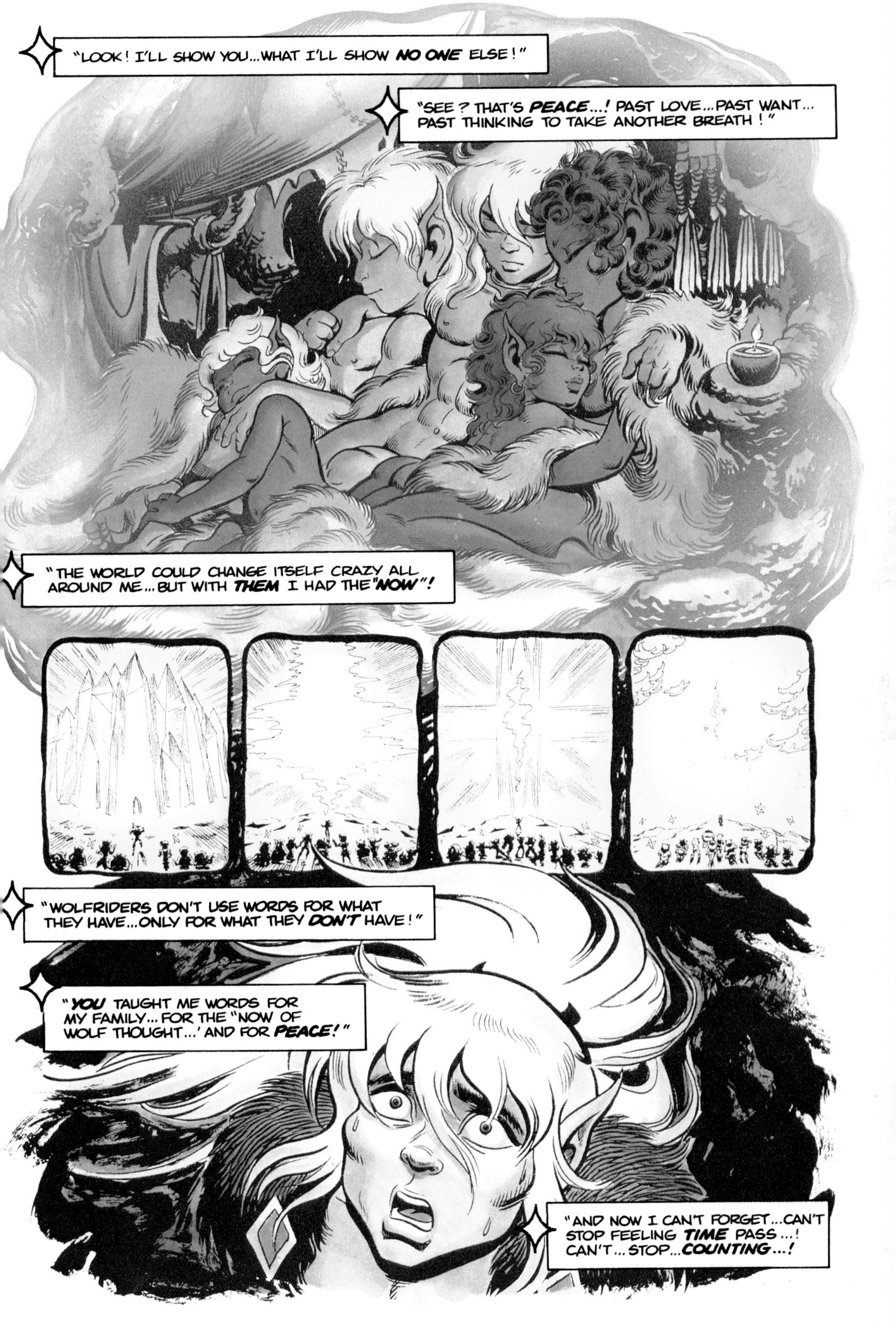
"LOOK! I'LL SHOW YOU...WHAT I'LL SHOW **NO ONE** ELSE!"
"SEE? THAT'S **PEACE**...! PAST LOVE...PAST WANT... PAST THINKING TO TAKE ANOTHER BREATH!"
"THE WORLD COULD CHANGE ITSELF CRAZY ALL AROUND ME...BUT WITH **THEM** I HAD THE "**NOW**"!
"WOLFRIDERS DON'T USE WORDS FOR WHAT THEY HAVE...ONLY FOR WHAT THEY **DON'T** HAVE!"
"**YOU** TAUGHT ME WORDS FOR MY FAMILY...FOR THE "NOW OF WOLF THOUGHT...' AND FOR **PEACE**!"
"AND NOW I CAN'T FORGET...CAN'T STOP FEELING **TIME** PASS...! CAN'T... STOP...**COUNTING**...!

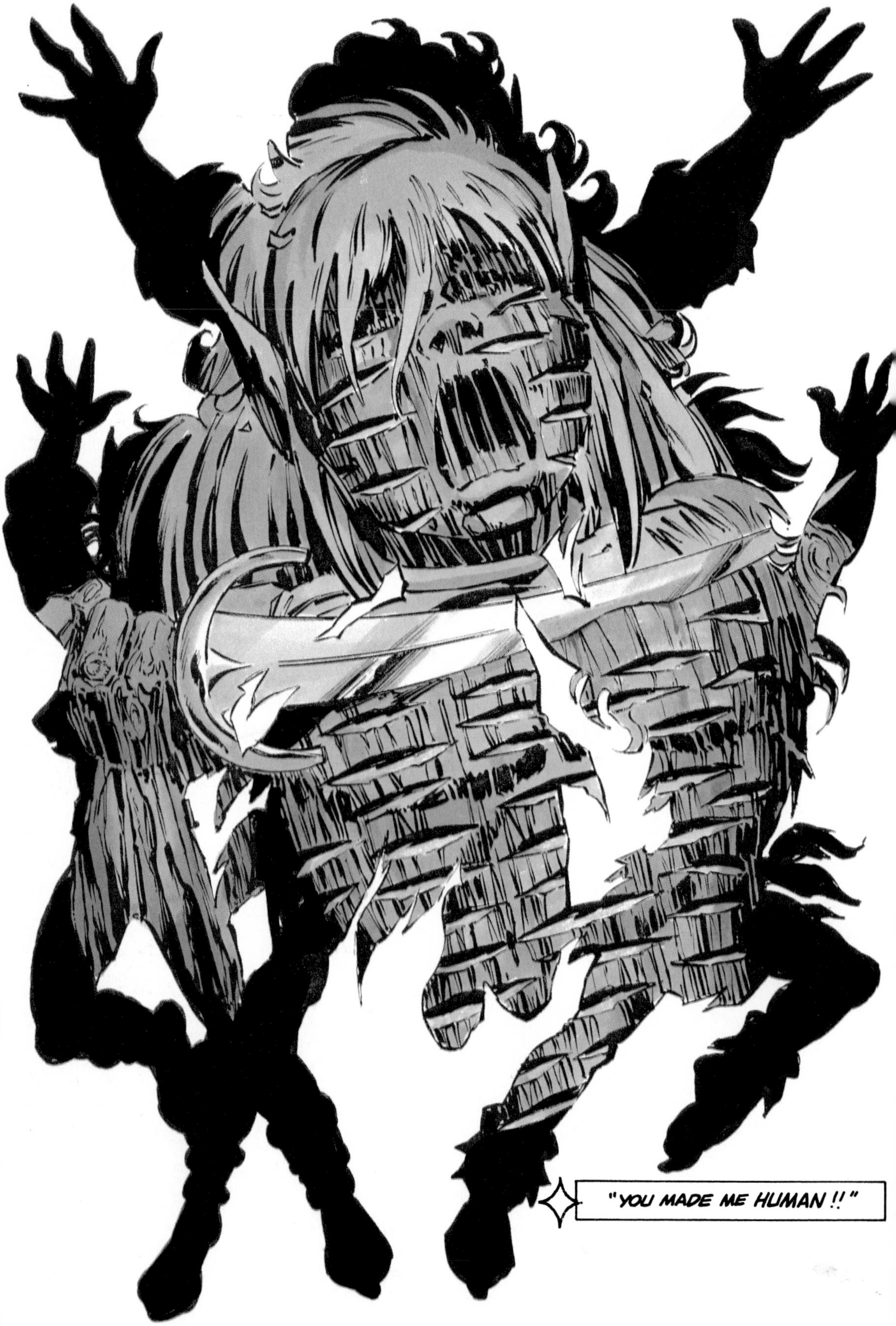
"YOU MADE ME HUMAN!!"

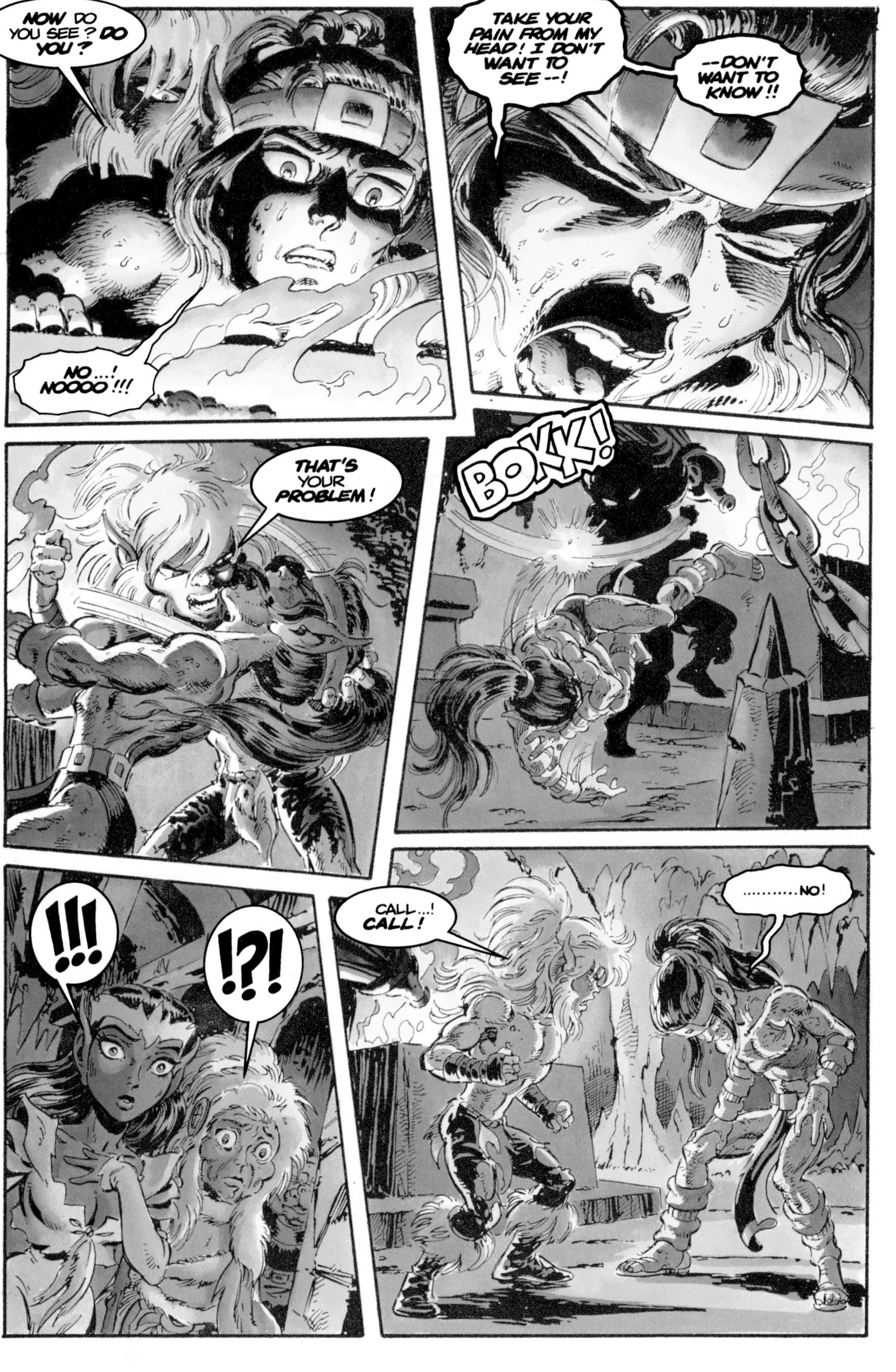
NOW DO YOU SEE? DO YOU?
NO...! NOOOO!!!
TAKE YOUR PAIN FROM MY HEAD! I DON'T WANT TO SEE--!
--DON'T WANT TO KNOW!!
THAT'S YOUR PROBLEM!
BOKK!
!!!
!?!
CALL...! CALL!
..........NO!

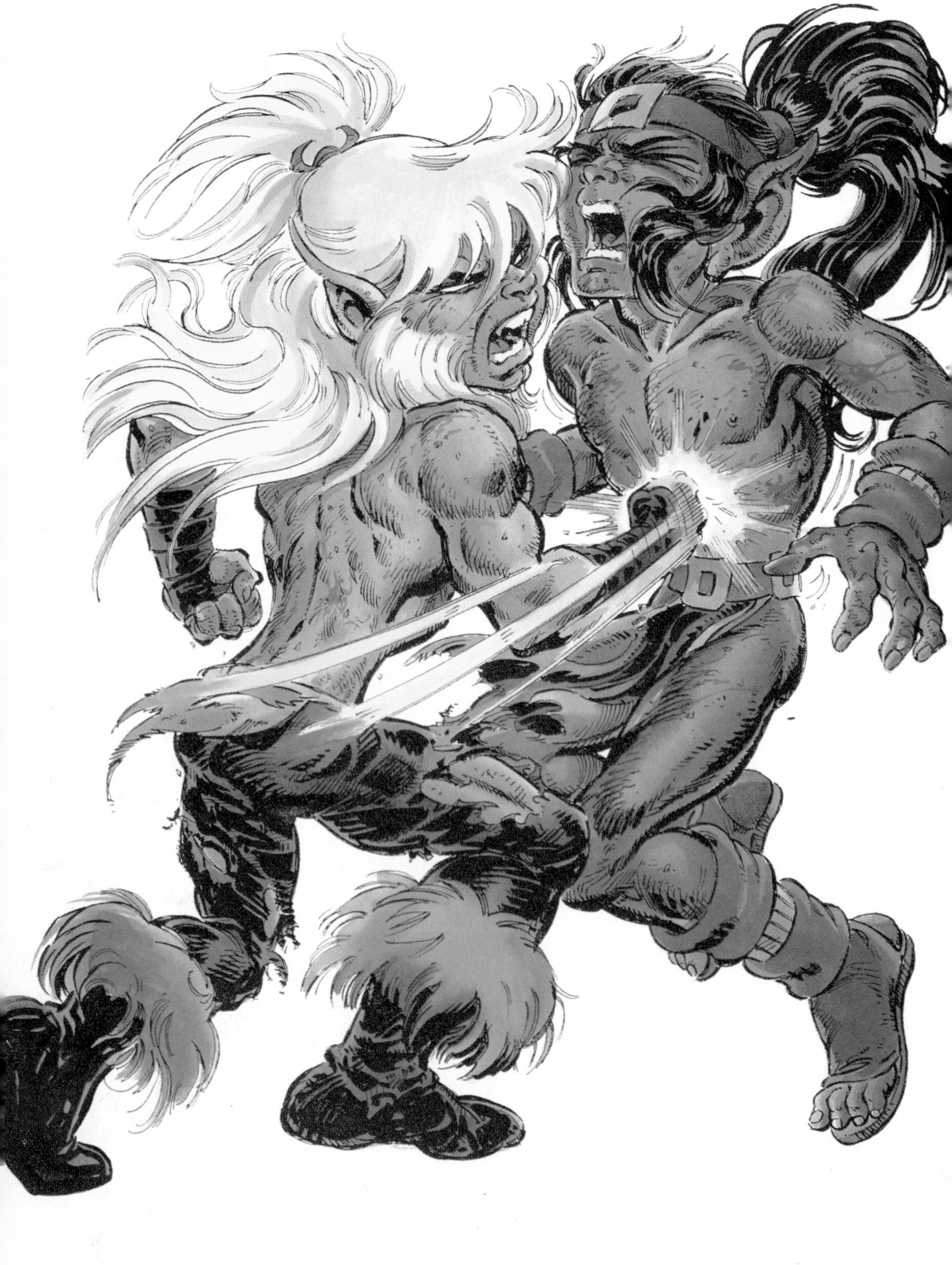

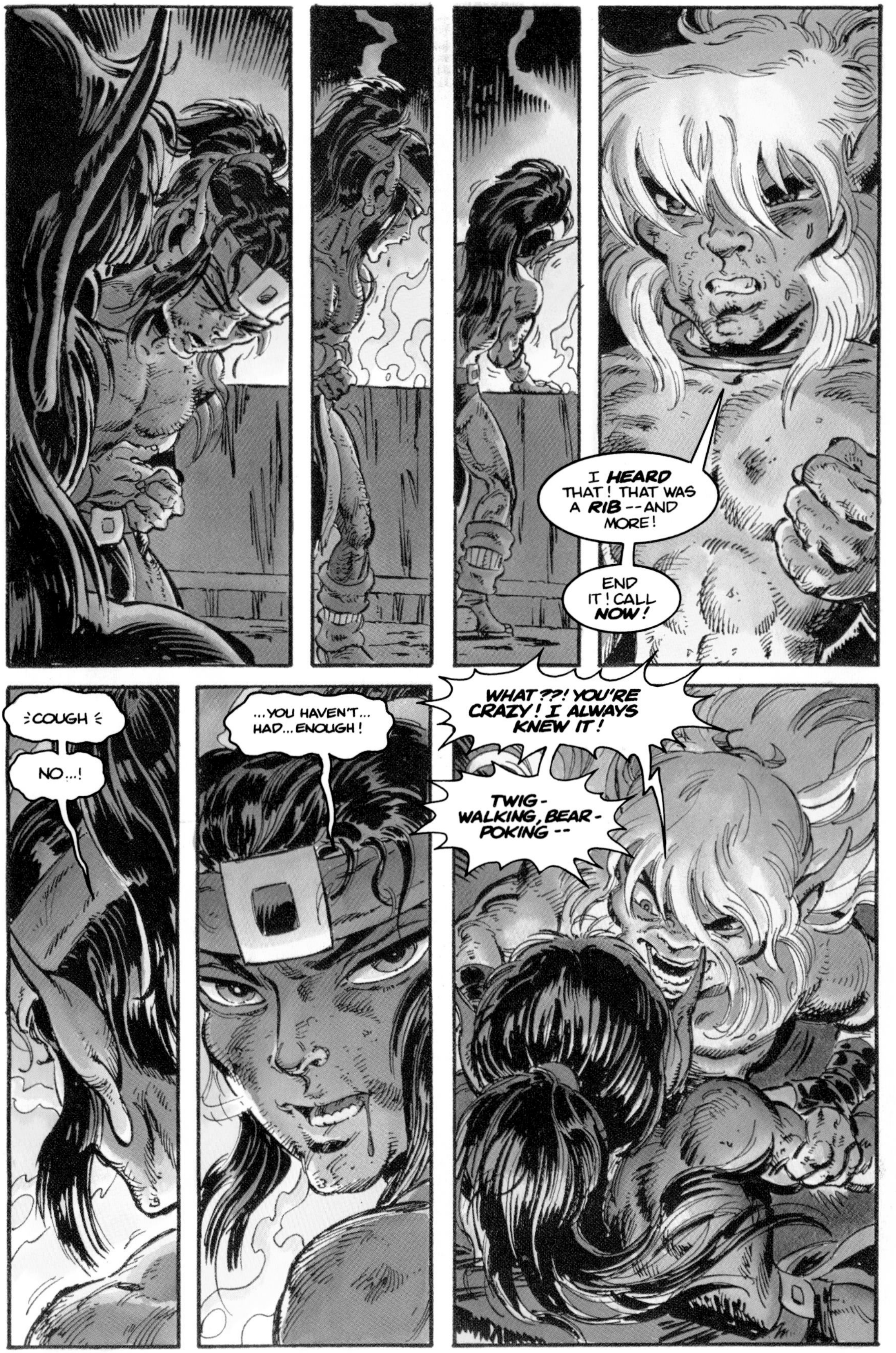
I HEARD THAT! THAT WAS A RIB --AND MORE!
END IT! CALL NOW!
COUGH
NO...!
...YOU HAVEN'T... HAD...ENOUGH!
WHAT??! YOU'RE CRAZY! I ALWAYS KNEW IT!
TWIG-WALKING, BEAR-POKING --

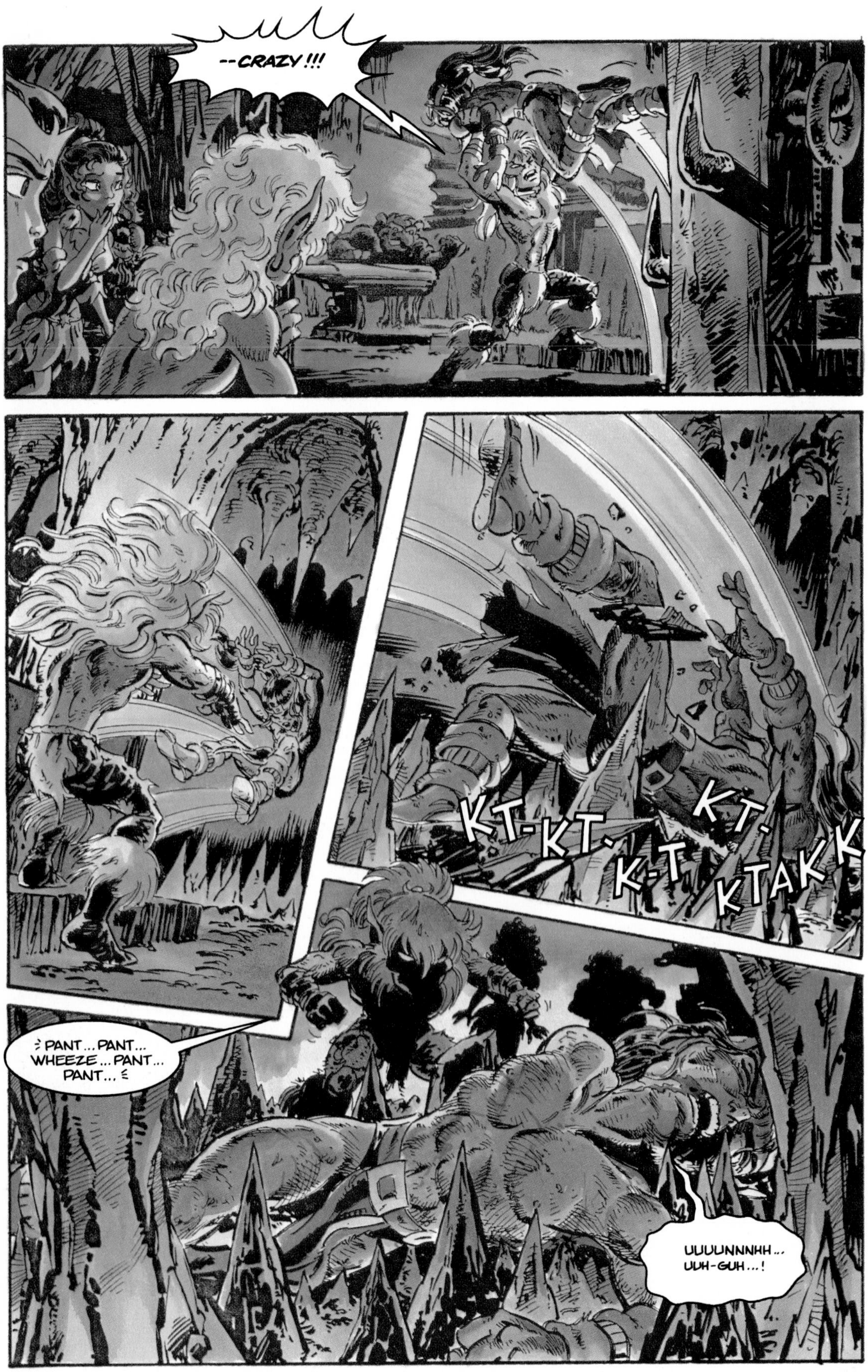
--CRAZY!!!
KT-KT-K-T KT-KTAKK
PANT... PANT... WHEEZE... PANT... PANT...
UUUUNNNHH... UUH-GUH...!

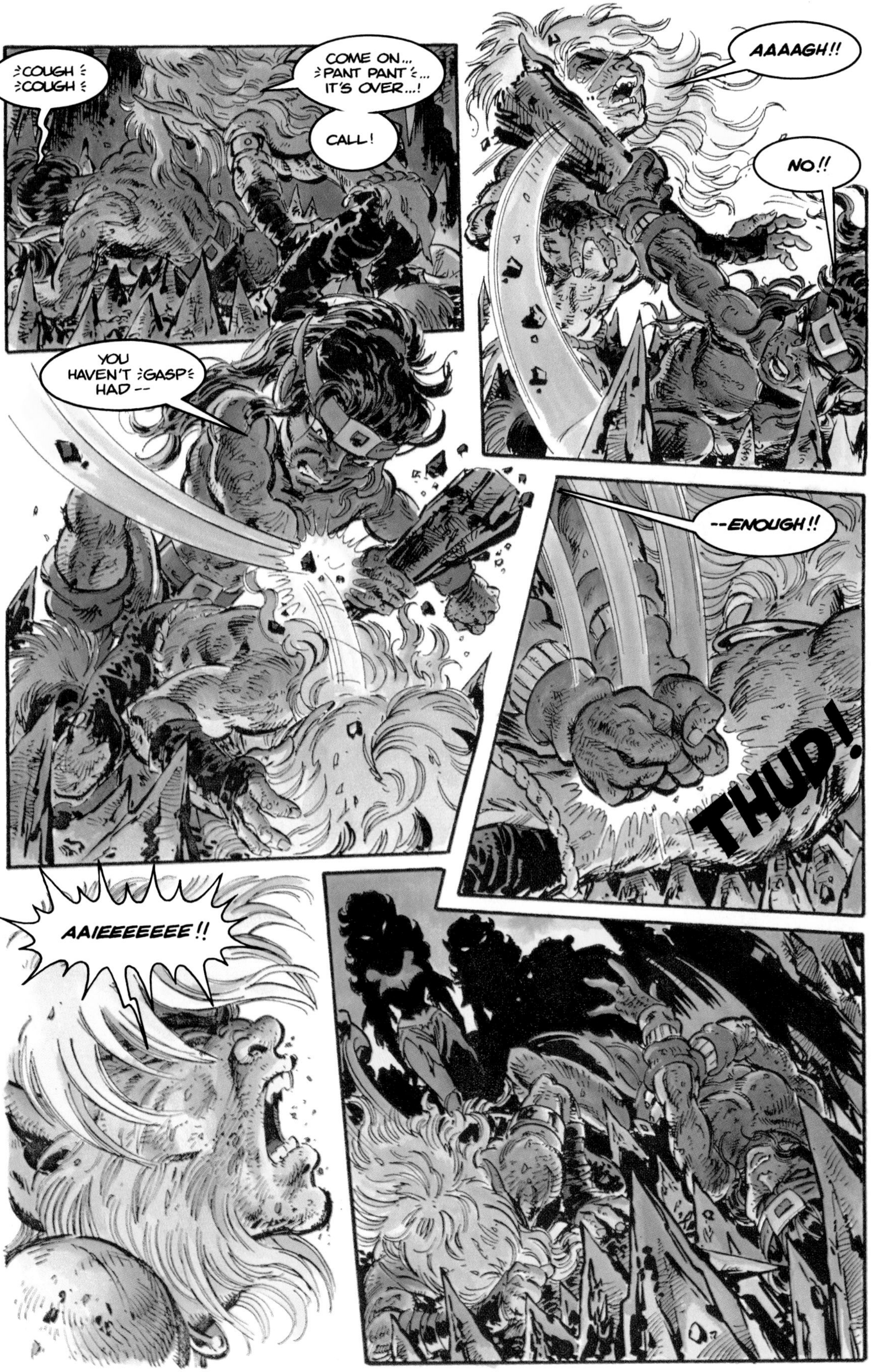
COUGH COUGH
COME ON... PANT PANT... IT'S OVER...!
CALL!
AAAAGH!!
NO!!
YOU HAVEN'T GASP HAD --
--ENOUGH!!
THUD!
AAIEEEEEEE!!

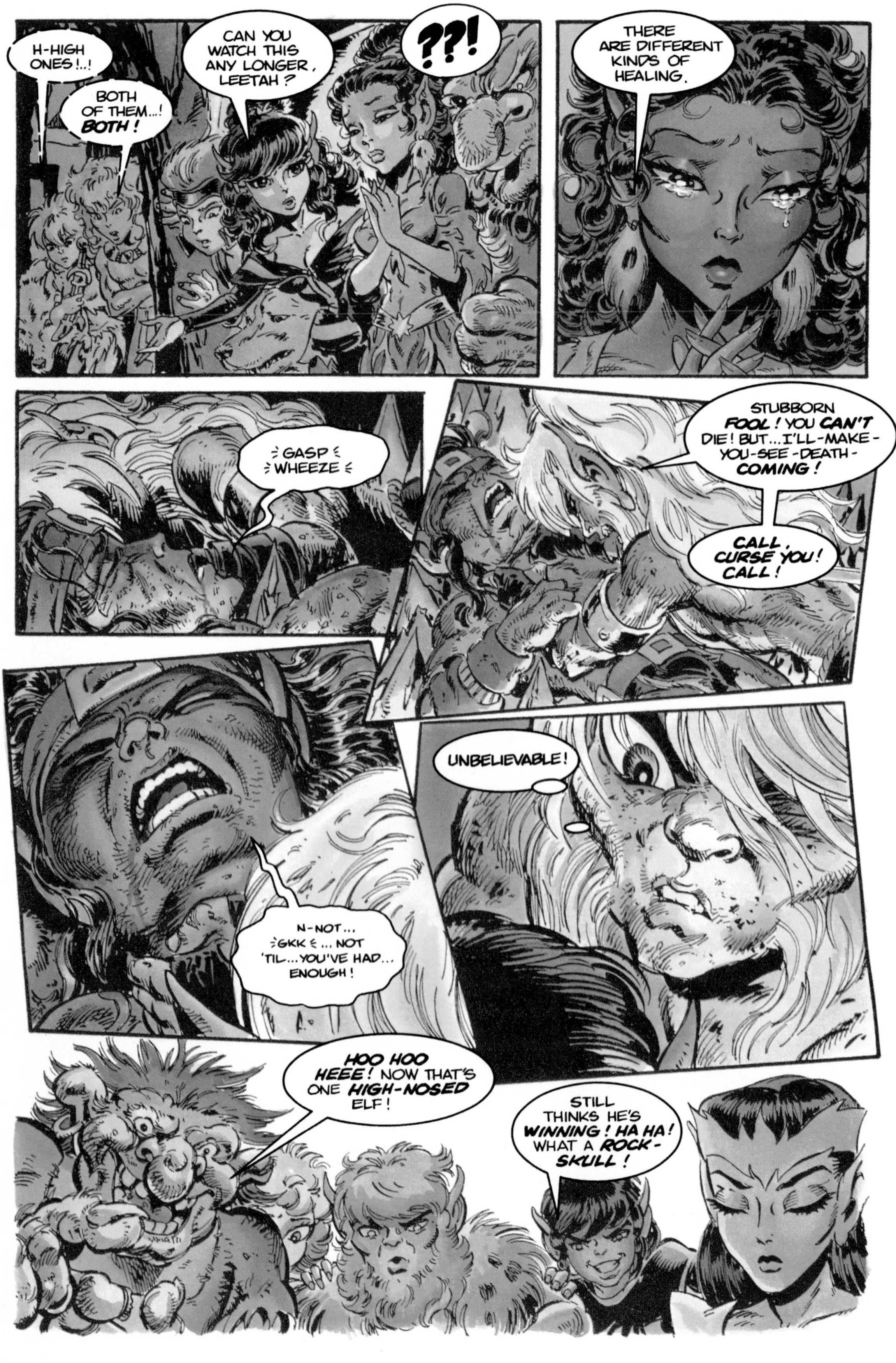
H-HIGH ONES!..!
BOTH OF THEM...! BOTH!
CAN YOU WATCH THIS ANY LONGER, LEETAH?
??!
THERE ARE DIFFERENT KINDS OF HEALING.
GASP WHEEZE
STUBBORN FOOL! YOU CAN'T DIE! BUT...I'LL-MAKE-YOU-SEE-DEATH-COMING!
CALL, CURSE YOU! CALL!
N-NOT... GKK ...NOT 'TIL...YOU'VE HAD... ENOUGH!
UNBELIEVABLE!
HOO HOO HEEE! NOW THAT'S ONE HIGH-NOSED ELF!
STILL THINKS HE'S WINNING! HA HA! WHAT A ROCK-SKULL!

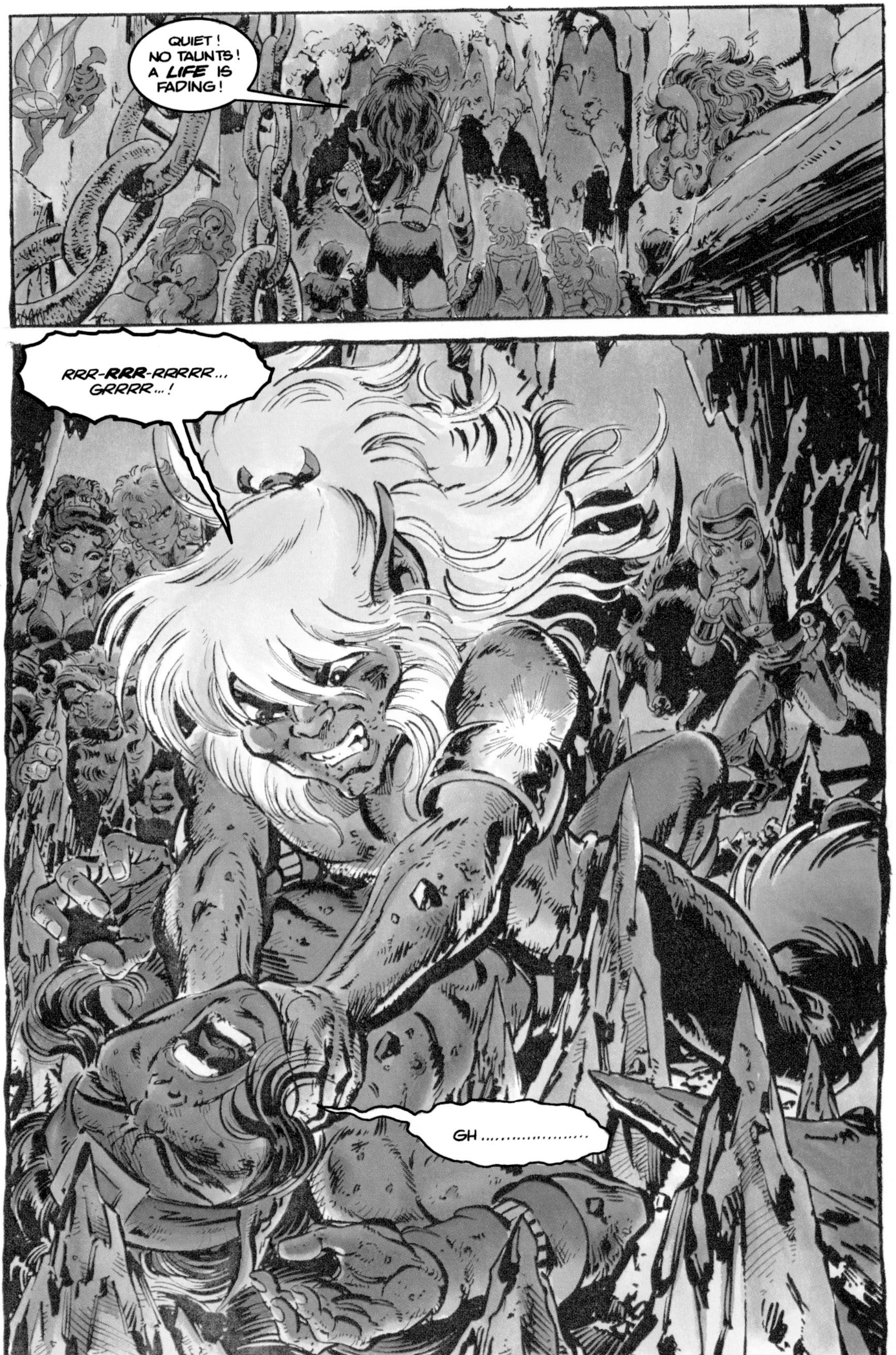
QUIET! NO TAUNTS! A *LIFE* IS FADING!
*RRR-**RRR**-RRRRR... GRRRR...!*
GH......................

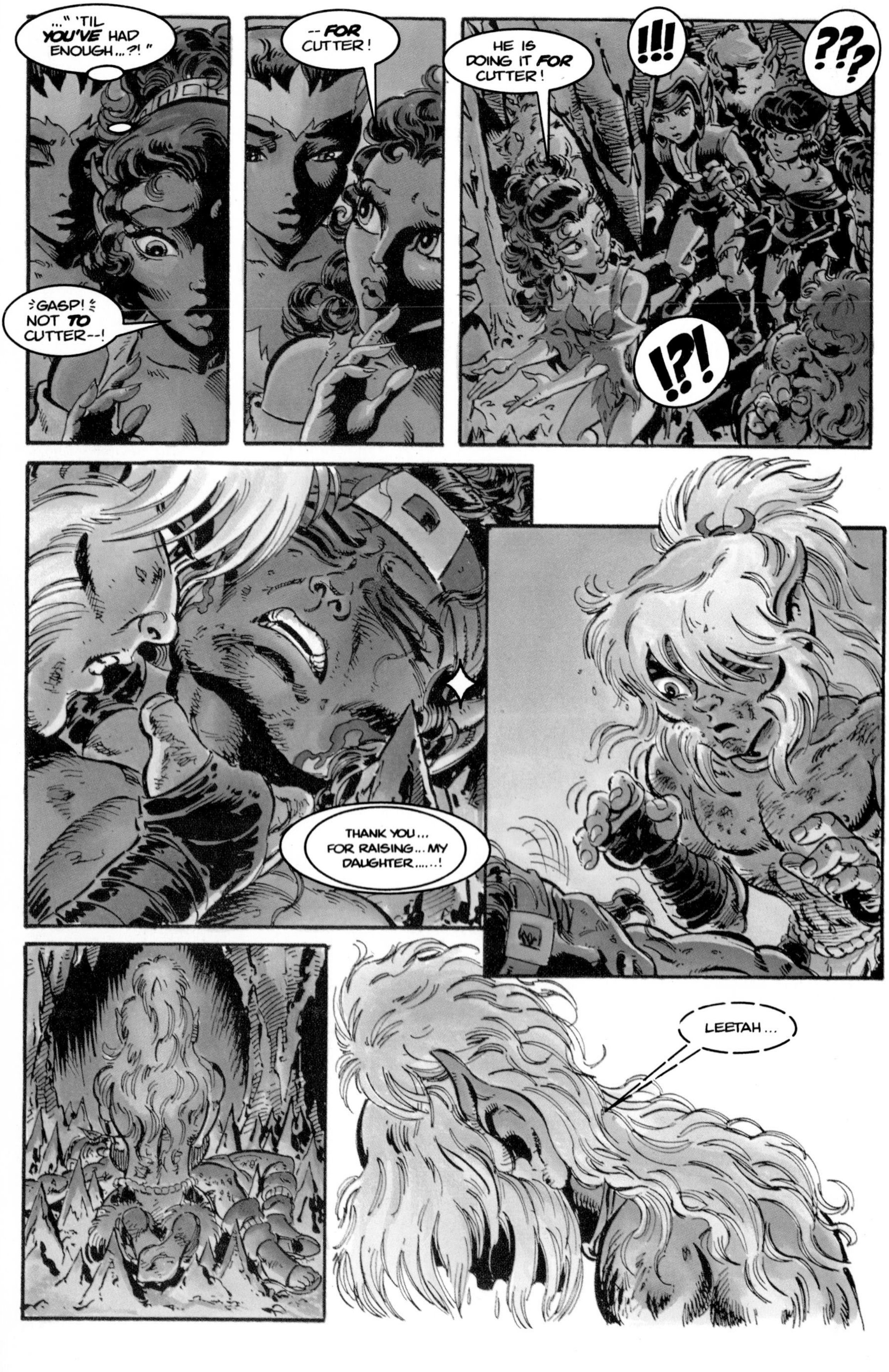
..." 'TIL YOU'VE HAD ENOUGH...?!"
⁝GASP!⁝ NOT TO CUTTER--!
--FOR CUTTER!
HE IS DOING IT FOR CUTTER!
!!!
???
!?!
THANK YOU... FOR RAISING... MY DAUGHTER.....!
LEETAH...

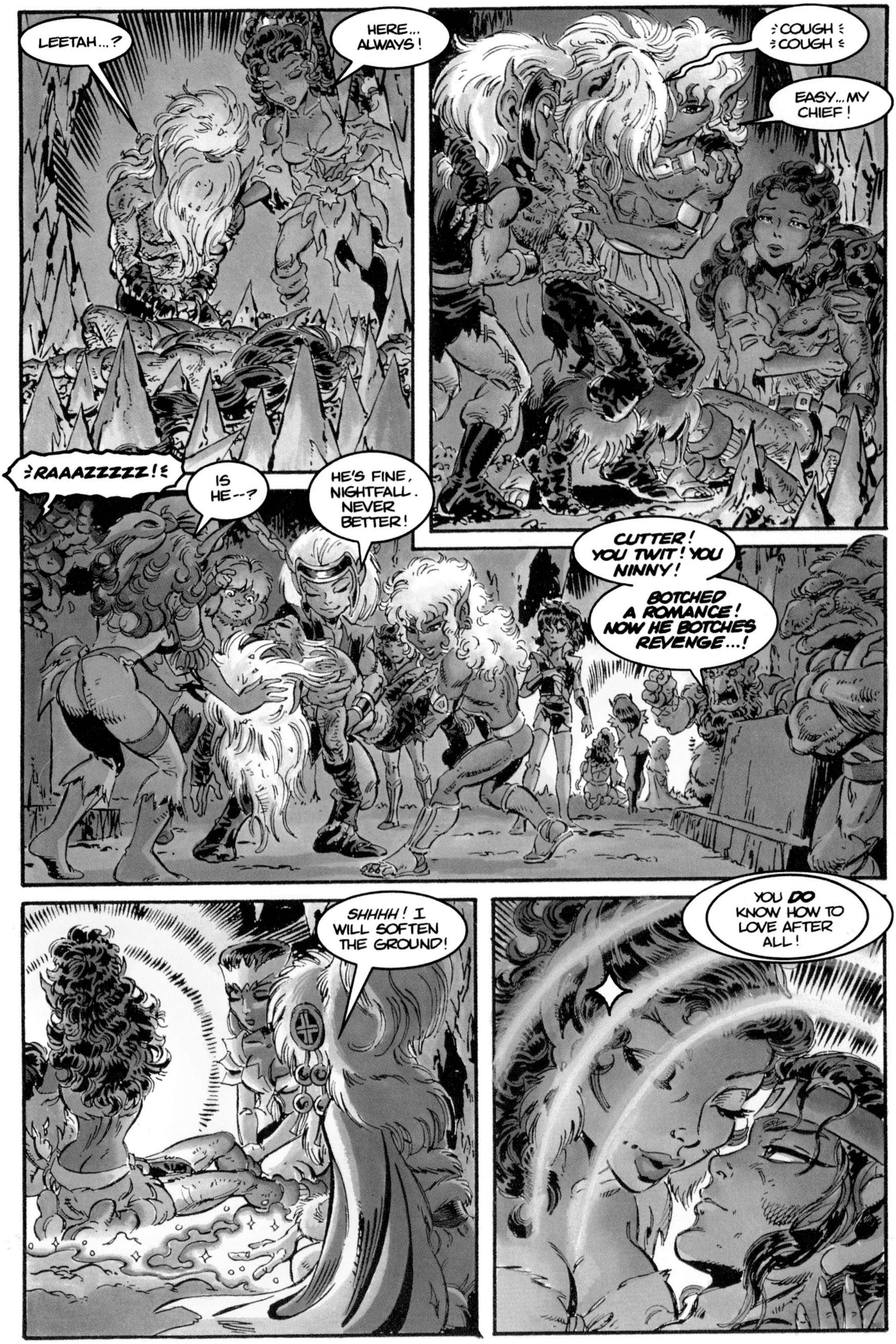
LEETAH...?
HERE... ALWAYS!
COUGH COUGH
EASY... MY CHIEF!
RAAAZZZZZ!
IS HE--?
HE'S FINE, NIGHTFALL. NEVER BETTER!
CUTTER! YOU TWIT! YOU NINNY!
BOTCHED A ROMANCE! NOW HE BOTCHES REVENGE...!
SHHHH! I WILL SOFTEN THE GROUND!
YOU DO KNOW HOW TO LOVE AFTER ALL!

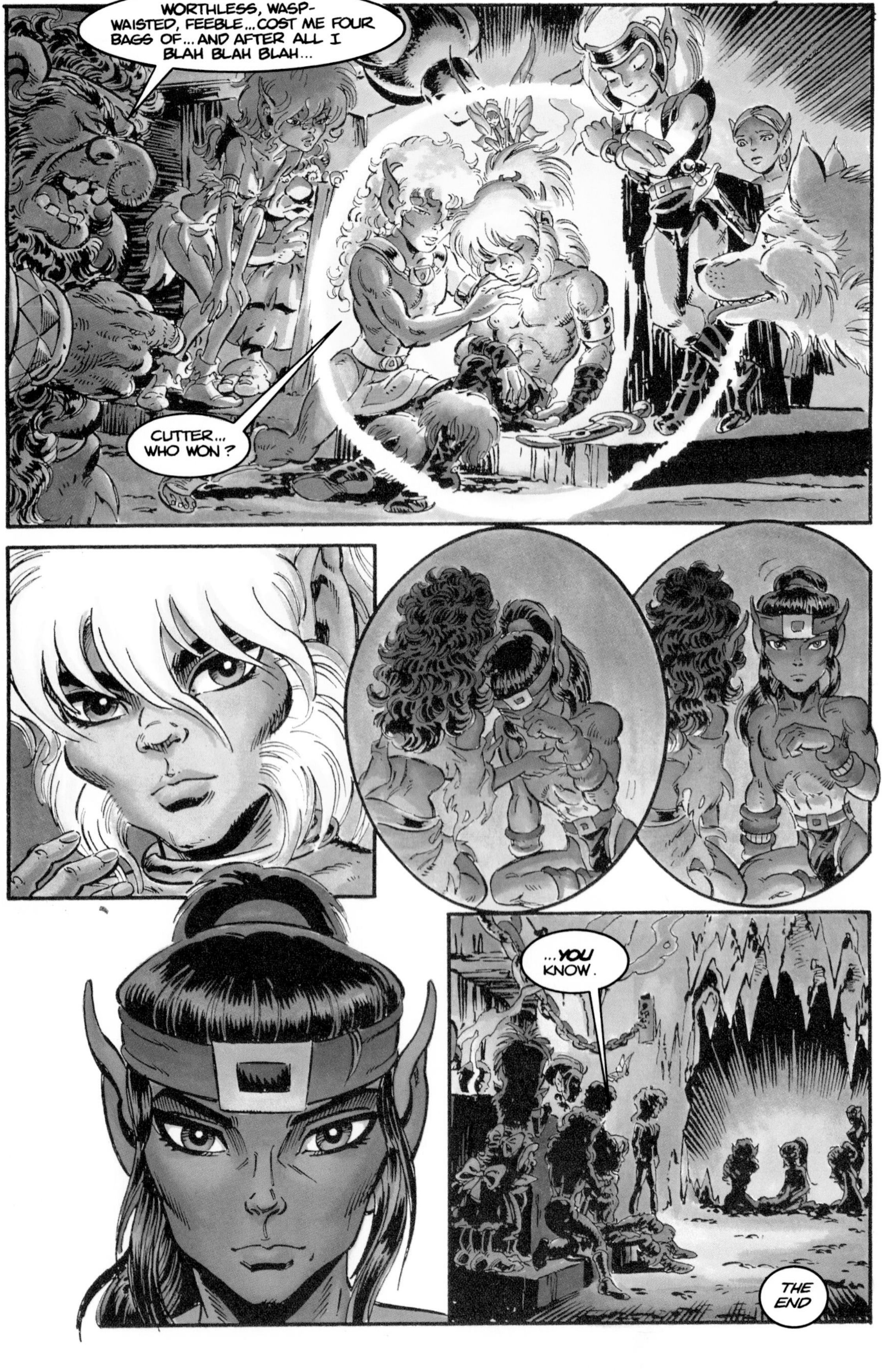
WORTHLESS, WASP-WAISTED, FEEBLE...COST ME FOUR BAGS OF...AND AFTER ALL I BLAH BLAH BLAH...
CUTTER... WHO WON?
...YOU KNOW.
THE END

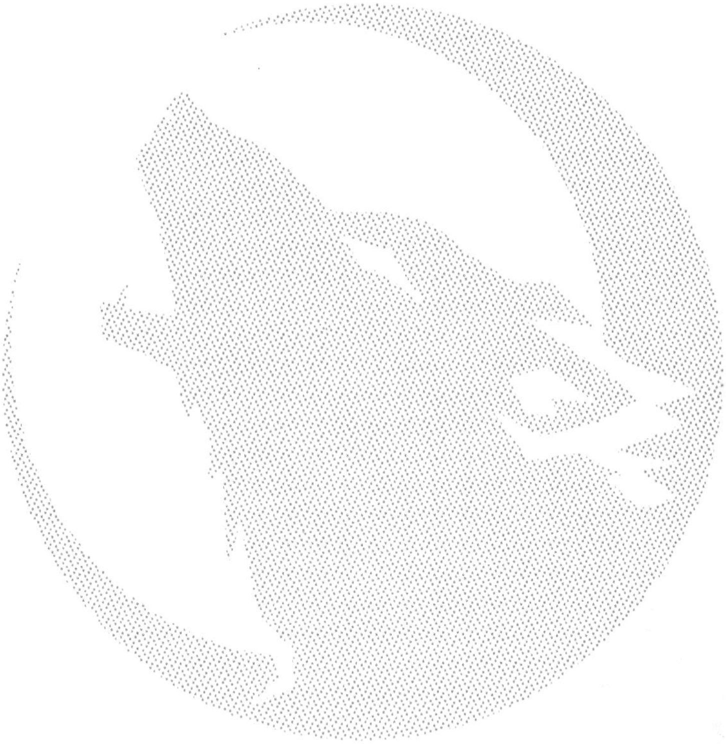

Cover Gallery

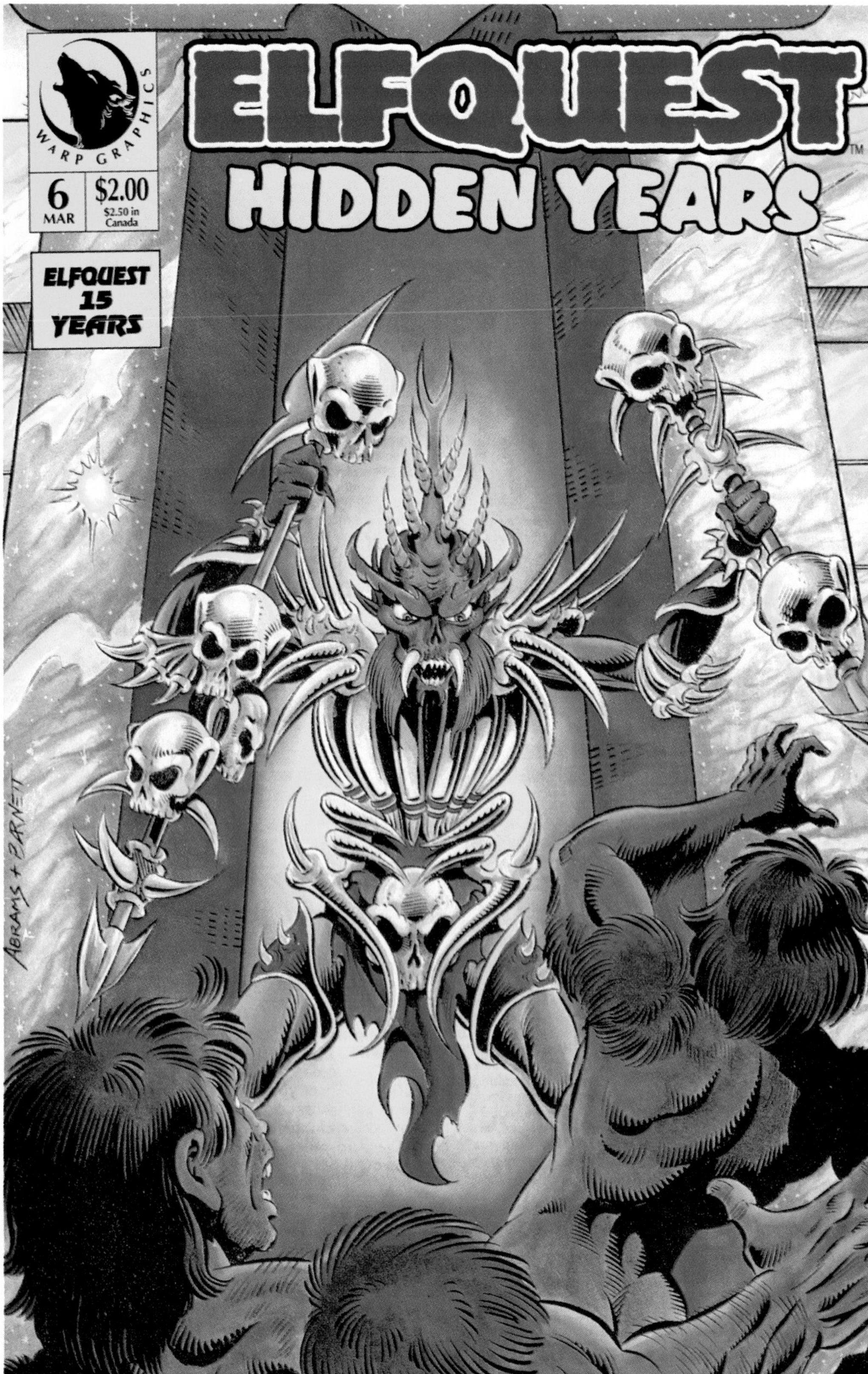

WARP GRAPHICS
ELFQUEST
HIDDEN YEARS
6
MAR
$2.00
$2.50 in Canada
ELFQUEST 15 YEARS
ABRAMS + BARNETT

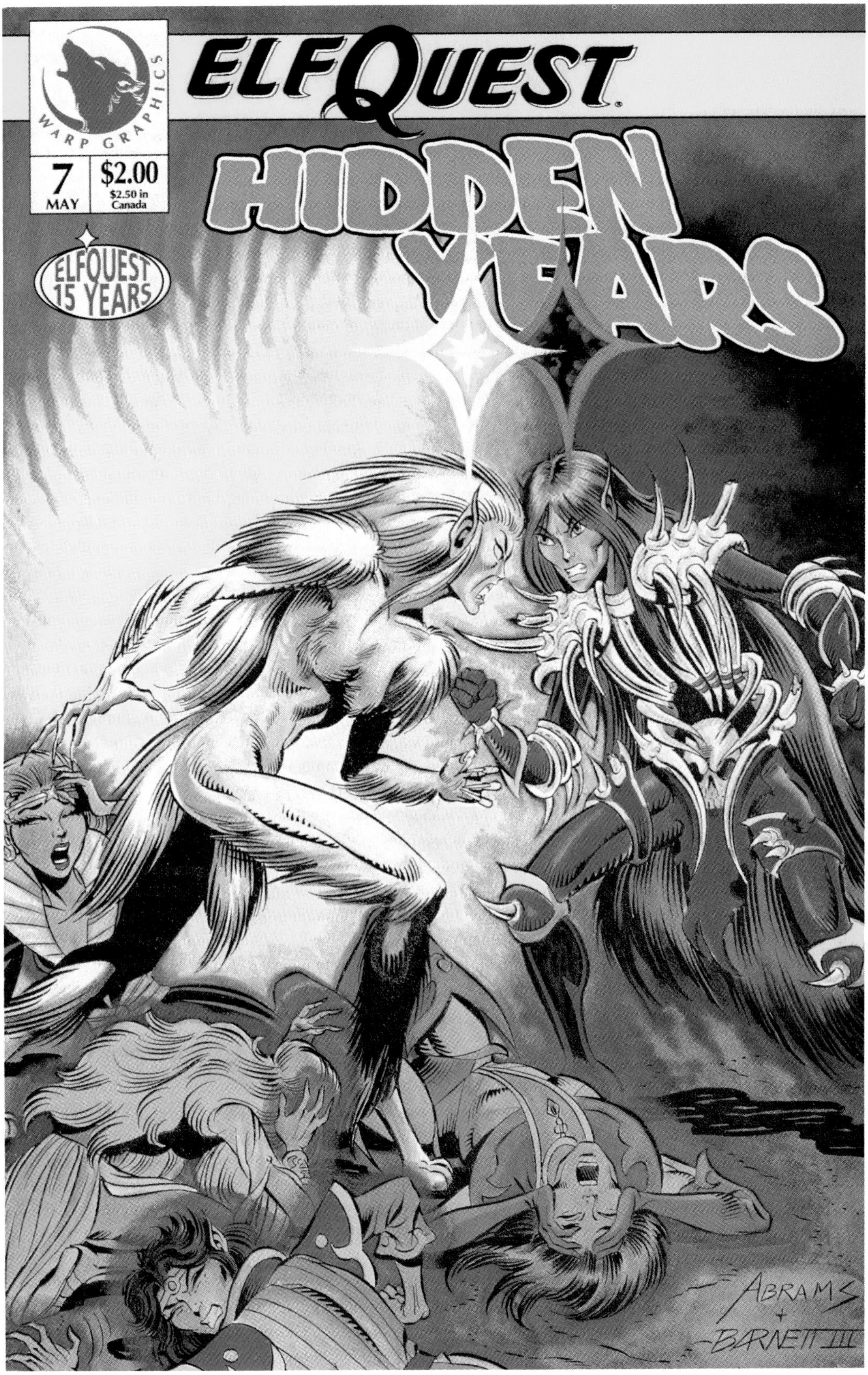
ELFQUEST
WARP GRAPHICS
7
MAY
$2.00
$2.50 in Canada
HIDDEN YEARS
ELFQUEST 15 YEARS
ABRAMS + BARNETT III

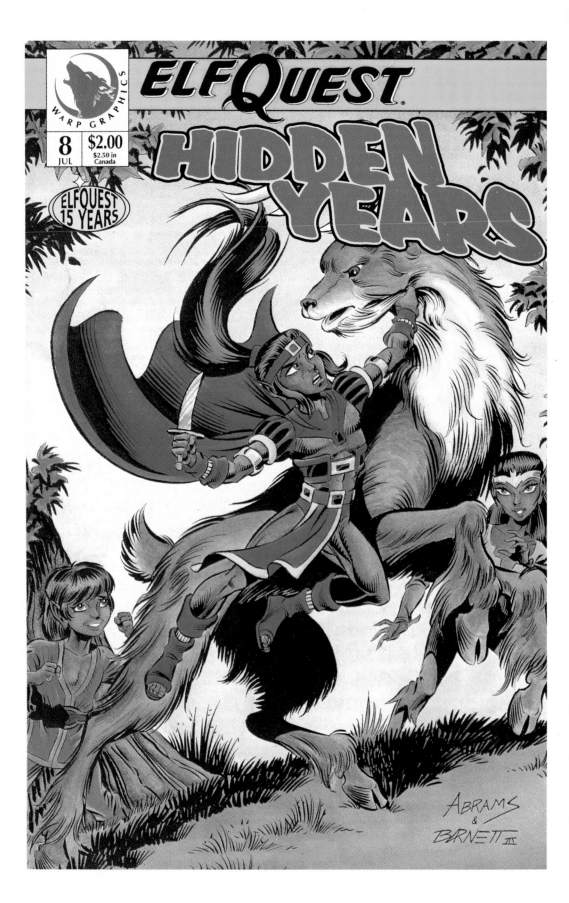

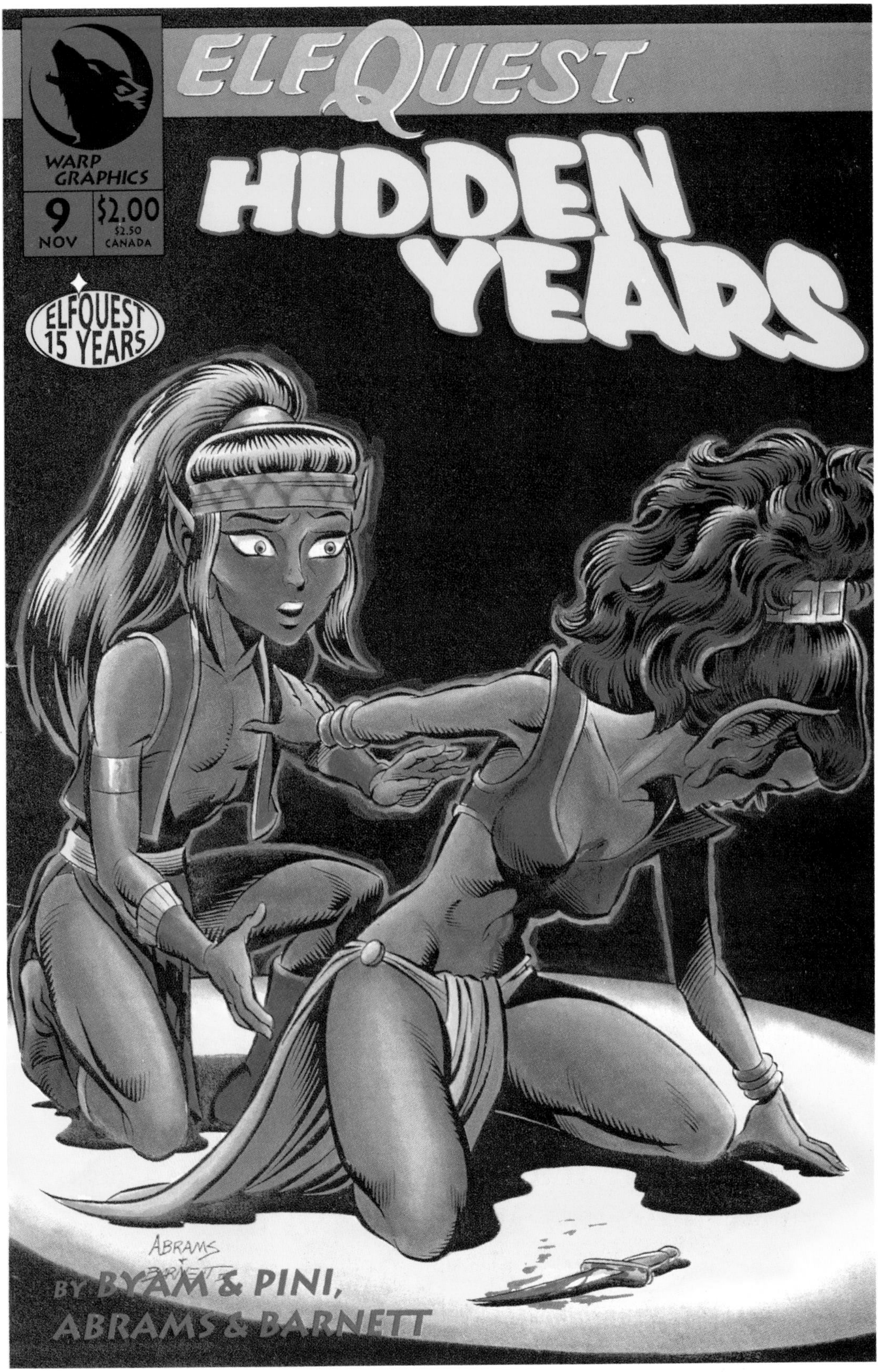

WARP GRAPHICS
ELFQUEST
9 NOV
$2.00
$2.50 CANADA
HIDDEN YEARS
ELFQUEST 15 YEARS
ABRAMS + BARNETT
BY BYAM & PINI, ABRAMS & BARNETT

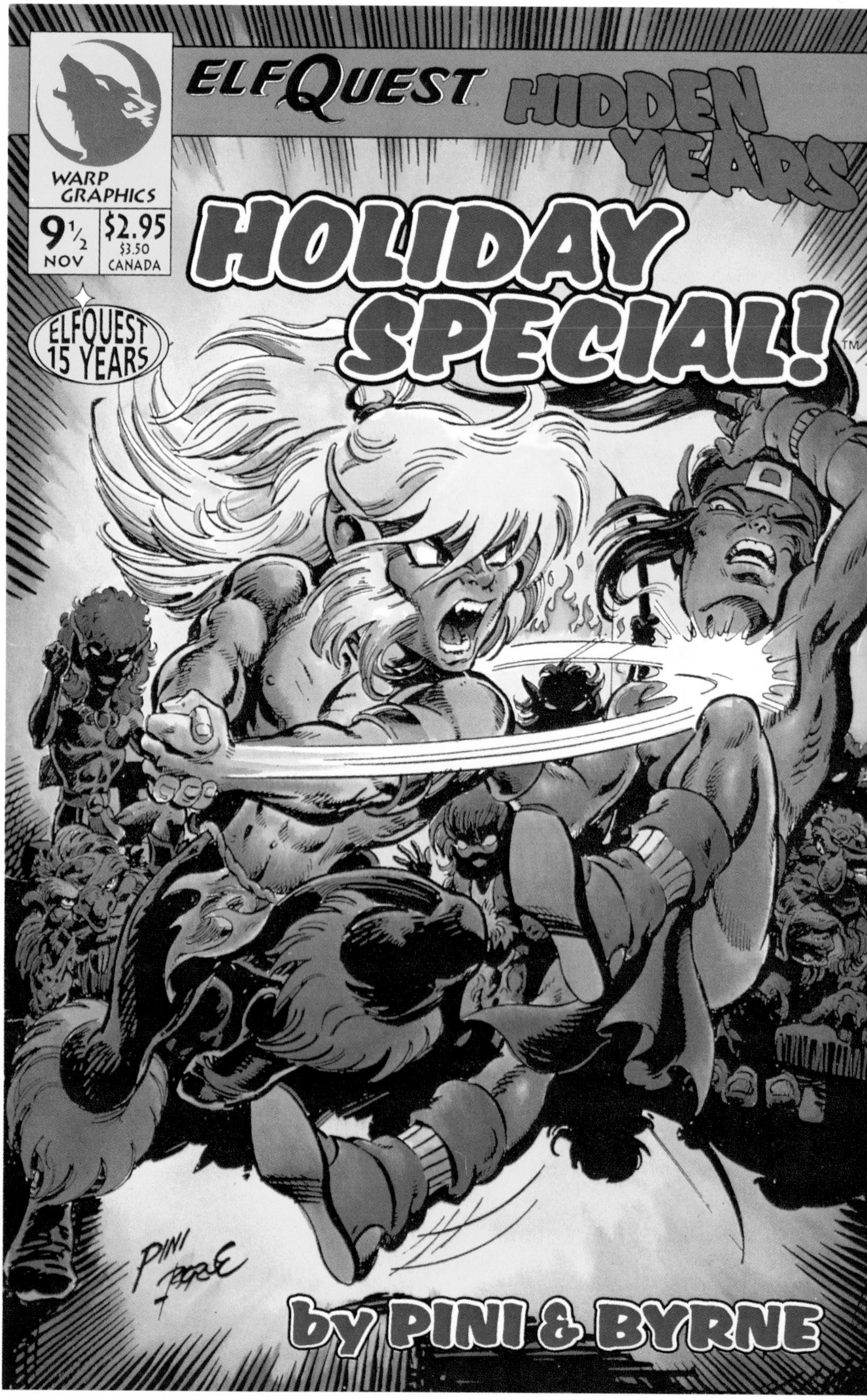
WARP GRAPHICS
9 1/2
NOV
$2.95
$3.50 CANADA
ELFQUEST
HIDDEN YEARS
HOLIDAY SPECIAL!
ELFQUEST 15 YEARS
PINI
BYRNE
by PINI & BYRNE